AF505427

Contested Learning in Welfare Work

Drawing on the field of cultural historical psychology and the sociologies of skill and labour process, *Contested Learning in Welfare Work* offers a detailed account of the learning lives of state welfare workers in Canada as they cope, accommodate, resist, and flounder in times of heightened austerity. Documented through in-depth qualitative and quantitative analysis, Peter H. Sawchuk's analysis shows how the labour process changes workers, and how workers change the labour process, under the pressures of intensified economic conditions, new technologies, changing relations of space and time, and a high-tech version of Taylorism. Sawchuk traces these experiences over a seven-year period (2002–2009) that includes major work reorganization and the recent global economic downturn. His analysis examines the dynamics among notions of de-skilling, re-skilling, and up-skilling, as workers negotiate occupational learning and changing identities.

Peter H. Sawchuk is a professor of adult education, sociology, and industrial relations at the University of Toronto. He studies, writes, and teaches in the areas of adult learning theory, the sociology and psychology of work, and Marxist political economy.

By Christopher James Tinkler

Contested Learning in Welfare Work

A Study of Mind, Political Economy, and the Labour Process

PETER H. SAWCHUK
University of Toronto

CAMBRIDGE UNIVERSITY PRESS
Cambridge, New York, Melbourne, Madrid, Cape Town,
Singapore, São Paulo, Delhi, Mexico City

Cambridge University Press
32 Avenue of the Americas, New York, NY 10013-2473, USA

www.cambridge.org
Information on this title: www.cambridge.org/9781107034679

First published 2013

Printed in the United States of America

A catalogue record for this publication is available from the British Library.

Library of Congress Cataloguing in Publication data
Sawchuk, Peter H. (Peter Harold), 1968–
    Contested learning in welfare work : a study of mind, political economy,
    and the labour process / Peter H. Sawchuk, University of Toronto.
        pages   cm. – (Learning in doing : social, cognitive and computational
        perspectives)
    Includes bibliographical references and index.
    ISBN 978-1-107-03467-9 (hardback : alk. paper)
    1. Human services.   2. Social service.   3. Employees – Training of.
    4. Civil service.   5. Public administration.   I. Title.
    HV40.S29   2013
    331.7′61361–dc23   2012042705

ISBN 978-1-107-03467-9 Hardback

In memoriam,
Alex & George

Contents

Figures and Tables

Figures

Tables

Series Foreword

This series for Cambridge University Press is widely known as an international forum for studies of situated learning and cognition. Innovative contributions are being made by anthropology; by cognitive, developmental, and cultural psychology; by computer science; by education; and by social theory. These contributions are providing the basis for new ways of understanding the social, historical, and contextual nature of learning, thinking, and practice that emerges from human activity. The empirical settings of these research inquiries range from the classroom to the workplace, to the high-technology office, and to learning in the streets and in other communities of practice. The situated nature of learning and remembering through activity is a central fact. It may appear obvious that human minds develop in social situations and extend their sphere of activity and communicative competencies. But cognitive theories of knowledge representation and learning alone have not provided sufficient insight into these relationships. This series was born of the conviction that new exciting interdisciplinary syntheses are under way as scholars and practitioners from diverse fields seek to develop theory and empirical investigations adequate for characterizing the complex relations of social and mental life, and for understanding successful learning wherever it occurs. The series invites contributions that advance our understanding of these seminal issues.

Roy Pea
Christian Heath
Lucy A. Suchman

Acknowledgements

This book could not have been written without the support of the many welfare workers of the Canadian Union of Public Employees in Ontario (CUPE-Ontario) who took the time to talk about their work life (and fill out surveys). But a union is also about the individuals who bring it to life. I want to thank Steve Leavitt and Bev Patchell, who helped make this research happen. Steve helped invent and get this research started while Bev was largely the one who kept things going, patiently responding to questions and clarifications up until the end. Other CUPE-Ontario activists, officers, and staff helped the research at points as well: Vicky Houston, Claudia White, Tim McGuire, Ron Wing, and Margot Young each contributed to this work.

To complete the research also required a talented and dedicated team of graduate student researchers: Trish Hennessy, Debbie Boutilier, and Anthony Tambureno likewise made this work possible. They have moved on to bigger and better things, and special recognition is due Debbie for her tireless shepherding of the survey in addition to the many insights that emerged from her own analyses and engagements with workers. Both Trish and Debbie completed dissertations related to the research data, and both pieces of work introduced important ideas to the research team and me personally.

Not involved in the research itself, but invaluable intellectual supports through ongoing conversations were David Livingstone, Milosh Raykov, Arlo Kempf, Youssef Sawan, and Sue Carter, who reviewed draft materials. Thank you to Chris Tinkler who produced a wonderful frontispiece based on our conversations about the research. Thanks to the anonymous reviewers of the manuscript as well as editorial and production support from Adina Berk, Eve Mayer, and Hetty Marx at Cambridge University Press. A warm thank you to Paul Adler, Michael Lavalette, and Anna Stetsenko who looked at these materials. Anna deserves special mention, however. Over a growing number of years now, her intellectual inspiration and support have been irreplaceable to me and her critical eye has continued to support this and other of my works.

And finally I thank my partner, Jill. Her ongoing support and especially her willingness to sit through meandering discussions of ideas about a project that for much of the time seemed to have no end in sight were personally sustaining.

Across these acknowledgements all the usual disclaimers about any errors being my own responsibility apply.

Abbreviations

ASAP	Automating Social Assistance Project
BA	Basic Allowance
BNA	Basic Needs Allowance
BTP	Business Transformation Project
BU	Benefit Unit
BUH	Benefit Unit History
CIMS	Comprehensive Income Maintenance System
CPO	Case Presenting Officer
CPP	Common Purpose Procurement
CUPE	Canadian Union of Public Employees (Ontario)
CVP	Consolidated Verification Process Worker
CWT	Caseworker Technology
ERO	Eligibility Review Officer
EVP	Eligibility Verification Process
ISAMF	Integrated Social Assistance Monitoring Framework
ISU	Intake Screening Unit
LBE	Local Business Expert
MAIN	Municipal Assistance Integrated Network
MSAP	Modernizing Social Assistance Project
ODSP	Ontario Disability Support Program (welfare assistance for those with disability)
OMSSA	Ontario Municipal Social Services Association
OPSEU	Ontario Public Sector Employees Union
OWP (OW)	Ontario Works Program (general welfare assistance)
OWT	Ontario Works Technology
PA	Participation Agreement
PNA	Personal Needs Allowance
PUE	Permanently Unemployable

PV	Priority Verification
RBC	Re-Budget Calculation
SAMO	Social Assistance and Municipal Operations Branch
SDMT	Service Delivery Model Technology
SIR	System Investigation Report
SSAS	Social Service Access Site (Algoma)
SSWCC	Social Services Workers Coordinating Committee, CUPE-Ontario
TCB	Transition Child Benefit
WAYS	Web Access to Your Services (Toronto)
WFCD	Welfare Fraud Control Database

1 Introduction

In 1923, on stage in New York City, for a white-collar worker named Mr. Zero, an entire world of work had been reduced to numbers and a job carefully mastered was being replaced by a profitable new "super-hyper-adding machine". In response he makes his first real choice in life. He takes extreme measures. He is sentenced to death and uttering his last earthly words to the jury he says, "Suppose you was me." In the after-life he is presented with yet another opportunity to make choices, and once again he is laid off. This time it is not for the reasons of profit. It is because of his refusal to make one choice rather than another: to accept rather than change the designs of his circumstance. Where exactly does a worker go when laid off from a job in the after-life? Why, back to earth. As his supervisor Lieutenant Charles explains to him carefully: Zero is to start all over again, to "learn all the wrong things and learn them all in the wrong way [and] about all the things you want to know, they'll tell you nothing at all".[1]

In terms of the human experience of contemporary occupational change there are many similarities to be found between Elmer Rice's play and the research on state welfare workers in this book. The introduction of a new "super-hyper" technology is one. A form of work reduced to a world of numbers, the disorienting sense of starting all over again, alienation, disbelief, confusion, anger, accommodation, consent, the possibilities of resistance (as well as the possibilities of resistance that are refused) are others. These are all themes defining the lives of the workers we will learn more about here. In doing so, we understand more about an occupation being re-made. Still, when compared to Mr. Zero, these welfare workers we meet do something very different. They make all forms of choices. They construct and solve an ocean of problems. Some consent, some accommodate, some resist, and some do one and then the other. And, for both better and worse, they learn. At times, it seems they learn *all the wrong things in all the wrong ways*. At others, they struggle to learn things that they care deeply about, and about which they are *told nothing at all*. In either case, in times of radical change, these workers must make it up as they go.

It is likely no coincidence that the themes of work change and alienation emerged for Elmer Rice in the age of public and political fervour in America in the first decades of the twentieth century over Frederick Winslow Taylor's Scientific Management. Taylorism was, and I will argue still is, a force to be reckoned with, if, that is, we release it from the many caricatures it has regularly endured. Fundamental to seeing Taylorism in this way is recognizing that it is a force that has always had to contend with thinking, feeling, knowing, choice-making, and acting workers. And at the centre of this lay the skills, knowledge, and expertise workers inherit and create, which are at the same time those that management desperately needs to shape and control.

Demonstrating further parallels still, Rice's body of work might also be used to highlight one final feature of this book. Rice is actually credited with having introduced the *flashback* narrative structure to American theatre. Common to movies and theatre today, it is a technique through which we are made acutely aware how the present and future depend deeply on the past. I too rely on flashbacks – a type of *memory work* approach – of a kind.[2] Workers I spoke with recounted their work lives and work practices. In their stories are found topics that were boiling in their thoughts at that moment as well as the topics that were suspended just beneath the surface of their thoughts. The flashbacks contained in these stories – whether they were from the day before, a week, a year, or decades prior – provide a major resource for researching as well as accomplishing the learning of occupational life. A robust analysis of learning in occupational life can and must attend to the dynamic relationships among knowledge content, experience, space, as well as time in the structure of narratives. It is in this way that workers' stories are the foundation of this research. These stories cannot be separated from occupational biography and distinctive social standpoints. And, although these lives never reach the dystopian depths of Mr. Zero's, the stories and their implications are no less dramatic.

Purposes of the Book

This book comes at a time of dramatic changes to the nature of public sector occupations around the globe (cf. Seddon, Henriksson, and Niemeyer

2010). In the context of profound pressures for state austerity at virtually every turn, I argue that studying such occupations offers an ideal opportunity to explore how questions of *price, worth, human need, and purpose* bear on the re-organization of learning in occupational life. We discover further detail on how public sector workers' learning is accommodating, contesting, and floundering *in times of change* like these. It presents a sustained example of the analysis of *mind* not simply as a thoroughly cultural and historical phenomenon, but as a thoroughly political economic one as well. I argue that too many have forsaken the dense and often intimate fabrics of mind in political economy: the fact that in every instance of our participation in political economy, in every arrangement of work we encounter, in every single product or service we produce, and amid the minutiae of our working lives are found our opportunities to learn one thing, or to learn another.

Specifically I explore the complex machinations that define the struggle for the meaning, purpose, and soul of a vital occupation in Western capitalism: *state welfare work*. This is an occupation charged with administration of the fault-lines among the state, the economy, and poverty. In many ways, it is an occupation that is virtually definitive of the challenges – and indeed the failures – of advanced capitalist societies in their ongoing recreations of the relationship between notions of human welfare and the poor. And I claim that work design, the labour process, and mind in political economy are central to our understanding in this regard. Combining and extending the now-classic observations of Piven and Cloward (1971) and Lipsky (1980), in this book we can begin to see more clearly how the state has learned and re-learned an important lesson: *to discipline the poor requires the effective disciplining of those who administer the poor*. That is, there is no state law, legislation, program, or policy that ever becomes reality without being polished, perfumed, mis-interpreted, distorted, or otherwise filtered through the lives of public sector workers and their labouring/learning processes.

While the 1970s and 1980s produced particularly remarkable engagements with the challenges and possibilities of social services work of this kind, I suggest an extended re-engagement of the type offered here has an important place. Today, even amongst many of the researchers taking up critical social and political economic questions about state welfare, state welfare workers themselves are far too often depicted as automatons, cyphers of the state, or simply scapegoats. While refusing to white-wash the failures, tensions, and contradictions, this research is among those that continue to serve as a counter-weight to the straw-man portrayals that have been made of the lives of these workers. The analysis shows how the job of state welfare work is charged with moral and ethical as well as financial implications (for workers, the poor, and the state itself). Deep within these working lives we find contested learning and an occupation that is more complex and more contradictory than even most of its practitioners themselves care to admit. In recognizing this we recover an interpretation of occupational knowledge as political economic struggle: an interpretation that, as Baines (2008) points out, links these forms of work and learning to something the political theorists Antonio Gramsci referred to as *trench warfare*.

In the most basic sense, I recover yet another story of workers struggling under *the pressures and the limits*, as the Marxist cultural studies scholar Raymond Williams used to say, of capitalism. However, it is the world of monopoly-finance capitalism, neo-liberalism, and austerity shrunk down to the everyday act of producing a welfare cheque. In the shrunk down beginnings of this analysis, we re-discover the agency and choice-making, but going further reveal an entry point into much broader processes that give new insights into how workers are faced with and face up to powerful techno-organizational and political economic machineries. We will see at times workers are thoroughly *engrossed* – even entranced – in the course of their near-manic search for the next technical fix on the job. At other times workers waver or shirk and drag their feet on the job and seem to wait on their own decisions about just what kind of welfare worker they will be. At still other times, facing the very same techno-organizational machineries, workers struggle to re-inherit a half-imagined tradition of welfare work which, like a train pulling away, seems to be a tradition getting smaller and smaller. To be sure, the dynamics of how these tendencies unfold are neither uncomplicated nor unrelated. I demonstrate the independencies of historical, political economic, sociological, and psychological dimensions of learning empirically. I demonstrate how and why it is that there is enormous variability in the trajectories of occupational knowledge construction. In this way certain claims about the stability and interpretability of working skill, knowledge, and expertise, too often presumed in research on learning, skill, and the labour process, are challenged. In their place, I make claims that the vicissitudes and contestations that make up workers' learning play a significant role in defining the meanings of skill and knowledge, as well as an occupation over time.

The details of *how* skill, knowledge, and learning unfold in the concrete and rapidly changing realities of contemporary public sector human services are central. In fact, the research presented in this book began at the same time that a major public sector restructuring of welfare services in Ontario (Canada) was officially launched in 2002. It was a change initiative that affected general welfare as well as welfare benefits associated with the disabled. Central to this radical, new, legislatively supported labour process was the introduction of alternative divisions of labour, work rules and procedures, human resource practices, and, notably, a new intra-net based computer system called the Service Delivery Model Technology (SDMT). This was a transformation that at its birth in 2002 impacted the administration of more than $1.5B in social assistance (over $2B in 2011) at an operating cost of approximately $177M per year ($247M in 2011); it directly affected more than forty-seven municipalities across more than 290 separate offices, approximately one hundred First Nations (Aboriginal) sites, and more than seven thousand state welfare workers at the time (6800 in 2011); and it was a transformation that severely affected the lives of approximately 670,000 of Canada's poorest citizens (more than 800,000 in 2011). Notably, this was an initiative that would also depend upon a public/private partnership with the consulting firm who designed the SDMT system and work process, and who over the period of study would be associated with the surrender of certified accounting licences by its parent company in one of the largest public fraud cases in North American history (Enron). We will see that the financing of this scale of transformation depended upon issuing payments to the consulting firm vis-à-vis a system of accounting for welfare cost savings (cost avoidance) embedded in the technology and labour process design themselves. And, I argue, this transformation process utilized a high-tech, contemporary Taylorization of the occupation that brought with it new expressions of contradictions to the lives of front-line state welfare workers, as well as managers and the poor.

The research for this book lasted for the first seven years of the change process (2002–9) with the bulk of data gathering taking place in the first five years. Ironically, five years was the time-frame that Fredrick Winslow Taylor specifically named, in his testimony to the 1912 United States House of Representatives' investigation of the effects of Taylorism, as necessary to produce a successful transformation to his method of working. The data gathering and the level of access provided to the research team were made possible by working closely with the union representing these state welfare workers (the Canadian Union of Public Employees-Ontario [CUPE-Ontario]). Events I explore here, and the level of access this partnership with CUPE-Ontario provided, offer an ideal opportunity to analyze the processes of construction and re-construction of skill, knowledge, and expertise in the course of large-scale technological and labour process change in the public sector. It also offers an opportunity to glimpse – within the dynamic relations of mind in political economy – the forms of consent, accommodation, and resistance that workers can undertake when an occupation is forcefully attacked.

I demonstrate the implications of the many layers and enormous variability in work skill within these change processes. The research tells of how thinking, feeling, knowing, and acting people *can* and *do* take many *divergent trajectories* within and towards forms of occupational expertise in the course of work activity itself. Workers cluster and are clustered together in groups, producing dynamics which regularly amplify their learning by way of distinctive *spheres of meaning and communication* and what are called *zones of proximal development*. Through these processes, they affirm and renew, alter and re-alter the trajectories of their learning. Not infrequently, they are learning across different trajectories of skill and knowledge development *at the same time*. Throughout we see how it is that they exercise distinctive forms of *agency*. They choose to focus their learning at some points in time and in some places, on some things rather than others, but this involves a struggle over the establishment of *horizons* of agency and choice. According to the theoretical traditions used in this book, I argue that these horizons are shaped deeply by the unfolding of activity and work space design conceived under the auspices of Taylorism. I show these horizons are shaped by an occupational heritage of past symbolic and material artefacts, and configurations of these artefacts, of state welfare work activity. And I explore how these horizons of possibility – horizons linked to a shifting landscape of key or leading forms of activity – are also shaped by an even more fundamental struggle over the contradiction among the needs of capitalism, the capitalist state, and the human use-values in the lives of clients and workers. We discover new insights into the structure of activity that explain the *processes* as well as the *limits* of control in occupational learning.

Labour Process Theory (LPT) and Cultural Historical Activity Theory (CHAT) are the two primary points of departure for the analytic approach I use here. Respectively, I will show that the tradition of LPT initiated by Harry Braverman – widely and divergently developed since – with its focus on the contradictions of divisions of labour, autonomy, control, and skill remains essential. However, I will also argue there are limits to the assistance that LPT can provide, on its own, in terms of realizing the research goals of the book. As I explain later, this is the case for several reasons. Despite the persistent concern for the dynamics of skill, knowledge, and control, in even the most penetrating studies of work, difficulties emerge in analyses of the dynamics of learning themselves. LPT studies increasingly recognize the importance of context, social and collective skill, knowledge formation, and even something called knowledgeability but then struggle to conceptualize them in close empirical study. Although it is a broad criticism, I nevertheless suggest that it is difficult to side-step the fact that too much labour process research depends upon, defaults to, or otherwise suffers from the persistent influence of reductionist models of human learning and development. Offered few other viable options, much LPT research continues to trade in proxies for learning and skill rather than practices (Warhurst and Thompson 2006).

Equally, there are also limitations to be found in the bulk of studies focusing specifically on work-based learning itself. Again, this is a very broad criticism. By way of introduction only, in the first instance, amongst those who research in the growing sub-field of work and learning generally, few researchers consistently draw on the rich findings and theories of labour process, sociology of work, and organizational and technological design. Only a select number adequately address the historical, political, and economic mediations that shape practice (see Sawchuk 2010a, b). Too often the character of the workplace is taken as pre-ordained even while, as it is so often remarked, work and employment are in a constant process of change. Even amongst the most robust studies of work-based learning – in fixating on worker *adaptation* – we only ever find half of the story of workers' learning lives. In reality, workers create as well as adapt. At the absolute minimum, they create the conditions of their own adaptation. Thus, conceptualizations of transformation – frustrated, limited, or realized expansively – must be addressed, but are regularly given short shrift. This point is hardly insignificant to the theorization of learning, and it summarizes the rationale for a turn toward CHAT in this case. However, even in this CHAT research tradition, the integration of critical perspectives that might inform a mind in political economy approach to the learning/labour process remains elusive.

Taken together, the types of limitations I allude to help explain why inquiry into conflict, cooperation, learning, and change languishes at a conceptual *impasse* on the question of work skill. As a contribution to breaking this impasse I claim that overcoming the limits within and across the two solitudes – of detailed studies of work, on the one hand, and detailed studies of work-based learning, on the other – is one of the first orders of business. It is in this context that I claim there is value to be found in introducing a CHAT approach into an empirically informed dialogue with the traditions of LPT research.

Outline of the Book

I emphasize here and elsewhere that understanding more deeply the human face of the *how* of workers' learning is likely a key stepping stone for developing new, robust theories of the labour process, and along the way issues related to social change as well. In these terms, cultivating the analytic means of balancing aggregated, proxy measures of occupational skill and attitudes with the details of the labour/learning process practices themselves is critical. This concern for the learning process has influenced both the research in this book and the sequence of presentation of findings. In fact, it is suggested that the quickest way to bury oneself at the skills impasse is to work from a traditional social science model that, for example, *begins* analysis with a pre-established set of social groups (e.g., based on work experience, gender, race, educational training) *and then* explores how learning and skill based on these groups emerge. Among other things, this type of imposition obscures the human agency and variability of lived practices (cf. Smith 1987). Indeed, learning produces group formation as well as unfolds from it; social as well as collective dynamics *are dimensions of* the learning process. My point is that a traditional social science model would make the mistake of using as a *resource for claims-making* (e.g., the existence of groups) the very things that should be the *objects of claims-making.*[3] If we are to take the active construction of human learning and along with it the active construction of the social world seriously, then we must proceed in a different way. In this book I purposively begin with the details of the occupational learning processes. I then proceed to test and extend findings with quantitative data.

In taking this approach I attempt to move decisively beyond descriptive accounts of on-the-job, informal, self-directed, or incidental learning that researchers have, by now, become less enthusiastic about given the limited answers they can actually provide on their own. Rather, by placing LPT and CHAT approaches into dialogue with one another, and supporting them with a small, selective range of additional conceptual resources, I attempt to sustain a series of claims about how skill formation, consent, control, and resistance unfold in diverse ways in the course of daily work life based on the agentive construction and re-construction of learning *within activity.* To be clear, state welfare workers we meet in this book are experiencing not only complex and contradictory work lives but also distinct and divergent trajectories of occupational development. While they are not ignored here, we nevertheless find that factors like educational attainment, workplace training participation, the use of advanced ICT, for example, do not speak to occupational learning with the type of analytic power that is conventionally ascribed to them. Such factors offer only very limited explanations of performance, coping, flexibility, and occupational learning as such. They certainly do not allow us to decipher the existence of the thing referred to today as *knowledge work* (a term that I ignore going forward for reasons that will become obvious). However, in orienting to the dynamic nature of work-based *activity* as the basis for how the *machineries of knowledge construction* are themselves *constructed* (Knorr Cetina 1999), we can nevertheless understand these and many other factors as matters of contradictory forms of mediation.

It is against this backdrop that the book poses and answers the following types of questions:

- What contribution does the everyday knowledge production of workers make toward defining their occupation *in times of radical change*?
- What are the means of organizational *control and its limits* in the context of the machineries of knowledge construction, the shifting shapes of mediated activity, and the agentive learning of *consent, accommodation, and resistance* in occupational life?
- What role might *Taylorism* play in contemporary work change?
- In what ways do unique *biographies and broader social differences* such as those related to education, social class, gender, race, and disability continue to shape occupational learning lives?
- And what is the role of the *contradictions of capitalism* in occupational learning within and beyond capitalism?

No doubt the basic story of occupational change underlying this research is already recognizable (perhaps eerily so), and the preceding questions offer a basic indication of what is to come. Likewise, whether or not the concepts and themes gestured at so far are more or less familiar, several of the basic arguments I will attempt to make are discernible as well. However, the following chapter-by-chapter outline provides some final, introductory points of clarification concerning the material contained in the book and its order of presentation.

Chapter 2, 'The Skills Impasse and an Activity Approach', provides the basis for the uses of LPT and CHAT in the book. It is divided into two parts. In Part 1 I establish a key rationale for the book in terms of a critique of what I call the skills impasse. This involves a brief interrogation of the origins and contemporary status of this impasse across indicative samples from sociology of work with special emphasis on developments in the

LPT tradition. I discuss the relations between theory and socio-economic changes from the mid-twentieth century to the present. I summarize recent trends regarding the increasing number of skill types and learning processes that researchers are identifying which I claim foment rather than resolve the skills impasse. Within this, LPT is positioned as a key framework through which robust analysis of occupational learning and development in times of change might proceed. In Part 2 of this chapter I outline a rationale for and substance of a CHAT approach to occupational learning and knowledge construction within labour process activity. I define and interpret its terminologies, points of emphasis, and highlight a type of impasse it too faces related to the role of contradiction in learning and human development. I conclude with a summary explanation (and definition) of several key terms important to the study of state welfare work in the remainder of the book.

The controversial and enigmatic concept of *de-skilling* is an important concern within this book. It is a concept that has both lurked in the shadows and emerged boldly into the light at various points in scholarly debate over several decades. Linked tightly with historical changes in work design, it is a concept that rose to prominence in critical scholarship in the second half of the twentieth century and more recently has tended to recede. I argue that to understand how de-skilling may still matter a great deal today requires a fresh look back at the idea that, for the most part, inspired it. In Chapter 3: 'Taylorism –an Enduring Influence', I demonstrate why studies of past, present, or future work arrangements under capitalism benefit from a re-consideration of the unique strengths and weaknesses of Frederick Winslow Taylor's Scientific Management. My argument is for moving beyond the dismissal of Taylorism. I draw on some original writings by Taylor and early studies of his efforts at implementation, as well as offer a critical summary of contemporary perspectives that have attempted either to refute or to confirm Taylorism's character, implications, or existence. Contrary to both popular belief as well as much scholarly literature, I argue that the defining features of Taylorism revolve around his understanding of the over-arching powers of three inter-dependent elements: materiality, task design, and the independent nature of worker culture and learning. As powerful as they are contradictory and under-estimated, these are basic features from which all other specific aspects of his approach flow, which can and have been systematized in a host of ways, which have appeared at various times in various organizations and sectors, but which can still be readily recognized today.

This book deals with a distinct occupation within public social services as well as a distinct labour process that is in transition. The historical specificities, in these terms, are vital and undergird the claims throughout the book. In Chapter 4, 'Historical Mediations in the Making of Taylorism in Contemporary State Social Services Work', I offer a sketch of the historical and international origins, as well as the ongoing tensions, that define state welfare work as part of the broader family of social work occupations in Canada. Included here is a critical overview of the Anglo-American influences on practice and the literature that has examined the different phases of change in state welfare labour process specifically. I argue these historical details are central to explaining the resources and conditions of both consent and resistance within the labour process as it exists now; hence, in many ways Chapters 3 and 4 initiate the empirical analysis of the book. I conclude the chapter with further description of the organizational change initiative with which these Canadian state welfare workers have had to cope. Here the role of occupational history, public sector austerity, neo-liberalism, and, broader still, globalized monopoly-finance capital are outlined as important elements of learning activity itself rather than simply the context in which it occurs.

In Chapter 5, 'Experiencing the De-Skilling Premises of Welfare Work', we find personalized and extended commentary by state welfare workers on their experiences of the labour process in terms of the division of labour, autonomy, control, and workload. Introductory elements of a CHAT approach are interwoven. We explore the evidence of Taylorization and what I refer to as the "de-skilling premises" of work activity, skill, and knowledge production. Notable impacts of the new labour process on learning seen here include changes in worker orientations to clients, worker participation in a rigid reconstruction of the fully biographical client/person as case and then caseload, as well as the emergence of new patterns of client/worker relations more broadly. Indeed, the initial case for understanding worker-client relations as lying at the centre of the occupational knowledge form targeted by Taylorist design is offered.

While Chapter 5 introduces the self-conscious dimensions of workers' experience of labour process activity, in Chapter 6, 'De-Skilling – Learning Welfare Work and the Mediations of Space, Time, and Distance' I turn attention to artefact mediation with a focus on less self-conscious aspects of the material relations of space, time, and distance. Spatiality has obviously been on the agenda of social research for some time now, but I argue the spatial dimension of occupational learning itself is still too often ignored empirically. Explicitly surfaced in the interview data we see the new labour process – that is, the newly spatialized labour process – to be as powerful as it is taken for granted within the occupational knowledge production process. Drawing on the work of sociologist Henri Lefebvre, we see how changes in office design, new rules of work, and new divisions of labour constitute new relations of what he termed conceived, perceived, and lived space. Attention to this seen but largely unnoticed dimension of activity helps to explain further, for example, many of the origins of the initial experiences that workers voiced in the previous chapter. I show that the mediations of space, time, and distance form a unique dimension of the newly implemented Service Delivery Model Technology (SDMT) system in state welfare work. Specific software functions produce new distances, new sequential arrangements in time, and new spatialized relations of supervision within which workers must operate. These operations appear at first blush as virtual, but their dynamics are nevertheless underpinned by concrete materialities which give them particular force. I show how these new space/time operations, in turn, play a role in constituting a dominant form of object-relatedness in activity with important implications for the establishment of different trajectories of learning.

Workers are never mere appendages to the machineries of either work or knowledge construction at work. They agentively and creatively act. This is far from a novel observation. However, in terms of learning, skill, and knowledge formation, their practices can be seen to revolve around abilities to make both personal sense and collective meaning of their work. I argue that this helps explain the variability of practice in a unique way. State welfare workers are shown individually and collectively to re-skill, though always in relation to the de-skilling premises of conceived space. Thus, in Chapter 7, 'Re-Skilling, Consenting, and the Engrossments of Administrative Knowledge', I demonstrate how workers in the same objective conditions learn in different ways. For some, the basic conditions of activity undergo processes of inflection at different points in time, in the course of establishing what are termed "administrative trajectories" of occupational development within activity. Key terms of reference incorporated into a CHAT analysis of the learning/labour process in this chapter include games, making-out, relative/repressive satisfactions, and, in particular, the dynamics of engrossment. We see that what these workers encounter is challenging. It requires substantial operational expertise. More specifically the labour process requires and shapes forms of what I call "repair-work/skill" and "sense-repair-work/skill". The construction of these forms of expertise is fragile and necessarily involves deviation from the organizational script: distinctive types of workarounds. We see it is through the learning of particular types of workarounds that the labour process is made flexible enough to accommodate a range of occupational identities at hand, undergoing change, and now in question. The data demonstrate how it is that many workers, far from bureaucratic caricatures, establish enormously rich, engrossing learning lives that produce limited (and limiting) forms of expertise. They struggle and learn forms of practice that accomplish a personal sense of individuated agency and control while generating and then satisfying an array of relative/repressive satisfactions. In particular we see that while complex forms of skill, knowledge, and administrative expertise are developed, their trajectory is defined by the establishment of the contradictions amongst operations and goals as a fixture of occupational learning within activity.

In contrast to the type of re-skilling, administrative identity, and object-relatedness of activity discussed in the previous chapter, in Chapter 8, 'Up-Skilling, Resisting, and Re-Keying for Craft Knowledge', the focus is on the active struggle to construct, re-inherit, and maintain oppositional orientations and trajectories of occupational learning through what is called the re-keying of activity. We see how activity undergoes inflection by groups and individuals who recover and reproduce modes of participation, identities, and object-relatedness as a form of welfare work "craft expertise". Seemingly mundane, upon closer examination these are not simple learning accomplishments. Workers struggle to construct service to a fully biographical client, they struggle actively to erode the secondary processing of clients into cases and caseloads, and, importantly, they struggle to rebuild client/worker relation as having an inherent use-value. Meeting clients' ongoing needs in opposition to the new prevailing structure of work rules, literal interpretations of legislation, and the more general strictures of the new Service Delivery Model Technology system, for example, constitutes defining elements of a specific trajectory of knowledge formation. These practices further illustrate how specific operations, goals, object/motives, as well as alternative, re-keyed leading activities unfold through individual and collective intervention. As with the activity discussed in the previous chapter, these workers are developing enormously rich, if turbulent, occupational learning lives. Complex forms of craft skill, knowledge, and expertise are observed. These are seen to have fragile beginnings that are more than capable of collapsing. Preserving and advancing them involve the ongoing production of what are called self-talk and we-talk mantras (discursive artefacts) capable of mediating a rejection of the types of relative/repressive satisfactions and engrossments seen in the prior chapter. Of particular relevance, trajectories of craft knowledge production are seen to be defined by the establishment of contradictions across operations, goals, *and* object/motive as a fixture of activity. Here the repair-work/skill and sense-repair-work/skill explored previously are joined by an analysis of what is termed "object-work/skill". A fundamentally more expansive, less limiting, and more contentious form of occupational knowledge is the result.

Further substantiating how the same objective conditions of work can and do result in divergent trajectories of occupational learning and development amongst contemporary state welfare workers, in Chapter 9, 'Divisions of Knowledge Production, Group Formation, and Occupational Enculturation', I focus on how different trajectories of learning are mediated by group formation practices in labour process activity. I explore the important effects – both those which are real as well as those which are imagined but treated as real – of changing entry level qualifications. In fact, we learn that the new labour process included a formal change in entry-level qualification. Conventionally, this would be taken as a prime indication of de-skilling. However, drawing on both qualitative and quantitative data analysis, we see in this chapter that amongst those hired since the introduction of the new labour process educational attainment levels actually tended to be highly similar. Despite this, we see that, mediated by the emergence of increasingly homogeneous spheres of group communication and learning, a functioning mythology of downgraded qualifications along with specific human resources practices shape how learning in labour process activity unfolds in divergent ways. The implications for inter-generational occupational enculturation, I argue, are pronounced. In the latter half of this chapter a range of key observations stemming from the qualitative analysis are tested by drawing on the province-wide survey of state welfare workers. Having established the detailed processes of occupational learning earlier, here we begin to recognize more clearly the influences of prior work experience as well as more subtle (though statistically significant) effects of class self-identification, union participation, computer literacy, and educational attainment on divergent trajectories of knowledge formation.

Building further on the details of the labour/learning process and the argument for multiple trajectories of learning, in Chapter 10, 'Understanding Prevalence, Roots, and Factors of Trajectories of Knowledge Production', I undertake a sustained testing and extension of broader dynamics of occupational learning using the survey data. Here I explore the character and explanations for emergent, alternative styles of career within the occupation of state welfare work. We first see how, as a snap-shot in time, the survey data can be used to approximate the prevalence of the different trajectories of learning amongst state welfare workers. Attention to key litmus test questions in the survey is necessary. We learn that one such question involves workers' views on, at the time, the proposed closure of the centralized provincial Intake Screen Unit (ISU) call centre system, a question which proved a salient expression of worker orientation to the new division of labour generally. Views on the closure of the ISU separated starkly in ways that were internally consistent within the data. I demonstrate a roughly even split across those engaged in trajectories of administrative and craft knowledge construction as well as a third trajectory of learning (termed "floundering") amongst those struggling to maintain a basic semblance of acceptable job performance. Next, the survey data are used to explore more deeply an influence that emerged in the qualitative analysis as a potentially important mediator of craft knowledge production: level of labour union participation in the workplace. The analysis shows that union participation constituted an influential, additional sphere of communication and learning that produces a more internally coherent, "amalgamated critique" of the labour process that, in turn, could mediate trajectories of knowledge production in specific ways. I conclude the chapter with intensive consideration of how the many different variables identified in the survey data interact by way of two factor analyses. The first produces a clear profile of the unique combination of mediations influencing the three core modes of participation in state welfare work activity: administrative, craft, and floundering trajectories of learning. Complementing this, a second factor analysis explores evidence of additional, broader influences on the pathways that lead toward and along these distinctive trajectories of occupational learning. In the latter case, I show how educational attainment, computer literacy, social work training, gender, disability, age, social class, and race do (and in some cases do not) seem to afford entry to the different trajectories of knowledge formation.

Finally, in Chapter 11, 'Mind in Political Economy and the Labour Process – a Use-Value Thesis', I look at how the conceptual and empirical work has laid the foundation for a distinctive, dialogical alternative for analyzing skill, work, technology, complexity, autonomy, and control. A specific Use-Value Thesis is summarized which provides the basis upon which I synthesize the core conceptual and empirical claims across the book as a whole. It speaks to an approach that emphasizes the core dimensions of contradiction defining occupational learning lives within advanced capitalism. That is, learning and development within activity are shown to be deeply shaped by the myriad instances of the mutually supportive and mutually undermining relationships between exchange-value and use-value. This key dialectical relationship, I suggest, offers a means to make more visible the existence of both powerful forms of control and the limits of this control in the learning lives of workers as thinking, feeling, knowing, choosing, and acting human agents. The key practices of repair-work/skill, sense-repair-work/skill, and object-work/skill are placed in relationship to broader historical, political, and economic dynamics. Likewise, I confirm the importance of the process through which human thought, meaning, and personal sense are shaped in the course of unfolding labour process activity and that, under certain conditions, such dynamics produce divergent trajectories of learning through which an occupation may be re-defined.

Data Sources and Interpretation

The sociologist George Psathas expressed an important point in speaking to the presentation of data.

> Here I would assert my phenomenological predilections for all these researchers. Bring us to the phenomena directly and as clearly and comprehensively as possible. Allow us to see for ourselves as much as you claim to have seen. This means bring us the actual observations, in detail. (Psathas 1996, p. 389)

Before attempting to present "actual observations, in detail", it is of course equally important to supply some details concerning how these observations were gathered and interpreted. This research deals with a radical shift in the labour process. In the course of it, a semi-professional occupation is being transformed into a job that seemed, to many workers, to be anything but that. For these reasons, workers and their union were eager to join with academic researchers to explore the issues. Arrangements for this research grew out of discussions with a president of a local union of CUPE-Ontario representing state welfare workers. Sitting at a table in the Cat's Caboose tavern, together we arrived at a focus and sketched a research design. Through him other local presidents representing workers employed across small and large welfare offices in urban centres, mixed urban/sub-urban locations, and dispersed rural settings were recruited. Agreements were established to report on the research to member representatives at provincial social services meetings, and a rotating group of key informants (including the local union presidents, some local officers, and union researchers) were set in place and eventually helped guide the interpretation of results.[4] Beginning in 2002, the core research was undertaken until 2007 and followed by continued consultation to the end of 2009. Notably, this is a period that both pre-dates and includes state responses to significant global economic crises beginning in 2008. In this way, the research captures information on change in workers' lives at a critical juncture.

Herein we find not only a multi-disciplinary dialogue, but a *multi-methodological dialogue* as well. The true heart of the analysis, however, is based on a series of lengthy, wide-ranging, open-ended "learning life history" interviews carried out by me and a team of graduate students with a purposive sample of front-line state welfare workers from multiple work sites (n = 75). Care was taken to reach the membership across all major demographic variables to mirror what was known about the population of welfare workers in Ontario generally. This included recruitment of workers active and not active within their union; the bulk of interviewees were not active in the union (see Appendix). On the basis of worker interest level, some of these interviews lasted only an hour or two. Others, however, lasted much longer and took place over multiple sessions. The focuses of these discussions were experiences of change; the state of their occupation; their perspectives on clients; the personal sense of the purposes of their work; their daily practices, skills, and learning; as well as their broader working and learning lives. These interviews resulted in a little more than two thousand pages of single-spaced transcription.

Formal interviews were not the only source of qualitative information for the research reported in this book, however. One of our team was assigned to spend time at welfare offices and took field notes. Other sources of insight emerged in more coincidental fashion. For example, as part of our recruitment strategy veteran workers were sometimes asked to host evening gatherings at their homes where a number of one-on-one interviews could take place. A group of three to four researchers would attend and general explanation of the research would be given in a living room. Then people would split off to carry out individual interviews where recording sound was adequate while other workers waited patiently, enjoying a snack. With the smell of fresh coffee, chili, or pizza in the air, we learned early in the research that sitting in on discussions between workers after the formal interviews would be particularly helpful to understanding both shared and differing concerns. It was at such times that the notions of divergent perspectives as well as divergent trajectories of learning first came into view. After their interviews workers would mill about in open discussion. (A teenager of the house might peer from the hallway, wondering why rooms quiet a minute earlier had all of sudden gotten so loud.) Stepping out into the autumn air to smoke cigarettes together we could listen to workers support and contradict each other about questions they had just minutes before answered definitively in an individual interview. Sometimes ideas were being heard by both the researchers and co-workers for the first time. Between puffs of smoke, a worker might duck her head in the door and yell out as if she were in the stands at her son's hockey game, 'I TOLD YOU IT WASN'T JUST ME, LINDA!' A round of laughter followed by a buzz of discussion would be ignited inside. Experiences like these not only were fun, but sensitized the research to multiple perspectives, realized, pending, hidden, shared, and often contradictory. An expression of the occupational culture – long built-up, usually unspoken, and now potentially in decline – was made at least partially available to analysis even as people put on their coats and carried away any leftovers wrapped in tinfoil.

These types of broader findings, along with the interview data, were further contextualized, tested, and expanded upon through the administration of a survey of a purposive sample of the population of state welfare workers in the province as a whole (n = 339). Importantly, this survey was designed to work in a conceptually unified way with the qualitative research in order to generate a more fully realized multi-methodology. Paper and pencil surveys were distributed to workers through the careful selection of union locals across Ontario to produce sample representativeness in terms of geography, urban, mixed urban-suburban, and rural settings and average office size. The response rate was 30 per cent. As always, the lack of true random sampling in this method recommends cautious attempts at inference for which support from the qualitative findings is crucial. As we will see, the quantitative analysis (appearing in the latter portion of the book) relies on descriptive statistics. I summarize results of a variety of cross-tabulations including, where relevant, indications of statistical significance (chi square testing of association), and, I also carry out factor analysis of these data.

Beyond our limited use of ethnography, each of the two central research instruments was designed to speak to themes stemming from *both* cultural historical psychology of work *and* sociology of work. They were designed, in other words, to mesh the analysis of mind in political economy and the dynamics of activity (e.g., mediating artefacts, operations/conditions, goal-direct action and objects of work activity, personal sense / meaning-making, zones of proximal development) with analysis of the dynamic structures of the labour process offered by sociologies of work and work system design (e.g., divisions of labour, task control, work routing, autonomy and complexity, changes in workload and work performance, office and technological design, surveillance and organizational management, political economic context). Taken as a whole, I argue that this type of mixed-methods design has the potential to begin to answer the types of research questions and analytic concerns posed here. Indeed, it is difficult to imagine other ways in which the expansive, historical, cultural, political, economic, as well as deeply personalized, even intimate, processes of adaptation, consent, resistance, and contestation underlying work-based skill and knowledge formation could be effectively embraced within a single research effort.

These notes on method help situate the research and lead us toward a brief statement on interpretation. In these terms, some additional comments on the approach to the interview data are particularly important. I begin with an observation by one of the most discerning students of human interaction in the sociological canon. In *Forms of Talk* (1981), Erving Goffman offers some enduring comments about the complexities and possibilities of how talk works, and what it can and cannot tell us analytically. On the question of interpretation of talk he notes:

> Although who speaks is situational circumscribed, in whose name words are spoken is certainly not. Uttered words have utterers; utterances, however, have subjects (implied or explicit), and although these designate the utterer, there is nothing in the syntax of utterances to require this coincidence. We can as handily quote another (directly or indirectly) as we can say something in our own name. (1981, p. 3)

He goes on to say that "it is not the perspective and standards that are peculiar or the words and phrases through which they are realized, but only that there are more roles than persons" (p. 80). The stories, the claims, the self-talk, the group-oriented we-talk, the confusion, the pleasure, fear, anger, and even the crises indicated in the interview data say a great deal, but cannot fully speak for themselves. Vital to the interpretation are recognizing and *making a resource of* the multiple voices (or rather the many standpoints) within people's accounts. As will become clear, the interpretation of interview data in this book is guided by the fact that the complexity of people's accounts – that is, the *structural arrangements within descriptive accounts* in addition to the opinions and experiences (and occasionally the facts) these accounts provide – is a crucial source of evidence as to the *structure of labour process activity*. Notably, recognizing that there are "more roles than persons", as Goffman points out, provides an opportunity to recognize contradictions and the potential for change. What comes into view here are skill formation, knowledge, and the deeper dynamics of learning/labouring processes in social service work. The general point is that this complexity provides an evidence base for understanding multiple subjects within social activity, and within the self. There are, in G. H. Mead's terms, an 'I' and a 'me' always at play within human thought, within human action, as well as the accounts people provide in research like this. Often, there is also an 'us', 'we', or 'them' to be considered in the mix as well. For the type of analysis I carry out, the production of differences in these terms signals important elements regarding the ongoing, unfolding structure of activity, and workers' *perceived* – as well as their *lived* – place within it. In this research, as with all other interview research, there are points that workers simply cannot self-consciously report, declaratively express, or reflexively formulate, but which are nevertheless analytically available in their accounts.

Taking talk seriously in these ways can be challenging to both the analyst as well as the reader. And in addition to what research instruments help to describe, the interview and the survey interaction represent distinctive, joint interactional accomplishments in themselves (e.g., Suchman and Jordan 1990). Again Goffman is helpful to us here in explaining the following: "When we speak we can set into the current framework of participation what is structurally marked as integral to another" (1981, p. 4). Thus, in the first instance we must recognize that interview-talk (or survey-response-talk) represents a participatory structure in its own right. However, using careful interpretation we can still detect clearly the relationship of interview-based accounts (and to a more limited degree survey responses) to the broader forms of work activity which they describe, *if*, that is, our methods do not disorganize these accounts beyond recognition. The methodological and interpretational claim here is that by using a loose, albeit guided, discussive approach, and by paying close attention to the structure of accounts we can accumulate evidence of the core mediations, key contradictions, objects of engrossment, and so on, of welfare work. This is a point already well explained by the Marxist-feminist standpoint theorist Dorothy Smith in her discussion of how one undertakes the study of everyday life generally.

> The simple notion of the everyday world as problematic is that social relations external to it are present in its organization. How then are their traces to be found

in the ways that people speak of their everyday lives in the course of interviews of this kind? We do not expect them to speak of social organization and social relations. The methodological assumptions of the approach we are using are that the social organization and relations of the ongoing concerting of our daily activities are continually expressed in the ordinary ways in which we speak of them, at least when we speak of them concretely. How people speak of the forms of life in which they are implicated is determined by those forms of life. Wittgenstein opposed the philosophical practice of lifting terms out of their original home and their actual uses in order to explore their essence. I am taking the further step of arguing that the way terms are used in their original context, including their syntactic arrangements, is 'controlled' or 'governed' by its social organization and that the same social organization is present as an ordering procedure in how people tell others about that original setting [...] Given that we do not disrupt the process by the procedures we use, open-ended interviewing should therefore yield stretches of talk that 'express' the social organization and relation of the [original] setting. (Smith, 1987, pp. 188–9)

Smith's discussion of concrete description, "active listening," and "reading through" the interview (or survey) data to examine the social organization of daily life, along with Goffman's observations on the significance of, for example, multiple roles and subjects within talk, are essential to understanding the way I analyze the data in the book. In this case, I suggest this way of looking at the research allows us to begin to see how multiple trajectories of skill, learning, and development occur in the everyday life of the labour process, to chart more clearly the relationship between work and mind in political economy.

And so, it should be clear now that this book attempts to address *both* the broader significance of the skill, knowledge, and learning of people's occupational lives *as well as* the minutiae. However, it is reasonable to ask the question, Why bother with the analytic weight of both? Why attend to, for example, the arrangement of cubicles, the things a worker says to herself, a worker's vacation coverage, her attachment to scraps of paper, or the number of mouse clicks a task requires *in the course of also* exploring how an occupation is being transformed and monopoly-finance capitalism impacts the state's regulation of the poor? Unlike the question, the first answer to it is short. These things are intimately and necessarily linked. The fact is that concrete thinking, feeling, knowing, and acting people arrive at the practices of consent, accommodation, and resistance by no other way except the accumulating minutiae of the learning of their diversely situated daily lives. And, anything we might meaningfully refer to as political economy is ultimately composed of the dynamics of these lives. Even people's most definitive moments of learning and personal change can only be understood in relation to the horizon that these minutiae establish (and can upset), and, as such, we find here a key starting point for interrogating matters of broader social, political, and economic significance. Among other things, I am speaking here of a point with epistemological and ontological undertones, and this gives rise to a brief closing disclaimer.

The book speaks to the fact that the questions of work and skill are complicated. This is mostly because human learning is complicated. What appears to us as skilled performance is always only a Dies Irae, a complex expression of an entire realm and history of individual, social and collective, self-conscious and un-self-conscious, deeply political, economic, and cultural *doings*. To make matters worse, only a slim proportion of these *doings* have learning as the goal, and as such typically go unrecognized by learners themselves. Learning, in other words, is made of a billion things – a murky tangle of tiny details as Vygotsky once said – and these include many things that are seen but unnoticed. Thus, for those knowingly or unknowingly committed to that amalgam of rationalism and individualism (and thus also to the notion that learning is *not* a phenomenon of the kind just described), I suspect that this abridged account of "a billion things" will have limited use.

2 The Skills Impasse and an Activity Approach

Introduction

The critique and conceptual integration in this chapter emerge directly from difficult questions posed by the state welfare worker data. In times of change like these, are the concepts of re-skilling, up-skilling, informal learning, tacit knowledge, knowledgeability, and so on, adequate to the task of addressing the workings of the machineries of knowledge construction in these workers' occupational lives? A first step toward responding to this type of question thus involves reassessing a number of conceptual approaches to work and change for their ability to illuminate, in particular, the *contradictory*, highly *variable*, and potentially *divergent* nature of labour/learning processes specifically. In fact, the evidence called for, in essence, a particular conceptual conversation across labour process, context, skill, knowledge, and learning. And what immediately became clear to me was that the *separation of analyses of work and analyses of the phenomenon of learning itself is the first barrier to be overcome* in moving forward with analysis in this book.

To deal with this separation effectively I claim it is necessary to take a moment to step back, to define several roots of the type of challenges that the analysis would otherwise continually bump against unwittingly. I argue that the data will highlight the need for an approach that is not entirely available in the existing sociology of work, or the Labour Process Theory (LPT) literature specifically; nor is it entirely available in studies of work-based cognition, communication, learning, or Cultural Historical Activity Theory (CHAT) specifically. Focusing on questions of work, skill, and knowledge as well as resistance, co-operation, and consent, in this chapter the basic goal is to establish a clear need for an understanding of the conceptual tools applied in the following chapters.

The chapter is broken into two parts. In *Part 1* I focus primarily on sociology of work and skill that has emerged post World War II. I claim the thinking can be understood as having moved across and within a series of distinctive contributions from *industrialism* and *post-industrialism theses*, prior to encountering its first major conceptual challenge in the work of Harry Braverman's *de-skilling thesis*. Building from the work of Marx, it was Braverman (1974/1998) that ostensibly launched the LPT tradition, and it was his work that initiated a crucial turning point. This development cannot be characterized as a series of paradigmatic successions, however. Rather, a variety of elements of each tradition have remained operative in the study of work, skill, and change, thus creating an admixture increasingly reliant on empirics and conceptual elaborations which have not, I suggest, resolved several core challenges faced by researchers today. Instead, the result has been what I refer to as a *skills impasse* (Sawchuk 2006c). Overcoming it begins with several points of recognition. These points include the fact that roughly equal proportions of robust and persuasive work/skill research demonstrate the following: that disempowerment and resistance occur; that forms of technological and socio-emotional, internal, and external forms of control occur; that in advanced capitalist countries increases in educational attainment continue to occur; that a phenomenon termed de-skilling likely occurs; that re-skilling of some description definitely occurs; and that up-skilling may occur under certain conditions. Over the past three decades – even amongst the strongest pieces of research – rarely is analytic integration considered across these phenomena, much less attempted in close empirical study. With exceptions noted later, in the place of conceptual integration, most often we find a continued trend toward the intensification of arguments about what does or does not constitute knowledge work, knowledgeability at work, traits as opposed to skills, and what might constitute a knowledge economy. Such arguments regularly include rehearsals of the classic and typically dichotomous distinctions between autonomy/control as well as complexity/routine. They involve confusion over the meaning of either knowledge- or technologically-intensive production, and whether the best means of assessing work change is to focus on the worker, the task, the job, the occupation, or workforce characteristics as a whole. I suggest that these types of dichotomies and points of confusion whisk us swiftly, and further, down the rabbit hole of the skills impasse. Moreover, I claim that the proliferation of additional forms of work, skill, knowledge, ability, competencies, performance, or practices does not constitute a viable opportunity for breaking this impasse. Far more often than not, this proliferation only serves to sustain the impasse at new levels of descriptive and empirical complexity. What may be needed now, it seems, are a different type of conceptual dialogue and with it an alternative possibility for integration. Here I am speaking of a dialogue based on a fundamentally *political, historical, contingent, agentive, and fully humanized* conception of work, organizational life, learning, skill, cooperation, conflict, and change. At its heart, I argue that movement toward breaking the impasse requires a basic, yet challenging, recognition that *the pervasive contradictions that shape work under capitalism are at the same time definitive of the learning process, and vice versa.*

To be crystal clear about the substance of this: I am speaking of the necessity for a robust theory of learning and human development that, as much as critical analyses of the labour process, revolves around the endemic contradictions and possibilities of occupational life under capitalism. Indeed, the bulk of the book is bent on demonstrating the myriad ways that this type of approach can be realized and applied. It culminates in what I term a "Use-Value Thesis" on the learning/labour process in the last chapter. It is an approach that seeks to understand the labour and learning processes within a potentially more unified analysis framed by LPT and CHAT, the latter introduced, contextualized, and interpreted in Part 2 of this chapter.

Part 1: Interrogating Research on Skill, Knowledge, and Work – Arguing for a Point of Departure

As George Orwell wrote, "what have you in common with the child of five whose photograph your mother keeps on the mantelpiece? Nothing, except that you happen to be the same person" (quoted in Hitchens 2010, p. 1). So it is that the sociologies of work and skill from the past are linked to the research questions we consider today. It does us no good to ignore history, and this includes the history of our ideas: history is never through with them or us.

This book will be preoccupied with the dynamics of *skill, knowledge, and learning* within the labour process. However, establishing the historical roots that still mediate (in both obvious and hidden ways) the terms of debate in research on the sociologies of work and skill is vital. To do this properly, at the very least we must go back in time to recognize that the two decades following World War II were especially important. These decades expressed the modern apex of sustained, affirmative thinking about the relations between work and skill within English language research, even while many of the ideologies underlying it were much older. It is an achievement deeply intertwined with the unprecedented effects of economic growth that began to unfold at mid-century. It is in this context that what became known in several distinct but closely related guises as the *industrialism thesis* (e.g., Dahrendorf 1959; Kerr, Dunlop, Harbison, and Myers 1962) posited the emergence of an economy, a society, and forms of employment in which *progress* was to be realized through diminishing conflict, increasing co-operation, and a flourishing economic life generally. Understood in conventional terms, it was a short-lived thesis. In the 1950s and into the 1960s, in many Western countries forms of social conflict grew, spilling both from and into workplaces; the panacea of more engaging and less alienating work began to lose what lustre it might have had; and, the ideals of worker-management co-operation at work remained elusive at best. By the turn of the 1970s economic crisis itself was renewed. In less conventional terms, however, the industrialism thesis set the stage for reconsiderations of a new role for skill, knowledge, and creativity in paid work that continues to echo in our research today. As Simpson (1989) pointed out (see also Ritzer 1989; Form 2002; Nolan 2003; Paradeise 2003; Abbott 2009), through the turn of the twentieth century and across the inter-war period, ethnographic research on work was telling a more complex story of occupations, working knowledge, and organizational life.[1] Nonetheless, it was in the post-World War II period that sociology of work, industrial sociology, and forms of organizational analyses took off as robust, sustained, and identifiable disciplines and sub-disciplines.

Virtually from the moment of its appearance however, the industrialism thesis was interrogated vigorously and, in the context of the contentious social changes under way, a *post-industrialism thesis* quickly emerged (e.g., Touraine 1971).[2] Here was presented a more complex vision of progress, a style of progress more difficult to achieve, one clearly admitting the declining relevance of industrial manufacturing, and, one admitting notions of a declining, increasingly programmed, society and culture as well. In this context, post-industrial thesis scholars had begun to establish the relevancy of new, technologically advanced labour processes, they opened the empirical debate on worker alienation in more expansive ways, and they again highlighted the possibilities of wider – and more skilled – participation in work life which was recognized, in the case of Touraine for example, as a double-edged sword. Daniel Bell's *The Coming of the Post-Industrial Society* (1973) likewise proved seminal. Further ratified in *The Cultural Contradictions of Capitalism* (Bell 1976), as in Touraine (1971), the labour process itself became a mere reflection, rather than a core source, of difficulty. Through Bell's work especially (as an English language source),[3] many researchers and policy makers alike gravitated toward and were provided a vocabulary for claiming that changes in culture, computerized technologies, growing educational attainment, and the possibility of knowledge-intensive work could – once again – produce social progress under the auspices of an evolving capitalism.

Across the industrial and post-industrial theses, and all the specific variations within them, what has been retained is the idea that routinized (and particularly repetitive, physically exhausting) work was being or would be – decade by decade – replaced by new forms that required greater use of information, knowledge, discretion, educational attainment, and training. These are themes that in one form or another continue to be seen in analysis today, and from which germinated notions of the knowledge worker and worker as symbolic analyst. Arguments regarding how more complex products and rising service expectations of consumers (often only marginally modified forms of the logic of the post–World War II era) would translate to more complex and engaging labour processes likewise contributed to revitalized perspectives of this kind. Indeed, notions of occupational skill and knowledge production were made an unproblematic resource and, in turn, a crucial object of inquiry and public policy. Amidst all of this, the notion of change *within the confines* of capitalism and the presumption that, in these terms, knowledge and creativity were to play an important role would become hegemonic in the minds of researchers, policy makers, even educators, and, lest we forget, many workers themselves.

My argument is that the continuities represented in the industrialism and post-industrialism theses have remained central to the range of seemingly new visions offered by most researchers concerning how work and change unfold. Referencing several post-industrialism concepts that were considered by so many to be deviations from the industrialism thesis, it is a already claim nicely summarized by Thompson (2003):

> What is striking … is the extent to which each vision of the new is dependent on an assumption of reciprocity, if not between all the actors, then at least between the component parts of the 'paradigm'. For example, flexible specialization and post-Fordist perspectives saw a unity or sequential flow across the different links in the 'design chain', beginning in markets and moving through firm structures, to work and employment. Equally, though in a different manner, knowledge economy theories rest on the assumption of a virtuous circle between companies, employees, consumers and society: 'a cleverer society that will, in turn, demand cleverer service, creating cleverer jobs, to create a sort of virtuous circle of increasing enlightenment' (Lewis, 2001, p. 10). Thus the emphasis on cohesiveness and positive connections between elements in 'the system' continues unabated. (p. 360)

Thompson's point is key. Hegemonic status was conferred on the virtuous circularity of capitalist relations even if in the case of the post-industrial writings of Touraine and Bell, in blurring the lines between work and society, the cohesive and positive connections were made more complex and more contingent. Across the continuities of the industrialism/post-industrialism theses we find, in other words, a persistent analytic drive toward working out the (normative and technical) systemic kinks of an otherwise acceptable political economy. And, crucial to us here, these were viewpoints in which particular presumptions regarding the construction of work knowledge figure prominently. Under the auspices of capitalist progress, learning and human development were to be understood as unproblematic, uncontradictory, as well as primarily adaptive.

Braverman's Departure and the Three Basic Clusters of Research at the Skills Impasse

It is only a small exaggeration to say that a monolithic germ cell growing from the industrialism and post-industrialism theses has remained intact within research on employment and skill over the last sixty years. Certainly proponents of post-industrial thinking would be quick to note distinctions. This research has incorporated understandings, for example, of globalization and dynamic sectoral (or niche) market effects on employment and occupational knowledge over time. In turn, these effects have been the subject of debate as either outlier cases, transient trends, or emergent trends, depending on the side of the skills impasse one occupies. Ideas of knowledge management have been explored and scrutinized. These distinctions are not inconsequential.

What is more consequential, however, is the fact that the work of Harry Braverman consolidated a critique that had been brewing for some time. In establishing what came to be known as the LPT tradition(s) he helped lay bare (rather than initiate) the character of the skills impasse in a variety of ways. With particular attention to Taylorism, in *Labor and Monopoly Capital: The Degradation of Work in the Twentieth Century* (1974/1998) Braverman recovered and nourished what in English language research at that time was a latent branch of Marxist thought: the study of the process of production itself. Braverman's LPT did not deny as relevant but nonetheless set aside subjective dimensions of work and workers to focus on the objective processes and outcomes of Taylorist divisions of labour. He re-analyzed the effects of the separation of conception and execution: the breaking up of workers' capacity for independent knowledge formation. These were expressions, he argued, of capital's necessary and inherent war on workers, explored in his case through the analyses of manufacturing and, to some degree, clerical work. He directly confronted both the industrial thesis and many features of the post-industrial thesis regarding the measurement and interpretation of work skill and knowledge and demonstrated that, on an aggregate level, the fragmentation of jobs generated new levels of managerial control and the degradation of otherwise higher forms of working knowledge. He did so, it should be added, with a pronounced scepticism of the value of higher education.

Braverman's work argued that the presumptions of progress within capitalist labour processes were inherently problematic. What ensued thereafter was a debate over whether employment was being up-skilled, re-skilled, or de-skilled. Confusion over the nature of learning and work skill – in fact, a lack of analytic attention to these phenomena in their own right – regularly undermined effective support for a variety of claims. To a greater and lesser extent, this has essentially continued in more detailed forms to this day. As Wardell, Steiger, and Meiksins noted twenty-five years after the release of *Labor and Monopoly Capital*: "to a casual observer it might have appeared as if, for every researcher who attempted to follow in Braverman's footsteps, another researcher attempted to challenge, if not discredit, Braverman's work" (1999, pp. 1–2).

To understand where we are today and why, extending several observations initially summarized by Thompson (1989), it bears considering how three distinct lines of argument emerged in response to Braverman. First, advancing what was often termed as an *up-skilling thesis* were the likes of Wood (1982), Hirschhorn (1984), Attewell (1987), Spenner (1983, 1988), and Zuboff (1988). Later, additional and distinctive contributions by Nonaka and Takeuchi (1995) and Frenkel, Korczynski, Shire, and Tam (1999), for example, would extend the application of basic principles in innovative ways (Nonaka and company virtually setting in train an entire industry of comparative studies of management and knowledge management). When attending directly to Braverman's challenge initially, these researchers tended to critique his pre-occupations with social class, with industrial craft skill, with Taylorism, and with the objective dimensions of the division of labour. Scholars noted Braverman's lack of attention to niche sectors where new skills were being established, where new technologies were being employed, and, in particular, they observed the seemingly crucial point of the rising levels of educational attainment of workers. How on earth could a de-skilling trend exist when workers in advanced capitalist countries were utilizing the latest computer technologies and becoming so educated? Wood (1982) took seriously the dynamics of control and skill and persuasively demonstrated that skill cannot be understood simply as a label used by management to divide and reduce the power of workers. Like others since, he demonstrated that task complexity, forms of autonomy, as well as educational requirements of employment mattered in their own right, and were unevenly linked to matters of managerial control.

In response to the challenge to Braverman's work, the approaches of LPT continued to evolve to produce a recognizable second cluster of research. Clarifying, extending, sometimes correcting, but otherwise comfortably situated within the orbit of many of Braverman's initial claims were contributors to the edited collection by Zimbalist (1979). Stretching the orbit of these debates further (indeed challenging many aspects of it), were key monographs by Friedman (1977), Edwards (1979), Burawoy (1979, 1985), and Littler (1982). Distinctive extensions of the LPT approach were likewise found in Pollert (1981), Westwood (1984), and Cockburn (1985) as well as the fascinating personalized analysis by Hales (1980) on the trials of intellectual work. Taken as a whole, they gave greater attention to the subjective dimensions of the labour process (such as worker consciousness, resistance, and consent), expanded the consideration of occupational types and sought to address Braverman's exclusion of gendered divisions. More than two decades after Braverman, contributions would continue to appear extending the reach of LPT further (e.g., Milkman 1998; Ritzer 1998). Some updated the argument in relation to manufacturing (e.g., Delbridge 2000) while others pointed toward the need to deal with an even larger number of occupations (e.g., Beirne, Ramsay, and Pantelli 1998; Baldry, Bain, and Taylor 1998; Hampson and Junor 2005). Together a more detailed understanding of command/control processes, new technologies as well as macro-economic factors, different forms of management, and globalization were explained in the context of variations of a general thesis oriented by themes of conflict and control, if not always assuming an absolute position on the matter of de-skilling as such.

A third major stream of argument stemming from the establishment of LPT directed attention to the question of subjective dimensions of the labour process in another way. While attention to subjectivity in the labour process had started to grow even within the first few years of the publication of Braverman (1974/1998), this stream of research organized a search party for the missing subject inspired by the work of Michel Foucault and others in either the post-Marxist, post-structuralist or post-modernist traditions. It was a cluster of research that took the processes of subjectification, social difference, discourse, and identity (as well as an encompassing conceptualization of power) to be central to understanding employment and social reproduction. Certain presumptions of progress inherent to industrialism/post-industrialism (and, as those in this stream argued, Marxist inspired LPT as well) were challenged. Prominent figures have remained Knights and

Willmott (e.g., 1990; 2007). Traditional boundaries between the workplace and society were problematized in a fundamental way. Broader circuits of production as well as consumption and identity were to be observed. The types of concerns that Braverman and others had shown for class struggle, political economy, as well as perhaps working knowledge and skill as such, slipped (and were sometimes forcibly plunged) beneath the waves. According to some (e.g., Tinker 2002), the dimensions of the labour process that ultimately defined it as capitalist were obscured. Influenced by post-Marxism and the work of Laclau, Willmott (2005) summarizes a key defence of the post-structuralist orientation, while earlier the O'Doherty and Willmott (2001) review of post-structuralist LPT offered a constructive synthesis on the basis of a critical realist perspective. The syntheses centred on efforts to maintain/re-develop a perspective on "the complex-media of capital–labour relations, that difficult space where work organization gets produced and reproduced in the everyday accomplishments of agency and social interaction" (O'Doherty and Willmott 2001, pp. 458–9). The earlier work of Storey (1985) was used to argue that Braverman's version of LPT not only had ignored the multiple forms of power and control, but that such dynamics were not related to the logic of capitalism and class struggle alone.

Up-Skilling/De-Skilling at the Skills Impasse

Although Smith and Thompson (1999) argued that it is misleading to allow the industrialism, post-industrialism, Braverman, and the various post-Braverman LPT debates to degenerate simply into an impasse defined by the up-skilling versus de-skilling argument, in many ways, in an increasingly disjointed way, it has done just that. Warhurst, Grugulis, and Keep (2004) maintain that "many of the academics involved in the up-skilling/ de-skilling debates have tended to talk past each other and certainly have avoided direct debate" (p. 5) which solidified the impasse further. Beyond the sources of confusion that Braverman himself pre-emptively identified (1974/1998)[4], amidst the impasse, theories of work were regularly becoming conflated with theories of management: from discussions of synergies, to quality production, just-in-time, lean, agile, and reengineered organizations, not to mention theories on the learning organization and then organizational learning – dense, new discourses regularly expressing many recognizable principles of industrialism/post-industrialism seeped into research as well as practice. Still, several contributions in the 1980s and 1990s on questions of work and change seemed to have the potential to end-run the up-skilling/de-skilling debate. Piore and Sabel (1984), Streeck

(1989), and Womack, Roos, and Jones (1990) for example demonstrated cases of a re-emerging or new forms of craft labour, multi-skilled occupations, and/or processes of re-professionalization that seemed to unsettle the stalemate, for a time. Critiques of these observations often centred on whether such patterns would last and/or spread widely; for the most part we might now conclude that they did neither. More recently the work of Felstead, Gallie, and Green (2002, 2004) and others (e.g., Nolan and Slater 2003; Warhurst and Thompson 2006; Delbridge 2006; Ackroyd 2009; Hampson and Junor 2010) have likewise sustained significant claims that, one way or another, suggest that complexity and increasingly skilled work may not co-vary with autonomy and control at all. Cracks in the skills impasse, in other words, have been and still are detectable.

In what is likely the most definitive summary of the current state of affairs to this point, Warhurst et al. (2004, p. 5) explain that some basic forms of consensus around skill and work have developed. They argue that researchers mutually acknowledge several key principles: (i) skill includes internalized capacities resident in the individual worker; (ii) skill includes job design, divisions of labour, technology, and control; and (iii) skill is socially constructed. These points are vital, as we will see. However, taking a look at this list in comparison to sources representative of the arguments for de-skilling, re-skilling, or up-skilling, it is difficult to conclude that a fundamental advancement in thinking has occurred over the last three decades. Littler (1982), for example, identified task elements, social construction, and control in his analysis of work/skill, while Spenner (e.g., 1983, 1988) fore-fronted the issues of complexity and control. Even the U.S. Dictionary of Occupational Titles (DOT; now the O*NET system) traditionally organized its interpretation of work skill in terms of the complexity of dealing with things, people, or data (in addition to its now very long list of job description terms). Indeed, the remarkable familiarity of the terms of debate surrounding Paul Adler's (2007a) *paleo-Marxist* attempt at conceptual integration on questions of skill and the labour process – a debate which involved many of the leading voices of LPT today – confirms this argument in a number of ways.[5] And instead of advancing toward some form of integrated analysis, the most pronounced trend in the debate is toward a proliferation of skill types.

> One of the most fundamental changes that has taken place in the last two decades has been the growing tendency to label what in earlier times would have been seen by most as personal characteristics, attitudes, character traits, or predispositions as skills. (Warhurst et al. 2004, p. 6)

It is a trend that dovetails with and perhaps depends upon a persistent tendency, again well summarized by Warhurst et al. (2004), that "because skill is difficult to quantify, proxies are used" (p. 5), not infrequently degenerating according to the maxim "what is easy to count gets counted and what is not gets ignored" (p. 10). Or, worse still, skill becomes simply "whatever employers want" (Lafer 2004, p. 118).

Breaking the impasse has proven more difficult than many imagined. Debates at the skills impasse tell us that workers may develop skill involving formal, informal, and tacit dimensions; that these skills may include hard, soft, technical, or social skills; articulation, emotion, authenticity, or aesthetic skills; and, that this regularly seems to involve something called knowledgeability. The identification of skill/knowledge types and content, on its own, does not get us far.

It is against this complex and uneven backdrop that I take a different tact in this book. Here what is typically understood as *skill content* takes a back-seat in analysis to the dynamic practices and processes that lead to its construction, and ultimately its functional meaning in the labour process itself. This is the point that initiates discussion in Part 2, and it is a point explained clearly by Hampson and Junor (2010). Attempting to overcome the *skilled/unskilled dichotomy* – what Hampson and Junor unassumingly refer to as *putting the process back in* – belies a crucial conceptual turn that I try to mirror in a variety of ways. That is, one can look long and hard, but conventional notions of skill content are difficult to find much less interpret. Processes, on the other hand, abound. Moreover, careful analysis of these processes likely reveals far more. And, in the range of ways they occur, the analyses of actual social practices show that skill, skill content and so on are difficult if not impossible to decipher on an individual basis. Indeed, a recognition of the limitations represented by individualized notions of learning are only the tip of the iceberg in consideration of what types of approaches may be needed to begin to break the skills impasse.

Part 2: Understanding the Occupational Learning/Labour Process as Activity

By way of introduction to Part 2 of this chapter I want to begin by building from the following excerpt:

> Activity theory seeks to analyze development within practical social activities. Activities organize our lives. In activities, humans develop their skills, personalities and consciousness. Through activities, we also transform our social conditions,

resolve contradictions, generate new cultural artefacts, and create new forms of life and the self. (Sannino, Daniels, and Gutiérrez 2009, p. 1)

Cultural Historical Activity Theory (CHAT) is a theory of human learning and development that conceives of "activity" as the *minimal, meaningful unit of analysis* for understanding the mutually constituting practices of thinking, feeling, knowing, and doing.[6] Whether CHAT is, for example, a deeply sociological form of psychology or a deeply psychological form of sociology is difficult to say. However, as we will see in the sections that follow, from this perspective, it is impossible to understand individual actors in isolation from the patterns of social relationships, or spatial relationships, or the processes of self-consciousness and un-self-consciousness, or in fact the myriad symbolic and material artefacts that mediate who people are and what they do.

There are of course many theoretical traditions in the human sciences that orient to people as socially constituted in one way or another; rarely, however, are theoretically and empirically robust notions of *human learning* offered by them as well. And roughly speaking, the reverse can be said about theories of human learning and development: that is, most simply do not meaningfully attend to the culturally, historically and materially constituted situations through which the bulk of human learning transpires in societies. In this sense, CHAT means to directly speak to the concept of *mind in society* (Vygotsky 1978). At the same time, what I hope to show in the sections of Part 2 is that the concept of activity – fully in keeping with Marx's concept of praxis, his famous Theses on Feurerbach, his move to turn Hegel on his head, and so on – goes one step further (in so doing expressing particular epistemological and ontological commitments). *Activity* is *not* just a conceptual tool to increase understanding amongst analysts. As the phrasing in the excerpt from Sannino et al. suggests, activity represents the real 'units' (or forms) involved in how you and I carry out our lives. That is, activity speaks to the *minimal unit of concrete agency* through which real, living, and breathing human beings (as either individuals or as a collective subject) act in and on the world, learn, develop, and become. And it is through activity, we might say, that people make history but not simply as they choose.

Necessarily, these introductory comments are general and somewhat sweeping. In a moment we will see that the concept of activity and the CHAT approach more broadly includes a host of associated explanatory terms. These are ideas that have been painstakingly established through both theoretical elaboration and a deep commitment to empirical exploration accumulated over the better portion of a century. And these are ideas that continue to be debated and modified. Importantly and in keeping with the approach I take in this book: these are also ideas that bloomed originally from inter-disciplinary dialogue. This dialogue involved a variety of European intellectual traditions, notably but not exclusively Marxism and dialectical materialist philosophy specifically (e.g., Cole and Scribner in Vygotsky 1978; Engeström 1987; Sawchuk, Duarte, and Elhammoumi 2006; Blunden 2010), and it produced a version of psychology that, from its inception, challenged the boundaries of its discipline, demanding, over time, an even deeper inter-disciplinary conception of human science. Indeed, for Vygotsky (1896–1934), Luria (1902–77), and Leontiev (1903– 79), an inter-disciplinary conception of human science seemed inherent. CHAT may have been born amidst the methodologies and debates of early twentieth century psychology, but for the likes of Vygotsky and company a range of fundamentally new questions were posed that stemmed just as often from their reading across a variety of disciplines including philosophy, linguistics, history, literary studies, biology, physiology, neurology, and so on. And since then CHAT has come to attract the attention of anthropologists, sociologists, political scientists, socio-linguists, communications studies scholars, human resource and management scholars, ergonomists, computer design engineers, and many others.

It is against this historical backdrop that I apply concepts from both CHAT and LPT in the course of analysis of activity in this book in order to explore what, why, and how people do things together in both cooperative and conflictual arrangements over time in a particular occupational context. However, as I signalled at the close of the prior section my investigation will proceed in a particular way with regard to skill and knowledge analysis. As Leontiev (1978) explained:

> the direction of investigation turns *not* from acquired habits, skills, and knowledge to activity characterized by them *but from* the content and connections of activities to which and what kind of processes realize them and make them possible. (Leontiev 1978, p. 113; emphasis added)

Through this approach we will see how experience – accumulated, transformed and embedded in both the self and the environment as artefacts and tools – shapes the limits and pressures of occupational development.

In the following sections I will move from the general and the contemporary issues and purposes through to the historical roots and the specificities of CHAT. We will begin to see more clearly how CHAT is a theory of mind, and along with it a theory of the machineries of knowledge construction, as a thoroughly *agentive, social, material, political, economic,* and *historical* phenomenon. It is a theory that persistently and forcefully directs attention to the importance of the units and forms of everyday life through which people's appropriation, use, and creation of artefacts (i.e., culturally) over time (i.e., historically) explains the potential and limits of their learning and development. With its concern for the *form* of productive processes, its concern for the configuration of the many cultural and material mediations of human practice, as well as its original concern for the fundamental importance of the division of labour specifically – I suggest that the potential overlaps between LPT and the CHAT tradition are pronounced. And, it is in this context, that the goal of Part 2 of this chapter is to provide the bases for intervention into the types of gaps, debates, and impasses outlined in Part 1.

The Departure Marked by CHAT and Its Family Resemblances to Other Traditions of Learning Theory

Perhaps the best way to begin to understand CHAT and the specific approach used in this book is to discuss the critiques of theories of learning and human development that gave and have continued to give rise to its relevance. Indeed, as I hope to show, many of these critiques can be rather easily linked to challenges faced by sociologists of work and skill, and labour process scholars specifically. In the following, I start with contemporary concerns that, I suspect, will be helpful for linking those of CHAT's originators (in early twentieth-century Russia) to research on work-based learning today. For it is through a careful appreciation of the analytic needs that CHAT research attempts to fulfil more generally that we can better imagine its use in this analysis.

Looking across contemporary learning and developmental theory, a critique of a series of limiting tendencies has become well recognized, if not fully appreciated and/or consistently acted upon. For my own part, these tendencies were summarized from the perspective of CHAT as a set of four interlocking biases: (1) individuation, (2) universalization, (3) ahistoricism, and (4) pedagogization/acquisition/adaptation (Sawchuk 2003a). Indeed, I argued that together these biases form a hegemonic bloc because of their mutually supportive character, which, in turn, produces effects uniquely suited to the major social institutions of advanced capitalism specifically. That is, these are biases of the practices of research and theory making that are, either directly or indirectly, linked to learning and human development;

and, they are also biases at work in the unfolding of social practice under advanced capitalism. I claim we can see these biases at play, for example, in the centrality of the *individualized* credentialization of learning, in the functioning of the labour market, and in methods of compensation and career progression. We can see them in the dominant legal frameworks that insist on an *ahistoric-universalized* treatment of social groups (through which disadvantage is allowed to multiply). We see these biases at play in terms of the production, monopolization, and legitimization of authority vis-à-vis forms of knowledge. Underlying such monopolization are the biases of *pedagogy*, individual *acquisition*, the myth of de-contextualized learning transfer, as well as notions of learning as defined by *adaptation*. In fact, resting within this bloc of biases – its glue, if you will – is what can been called the *Cartesian bias*: a series of consequential separations between mind and body, between the internal and external, and between the subjective and objective dimensions of human life. And it is this set of mutually constituting biases that, I argue, undermine the possibilities for developing a coherent understanding of skill, knowledge, and learning in the labour process.

Some, much or most of this critique will be familiar to a range of critically-minded researchers across many of the social sciences. More to the point we find increasing recognition of some (though rarely all) of these types of biases amongst labour process researchers when, that is, concern turns to the concrete processes and practices of skill and knowledge formation themselves (cf. Warhurst and Thompson 2006). In fact, in terms of those who specialize in learning and development research specifically (within but mostly beyond workplaces) we can also see that over the last three decades a host of similar critiques have been produced. Unsurprisingly, many of these have depended, in whole or in part, upon the work of Vygotsky (e.g., Rogoff and Lave 1984; Engeström 1987; Lave and Wenger 1991; Hutchins 1995; Cole 1996; Illeris 2002; Barley 2005; Stetsenko, 2009; Niewolny and Wilson 2009). More important still, these types of criticisms – their identifications of biases that undermine our understanding of skill, knowledge, learning and development – are likewise traceable in even earlier and more foundational works.

Vygotsky's work at the turn of the twentieth century was built on a very similar set of concerns. These concerns emerged from his original criticisms of Piaget, Freud, behaviourialism, operant conditioning, as well as variations of gestalt theory, for example. Indeed, both Vygotsky and his colleague Luria explicitly criticized the Cartesian bias of theories of thinking, learning, and development (e.g., Luria 1976, p. 19; cf. Blanck 1993,

p. 37). In the broadest sense, Vygotsky's interest was to develop a theory of mind in society based upon anti-reductionist and anti-Cartesian principles. Still, understood in this way, it is not quite accurate to say that even in the first decades of the twentieth century, Vygotsky, Luria and Leontiev were alone in holding such interests. There were other giants of learning theory at work at this time offering perspectives which continue to echo loudly today and which show many similarities. To understand the similarities as well as the differences we can turn to the discussion offered by Stetsenko (e.g., 2008).

Taking the example of key figures from the first half of the twentieth century who (both implicitly and explicitly) remain seminal to understandings of learning theory today, Stetsenko offers us a comparative exploration of the works of Lev Vygotsky, John Dewey and Jean Piaget. It begins with what I will call a series of strong family resemblances. These resemblances include what she refers to as a shared *relational ontology* of learning and human development: "the notion that social and psychological phenomena are processes that exist in the realm of relations and interactions – that is, as embedded, situated, distributed, and co-constructed within contexts while also being intrinsically interwoven into these contexts" (2008, p. 477). For those who see few differences between, for example, Dewey and Vygotsky, here is likely the first of two main reasons why. A second family resemblance deals with skill, knowledge, learning, and social action, and more specifically the relation of each to people's active engagement in the world around them. This is something Stetsenko refers to as *action-centredness*. What we see here is that skill, learning, and development – for Piaget, Dewey, *and* Vygotsky – necessarily involve increasing elaboration of successive practices in which learning cannot be considered a passive transmission of knowledge. People learn through active social interaction in the world. Practice – that is, *doing* – is not ontologically separable from learning and human development. It was this perspective in particular that placed these three figures in direct opposition to the powerful commonsense views, then as today, of de-contextualized learning, the learner as individual, and mind as container.

However, drawing on Stetsenko (2010) these observations lead us in turn to one final, crucial point related to Vygotsky and the CHAT tradition more uniquely.

> Lev Vygotsky laid foundations for a theory that potentially represents the next step after establishing the situated and active nature of development and learning because development, in his approach, can be conceptualized as the transformation of socially shared and fully contextualized activities into internalized processes without positing any ontological breaks between internal and external, social and

individual, and continuity and change (or transmission and transformation). He understood all of these putatively dichotomous constructs as interrelated (opposite but not disjunctive) poles on one continuum of a unified reality of *collaborative trans-formative practice*. (p. 8; emphasis added)

In this excerpt the break between Vygotsky (CHAT) on the one hand, and the two other seminal approaches to learning, on the other, is identified. And likewise, in it we also find an important means of challenging the barriers between the analysis of the work (and indeed, a more politicized analysis of work), on the one hand, and analysis of learning on the other; the type of conceptually unifying first step recommended earlier as necessary for breaking the skills impasse. Effectively breaking this impasse, in other words, begins by effectively reconciling the concepts of labouring and learning. This, in turn, requires a recognition of the many biases that shape our understanding of skill and knowledge, but also revolves around recognizing the relationship between internalization and externalization, contradiction and change, and, in particular, the mutually constituting dynamics of adaptation *and* transformation. It is with this type of approach, I argue, that we can begin to appreciate a broader concern for the cultural, historical, *and* material dimensions of learning, the fully situated nature of skill and knowledge practices, *as well as* the dimensions of labour process activity definitive of capitalism specifically.

It bears emphasizing that in analyses of skill formation, the ontological presumption of learning *as adaptation* can be startling in its ubiquity once we focus our lenses just right. We might go so far as to say that learning as adaptation is pre-given to our consciousness, not only as researchers but as contemporary institutional actors (as a modern *well-schooled* population). In educational institutions, for example, it virtually impossible to deny that *adaptation* (i.e., socialization) is not the organizing principle, and much the same can be said about work-based training. In only slightly more convoluted ways, it may also be said of a great deal of on-the-job or informal learning where these types of practices are directed by organizational scripts. The adaptation bias is (whether implicit or explicit), in this sense, among the most powerful biases undergirding both mainstream learning theory as well as the skills impasse, underlining all the more the relevance of a turn toward CHAT. Indeed, while Vygotsky, Dewey, and Piaget all oriented toward a social relational ontology as well as action-centredness, following Stetsenko, both Dewey (disproportionately concerned with continuity and the learner as navigating the world via transactions) and in particular Piaget (with his concern for equilibrium and assimilation) can be characterized as offering perspectives that are more adaptive rather than transformational.

Vygotsky wrote of the continual transformations, as well as adaptations, of human life taking place through processes of internalization and
externalization, thought and action. In comparison to Dewey and Piaget
(and Mead), more detailed attention was paid to conceptualizing the social
structure of practical activity by Vygotsky (e.g., zone of proximal development) and Leontiev (i.e., activity). For Vygotsky these transformations were
inherently political and were sometimes highly contentious.[7] Drawing on
dialectical materialist thought, Vygotsky and followers like Leontiev specifically interrogated the inseparability of adaptation and transformation
in terms of individuals, groups, societies, and social change. Under specific
concrete historical conditions, human needs, objects, motives, and forms of
mediation are reorganized by, and in turn reorganize, social relations and
interactions. Like Dewey and Mead in particular, Vygotsky rejected the
privileged role of self-consciousness over being and practice.

> ideas readily live in harmony with one another, yet they violently collide in space....
> The dynamics of a real situation, when converted into the fluid dynamics of thought,
> reveal a situation's new features, new opportunities for movement, association, and
> communication among sub-systems. However, this direct motion of dynamics
> from the actual situation to thought would be quite useless and unnecessary, if the
> reverse, the backward transition from the fluid dynamics of thought into rigid and
> firm dynamic systems of real action also did not exist. The difficulty of implement-
> ing a set of intentions is directly related to the fact that the dynamics of an idea, with
> all its fluidity and freedom, must be transformed into the dynamics of real action.
> (Vygotsky *Collected Works*, Volume 5, as quoted by Zinchenko 2002, p. 19)

Inspired by what is arguably Vygotsky's master work (i.e., *Thinking and
Speech*, 1987), but fleshed out and extended across the breadth of the volumes
of his collected works, these are the precise points that would later become
elaborated – in diverse and occasionally divergent ways (see Sawchuk and
Stetsenko 2008) – in the work of others such as Luria, Galperin, Davydov,
Wertsch, Engeström, as well as Stetsenko. They would lead toward a more
fully realized theory of activity. And, they are points that were elaborated
by Leontiev in particularly fruitful ways for us here.

From Mediation to Activity

In the context of this book's themes as a whole, it remains important to
interrogate the seminal concerns, criticisms, and concepts that established
the CHAT tradition. They will be recovered, applied and elaborated vis-à-
vis the proposed dialogue with LPT across the analysis of skill, knowledge,
expertise, and learning practices of state welfare workers going forward.

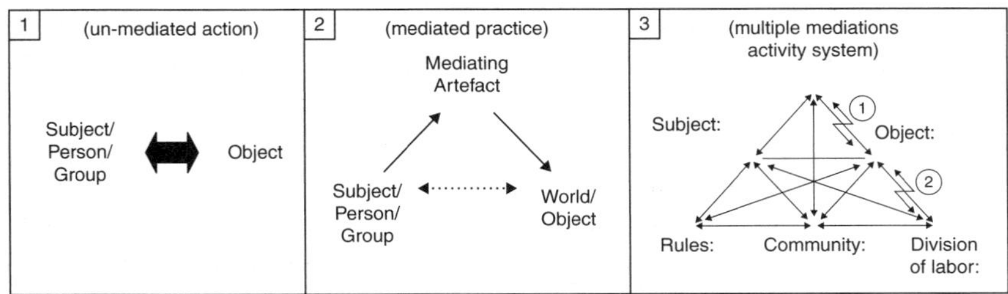

Figure 2.1. Relations among non-mediated action, mediated action, and activity concepts.
Note: Modified from Sawchuk 2007a, p. 205.

In this section, however, I begin with the analytic break in understanding thinking, learning, and human development afforded by one of the foremost principles of CHAT embedded within the concept of activity: *mediation* (Figure 2.1).

For Vygotsky and others since, the principle of mediation directs our attention to a very basic but important fact. People always, and without exception, act on (and are acted upon), think about, feel, perceive and experience the world *through artefacts or tools of some kind*. This is a process (though still occasionally ignored) that is more and less recognized in a variety of theories of learning, development, and, indeed, theories of social action in other social sciences. Rarely, however, are the dynamics and implications of artefact mediation for learning analysis accorded the centrality seen in the CHAT tradition. In CHAT analysis, artefacts include an enormously large range of items: from physical tools and technologies to spatial or temporal properties of the environment; from language, narrative, and non-narrative aspects of discourse or ideology to organizational rules, divisions of labour, or norms; from specific cognitive or affective schema to desires, fears, or other elements commonly associated with personality, subjectivity, or identity. While Vygotsky is often associated with the processes of sign-mediation, in point of fact material dimensions of mediation whether it was by the use of simple objects (e.g. people's use of simple objects such as string tied around one's finger or knots in a handkerchief to mediate memory and thinking), or the use of more complex tools were also important to his thinking. At the same time, CHAT analysis makes additional demands of this concept of artefact mediation. It requires attention to the history of artefacts (e.g., their history of design, production, reproduction, and alteration in use) in order to understand the effective tendencies – the affordances, inhibitions, and prohibitions – of mediation. And it is in this way, artefact mediation places human thought, feeling, and action in constant symbolic and material communion with a past that produces both limits and pressures.

To understand better this principle of a CHAT approach to skill, knowledge and learning in relation to the labour process we can take a classic example from manufacturing. Those in the LPT tradition will undoubtedly remember the work of Noble (e.g. 1984). A CNC lathe[8] affords very specific work practices that contrast to the Record/Playback lathe as Noble demonstrated in his detailed history of the development of production technologies and computers. Many studies of technology attempt to do the same thing, but Noble's extended research and commentary makes it particularly easy to see that all tools, all artefacts, are from somewhere, were made under certain conditions, emerged from specific sets of power relations, goals, and purposes. They are objects within a historical scene of struggle: what Feenberg (1991) referred to as a contested parliament of things. The implications are considerable for learning and skill. And, these were points Vygotsky too took time to emphasize in his concern for the historical approach (including historical in terms of an individual, as well as for an artefact, a human group, or humanity as a whole). The histories of human change (including, learning and development) are inseparable from the histories of the production of the things – the conflicts, the co-operations, and ratifications endemic to them – which mediate ongoing practices, goals, interests, attention, dis-attention, engrossments, investments of energies, and so on. And just as we might say that our prior learning experiences can either expand *or* limit the horizons of our practices, so too the historical features embedded in the symbolic and material artefacts that surround us are central for understanding how human practices are expanded, limited or otherwise shaped through processes of mediation. Vis-à-vis the histories of artefacts, history can be seen to live within and around people, at each moment, in the present. Artefacts and their various forms of configuration in activity represent the history we encounter, reconfigure, and make, but again, not simply as we choose.

How did Vygotsky and colleagues arrive at such claims? An answer to this question requires some attention to how they worked. I have referenced already that Vygotsky carried out extended and detailed criticism of existing theories of his day, but his extensive and creatively conceived empirical work is equally important. Much of this empirical work used experimental designs isolating and testing particular learning dynamics or mechanisms that were, in turn, persistently interpreted through the lens of his broader, situated view of learning and action. He undertook empirical study of those with impairments and those without, as well as children, youth and adults. In each case what was confirmed in distinct ways was that the inner world of cognition, emotion, learning, and development was inextricably and deeply integrated with the structure and dynamics of the outer world of concrete social and material relationships. And agentive transformation of the world, including those carried out by of children and those with impairments, was critical to a full understanding of the learning process.

Moving forward in the book it will become clear that central to understanding the Vygotskian approach to learning were the claims of how learning and development unfold *not from part to whole but rather from whole to part*; a claim that more or less ran in direct opposition to those of Piaget (e.g., Vygotsky 1987, p. 88). This principle of *wholeness* has a crucial link to the research in this book, and it also has a special relationship to the role of play in Vygotskian thought as well. For Vygotsky, the notions wholeness and his conceptualization of play were among several key turns of thinking that helped lead him and colleagues toward the ideas we connect to the activity concept as we know it today (e.g., Vygotsky 1987, pp. 124, 126). And, in terms of the research in this book, it is the wholeness of learning and activity, a conceptualization of skill, learning, play, and linked with them a theory of work as *games* (Burawoy 1979) and *engrossment* (Knorr Cetina 1999), that will prove to be quite central.[9] Also assisting Vygotsky's transition to the concept of activity was the transition of his views on the questions of meaning, sign-mediation, and communication. Initially using sign-mediation simply as a means to challenge the stimulus-response psychology of that day (e.g. Vygotsky 1997, p. 79; 1978, p. 40) by 1933–34 Vygotsky was explaining how psychological functions depended on explanatory principles found in "social systems of interaction and action" (Minick in Vygotsky 1987, pp. 17–18). Again expressing this notion of wholeness in his analysis, conceptualizations of *communication* (that is, a larger whole involving active social relations) came to envelop Vygotsky's earlier concerns for meaning and sign-mediation: for example, "it may be appropriate to view word meaning not only as a unity of thinking and speech, but as a unity of generalization and social interaction, a unity of thinking and communication" (Vygotsky 1987, p. 49). Indeed, these were further points of departure that go hand-in-glove with the emergence of other Vygotskian concepts including zone of proximal development (i.e., the distance between developmental as determined by independent problem solving and the level of potential development vis-à-vis collaboration with more capable peers) and many others.

In general terms, we can say that these and other conclusions initiated the concept of the *mind* as not simply an internal phenomenon, but an inherently externalized one as well: *mind-in-activity*. Here was an approach to knowledge, skill, personality, learning, and development dependent on configurations of mediations by external symbols and material artefacts, historically situated, social, and yet thoroughly agentive. Perhaps most important for us here is that, following these types of observations, Vygotsky and especially Leontiev quickly arrived at the realization that a theory of mediation was, on its own, inadequate to the task of providing a proper account of learning and knowledge formation. This is precisely the transition of thinking summarized by Figure 2.1, wherein by plate 3 we find something that is a familiar sight for many CHAT scholars: the triangular model of multiple mediated actions representing the basic elements of an activity system. Here we see a representation seeking to express not only a system of learning and development but also a system of production central to which are the powerful mediating effects summarized under the categories of rules, community norms and the division of labour. Indeed, exemplified by Leontiev's conceptual allegory (i.e., the division of labour in a primeval hunt discussed in the next section), the potential overlaps between CHAT and LPT are difficult to ignore.

Key Concepts of the CHAT Tradition

This backdrop provides us with an entry point into many of the key analytic concepts of the CHAT tradition that will emerge again and again throughout the book, juxtaposed, elaborated upon, and placed in dialogue with key findings and concepts of LPT research past and present. Building upon this backdrop, we turn to one of Vygotsky's most prominent colleagues, A. N. Leontiev, for some additional definition of the core term. *Activity* as,

> the minimal meaningful context for understanding individual actions.…In all its varied forms, the activity of the human individual is a system set within a system of social relations.…The activity of individual people thus depends on their social position, the conditions that fall to their lot, and an accumulation of idiosyncratic, individual factors. Human activity is not a relation between a person and a society that confronts him [*sic*]…] a person does not simply find external conditions to which he must adapt his activity, but, rather, these very social conditions bear within themselves the motives and goals of his activity, its means and modes. (Leontiev 1978, p. 10)

Leontiev goes to explain:

> Activity is a molar, not an additive unit of the life of the physical, material subject. In a narrower sense, that is, at the psychological level, it is a unit of life, mediated by psychic reflection, the real function of which is that it orients the subject in

the objective world. In other words, activity is not a reaction and not a totality of reactions but a system that has structure, its own internal transitions and transformations, its own development. (Leontiev 1978, p. 50)

Amidst the contingencies and complexities of the flow of everyday life, the CHAT concepts of activity, motive (or rather object/motive), goals, and so on, are central to my claims about skill, knowledge, expertise, and trajectories of learning in the labour process. As we will see, the concept of object/motive especially forefronts the mutuality and structure of shared and contested, un-self-consciously as well as self-consciously held, purposes. Likewise, in the analysis in this book, objects, object/motive, and the object-relatedness of activity are not static and cannot be taken simply as a given. Rather, they are constantly undergoing challenges and changes producing variation in the unique ways that individuals and groups participate, learn, and construct knowledge within the labour process.

In order to understand each of the preceding concepts and my application of them clearly I begin with a discussion of term *object*. In CHAT analysis, the term *object* in the concept of object/motive is not be understood as either simply a thing (original Russian word *objekt*) or a personal objective. Rather, in CHAT theory the term *object* can take on a more expansive, specialized meaning expressed by the Russian word *predmet* (see Kaptelinin 2005). In this latter sense, the object/motive relates to a broader, socially constructed need, meaning, and relevance implicating, but not defined only by, personal sense-making. The object/motive, in other words, includes but is not reducible to individual intentionality, outcomes, and perception. The object/motive mediates individual and collective attention (and dis-attention), perceptions, efforts, meaning-making, and the myriad practices, both profound and mundane, of problem-solving and learning. And, it can be added, it has vital implications for understanding instances of consent, accommodation, cooperation, as well as conflict. A CHAT perspective argues that wherever we find patterned human practice, we find people adapting to *and* transforming the objects/motives of activity in ways that may be mutually supportive or mutually undermining of this patterned practice. In my analysis later on we find people actively negotiating and altering their relationship to various object/motives of labour process activity specifically. Noting my earlier comment that activity speaks to the minimal unit of concrete agency, workers are constantly learning to both accept and challenge the purposes of their work (and working lives), and it is the relationship of their many practices to the object/motive of activity that allows (them and us) to make concrete sense of various skills and knowledge. This formulation, I argue, provides the potential for new insights into the divergent knowledge forms as well as the difficulties and successes workers experience in terms of work performance.

As Leontiev (1978, p. 62) put it, "it is understood that the motive may be either material or ideal, either present in perception or existing only in the imagination or in thought." Moreover,

> [a] basic or, as is sometimes said, a constituting characteristic of activity is its objectivity. Properly, the concept of its object (Gegenstund) is already implicitly contained in the very concept of activity. The expression 'objectless activity' is devoid of any meaning. Activity may seem objectless, but scientific investigation of activity necessarily requires discovering its object. Thus, the object of activity is twofold: first, in its independent existence as subordinating to itself and transforming the activity of the subject; second, as an image of the object, as a product of its property of psychological reflection that is realized as an activity of the subject and cannot exist otherwise. (Leontiev 1978, p. 52)

Neither personal nor collective need, as such, is conceivable in isolation from objects (*predmet*) and object/motives in the CHAT approach. Paraphrasing Leontiev closely, Miettinen (2005, p. 54) explains, "need becomes a motive capable of directing actions only when it finds its object"; and hence going forward in this book I talk about a *nexus of need/ motive/object*. Kaptelinin (2005) explains it further, noting the object of activity is both a projection of the mind onto the world *and* vice versa. It is, in his phrase, "the sense-maker," providing the "means [for] anchoring and contextualizing subjective phenomena in the objective world" (Kaptelinin 2005, p. 5). It is in this context that in CHAT analysis we use the term *object-relatedness* of activity: all aspects and dimensions of activity are related to the object/motive, albeit in a variety of ways and in a variety of internal configurations that speak to distinctive experiences and trajectories of learning.

Building upon the concepts of object/motive and the object-relatedness of activity, we can more clearly see how CHAT analysis distinguishes, first, between *action* and *activity*. An action is conducted by an individual or group to fulfil some *self-consciously held goal*. We are speaking here of the realm of reflexive awareness, intentionality, what people explicitly understand and can describe themselves to be doing (and sometimes learning) within activity. But the point of CHAT analysis is that analysis of self-conscious, reflexive awareness and intentionality, on its own, cannot generate an adequate understanding of what is in fact going on. Moreover, nor is it the case that actors themselves rely exclusively on these in the course of their practice, learning, and development. Thus, while people have self-conscious intentions and carry out goal-directed action, these take the form they do in relation to an activity as a whole; a social formation composed of a specific configuration of internally related mediations including divisions of labour, conventions, rules, expectations and roles – that is, an *object/motive* of some type.

Another key CHAT concept that will be used again and again in the book is the term *operation*. The concept of operation is distinct from activity and action. It refers to un-self-conscious practice in direct response to the conditions of activity. In relation to their execution, operations cannot be self-consciously (or reflexively, or declaratively, etc.) formulated. They are un-self-conscious and tacit, though this does not mean operations lack the exercising of human agency. They involve responses to conditions that are in fact *seen but unnoticed*. As we will note in the analysis, struggles to construct occupational knowledge bear heavily on the conditions – based upon work design or set of production technologies, for example – with which workers must cope on a daily basis.

Leontiev's (1981) oft-quoted conceptual allegory of the primeval hunt referenced earlier still provides a classic illustration of the role of operations in relation to goals/actions, and object/motive in activity in this sense. As he notes, within a hunting party, there can be those who beat the bushes and scare the game toward others; and here the *object/motive* of *activity* is the provision of food and clothing even while the conscious *action* and *goal* for the bush-beaters themselves is actually to *drive game away* involving certain *operations* tacitly mastered and undertaken in response to given *conditions and materials*. Both the technical and the social divisions of labour embedded in this hunting labour process – and in turn the significance of the separation of design and execution, complexity and autonomy, technological mediations, power relations, and so on – are all inextricably and simultaneously implicated. Individual practices, in keeping with the basic definitions we began with here, simply are not meaningful without reference (explicit for the analyst and implicit for the actor herself) to the different dimensions of activity as a whole.

> An analysis leading to an actual disclosure of sense cannot be limited to superficial observation.... After all, from the process itself it is not evident what kind of process it is – action or activity. Often in order to explain this, active investigation is required: substantiating observation, hypothesis, effective verification. That to which the given process is directed may seem to be inducing it, embodying its

motives; if this is so, then it is activity. But this same process may be induced by a completely different motive not at all coinciding with that to which it is directed as its results; then it is an action.[...] In spite of what it seems to be from the superficial point of view, this is a way that confirms the objectivity of its bases to a high degree inasmuch as this way leads to an understanding of the consciousness of man [*sic*] derived from life, from concrete beginnings, and not from the laws of consciousness of surrounding people, not from knowledge. (Leontiev 1978, pp. 173–4)

As indicated by Leontiev in this excerpt, CHAT entails the forefronting of practices, concrete processes, and (it could be said) social *being* over *consciousness*. It is materialist in this way.

Attending to activity as a whole – the principle of wholeness and the object-relatedness of activity – implies a specific type of mutuality among concepts, dimensions, and moments. Here I am speaking of the centrality of dialectical thought in CHAT analysis; that is, a recognition that human learning and development depend upon mutually constituting and mutually undermining relationships, operating across a range of levels of generality, understood as involving multiple social standpoints, constantly in motion, over time (cf. Ilyenkov 1982; Ollman 1993). Thus, in this sense at the heart of the matter of a CHAT approach are not the individual concepts alone, but their dialectical integration, what Galperin referred to artfully as the elusive "blue bird" of analysis (see Arievitch 2003, p. 283). It is an intellectual aspiration that, likewise, Leontiev (1978, p. 67) said remained both crucial and far too often under-realized. It involves recognizing the internally related way that the processes of transformation of object/motives express a series of constantly emerging object-related forms of activity involving what people think they are doing (i.e., goals/actions), how they go about doing what they do (i.e., operations), and the myriad, mediating artefacts involved in each instance of practice. And it is an approach, as Stetsenko (e.g., 2008, 2010) reminded us earlier, that seeks to address the dialectical unity of the processes of internalization/externalization, adaptation/transformation, and learning/doing.

It is the dialectical materialist nature of CHAT that requires careful attention to change as emerging from the dynamics of contradiction. Skill, learning, and knowledge production are defined by the contradictory and relationally patterned ways (i.e., the form) in which a configuration of actors and artefacts mediate interaction with the world producing, at times seemingly stable and at others rapidly shifting, patterns of object-relatedness in activity. It is an approach that inherently draws our attention toward not simply the *limitations* of the world around us, but the degrees of *freedom* afforded by specific meditational processes (i.e. that people may appropriate artefacts and use them in unexpected ways). Specifically, it draws our attention to the freedoms afforded by the shifting *organization of meditations and object-relatedness* as a whole, the shifting *configurations* of actors and things, and thus also to the many unique modes of participation of individuals and groups within activity.

Contradiction and Dialectical Thought in the Learning/Labour Process: Promises and Impasses in CHAT Analysis

CHAT research that draws effectively upon dialectical thinking pays close attention to the relations among things (e.g. actors and artefacts) – that is, their interconnections – as definitive of these things. This way of thinking undergirds discussions of terms such as object-relatedness, or what I called the principle of wholeness in Vygotsky's approach earlier in this chapter. Translated into the language of a dialectical materialist philosophy I am gesturing at terms such as concrete totality and what is called a philosophy of internal relations (Ollman 1993). Particularly important to my discussion at this point however, CHAT research that draws effectively upon dialectical thinking likewise highlights the way that *contradictions* in activity express a unity of opposites, necessary to the identity of the activity, locked together in a series of mutually supportive *and* mutually undermining relationships. This conception of contradiction was important to the founders of CHAT (Vygotsky marking the point even in his original doctoral dissertation in 1924), and many contemporary CHAT researchers have referenced the importance of dialectical contradiction as well. It is a concept that will be central to analysis in the book, and it figures explicitly in the synthesis I offer in the Conclusion.

To situate more clearly the application of this concept of dialectical materialist contradiction to labour process activity however we can look toward some introductory comments provided by Engeström (e.g., 1987, 2006; Engeström and Sannino 2010). For him, contradictions are linked inherently to processes of value production under capitalism, and he notes how activity under capitalism is necessarily infused with the dual nature of the commodity form.

> Activity theory is a dialectical theory, and the dialectical concept of contradiction plays a crucial part in it…. In capitalism, the pervasive primary contradiction between use value and exchange value is inherent to every commodity, and all spheres of life are subject to commoditization. This pervasive primary contradiction takes

its specific shape and acquires its particular contents differently in every historical phase and every activity system. Most importantly, contradictions are the driving force of transformation. The object of an activity is always internally contradictory. It is these internal contradictions that make the object a moving, motivating and future-generating target. (Engeström and Sannino 2010, pp. 4–5)

In figuring the connection among contradictions, the commodity form, learning, skill formation, and activity, Engeström confirms for us again, "problem solving and reflection-in-action at individual or dyadic levels" alone simply "will not suffice" (2006, p. 194). Indeed, nor will a general recognition and description of social interaction within the labour process suffice either. Engeström and colleagues clearly establish the point that the unit of analysis must necessarily be expanded beyond simply individual learning to the level of learning-in-activity inherently shaped by contradictions. And they add that what are called primary contradictions (those contradictions between use-value and exchange-value production processes) are likewise supported by a range of others. For example, Engeström's (1987) own description provides for secondary contradictions expressed, for example, in a hierarchical division of labour and the specific structure of organizational life; tertiary contradictions related to the introduction of new object/motives by what he refers to as representatives of culture (i.e., people in charge); and even quaternary contradictions that speak to the inter-relations of a particular system of activity with neighbouring systems of activities.

Yet, in these terms and despite these principles of analysis, gaps in CHAT research on work, organizations, vocational education, and learning remain, as pointed out by a variety of CHAT researchers and others carrying out closely related socio-cultural learning research (e.g., Avis 2007, 2009; Langemeyer and Roth 2006; Sawchuk and Stetsenko 2008; Niewolny and Wilson 2009; Martin and Peim 2009; Fenwick, Edwards, and Sawchuk 2011). Many of these gaps relate directly to either missing, incomplete or limited appreciation of contradiction – and hence power, conflict as well as cooperation – within activity. Peim (2009) and a number of others describe CHAT research on work and learning as regularly tending toward a type of apolitical localism which supports an orientation toward a managerialist "ethic of improvement" (p. 167). Likewise, Warmington (2008) suggests a concern for the CHAT tradition becoming "domesticated" (p. 17) and less critical of power dynamics. Niewolny and Wilson (2009) inquire into the under-realized promise of a critical CHAT learning analysis, while in Sawchuk and Stetsenko (2008) a summary of distinctions between what are termed canonical and non-canonical streams of CHAT echo similar themes of potential for critical analysis that often goes unfulfilled. Too infrequent, it seems, are linkages drawn among occupational life, human learning, and the contradictions of either political economy or society more broadly.

Earlier in this chapter I described a type of "skills impasse" within sociology of work. Here I argue that CHAT research may suffer from a type of *impasse* of its own, and a key element of this problem is the particularly uneven level of empirical attention to the core contradictions within activity which are definitive of capitalism as such. Avis (2007, 2009) notes that, even when CHAT scholars analyze contradictions, it is typically within more narrowly conceived confines of organizational life. Regularly, in other words, the concern for *primary/core contradictions* is prematurely foreclosed (or ignored altogether). As Avis explains, in turn these types of gaps give rise to a host of other tendencies to emphasize, for example, reproductive rather than contested dynamics of learning. Taking examples from Engeström's work specifically, Avis (2007) argues:

> Processes of transformation are Janus-like; they can both secure the interest of capital or align with radical interests. Whilst Engeström argues 'the mightiest, most impersonal societal structures can be seen as consisting of local activities carried out by concrete human beings with the help of mediating artefacts' (1999a, p. 36). This insight fails to be translated into wider societal interventions that challenge capitalist relations. Although the notion of social practice is fully theorized, with respect to the activity system(s) under investigation, in its application it is *truncated* and veers towards a conservative practice, becoming in effect *'bourgeoisie' transformation*, or in Gramsci's terms, a form of transformism. Whilst change occurs, it secures the interests of capital rather than being forcibly tied to an emancipatory project (Gramsci, 1971, p. 58, 106; Johnson & Steinberg, 2004, p. 13). This tendency is in part a consequence of the focus upon secondary contradictions but is also a failure to engage in a wider politics.... Although the *recognition of primary contradictions could herald wider emancipatory possibilities, these are effectively bracketed.* (Avis 2007, p. 163; emphasis added)

I suggest that to fulfill the promises of CHAT in these terms a careful re-articulation of dialectical materialist thought will be helpful. The contradictions I advocate dealing with in this book are seen across the relations of global economics and nation states all the way to the dynamics of organizations, occupations, groups, and individuals within the labour process. But how, exactly, are these seemingly different "levels" of analysis and "types" of contradictions to be inter-related dialectically? As basic as it may be, I think it is worth quoting Bertell Ollman (1993) at some length on the question of *levels of generality* in dialectical analysis.

> Starting from the most specific, there is the level made up of whatever is unique about a person and situation. It's all that makes Joe Smith different from everyone else, and so too all his activities and products. It's what gets summed up in a proper name and an actual address. With this level – let's call it level one – the here and now, or however long what is unique lasts, is brought into focus.
>
> Level two distinguishes what is general to people, their activities, and products because they exist and function within modern capitalism, understood as the last twenty to fifty years. Here, the unique qualities that justify using a proper names, such as Joe Smith, are abstracted out of focus (we no longer use them), and abstracted into focus are the qualities that make us speak of an individual as an engineer or in terms of some other occupation that has emerged in modern capitalism. Bringing these slightly more general qualities into sight, we also end up considering more people – everyone to whom such qualities apply – and a longer period, the entire time during which these qualities have existed. We also bring into focus a larger area, usually one or a few countries, with whatever else has occurred there that has affected or been affected by the qualities in question during this period. Marx's abstraction of a 'particular branch of production' belongs to this level.
>
> Capitalism as such constitutes level three. Here, everything that is peculiar to people, their activity, and products due to their appearance and functioning in capitalist society is brought into focus. We encountered this level earlier in our discussion of 'production as a whole.' The qualities that Joe Smith possesses that mark his as Joe Smith (level one) and as an engineer (level two) are equally irrelevant. Front and center now are all that makes him a typical worker in capitalism, including his relations to his boss, product, etc. His productive activity is reduced to the denominator indicated by calling it 'wage-labor', and his product to the denominator indicated by calling it 'commodity' and 'value.' Just as level two widens the area and lengthens the time span brought into focus as compared to level one, so too level three widens the focus so that it now includes everyone who partakes of capitalist relations anywhere that these relations obtain, and the entire 500 or so years of the capitalist era. (Ollman 1993, p. 55)

Perhaps most helpful of all, however, is what Ollman goes on to say immediately thereafter:

> all the human and other qualities discussed above are present simultaneously and are equally real, but that they can only be perceived and therefore studied when the level of generality on which they fall has been brought into focus…. The dynamics of any power relationship lies in the historically specific conditions in which the people involved live and work. To abstract the bare relation of power from these conditions in order to arrive at conclusions about 'power in general' … ensures that every particular exercise of power will be out of focus and its distinctive features undervalued and/or misunderstood. (Ollman 1993, pp. 56–7)

Following this type of attention to levels of generality as well as extension in dialectical analysis, we can likewise see that there is a need (which Marx satisfies in his own way) to find "preferred abstractions [i.e. concepts] for treating human beings" that provide the "necessary ties to the kind, range, and above all levels of generality of the phenomena [we seek] to explain" (Ollman 1993, p. 59).

As the minimal unit of both meaningful analysis and concrete human agency, an empirically informed conceptualization of the contradictory nature of *activity* and *value generation in activity* are, I hope to demonstrate clearly, "preferred abstractions" of this kind. It is in this way, as realized through our activity, that capitalism bears down on human life (and hence occupational learning as well), and it does so in multiple ways and at multiple levels of generality that are "present simultaneously and are equally real," as Ollman says.[10] In terms of the reproduction of the complex relations of social class – infused as they always are with other forms of social difference in the course realization – the dynamics of use-value, exchange-values, commodification, and estrangement/alienation (cf. McDermott and Lave 2006) become central to the nexus of need/motive/ object. From a thoroughly dialectical and materialist perspective, these are mutually constitutive and mutually undermining elements *of the same relation*. Use-value generation, even those forms buried deep within the most exploitative realizations of the nexus of need/motive/object definitive of capitalism, speaks to a range of fundamentally transformative possibilities nevertheless. In speaking of use-value, exchange-value, and contradiction, it is important, then, to provide clarity as to the inherent mutuality of what would appear otherwise as distinctive types of contradiction. To deal with this, in this book I speak of *core and peripheral dimensions* of contradiction as an invigorated attempt to maintain this sense of mutuality, as dimensions *of the same relation* at different levels of generality.

Still, it is not likely the case that simply having a critique in hand and a plan to think more dialectically about contradiction in activity is enough to deal with either the skills impasse I have described or to fulfil the types of unfulfilled promise of CHAT analysis that I have just suggested. Rather, to support the approach in this book properly it is important to look briefly at research that has actually dealt with expressions of core contradictions at different levels of generality as well. This, I believe, will help ground some of the otherwise abstract points just raised. While there are many resources we could draw on to do this, for my purposes, three indicative examples stand out despite the fact that they link to CHAT analysis only lightly if at all. One emerges directly out of LPT research while the others are linked to vocational education and occupational life research. They each speak to dialectical contradictions relating capitalism to work-based learning practices, skill and knowledge formation, but they do so at three distinctive levels of generality: global/historical, organizational, and personal.

The work of Adler (e.g., 2005, 2006, 2007a,b) summarizes substantial explorations of the labour process in which he highlights several points of confusion that surrounds the up-skilling/re-skilling debates that were discussed previously in this chapter. In it he takes much of the LPT corpus to task for, on the one hand, what he sees as the drift toward a contingency approach and the abandonment of a more searching Marxist analysis, and, on the other, a failure to account consistently for the implications of aggregate upgrading trends in worker education levels and work-based skill requirements. Adler's research highlights the evidence of persistent growth in educational participation over the last fifty years in the United States and United Kingdom (see also Spenner 1988; Myles 1988; Felstead, Gallie, and Green 2002, 2004; Livingstone 2004). Building on his studies of auto manufacturing and, perhaps especially, global software design he offers a Marxist perspective that recommends the importance of recovering a consideration of labour process, learning, and development in terms of the *contradictory relations between the socialization of the forces of production and capitalist relations of production*. In these terms, here we find a key perspective on the core dimensions of contradiction at a particularly broad level of generality addressing a long, historical arc that, as we will see in the analysis going forward, applies to state welfare work activity in this book as well. Adler's argument speaks to the continuously growing, aggregate socialization of work processes (the expansion of the complexity of the social and technical division of labour) and its interaction with the expansion of the privatized relations of production (private ownership, its requirements for capital accumulation, and its impact on work). This type of classic dialectical contradiction, he shows, produces changes in skill and knowledge that, consistent with Marx, speak to the transformation of capitalism in terms of the growing capacity of workers not only to produce things, services, and surplus value, but to expand their knowledge, sometimes in critical ways. He forefronts the overall socialization and growing *interdependence* that global production systems and shared conditions necessarily establish. This interdependence, he argues, decreases isolated and particularistic design and practice. In doing this, Adler recovers what he calls a paleo-Marxist perspective on the labour process.[11] That is, the forces and relations of capitalist production create conditions for historical change because they are inherently antagonistic and contradictory, dependent on dialectical conflict over work relations between capital and labour. They produce new forms of transformational potential in occupational life as well as transformational potential in an increasingly globalized world.

A second type of example that helps ground my general discussion of contradiction in labour process activity is provided by Marxist-feminists research in the field of vocational education and work research. Jackson (1994) focuses on very different dimensions of contradiction in occupational life. She presents a critique of the presumptions that pervade dominant understandings of skill specifically, influenced by the standpoint theory and sociology of everyday life of Smith (e.g. 1987). In Jackson's analysis of the relations of vocational education and the construction of skill in the organization of capitalist employment, she discusses the way in which dominant understandings necessarily

> [treat] knowledge and skill as naturally occurring phenomena, locatable empirically by examination of work processes in the world around us. In this mode, [knowledge and skills] are constructed as stable objects which stand outside the learner, and can be discovered in the form of 'tasks' to be mastered. Such tasks and their mastery are seen to be unambiguously definable and accessible to evaluation in a systematic and unambiguous manner.... 'Performance' becomes a form of action from which the 'knowing subject' has been removed for all practical purposes. It is a moment of abstraction, a separation of subject and object, a rupture in the internal continuity of knowledge and action. It is precisely this separation that provides for the possibility of external definition and control – it creates a position for authority outside the moments of teaching and learning from which these activities may be defined, measured, and evaluated for someone else's purposes.... But I will argue here that it [also] has the effect of disorganizing [activity] for the purposes of the individuals whose 'need' is to master it as a form of practical action. (p. 344)

This type of approach points to the contradictory gap between design-based, managerial, or educational understandings of occupational knowledge and the actual, practical skill within organizations. It speaks to how these dominant presumptions actually have a "disorganizing" effect on the potential of workers to collectively work, learn, and develop according to the direct satisfaction of their practical interests and broader social concerns.

This is a point that has since been updated, developed, extended much further in the work members of the VET (Vocational Education and Training) and Culture Network, where, in Seddon, Henriksson, and

Niemeyer (2010), for example, we find that the work of another key Marxist-feminist standpoint theorist (Frigga Haug: e.g. Haug 1987) helps orient an analysis of the notion of *disturbed work* as a fundamental feature of organizational life under flexible capitalism. "Disturbed work" refers to the re-shaping of traditional patterns of labour process,

> through, for example, the organisation of skill, the categorisation and orchestration of work practices and the development of people's capacity to labour [which] have practical effects in the way people see themselves and on the ethical understanding of good practice that underpin their occupational identities.… These disturbances play out in ways that destabilise occupations, their collective organisations and activities and the individuals that make up established occupational groups. (Seddon, Henriksson, and Niemeyer 2010, pp. 1–2)

It is a perspective that argues for an analysis that recovers people, in the context of particular forms of contemporary capitalist organizations, as fully biographical, living subjects of their labouring, rather than strictly objects of control.

A third and final type of example that helps ground my discussion of contradiction in labour process activity is provided by Rikowski (e.g., 2002a, 2002b). He links broader Marxist theory to an analysis of work skill and vocational education as well. However, the dimension of contradiction that he highlights relates to the complex relations between *labour-power* and *personhood*:

> labour-power is a complex phenomenon with inherent contradictions and tensions that become incorporated within personhood – given labour-power's fusion with the person of the labourer.… However, as well as these diverse aspects of the unified social force that is labour-power, there is a deeper rift that de-stabilizes labour-power and the person within which its force flows. Labour-power, which takes the form of human capital, is at odds with the person (de facto with itself) as not-labour-power; the person with interests, desires, motives (with dreams even) that run counter to the subsumption of the self as labour-power. The antagonistic labour-capital relation is a relation within personhood too in capitalist society. Our existence as labour against capital (as opposed to labour within and as capital) places a limit on the capitalisation of our souls. (Rikowski 2002a, pp. 15–16)

Rikowski (2002b) goes on to provide a series of qualities, attributes, and aspects of *labour-power*, recalling Marx's original claims of its singularly unique ability (against all other commodities) to create *both* use-value *and* exchange-value. In this way he helps us identify another aspect of this core contradictory relationship: "The labour-power of the labourer is under the sway of a potentially hostile will, a will that also exists against capital as well as within it." Workers, in other words, "also have the capacity to use their precious commodity in non-capitalist productive forms as labour beyond capital" (2002a, p. 8). These points are not unfamiliar to the LPT tradition, as Thompson (1989) noted some time ago in his authoritative summary: "the quest in capitalist labour process to manage and control these types of indeterminate qualities of labour power to secure valorization vis-à-vis commodification has been long-recognized" (pp. 241–2). And yet, as Rikowski makes clear, it is a quest, both realized and sometimes rejected, that is inseparable from the personhood of the labourer.

These three different types of examples of research on skill and the labour process dealing with (respectively) global/historical, organizational, and personal "levels of generality" are meant to ground the principles of dialectical materialism and the concept of contradiction. Going forward, I claim that attention to different dimensions of contradiction in activity is critical to carrying out an effective analysis of occupational learning, skill, and knowledge undergoing change. Understanding this requires attention to the simultaneity of different levels of generality in analysis. I argue that different relations of contradiction (involving object/motive, goal and operation) within activity have profound significance for understanding the dynamics of mind in political economy as highly *variable* and potentially *divergent*. And as I also hope to show, variations and divergence in occupational learning are matters which are definitive of the achievements of resistance and control (and the limits of both) as well.

Conclusions and Definitions

I began this chapter by interrogating and placing into dialogue several traditions of work and skill analysis in order to outline what I called a *skills impasse*. I argued its roots were established some time ago, and in ever elaborating form a skills impasse persists today. This impasse involves foundational concerns regarding the nature of labour process change including job and task complexity, autonomy, and whether or not an occupation is de-skilled, re-skilled, or up-skilled. While some of these terms have from time to time lost their analytic precision, I argue they remain important for answering questions about the nature of an occupation, a sector, a labour force, or an economy. To be clear, the approach taken in this book does not view the bodies of research stemming from the industrialism or post-industrialism theses, Braverman LPT, or alternative streams of post-Braverman LPT as a series of errors to be overcome. As I hope to show, there are conceptual and empirical insights from each that, to my mind, simply cannot be dismissed. Certain approaches to LPT do, however, serve as an especially important compass for the investigation, and with special attention to them I suggested here that breaking this skills impasse likely would require a dialogical approach incorporating a robust theory of human learning itself.

In turn, this led to a discussion of the bases for understanding and incorporating a CHAT analysis into debates of sociology of work and LPT specifically. Along the way I interrogated and attempted to explain the origins and key concepts of the CHAT tradition including their emergence in relation to certain theoretical criticisms. I took some time to highlight a set of key biases which formed an interlocking, mutually sustaining bloc of dominant tendencies in mainstream learning analysis to which CHAT offers an important series of responses. We saw, however, that CHAT may be subject to an impasse of its own in several ways leading to a series of unfulfilled promises. Important for achieving its potential in the context of the type of analysis I provide in this book is attention to dialectical and materialist thought, and, in particular, key expressions, dimensions and relations of contradiction in activity with attention to multiple levels of generality.

The type of interrogation, explanation, and proposal for a dialogical approach has given rise to several distinct sets of analytic concerns, many of which have essentially only been referenced to this point. As such, an additional set of summary remarks (and definitions) are necessary for moving forward. The first set of remarks briefly deals with the notion of occupational learning *trajectory* (cf. Edwards and Mackenzie 2005, 2008). It is a term that figures prominently in Chapter 1, relates closely to comments in this chapter, and will continue to be central. In fact, in virtually every scientific conception of learning there is suggested some notion of a learning trajectory as a means of addressing the accumulating nature of skill and knowledge development over time. Based on the many features of the CHAT approach just discussed, the analysis of trajectories of learning within activity will allow us to understand additional mediating elements (e.g., a mediating sequential structure) that shapes the direction of the refinement of learning capacities. The implication of this concept, of course, is that it speaks to supports as well as limits for occupational learning, as we will see. In this analysis I claim that people do not simply construct and participate in occupational activity in general, but construct and participate in a series of distinctive trajectories of learning within activity.

A second series of definitions includes the existence of three key forms of work/skill that are essential to understanding occupational learning and development within activity. I argue that taken together, these forms of work/skill become particularly relevant in attempting to address what has been called *knowing* in a system of *fragmented knowledge* (Bruni, Gherardi, and Parolin 2007) in which labour process re-organization is re-introducing new pressures to de-skill, re-skill and up-skill. I claim the forms of work/skill practices that chart changes in the labour/learning process most effectively in times of change are *not* the myriad *skill types* (e.g., technical skills, literacy skills, language skills, inter-personal skills, emotional skills, articulation skills) that have been identified in the literature as much as three integrative forms of work/skill practices in activity which I call repair-work/skill, sense-repair-work/skill, and object-work/skill. They mirror the basic CHAT analysis of operation, action, and activity and appear again and again throughout the book.

Repair-work/skill refers to those practices supporting internalization and externalization associated with the repair of conditions that actively maintain but otherwise leave undisturbed the organizational meanings, personal sense and broader purposes of activity for a worker. All workers necessarily engage in these practices within activity. They are unavoidable and entail the everyday coping with the general contingencies of the labour processes. Destined to become tacit and un-self-conscious in nature, these practices emerge from and quickly return to what, in the CHAT approach, is referred to as operational practices, or simply operations. In contrast, *sense-repair-work/skill* refers to those practices supporting internalization and externalization associated with the repair of relations between the organizational meanings and personal sense within activity. I argue these practices are particularly but not exclusively important in times of change. Under conditions of labour process change (as opposed to simply the on-going contingency of the labour process), this type of practice revolves around what are termed peripheral dimensions of contradiction. Specifically, sense-repair-work/skill is distinguished as revolving around the *contradictory relations between operations and goal-directed action* within activity. It is signalled, for example, by the processes of workers actively constructing a new means of alignment among their sense of tasks, their work, and their identity within the labour process. Finally, *object-work/skill* refers to those practices supporting internalization and externalization associated with the dynamic and *contradictory relations across operation, actions, and object/motive of activity as a whole*. As in the prior two types of practice, object-work/skill involves a host of skill types as well as formal, informal, and tacit learning processes commonly dealt with in the literature. What distinguishes it is that these are practices in which workers question and may actively resist pre-given or designed organizational arrangements, meanings, and purposes. Incorporating more self-conscious forms of agency and counter-control across activity as a whole, it is a process that integrates in diverse ways the centrality of the core, contradictory dynamics of the capitalist state and capitalist society more broadly. I seek to demonstrate that these three forms of practices provide new levels of clarity in understanding occupational learning, allowing us to discern the dynamics of individual, collective, and occupational change as a whole, for the most part irrespective of what are conventionally understood as the distinctive learning processes or skill types involved.[12]

As important as repair-work/skill, sense-repair-work/skill, and object-work/skill are to the establishment of distinctive trajectories of occupational learning and development in this analysis, the same can be said about what I will refer to in the book as processes of engrossment, re-keying, and workarounds. Going forward and building on the work of Knorr Cetina (1999), I argue that different forms of *engrossment* (i.e. the establishment of a sustained, individuating, reciprocal relationship between a person and particular types/configurations of artefacts) implicate distinct relations and dimensions of contradiction within activity. Defined in this way, through the construction of engrossments we will see specific patterns of attention/dis-attention and mediation that tend to (re)produce the learning of consent. As a contrasting dynamic and building on the work of Goffman (1974), the learning of resistance that we see in the book is said to involve the practices of *re-keying* (the transformation of an overall frame of pre-conceived/designed meanings called the primary framework) of labour process activity which implicate very different patterns of attention/dis-attention, mediation, as well as distinctive relations of contradiction in activity. Re-keying speaks to an important shift in what CHAT refers to as the *lead activity*. Agency, creativity, skill, knowledge, and expertise are exercised and generated across each trajectory in this research through the dynamics of artefact use, appropriation and creation informing the dynamics of engrossment and re-keying. Notably, and perhaps particularly in times of change, both engrossment and re-keying (and in turn two of the three trajectories of occupational learning I address) involve rule-bending, rule-breaking, and workarounds. These wide-spread practices take different forms. In fact in this book I offer further support for the rejection of conventional notions of rule/procedure-following (even amongst those workers most committed to reproducing bureaucratic outcomes). While in itself this claim is hardly novel, I will nevertheless demonstrate how it is that some workers are busy *working around* the *ordering* of operational rules and procedures of the labour process (vis-à-vis repair-work and sense-repair-work) while others are busy *working around* the labour process as a larger and more consolidated whole (vis-à-vis repair-work, sense-repair-work, *and* object-work). Taken together, I demonstrate that recognizing divergent trajectories of learning – constituted by the three work/skill types as well as patterns of engrossment and re-keying through which lead activities shift – provides a means of penetrating more deeply into the traditional LPT conceptions of consent, accommodation, resistance, de-skilling, re-skilling, and up-skilling. Each of these terms will be further discussed and, more importantly, applied going forward in this book.

3   Taylorism – An Enduring Influence

Introduction

> It was practically like playing a game of chess in which four to six hundred men were moved about so as to be in the right place at the right time. And all this, gentlemen, follows from the *one idea of developing the science of shovelling*. (Frederick W. Taylor; emphasis added)[1]

As the excerpt indicates, a great deal can follow from a key idea applied to a key task. Changes at a well-selected leverage point, in other words, can form the basis of systematization that reverberates across an organization, and sometimes beyond. Braverman (1974/1998) shed light on a series of important questions regarding the power of Taylorism, but even here we do not see enough of the detail that might better foreshadow an argument for its endurance. I argue that Scientific Management, or Taylorism, has remained largely misunderstood for some time. It is a concern that is not new. As Craig Littler (1982) observed in one of the key early texts of the Labour Process Theory (LPT) tradition:

> It is important to question the conventional version of Taylorism, which maintains that Taylor knew nothing of, nor about, work-groups, and their significance for the organization. According to the accepted version Taylor adopted an economistic view of working-class motivations, such that the only point of contact between managers and men is the pay envelope (cf. Thompson, 1913, p. 631). This is a superficial level of analysis. Taylor knew all about work-groups. He knew about solidarity [in] work-groups. He knew about their significance in regulating output; he called it 'systematic sold[i]ering' [*sic*] because he did not like it. (Littler 1982, p. 55)

The era in which key researchers first began to assemble elements of the argument I present here should be recognized, in part, because the texture of the debate has been forgotten or fore-closed by so many today. In this regard, a recovery of Littler's comments serves as a relevant reminder. Here in this short chapter, however, I seek to clarify the matter further in terms partially inspired by a Cultural Historical Activity Theory (CHAT) approach. I suggest that with special attention to the potentially critical role played by occupational learning, we can extend Littler's (1982) observations about "human relations", "work-groups", "solidarity", and occupational cultures to find a new opening for making the case that Taylorism may be an enduring force. Against this backdrop, it can be argued that Taylor likely understood what lay at the very heart of capitalism more deeply than his otherwise derivative notions of market economics or his somewhat lacklustre attempts at systematization of his core ideas suggested. Specifically, he understood that the basis of managerial power *at the point of production* rested in challenging the semi-autonomous, socially and culturally embedded nature of the machineries of worker knowledge construction materially, in terms of task design.

From the beginning, however, we need to clarify the ways in which Taylorism has been and could be defined. Taylorism is conventionally earmarked by the separation of design from execution (e.g., Braverman 1974/1998). It is a work design approach rooted in the re-organization, first, of a key task or discrete set of tasks identified as *both* central to a particular series of work practices *and* which presented the opportunity for the application of new technique or technology. It was described as *scientific* because its purpose was eventually to provide the basis for detailed measurement and mathematical calculations regarding ongoing changes to production output in response to capitalist markets. It was a key germ cell idea which, in turn, could be systematized and complemented in a variety of ways implicating diverse forms of labour process rationalization more broadly. In terms of the germ cell idea of changes to key tasks, the principles of evaluation were the centralization of decision-making and an ensuing search for and elimination of time, motion, and discretion that were not directly productive of organizational output (in generic terms, surplus value).[2] These basic elements are infamously and, as I show, somewhat ambiguously summarized by Taylor's six principles in *Principles of Scientific Management* (1911/1947; hereafter cited simply as *Principles*): shift decision-making from worker to management; use scientific methods to analyze work and re-design; provide detailed description of best practice and establish production outputs/wage system; select the best worker for the job; train workers; monitor their activities. These were principles which Taylor elaborated upon as he pitched his services to potential clients of his consulting business. I argue in the following that (perhaps by design) they hide much that is central to the enduring power of Taylorism.

I suggest that in itself, this list of six principles is underwhelming, particularly so, if we were to agree on some additional facts. Indeed, on the surface each of the following facts undermines the notion of Taylorism's enduring significance. In plain-speaking terms, the first of these facts to recognize is that no form of Taylorist work re-organization (including those guided by Taylor personally) has ever completely shifted decision-making from workers to management as Taylor's system ostensibly required. The second fact is that the linkage between outputs and wages was and has remained a central element of the employment relation with or without the interventions of Taylorism. Third, the record keeping and cost-accounting procedures he incorporated were equally unoriginal. The fourth fact concerns the place of time-motion studies that Taylor carried out in his private life, in his work as a tradesman machinist, in his work as a shop foreman, and most famously as a private consultant. That is, what he called detailed *unit time study* – as distinct from preliminary, much more ad hoc *standardization* or *standards work* – was unevenly completed and applied. A point I will return to later, this fourth issue might be thought of as particularly consequential, in part, because detailed time-motion study (i.e., unit time study) is so often set as the sine qua non of Taylorism. Perhaps tied with his need to guard proprietary knowledge as the basis of his consultancy business, for now all this is to say that a check-list of the application of Taylor's "principles" – especially where an emphasis is placed on unit time study – is unlikely to support an argument regarding Taylorism's unique qualities, and by extension its persistence today. Many of Taylor's six principles pre-dated him (and in some cases pre-dated capitalism), and Taylorist re-organization as described in these principles was, for all intents and purposes, never fully realized.

These facts make any claim that Taylorism is enduring counter-intuitive. Indeed, they partially undermine the very existence of such a system. Thus, an effective argument for the endurance of Taylorism must take unique tact. It must explore the unstated principles beneath the stated principles. This involves establishing a different standard from which to make judgements. In doing this in a particular way, I argue that we may come to see that Taylorism has very likely remained one of the most important, enduring, *materialist* expressions of work design *under capitalism*, from the *standpoint of capital*, since the decline of craft production. Specifically, I claim the principles of this alternative standard should revolve around the combined focus on (a) key task sets, (b) material practice, and (c) the capacities of autonomous worker learning/culture. Finally, I argue that fundamental to effectively applying this standard is the realization that Taylorism *cannot* be understood as a *project* in the conventional sense of having a beginning and a recognizable end. Eliminating this pre-conception as a measure of the existence and persistence of Taylorism is critical. What I mean by this is that as a particularly coherent expression of the contradictions of class struggle (from the standpoint of capital), Taylorism is necessarily and permanently incomplete. It must continually respond to capitalism's need for the magic of human labour power, *and* in attempting to tame it toward the point of non-existence it must always fail (cf. Cressey and MacInnes 1980). And none of this undermines the claim that it exists or persists.

For these and other reasons I argue that Frederick W. Taylor's Scientific Management system remains an entirely relevant frame through which to begin to understand contemporary changes within advanced capitalism, and the dynamics detailed in this book specifically. I suggest that it is because of the effectiveness of this unique combination of concerns, largely original to Taylor, that Taylorism has been absorbed, re-absorbed, and re-articulated by researchers, consultants, work and systems design engineers, as well as the common manager so readily. In this way, Taylorism has been a victim of its own success: its defining features have become invisible as they have entered into a widely held common sense. As we will see, under capitalism – wherever a viable, key, material task-based innovation is available – some variant of Taylorism is consistently attempted and genuine deviations from Taylorism have virtually always been erratic and unsustainable. Moreover, in this chapter I show (contrary to popular wisdom of a great deal of research literature), how and why Taylorism is equally at home in early twentieth-century manufacturing, the carrying of pig irons, or the shovelling of ore, as it is amidst the complexity of early twenty-first-century, computer-mediated human services. Among the implications for the discussion as a whole we begin to see how de-skilling, as well as re-skilling and up-skilling are distinctive, and yet also mutually achieved phenomena of labour process activity.

Origin and Meaning: Materiality, Tasks, and Learning

> *Mr. Tilson*: Wherein is the power for bad then in scientific management?
>
> *Mr. Taylor*: The mechanism of scientific management is a big engine, Mr. Tilson [and] it may do a durned lot of harm ... just as if you were to turn a locomotive loose on the streets and say 'Let her go.' (*Testimony* 1912/1947, pp. 189–90)

Amongst academics there has been no shortage of commentary on Taylor, and over the course of a century of consideration and re-consideration, the meaning of his work has proven enormously flexible. Its populist expressions, its politicization in the U.S. House of Representatives hearings and in the course of the Eastern Railroads case,[3] its influence within two key American administration cycles (Hoover and Roosevelt), and, for a significant portion of the last century, its sustained appearance in popular magazines and newspapers as well as trade journals: all these contributed to the multiple forms of interpretation Taylorism has experienced. In the face of both general public pressure as well as contention on the shopfloor, however, in his own day Taylor was forced to concede that his system could unfold in many different ways, and perhaps even do "a durned lot of harm".

Taylorism is typically discussed in terms of Taylor's formally stated principles, though in different publications (and no doubt in the course of consultancy work as well) there emerged at least two variations on these principles.[4] One thing that did not change however, Taylor regularly rehearsed the received wisdom of (labour force and commodity) supply and demand as a central response to contradictory elements of his work. Both the problems to which he responded and the solutions which he provided, when pressed, were consistently referred to this level of explanation. It is a rationale easily recognizable in contemporary life, and in part constitutes one of the many (minor) explanations for Taylorism's continued fit with the common sense of production and experience of economic life under capitalism generally. Taylor was individualistic, dogged, unyielding, and obsessive.[5] In this sense, he was capitalism in the figure of an energetic, living, breathing person. And at the heart of his concerns was the desire to develop a means of overcoming the collective, deeply cultural forms of working skill and knowledge that he had seen and experienced as enormously powerful. In these term, the goal was the appropriation and control of what he called *workers' rule-of-thumb or traditional knowledge-making*.[6] To do this he proposed observation of this working knowledge and then re-inscription of it through the reorganization of key tasks to which, according to Taylor, time-motion and output measurement (i.e., unit time study) could then be meaningfully applied. His writings in *Principles*, his three-day testimony before the Special Committee of the House of Representatives (*Testimony* 1912/1947), as well as many of the papers he delivered to the American Society of Mechanical Engineers (ASME) (collected for the most part within *Shop Management*, 1903/1947) will be central to the analysis that follows, an understanding of which is important to the remainder of the book.

Along with those who have bothered to look at Taylor's work closely for its apparently positive consequences (e.g., Nyland 1996, 1998), for its sustained negative consequences (e.g., Braverman 1974/1998), or for both (e.g., Aitken 1960), I argue that Taylorism represents the spirit of *capitalism as rooted in the material realities of production itself* (cf. Meiksins Wood 1999).[7] It emerged as such at a specific place and point in time that allowed it to develop, that is, American industrial capitalism at the turn of the twentieth century. As Braverman (1974/1998) and others (including Taylor himself) have noted, Taylorism is an admixture of the work of many, many others stretching from his contemporaries like Henry R. Towne and others within the ASME community of the period all the way back to Charles Babbage, Andrew Ure, and perhaps even Adam Smith. It was a system of thinking that eventually culminated in and was developed further by members of an off-shoot organization of ASME: the Taylor Society.[8] It seems clear from Taylor scholarship that its revolutionary nature primarily derived from its circulation of continually evolving, *material techniques* of management in relation to workers' knowledge production capacities specifically.

It is relevant to note that beyond Taylor's (various sets of) principles, he included and subsumed many other elements of managerial practice. Indeed, many subsequent management practices have been mistakenly thought to represent a departure from his approach. Taylor incorporated elements of modern cost accounting systems. And although he bristled at management by incentive alone, throughout his writings inducements retained a relevant, if subordinate, role (*Shop Management*). Typically forgotten, incentives were broadly conceived of by Taylor as not simply pay increases[9] but also promotion, shorter work hours, better surroundings, the intrinsic motivation of efficient work, and even notions of better human interrelations. Nor did Taylor eschew the powerful contributions of organizational trust and commitment. He recognized the importance of such matters, though always within the confines of the Taylorist system.

Importantly, Taylor recognized the successful application of his method of workplace change involved a two-front war.[10] In one sense, his was likely more a capitalist, as opposed to a managerialist, approach. That is, his system was designed to challenge the inherent capacities of worker self-management and knowledge-making *as well as* what he called the learning, knowledge, and ordinary initiative of local management. The effects of both of these forces – up to the point of the achievement of what Taylor regularly referred to as a "complete mental revolution" (amongst all parties) – were fundamentally problem-ridden and contradictory. Taylorism in this sense spoke directly to the challenges of production management *as faced by capital* rather than those faced by simply production managers as such. Undoubtedly, this was a point that explained how he earned admirers always at least one step removed from the nitty-gritty of the workplace, among owners and upper management, in the broader Technocracy movement of the period, amongst the inter-war period proto-Keynesians of the U.S. government, as well as in early Soviet Russia and the Samuel Gompers–led American Federation of Labor (Nelson 1980; Waring 1991; Pabon 1992; Nyland 1996, 1998). Across multiple instances of appropriation as well as through its implicit and explicit recognition of the forces actually at play in organizations, Taylorism can be seen as materialist and practice-based starting from achievements at the task level. Its contradictory nature in this sense is not a failure of his system, but rather a reflection of the contradictory reality of work (including the work of operational management) under capitalism. It is, in other words, inherently and particularly reflective of a complex *capitalist praxis* in the broadest sense. And, in this way, it remains in large measure more insightful on the challenges of work re-organization than many other contemporary work change perspectives (cf. Thompson 2003).

As indicated from the start, however, perhaps most importantly of all, what we find within Taylor's thinking about working knowledge is a deeply rooted recognition of the power of workers to develop knowledge and expertise within the labour process and beyond. Here we arrive at a point of argument that perhaps most clearly contradicts popular wisdom today. Though Taylor criticized the seemingly unsystematic nature of workers' knowledge and regularly spoke of the need to consolidate what he referred to as *brain work*[11] in his planning offices, he also expressed his belief in workers' general capacity by reference to his own life as well. In his testimony to the U.S. Congress, for example, he explicitly remarks that his family's wealth had but one value to him: it freed him up to learn rather than simply earn (*Testimony*, p. 112). More importantly, all of his writings drew extensively, both implicitly and explicitly, on the two apprenticeships he completed (pattern-maker, machinist), and he ruminated consistently on the learning process of "observing," "imitating," "asking questions," arguing that knowledge is "transmitted from hand to eye and comparatively little is learned from books" (*Testimony*, pp. 34–6).

> The knowledge which every journeyman has of his trade is his most valuable possession. It is his great life's capital, and none the less valuable – perhaps even more valuable – from the fact that it is attained in the old-fashioned traditional way rather than through such study as is to be had at school or college. (*Testimony*, p. 36)

Indeed, from unexpected places, we find recognition of working knowledge as human capital, and yet alongside it we find criticisms of formal education and abstract theory that would in many ways mirror the cultural forms of working-class knowledge of the day. Moreover, Taylor provides remarkably familiar and clear gestures toward a theory of learning as a guided form of participation. People learned best in situ, grounded in what Taylor called *object lessons*: that is, *learning-in-doing*.[12] Clearly, according to both Taylor and Taylor scholars such as Nyland, Taylor's early experiences beginning in 1886 at Midvale Steel (where he advanced from day-labourer all the way to foreman of the shop) remained the defining object lessons on the ingenuity and resourcefulness of worker culture. These lessons on the inherent relationship among learning, knowledge, and power were, it seems clear, formative. While his notions of learning-in-doing and pedagogy were directed in a specific way, it is nevertheless striking to contrast Taylor's articulations of the fluid and creative potential of workers' learning with those of early Human Relations Movement scholars like Elton Mayo – thought to have represented a major (humanist) break with Taylorism – where worker practices, by comparison, appear both mechanical and largely instrumental (cf. Waring 1991; Braverman 1974/1998, p. 69f).

In fact, Taylor had arrived at the notion that it was workers' knowledge development capacities in the labour process (linked also with their learning together within their communities outside the workplace) that were a crucial fulcrum across which the balance of power was decided. Braverman (1974/1998), of course, registered a critical feature of this point, but at the same time stopped quite short of recognizing Taylor's awareness of workers' learning capacities as such. I argue that Taylor's perspective on workers' learning has played an important role in Taylorism's longevity; and that Taylor's writings included persistent references to individual cognitive/motor as well as socio-cultural, economic, and occasionally even psycho-dynamic dimensions of learning in which workers' capacities were understood as natural, effortless, highly flexible, and embedded in collective life. Taylor understood that workers' learning was formidable. As he makes clear, given the countervailing power of workers' learning, only techniques to control it through the material mediations of an equally powerful standardizing science of task management[13] would be adequate. A perspective peppering his writings liberally, it is a view summarized by the following:

> This one best method and best implement can only be discovered or developed through ... the gradual substitution of science for rule of thumb through the mechanic arts.... The ingenuity of each generation has developed quicker and better methods for doing every element of the work in every trade. Thus the methods which are now in use may in a broader sense be said to be an evolution representing the survival of the fittest and best of the ideas which have been developed since the starting of each trade. However, while this is true in a broad sense, only those who are intimately acquainted with each of these trades are fully aware of the fact that in hardly any element of any trade is there uniformity in the methods which are used. Instead of having only one way which is generally accepted as a standard, there are in daily use, say, fifty or a hundred different ways of doing each element of work. And a little thought will make it clear that

this must inevitably be the case, since our methods have been handed down from man to man by word of mouth, or have, in most cases, been almost unconsciously learned through personal observation. Practically in no instances have they been codified or systematically analyzed or described. The ingenuity and experience of each generation – of each decade, even, have without doubt handed over better methods to the next. This mass of rule-of-thumb or traditional knowledge may be said to be the principal asset or possesion of every tradesman. Now, in the best of the ordinary types of management, the managers recognize frankly the fact that the 500 or 1000 workmen, included in the twenty to thirty trades, who are under them, possess this mass of traditional knowledge, a large part of which is not in the possession of the management. The management, of course, includes foremen and superintendents, who themselves have been in most cases first-class workers at their trades. And yet these foremen and superintendents know, better than any one else, that their own knowledge and personal skill falls far short of the combined knowledge and dexterity of all the workmen under them ... the managers assume new burdens, new duties, and responsibilities never dreamed of in the past. The managers assume, for instance, the burden of gathering together all of the traditional knowledge which in the past has been possessed by the workmen and then classifying, tabulating, and reducing this knowledge to rules, laws, and formulae which are immensely helpful to the workmen in doing their daily work. (*Principles*, pp. 25, 31–2, 36)

In few other early sources do we find such explicit orientations to notions of, for example, knowledge management. However, the issue that is most central to the argument here is that Taylorism was a capitalist *and* materialist science of working knowledge, its codification, appropriation, control, and re-inscription. In this regard, most often noted is the fact that this approach produced a fundamentally new role for management and work designers. Chapters 2 to 4 of Braverman (1974/1998), for example, argue this explicitly. But understanding the nature of such roles, whether wholly or partially invented by Taylor, is aided by recognition of the concrete effects on practice as revolving around specific centre-points of knowledge production.

Taylorism would provide a *thoroughly materialist* counter-balance to management's relative lack of knowledge and lack of control vis-à-vis a coherent system of sustained, object-lesson-based labour process pedagogy at the task level. As involving a two-front war, it spoke to the inherent contradictions of both learning and the practical management of it. In fact, Taylor recognized how work in capitalism under *pre-Taylorist* management could undermine the natural learning capacities of workers and eventually render them too "dumb"/disinterested, or, more often as he saw it, too "selfish" to engage productively in any type of labour process. Moreover, when workers refused to be dumbed-down in this way he likewise understood their energies were naturally realized in forms of resistance, recalcitrance, and soldiering (e.g., *Principles*, p. 102). Careful inspection of his writings reveals that he clearly understood the natural ingenuity, the communication structure, the seemingly effortless developmental patterns that could and did emerge amongst workers, and the powerful forms of knowledge for alternative choice-making and resistance that such practices engender.[14] These types of considerations belie the more superficial, but persistent, view that Taylorism is *only* the separation of design from execution by scientific study of work processes.

Yet another key issue concerns the matter of work study. This may be particularly important given that so many researchers have continued to assume that where there is no detailed time study undertaken Taylorism does not exist. Here the work of Aitken (1960) is particularly valuable. Drawing on personal papers and the enormous collection of detailed records surrounding one of the most infamous implementations of Taylorism (at the Watertown Arsenal beginning in 1909), among other things Aitken provides are insights as to how and why many of the standard presumptions surrounding Taylor's time studies are misleading. In the introduction I alluded to how Taylorism involved two distinct phases and types of work study. Aitken's study clarifies Taylor's own, at times somewhat elusive, statements in this regard.[15] Detailed and sustained time study – what Taylor most often referred to as *unit time study* – only appeared in the final stages of the Taylorist change program. It was to be used once the Taylorism system of work and task design had been established. In this regard we could say (as Taylor himself suggested) that *Taylorism was what made time study relevant, not the other way around.* An extremely telling comment, the explanation for it is not complicated: Taylor and associates knew that to carry out detailed time study of a task or labour process which was *not* already re-organized was simply to study an array of factors that could and did vary enough as to make the effort pointless.

We can add that, even in the course of implementations under Taylor's own guidance, the notion of objective decision-making itself was ambiguous. Aitken's (1960) analysis makes this point quite clearly as well. His was one of the first robust study to demonstrate definitively what some, then and since, have suspected: Taylor's techniques involved many *rule-of-thumb* approaches themselves. As much as Taylorism can be defined by the razing of the conditions of workers' knowledge production, it was in reality best understood as an attempt at the transfer of subjective judgement, situated rule-of-thumb action, and learning to the work design office. Finally, it bears mentioning that judged by its own standards (as opposed to ours here) the Taylor system was never made fully functional at the Watertown Arsenal, or likely anywhere else either.

> The Taylor system was adopted in the arsenal in the expectation that it would bring about reductions in costs of production and in general raise productivity. To what extent were these objectives realized? Something depends on the date at which comparisons are made. When was the installation of the Taylor system complete? In a sense, it never was complete: The Taylor ideal was not fully realized at Watertown – or in any other plant, for that matter – and there is ample evidence that, even when the system at Watertown was regarded by those in charge as fully installed, there were many deviations from the formally prescribed methods. (Aitken 1960, p. 186)

Aitken (1960) introduces an additional point of relevance in the preceding excerpt as well. That is, rule-bending, rule-breaking, and workarounds amongst workers, supervisors, as well as management, and, not infrequently, in collaboration with one another existed even under the most intensive and scrutinized attempts at implementation of Taylorism. Once again, expressions of contradictions across capital, practical management, and workers come to the fore.

> Since the new system did not always work as it should, particularly in the early days, the gang bosses sometimes found themselves stepping outside their formal role to unsnarl difficulties with the planning room and perform functions which were formally outside their jurisdiction. This even extended to routing. The gang boss of the south wing of the machine shop stated in 1911, for example, that the routing system 'has not worked out as it should have worked out, and I still have many duties to perform….' This is one of several items of evidence which suggest that the way things were done at Watertown under the Taylor system did not always coincide with the [principles Taylor] described. (Aitken 1960, p. 133)

Remarkably enough, examples from the Watertown Arsenal, in fact, can be overlaid directly with the types of local office responses seen in the state welfare work analyzed in the remainder of the book.[16] They raise the question of how much Taylorism has always implicated the organization of conflictual as well as cooperative, rule-of-thumb practices of workarounds and judgment, whether these are best understood as true deviations from Taylorism or rather to be viewed as living elements of it. Something meaningfully referred to as Taylorism – if judged by a more insightful standard – did and continues to exist, I argue, despite (and perhaps even because of) the ambiguities between rhetoric and practical function. As we have seen, this "something" is not likely identifiable by reference to the stated principles of design offered by Taylor, notions of scientific practice, or any of the other mainstream elements of definition.

It is more than likely these types of failed principles of definition have in fact led to the prevalent and premature announcements of Taylorism's demise, and in these terms Braverman (1974/1998) continues to stand as one of the most prominent voices of opposition. He famously rejected the idea of Taylorism's demise, while igniting a series of critical re-examinations of it even if these subsequent efforts have proven uneven. Thus by way of transitioning to a discussion of contemporary research it is worth taking a moment to consider again the work of Littler (1982) as one of the three major critical advances that followed quickly on Braverman's heels.[17] Using a historical and comparative international approach, in *The Development of the Labour Process in Capitalist Societies* (1982) Littler argued that "[a] simple model of craft-deskilling with F. W. Taylor as the devil incarnate is not tenable" (p. 187). True enough. However, Littler went on to define Taylorism as a form of organizational rationalization and bureaucracy.

> Taylorization, as I have persistently argued, represents the bureaucratization of the shopfloor, substituting manager-subordinate relations for those of the independent petty-bourgeois contractor. The fabric of control and coordination is woven afresh out of hierarchy, rules, a systematic division of labour and written records and communications. (Littler 1982, p. 188)

While correctly challenging the many presumptions about Taylorism, what is also clear is that emphasizing the *systematization* of Taylorism likely helped serve to define it out of existence. To be clear, I argue that rationalization and bureaucracy are *not the source* of Taylorism's magic at all. Taylor's *system* of rationalization/bureaucracy was particularly ineffective as well as unoriginal. Advances in *systems* of rationalization/bureaucracy long pre-dated Taylor, while innovations in *systems* of rationalization/bureaucracy have continued to emerge to this day. What is important here, rather, is the recognition of *what* is being systematized. It was Taylor's unique focus on the capacities of *worker's learning* which he understood formed the key source of counter-control. Rationalization and bureaucracy can, and usually do, formally ignore this capacity (even as the studies that have demonstrated the lively unpredictability within bureaucracies are legion). In contrast, Taylor recognized that any hope of control of this capacity lay in the *material* arrangements of key *tasks* and tools.[18] One of the keys to an alternative appreciation of Taylorism that would allow the claim of power and endurance thus revolves around attention to the relations of *learning/materiality/task design*. Neither general models of bureaucratic labour process rationalization, nor the models of Bedaux or Ford that Littler (1982) mentions specifically, can be said to have been oriented by this set of relationships in the same way. These relations of learning/materiality/task design thus loom as the heart and soul of any attempt to systemize them.

Persistence and Contemporary Expressions

Having discussed the work that Taylor carried out himself, it now makes sense briefly to address Taylorism's persistence in contemporary work situations. Pabon (1992) provides an impressive account of Taylorism's influence in American business during the inter-war period through to its key role in both the Hoover administration and the Roosevelt New Deal era's drafting of its National Recovery Administration policies and Industrial Code.[19] Taylorism's influence, in this sense, ran and runs deep in both private and public sector life beginning but not ending with America. However, as to its influence in the post–World War II era, as Waring (1990, 1991) shows, Peter Drucker – arguably the most prominent management writer and consultant of the last fifty years – explicitly recognized the centrality of Taylor's thought as underlying and anticipating a range of contemporary management approaches (Waring 1990, p. 205). Waring goes on to show how "Druckerism, rather than being anti-bureaucratic and a genuine alternative to scientific management, proposed new Taylorist techniques" (1990, p. 207). The heart of Taylorism would be retained: "Taylorism, reborn and transformed, was alive and well after the Second World War" (Waring 1990, p. 230). Many others have likewise confirmed that "managerial interest in scientific management has not waned since Taylor proposed it in the late nineteenth century" (Wagner-Tsukamoto 2007, p. 105).

Over the last twenty-five years, in fact, a range of studies have continued to demonstrate that key elements of Taylorism have been actively taken up or stubbornly persist as a core influence in organizational management and change. An example of a helpful piece of work in this regard can be found in the international comparative analysis by Pruijt (1997, 2000), who took on the challenge of reviewing 150 case studies from across Northern/Western Europe (in a variety of sectors), each involving attempts at *anti*-Taylorism.[20] The analysis shows that in the vast majority of attempts at supplanting Taylorism – whether cooperatively undertaken by both workers and management or implemented top-down – the interventions proved exceedingly fragile and were abandoned. Often, in fact, Taylorism has been specifically contrasted with a range of contemporary management schemes. These include business process re-engineering, high performance work, flexible specialization, the use of quality circles, and Total Quality Management. Turning toward studies of them in practice, however, we find that to the degree they are successful they function alongside features that are either largely consistent with or indistinguishable from the type of alternative definition of Taylorism provided here. Take, for example, the study by Giordano (1992). He attempts to demonstrate the death of Taylorism through the implementation of quality circles and new computer technologies. It may be a particularly pertinent example as quality circles are conventionally thought to represent co-determined knowledge development. We learn from Giordano, however, that the impacts on the labour process are "complex, contradictory and multi-dimensional. The comparable effects on the skills of machinists, methods, drafters and design drafters are not uniform, nor can it be simply categorized as de-skilling or upgrading" (p. 200). In fact, it becomes clear in the analysis that quality circle techniques are largely a supplementary attempt to obtain labour cooperation in the context of an otherwise intact Taylorized labour process: in practice, quality circles proved to be much more an extension of Taylorism rather than a departure from it. Similarly, Total Quality Management (TQM) has also been sometimes thought to have represented an alternative to Taylorism. Exploring contemporary Work Study Engineers (WSEs) for example, Jones (1997, 2000) notes, "since the time of Taylor it has been the responsibility of the time study man or the work study engineer to ensure that improvements made by workers are revealed to management" (2000, p. 632). And yet, Jones's fascinating participatory observation research into WSE sub-culture *within a TQM initiative* goes on to confirm in still another way how a supposed alternative likely does not represent a break with, but rather a further elaboration of, Taylorism: "Tayloristic techniques are now applied by the workers themselves as part of a TQM programme rather than by WSEs" (1997, p. 14). Other examples abound including Stoney (2001) identifying Taylorism's persistence within the context of Business Process Reengineering, and Niepce and Molleman's (1998) similar conclusions in terms of Lean Production and socio-technical design. While no doubt it has been supplemented, surrounded, framed, re-articulated, re-systematized and up-dated by new forms of management and design, evidence suggests it to be a uniquely and stubbornly viable feature of working life in a variety of settings. Taylorism, it seems, is not such a fragile relic of an age long past.

Beyond the endurance of Taylorism that these and other studies seem to suggest, we find an important question raised by Lomba (2005) in a review of research examining the meaning of *neo-* as opposed to *post-*Taylorism. This distinction is said to revolve around the interpretation of the break with mass production understood in terms of the practices of material flow, work routing, the recognition of the distinction between real and prescribed work, and the emergence of managerial interest in consulting workers on task design (pp. 72–3). Much like the review of Pruijt (1997), however, a close inspection of Lomba's findings reveals how unevenly, if at all, the core principles of Taylorism have been truly altered. Indeed, coherent notions of either neo-Taylorism or post-Taylorism are not easily discerned. Still, attempts at further specification of Taylorism do not stop there. Adler's influential studies at the NUMMI auto plant (e.g., 1995) arrive at the conclusion that employees were the ones working the stop-watch, monitoring, and re-designing their work, giving rise to the notion of *democratic* Taylorism.[21] The seemingly endless morphology of a still recognizable Taylorism and the persistent interest in further specifying it, along with the definitional confusion and clarifications discussed previously, perhaps explain why opinions on Taylorism tend to swing so widely and some have even wondered whether Taylorism ever existed at all.[22]

Against this backdrop, what further can be said of the frame of reference, the principles, and standards of judgment for a claim that Taylorism remains with us today? Following the work of Aitken (1960) again, and in light of this examination of contemporary expressions, we can reiterate more clearly how Taylorism must be considered a *process* rather than a *project*: a necessary and persistent *attempt* by capital and its work designers to respond to the internal contradictions of the capitalist mode of production. Looking at it this way cements the importance of recognizing the inherent political economic standpoint of Taylorism, a point that Braverman to his lasting credit went to great pains to clarify. But more importantly, this type of *processural* emphasis underscores the point that this standpoint must be *constantly renewed in the course of the living contingencies of practice* within concrete, cultural-historical relations of practice, learning, knowledge formation, and development. In this sense, Taylorism must involve constant learning and re-learning, by management and designers as well as workers. Thus, as an additional clarification to certain readings of both Braverman's and Taylor's work, we see that it is also the emergence of a clear articulation of capital's standpoint *in the material dimensions of production itself* that has so effectively undergirded Taylorism's unique form of attention to learning and task design. The characterization that emerges is of a deeply pragmatic, practice-based, and social constructivist Taylorism in need of constant rearticulation. And in a broader way, Taylorism as a *progenesis* – a type of man-child – of capitalist praxis to be taken up amidst the contradictions of working knowledge, pedagogy, and learning when the conditions are correct.

Given this re-specification of Taylorism, the question of its application in the case of contemporary state welfare work now can be more clearly previewed. Further answers to this question are to be found in the remaining chapters. But for now, in connection to the enduring features of Taylorism that I have tried to establish, the classic study by Hugh Aitken (1960) is again relevant for introducing some basic points. Aitken's work is in fact doubly relevant to us here for its focus on the implementation of Taylorism in the public rather than the private sector (i.e., the Watertown Arsenal was a government facility). This is a distinction, he argues, that is not nearly as relevant to the concrete practices of the labour process as is conventionally presumed (pp. xv–xvi). A point that is likely more central and that will emerge again and again, as we will see going forward, is how in the re-organization of the labour process of state welfare work the new production technology (called SDMT) can be understood, in Taylor's terms, as a virtual *planning department*. Specifically, SDMT plays a particularly important role in attempting to control the labour process through (what Taylor called) *routing work*, itself linked tightly with new cost accounting capacities in welfare work management and the case review process.[23] Routing work refers to the sequencing procedures and the control of movement of materials that stem from and help realize the potential of a specific task re-design within a new division of labour. In point of fact, forms of work routing control were critical to Taylorist systems, and even more importantly it was the defining element of the all-important preliminary work analysis: that is, *standards work* as opposed to *unit time study*. Beyond the initial task design and standards work, we find further parallels. For example, we will see how the SDMT system also serves the functions of *route-sheet clerk* and *production clerk* (see Aitken 1960, pp. 125–34); likewise we will see the ways in which SDMT and the state welfare labour process depend upon analogues of the types of forms and cards described by Taylor in *Shop Management* (1903/1947). This is so even if, in the case of SDMT, these forms and cards appear as screen-based texts and software functions. Moreover, as we will also discover, what are called SDMT's *Task List* and *Note* functions operate as virtual replicas of Taylor's *job cards*; client numbers (and what are called Participation Agreement [PA] numbers) and other identifiers function in the exact same manner as the information contained on what Taylor referred to as *move cards* and *move tags*. In each case (despite their attachment to people as opposed to things) they are designed, made to circulate, are routed, and controlled, all in accordance with task standards, in classic Taylorist fashion.

These types of specific parallels will be worthwhile to recall in reading on in this book, and they will be mentioned from time to time. However, one final and somewhat broader point of comparison between Taylorism and the contemporary state welfare labour process at issue here is important to mention. It revolves around the initiation of broader re-organization based on a *particular technology* as linked to specific series of task re-designs. To understand its implications properly it will be helpful to put it in historical context in terms of the work of Taylor himself.

In the American fabrication industries at the turn of the twentieth century, Taylor's introduction of *high-speed steel* had enormous significance.[24] Indeed, Aitken (1960) is not alone in claiming that high-speed steel was not only a major industrial achievement in itself, but likely funded Taylor's consultancy. High-speed steel allowed – *under the correct conditions* – fantastic increases in output (i.e., between 200% and 1000% increases in output speed in industrial lathe work).[25] However, what is important to us here is not necessarily that the use of high-speed steel was an important new material technology, but rather that it came to be linked by Taylor to a very specific task re-design that, in turn, *necessitated the restructuring of specific task sets and then work more broadly in order to make the most of the gains in output it could potentially provide.* Thus it could be said that, building on the principle of the relations of learning/materiality/task design, central to the process of Taylorization were the identification of a key technology and with it specific task sets, followed by the effective re-organization of the labour process. Just as I began this chapter highlighting the notion that a specific task may reverberate through the organization of work as a whole, we see how this was clearly the case with metal turning as mediated by the use of high-speed steel. In the case of state welfare work we again have a crucial parallel: task set identification and the application of standards work linked to the vastly expanded work routing and information transfer capacities of the SDMT intra-net technology. In other words, just like the introduction of high-speed steel, it was through the unleashing of SDMT's unique powers *on the bases of learning, materiality and task design* that Taylorism could be made to take root in the state welfare labour process.

Conclusions

With only a small number of exceptions, much (though not all) of the preceding discussion has focused on manufacturing work. However, Taylorism – even at its birth – was never meant to be, nor was limited to, the factory (*Testimony*, 1912/1947, p. 126). Two different American presidents sought to apply it to public sector administrative work vis-à-vis the life of the Hoover Commissions. Clearly, as Taylor mentioned in his testimony to the U.S. Congress, applications of his approach could easily be made to reach into white-collar and even professionalized labour processes (e.g., p. 126). Braverman (1974/1998) himself took efforts to summarize a history of advancing Taylorism in office work up to the 1970s. In fact, as regards de-skilling and de-professionalization in white-collar occupations, Braverman (1974/1998, pp. 207–16) likewise outlined clearly the regression over time from specialized occupations involving significant levels of craft knowledge, complexity, autonomy, and control toward occupations where these were significantly undermined if not obliterated beyond recognition. Though in the contemporary context we must include computers and advanced ICT rather than just paper within the "stream" of information – the state welfare workers that we hear from in this research would likely easily recognize Braverman's summary of Taylorism in the office:

> here the productive processes of society disappear into a stream of paper – a stream of paper, moreover, which is processed in a continuous flow like that of the cannery, the meatpacking line, the car assembly conveyor, by workers organized in much the same way. (1974/1998, p. 208)

While we will detect elements of both batch and continuous flow production in this research, what I have argued to be the genuine principles of Taylorism based primarily on his unique, combined appreciation of learning, materiality and task design is observable, and remains both flexible and powerful. At the same time, however, we might pause to consider the limits of this form of power. In this regard, what Leontiev (1978) said about technology (and here we can include the socio-technical machineries of a Taylorist work system) is highly relevant and links us directly to the analysis to come. Technologies represent "thought in their exteriorized forms separated from human activity and transferred to machines," *but* such systems "are *only ways and means* of thinking, and *not* thinking itself" (p. 28; emphasis added). From this perspective on learning in labour process activity, Taylorism should be understood as a *premise*, though a premise correctly linked to the notion of "de-skilling" because it is designed specifically in order to appropriate working skill and knowledge. I argue it is a flexible and powerful premise for labour process activity that has endured. However, it is *not* labour process activity itself. People must, as CHAT researchers such as Holland, Lachicotte, Skinner, and Cain (1998) have put it, figure the landscape of their activity in terms of an identity; they must participate in the labour process, in other words, personally. When they do, necessarily, a large series of challenges that I argue Taylor was well actually aware of emerge. And, these are challenges that should be considered as inherent to a functioning definition of Taylorism itself.

This notion of the human figuring of designed labour processes can be extended still further with regard to the role of contemporary production technologies. As Durand (1990) points out, "the application of IT multiplies the possibilities of appropriation of worker's *savoir-faire* and its objectification" (p. 416). He goes on to point out that with more complicated technologies come new realms of intervention – and learning – for workers:

> Careful observation shows that the new production technologies, along with the high performances demanded of them, multiply the possibilities of breakdown. Put simply, they render fragile the production process. And of course, the human skills necessary to tackle and control problems in that process continue to grow. (p. 417)

Anomalies, break-down work, workarounds, instances of irregularity, and so on – all these obviously demand persistent and sometimes complex skills of intervention by human actors. As we will see, in state welfare work, by its very nature, "deviations from the routine" and "break-down work" are features that may be particularly important. This is assured not simply because of new technologies or the contradictory nature of Taylorism, but also in the case of the empirical focus of this book by the sheer weight of unpredictability and irregularity in the lives of clients. As such, and all the more even, here we see the argument *against* understanding the dynamics of de-skilling, re-skilling and up-skilling as mutually exclusive. We will see that rule-of-thumb knowledge production – the capacity of workers to learn in their own ways – can and does continually reassert itself in creative forms of *both* consent *and* resistance. Far from deviating from a theory of Taylorism, however, I suggest these are processes for which this system of work design was built, and within which it has always functioned. Many researchers have sought to qualify or re-specify Taylorism while others have proclaimed its premature demise. The premises of Taylorism remain intact, however, even as the processes that emerge from it remain as unstable and contradictory as ever.

4 Historical Mediations in the Making of Taylorism in Contemporary State Social Services Work

Introduction

In this chapter I interrogate several closely related strands of occupational history. In doing so I seek to identify and establish the historical character of a series of key occupational artefacts shaping contemporary labour processes, learning, and occupational identities of state welfare workers. This occupational history is uneven and complex. British and American influences, as well as factors relatively unique to the Canadian context, are involved. It is a history that necessarily implicates broader social policy, economy, and politics. We learn, in fact, how this history of *state welfare work* is deeply intertwined with historically evolving occupations of *social work* as well as volunteer charity work. Indeed, this relationship has been the subject of intermittent discussion (albeit amongst professional social workers primarily) for fifty years or more in Canada. But it is a point that gains additional significance as we move forward in the book, particularly where we find something I refer to as the *ideals of social work* mediating and serving as an important point of reference in the enthusiasms, preoccupations, negotiations, and struggles of state welfare workers in these contemporary times of change.

I begin with a summary of the broader and longer-established occupations of social work and to a more limited degree volunteer charity work in Canada, highlighting key influences, dynamics, and turning points. Mid-way in the chapter I turn to a brief overview of leading accounts of social work as well as state welfare work labour process change, during which I summarize details related to welfare policy, inter-governmental relations, the vagaries of private sector contracting, as well as the types of production technologies that have further supported the changes implemented beginning in 2002 in Ontario (Canada). Each section helps substantiate an overall claim: a critical turn in state welfare benefits delivery has been mediated by the contradictory nature of the capitalist state vis-à-vis specific shifts in forms of managerial control, in patterns of occupational knowledge-making, and in the balance of knowledge/power at work. It is a critical turn toward a new assertion of control across workers and clients depending significantly upon an application of Taylorist work design. And yet amidst this we can also detect important mediations by occupational artefacts with a history of production and reproduction beyond state welfare work.

What becomes clear in this look across occupational and labour process change is that the nature of state welfare work, like that of social work more broadly, depends significantly upon how distinctive orientations to client need and societal need are negotiated, accommodated, and contested. Deeply implicated are the dynamics of contradiction among commodification, alienation, and humanization: that is, the contradictions between use-value and exchange-value. In fact, the clash of needs and values related to these contradictions has been the subject of debate in the occupations of social work and state welfare work for a significant length of time in Canada and elsewhere. Indeed, this set of occupations has likely produced one of the most sustained critical debates about the political and economic purposes of their work that one is likely to find. Even more to the point in this book, these debates have helped produce a host of mediating artefacts (e.g., symbols, codes, discourses, ideologies, rules, protocols, and a host of other occupationally-specific tools) that shape contemporary occupational activity. In an analysis of occupational knowledge in activity, understanding the origin and substance of such artefacts matters a great deal. Thus to be clear, the intention in this chapter is *not* to set the *context* for the dynamics of contemporary occupational knowledge production, but rather to support the position that these historical elements are fully and actively inherent in how this knowledge production currently functions, its pressures and limits. With this chapter as well as the previous one, in other words, the empirical analysis of learning has already been set in motion.

"Dig Where You Stand": Origins of the Objects of Canadian State Welfare Work[1]

If we hope to understand the mediations of skill, autonomy, complexity, control, and the concrete realities of workers' lives in a serious way – then the historical dimensions of practice within the labour process are crucial. Every mediating artefact has a biography; and history provides essential evidence as to the origin and hence character of the contradictory mediations shaping present learning and development. A cultural historical approach to work, human learning and development explicitly depends on recognition of the myriad, mediating symbolic and material artefacts within activity *over time* to help explain the production, reproduction and transformations of working knowledge. In this brief opening section of the chapter I focus on three main points of recognition specifically: (i) recognition of mediations stemming from international influences tied to the early attempts at welfare state formation in Canada; (ii) recognition that mediation of impulses toward alleviating poverty in early capitalism were ensconced in class, gender and related contradictions vis-à-vis volunteerism and charity work in Canada which in turn were shaped from the start by concerns for organizational efficiency; and (iii) recognition of contradictory mediations related to professionalization, state bureaucratization, as well as more radical perspectives stemming from the field of social work with implications for the role of direct, sustained engagement with clients in occupational knowledge production and control. Each of these forms of mediation will emerge in various guises and situations in my analysis of state welfare worker learning going forward in the book.

In order to understand the history of state welfare work in this way however, we face some challenges. First, no coherent, consolidated historical examination of state welfare work in Canada currently exists. In the Canadian context, reference to the changing dynamics of state welfare work over time usually are only found in fragments, dispersed across discussions of the welfare state, and/or changing social policy. Second, we face the challenge of having to trace the historical impacts of separate ancestral types of work (i.e., volunteer charity work and social work) which both pre-date the occupation of state welfare work and have, of course, each continued to this day.

The substance of these challenges will become clear as I proceed, and building on these introductory comments I begin with several basic observations. The state welfare work occupation as we know it today is very much a late-comer to a complex family tree in Canada. As I indicated, this family tree is composed primarily of social work related occupations, but its branches and roots are influenced deeply by the nature of public sector human services work and state bureaucracy, as well as volunteer charity work. In fact, as we will see still later in the chapter, the state welfare work occupation was formed across multiple jurisdictions, and across the complex and uneven negotiation of federal, provincial, and municipal responsibilities associated particularly but not exclusive with the Canadian post-World War II welfare state.[2] As we will also see going forward in this book, each and every one of these dynamics I identify here continue to mediate occupational practice, and occupational learning; however, one final point I make to begin is that volunteer charity work, social work and state welfare work in Canada were influenced in powerful ways by Great Britain (as Canada is part of the British Commonwealth). And many, though not all, of these influences are likewise linked to early attempts at initiation of a type of welfare state apparatus, i.e.

> Canada's welfare state was born in the late 19th century, and its birth mother was Great Britain.... In the early 20th century, the British economic theorist John M. Keynes claimed that government must become actively involved in welfare economic policies by 'exercising a guiding influence on the propensity to consume, partly through a scheme of taxation, partly by fixing the rate of interest, and partly perhaps in other ways' (e.g. extensive social services, public investment programs, and cooperatives between public and private enterprises) (Keynes, 1960, p. 378). Keynes's thinking culminated with *The 1942 Beveridge Report* by Sir William Beveridge, which was the scaffolding document for Great Britain's welfare, health, and old-age programs, all of which Canada adopted and modified to suit economic realities and political infrastructures. (Holosko and Leslie 2001, p. 201)

Distinct from the making of a welfare state as such and as seen through the looking-glass of the history of the Canadian Association of Social Workers (CASW), Jennissen and Lundy (2008, 2011) comment that the emergence of the occupation of social work in Canada emerged from the nineteenth-century traditions of Christian Charity Work. Remarking on the link among early capitalism in Canada, the emergence of social work, and eventually state welfare work, they indicate:

> social distress caught the attention of well-meaning citizens, primarily women from wealthier backgrounds, who responded to the underprivileged through charity work based in Christian morality. Both the Charity Organization Society (COS) and the Settlement House Movement (SHM) were part of this tradition. Charity work was an acceptable activity for women because it was regarded as an extension of the caring role assigned to them: 'As guardians of the home, their natural charitable and benevolent abilities could be applied to society's problems.' (Jennissen and Lundy 2011, p. 2)

Powerful, contradictory goals embedded in the identity of forms of social/caring work were forged, in other words, amid these deeply gendered, religious and class laden contexts (obviously laden with matters of race and ethnicity as well). Still easily recognizable amongst the state welfare workers we meet in this book I argue, inextricable linkages between ancestral forms of work and broader social and economic purposes were established some time ago in Canada. And these linkages would mature (sometimes in self-consciously politicized ways), but also take root in work design, expectations, objects, techniques and technologies, labour processes, and so on.

Extending these basic points further, Tsui's (1997) review of the historical development of management of social work *beginning with* early forms of volunteer-based charity work organizations in North America establishes a key point relevant to parallel developments in (English) Canada specifically vis-a-vis the Charity Organization Society (COS). Likewise distinct from the dynamics of establishing a welfare state, she demonstrates how by the end of the nineteenth century, despite the bases of charity work in the upper-middle-class, female volunteer labour, applications of classic forms of administrative supervision and management could be found. In this sense, the modern contradictions of control were lodged deeply in the genetics of the occupation of social work, and through it state welfare work, from the beginning. COS serves as a primary example, and its establishment pre-dated a recognizable attempt at the creation of a welfare state in Canada. Indeed, Tsui goes on to trace a lineage of administrative control – shaping volunteer labour experiences, recruitment, and how and why people engaged in the work – all the way from the nineteenth century through to the 1980s and early 1990s with the establishment of what became known as the *New Public Management* (NPM). This analysis leads right to the doorstep of the research in this book. And it helps explain a much longer trend of intensification (not the creation) of an approach to work re-organization and management of government favouring private sector market/capitalist principles. In other words, the seeds of yet another important set of contemporary contradictions – shaping visions of need, motivation and occupational purpose that mediate practices – is clearly detectable historically.

Still, dynamics of either welfare state formation or managerial control dating back to nineteenth century volunteer charity work are not the only sources of mediating artefacts we will encounter in this book. Workers themselves, and especially social workers, played a role in directly shaping the future. As early as the 1920s Canadian social workers pursuing the initial path toward professionalization would initiate a powerful mediating vision (and debate) that would in turn continue to echo loudly in occupational learning of state welfare workers here. It is notable that efforts to professionalize the social work occupation built upon the establishment of Canada's first university-based Schools of Social Work a decade earlier, and, in turn, the creation of the CASW itself (in 1926). Forty years later, the drive for professionalization was further advanced with the establishment of the Council of Social Work Education in Canada. The mutually defining nature of professionalism, specialized education, clearly defined knowledge forms, and occupational entry requirements clearly shape the attitudes of welfare workers in this book despite the fact there is little if any formal linkage between the occupations as such.

In fact, these types of contradictory dynamics have been the subject of research literature on the professions, occupational knowledge and work organization for some time (e.g., Parsons 1954; Scott 1966; Haug 1973; Derber 1982; MacDonald 1995). Though this scholarship has tended to fixate on elements such as codes of ethics and standards of practice, it has also regularly observed important tensions between professional knowledge development and the dynamics of market competition.[3] The consensus in thinking in this regard has been that market competition undermined the neutrality of specialized knowledge forms; and moreover, neither were state bureaucracies felt to be a positive influence. Autonomy in the labour process, here with a special link to learning and knowledge production, were understood to be definitive of the very notion of professionalism. However, what may be even more crucial for our understanding is that, in terms of the development of occupational knowledge forms in the human service professions specifically, what is likely equally definitive is the role of *direct, unimpeded, expansive, and ongoing engagement with clients* specifically (Abbott 1986, 1988). This, according to Roach Anleu (1992, p. 24), was central to realizing forms of social service "ideals". Learning dynamics on the job itself also mattered deeply. Qualified in terms of the themes of this research specifically, we see here that when state welfare workers draw on the mediating resources of "professionalism" or something called "social work ideals", they appropriate supports and limitations that are both more specific and more historical than they often realize.

Workers have not only influenced the nature of this family of occupations vis-à-vis the ongoing drive for professionalization. Other competing representational artefacts can be found. Historically laying in tension with the drive for professionalization in fact were other opposing visions of the social work occupation. Jennissen and Lundy (2011) summarize the point made by one prominent voice in the debate speaking in the 1930s (a leading Canadian social work educator named Harry Cassidy):

> social workers had taken the role of the 'stretcher bearers of society' who respond to the casualties of the system but do little to strike at the roots of the problem: the deplorable economic conditions. [Cassidy] called on social workers to 'wage unremitting war against the social crime of poverty.' (Jennissen and Lundy 2011, p. 50)

Indeed, likewise reflecting on the writings of key individual leaders in the early establishment of Canadian social work, Moffat (2001) emphasizes that separate from the drive for professionalization a broader and more critically minded concern for the public good was equally well established. Thus, distinct from the drive for professionalization, a more radical (humanist, socialist and occasionally explicitly communist), impulse had been brewing for some time constructing and re-constructing a host of alternative representations, tools, skills and knowledge forms. These were elements likewise expressed clearly in the American rank-and-file movement (1920s and 1930s) which at one time exercised influence comparable to the drive professionalization (e.g., Reisch and Anderws 2001), and which influenced practices and debates in Canada (Jennissen and Lundy 2008). And here again we will find another series of contradictions easily detectable in the lives of state welfare workers in this research.

As we turn to the post-World War II period, each of these identifiable sources of contradiction and mediation I have noted thus far could be seen vascilating and competing in a new environment (for social workers as well as a fledgling state welfare occupation). Emergent at this time were additional themes revolving around what Clarke and Newman (1993) called bureau-professional regimes and Harris (2003) summarized as bureau-professionalism. The addition of bureaucratic managerialism, new hierarchies within the work, mixed with modulated notions professionalism with links to local/direct service delivery entered the mix. This was a time in Canada when social workers (and their new associations) were becoming more deeply embedded in the workings of the expanding government bureaucracies of the 1950s and 1960s, and a more fully realized form of the capitalist welfare state. The key contradictions (including those related to gender, social class and charity as well as professionalism and radicalism from much earlier) evolved and some instances sharpened further. The forms of occupational knowledge and the fight for occupational identities became entwined and realized within an even broader and intensive period of change in Canada and elsewhere. Many of the contradictions unique to large-scale public sector human services labour processes, and as we will see state welfare work specifically, gained further complexity.

I argue that this historical sketch of contested, competing, and contradictory artefacts and objects of contemporary state welfare work outlined here will deepen an understanding of learning, skill, and knowledge formation within labour process activity going forward. The origin of key mediating artefacts (e.g., the techniques, ethics, expertise, representations of an occupation, etc.) that constitute workers' distinctive forms of engagement in activity (e.g., as carrying out an act of charity, waging war against injustice, becoming a knowledgeable bureau-professional, and so on) has been the focus. I suggest in fact that this history helps open the way for recognition of the unique tension in the use-value of the state welfare work in the context of the development of the Canadian capitalist state today. Once again it is worth noting: it is entirely commonplace to hear the workers I spoke to between 2002 and 2009 evoke and utilize, in whole or part, the artefacts and objects of activity shaped by these streams of history.

Phases of the Labour Process and Occupational Change in State Welfare Work

Some time ago Tudiver (1982) predicted the incursion of Taylorism into public sector social services in Canada, the United States, and the United Kingdom. He argued that fiscal crisis, neo-liberalism, and state austerity went hand in glove with what at that time were only the early murmurings of the NPM approach in Canada. But even in the early 1980s, such dynamics were beginning to put enormous pressures on state welfare labour processes as well. Tudiver cited the contradictory position of social service workers in terms of the relations between human needs, on the one hand, and intensifying managerial control, on the other. These were matters, as we saw previously, which were hardly new but which continued to take on alternative forms in new historical phases of the development of the public sector labour processes specifically. His analysis and others such as those of Corrigan and Leonard (1978), Simpkins (1983), Jones (1983) and Cousins (1987) in the United Kingdom were prescient in many ways, and tell us a great deal about state welfare work. Updating and expanding these observations, the study of three Canadian provinces by Baines (2004a) confirmed many of these early suspicions noting the role of Taylorism, the fertile soil provided for it by the NPM, and the relationship of both with the dynamics of de-skilling in social work. Likewise, with a focus on the privatization of state social work in Canada and England, Carey (2008) notes the following:

> conspicuous attempts to maximize labour efficiency, reduce staffing levels and other resources, downsize organizations and severely limit formal provisions within social care. In addition, managerial control and regulation has significantly increased, and once complex social work tasks have been broken up and condensed into simple and easy to regulate Taylorist care/case management procedures. (p. 83)

In fact, the works of Carey make a strong case for the comparability of changes in public service labour processes in Canada and the United Kingdom directly, and this provides our discussion with an important point of departure. The UK context following the 1960s provides, in other words, a basic framework of phases in labour process change through which we can better understand the Canadian context, as we will see. Thus, in this section I draw on, briefly interrogate, and seek to extend these analyses, concluding with discussion of key studies of state welfare work, and changes in worker responses to different forms of managerial control.

Austerity in the welfare benefits systems have advanced rapidly in Britain since the crisis of 2008, but in observing the British experience, Carey's cluster of studies have documented three basic phases of changes since 1970 that bear on our understanding of contemporary skill, learning, control, and worker responses in the welfare labour process. He shows that the 1970s was characterized by a labour process featuring *controlled discretion* – what Friedman (1977) referred to as *relative autonomy* – in which residual effects of professionalization, demographics, and large bureaucracies allowed the retention of purpose or object-relatedness in terms of clients, their social context and needs. Separate studies detailing this decade, by Parsloe (1981), for example, more or less confirm that the type of labour processes, as well as these types of social work ideals, were alive and well despite the threatening clouds that loomed on the horizon. Recalling the earlier social work rank-and-file movement and communist-inspired activism, it was in this period that some of the most clarion expressions of social worker *as activist*, serving human needs directly, were recovered and synthesized. This was expressed clearly, for example, in the Bailey and Brake collection (1975) as well as in the Corrigan and Leonard (1978) discussion of the issue of class solidarity amongst social workers, working-class clients, and communities (many of the themes re-examined again in Lavalette 2011). The Canadian context in fact paralleled most of these changes rather closely. In both instances, here was a period that was still rich with the conditions, artefacts, goals, and object/motives that could (potentially) serve specific forms of progressive occupational learning and knowledge production.

By the mid-1980s in Britain we see a period during which the labour process comes to be dominated by attempts at new forms of organizational procedure and managerial discipline (e.g., Cousins 1987; Clarke and Newman 1993). This period represents the emergence of NPM for example. As in the earlier phase, distinct parallels can be seen in the Canadian context. For state welfare workers specifically, this signalled a pronounced frontal assault on elements of autonomy in terms of labour process design, though the actual changes stemming from this assault proved limited. Carey argues that the key limitations to managerial control at this time lay primarily in the "paradoxical role fulfilled by the state" (2009, p. 507).

> despite extensive marketization within many areas of state welfare (including social work), the relationship between the market, civil society and the state 'is always problematic'. This is because capitalist growth depends on the state's capacity to regulate populations and facilitate social (and therefore political and economic) *reproduction* – such as through the education, health and social services. (2009, p. 509)

Cousins (1987) likewise summarized the views of the state in this regard.[4] Building from my discussion of Taylorism in the prior chapter, what remains vital beyond the "problematic" role of the state, limitations to managerial control in this period rested primarily upon residual commitments to bureau-professional regimes based largely on the fact that the state had not yet identified – and nor was it able/willing to finance – an adequately *materialist* approach to change *within the labour process itself*. That is, despite growing financial crisis and a resurgent conservative politics, the state in various countries (including the United Kingdom and Canada specifically) was still not yet in the position to envision how new levels of regulation of the poor could be achieved through new forms of regulation of those who administered the regulation of the poor *by drawing on the lessons of capitalist production themselves*. Different interpretations aside, the works of Pithouse (1987), Dominelli and Hoogvelt (1996), and, somewhat more influentially Harris (e.g., 1998, 2003), all verify the period of the mid-1980s as only partially successful in its achievements of intensified managerial control in state welfare work or similar social work occupations. Relative autonomy necessarily, according to labour process design, persisted.

Both in Britain and in Canada, the third phase of work change might be described as the state's re-doubling of its efforts. That is rather than attempting a fundamental change, it intensified its approach according to the already existing strategy. It is notable for its retention of many bureau-professional assumptions even as forms of hyper-regulation and surveillance were embraced (Cousins 1987; Carey 2009).

> Throughout the 1990s SSWs [state social workers] increasingly became identified in Britain as 'care managers' or 'case managers'.…As a consequence, quasi-professional social work became highly bureaucratic, with only tenuous links held to its relatively more engaged or 'hands on' approach of the past … in *practice* much of the support provided by care/case managers for an expanding 'social care industry' has tended to

> be administrative…. [State social work] is now predominately made up of a 'bureau-cratically compliant workforce' that is increasingly disenfranchised and alienated. (Carey 2009, p. 506; emphasis in original)

On the basis of what we have already seen in the previous section, in some ways this under-appreciates what almost a century of sociology of professional occupations has told us about the effects of bureaucracy. As bureaucratic, as administrative, as compliant (and as alienated) as workers were, the design of the labour process itself was simply not yet able to fully divest the state social and welfare work occupations of key elements central to their forms of knowledge production and identity.

I will argue in this book that the most definitive changes facing state welfare work in countries like Canada and the UK are shaped by the nature of the capitalist state, the contradictory drive to maintain professionalism as well as the persistence of an inherently humanizing, more radical socializing perspective in the occupation. However, I will also claim that the uneven dynamics across these elements are realized in relation to the tried and tested techniques of narrowing task design and establishing newly regulated and increasingly complex divisions of labour that limit – both symbolically *and* materially – *ongoing occupational learning* within the labour process itself.

In this sense, the work of Carey and a discrete number of others stand quite separate on the contemporary research scene in allowing us to think also in terms of the implications of a distinctive shift in something that will prove crucial in the preceding analysis: the *object-relatedness* of cultural historical activity. For example, Carey effectively highlights the links among the loss of *real social work* (2009, p. 525), changes in skill, and the dynamics of the labour process specifically. Fitzgibbon (2008), likewise, confirms the loss of the *wholeness of client contact* as central to changes in skill and loss of meaning, adding that these resulted in poorer, less accurate (and more punitive) client assessments as well. And, though remaining unconvinced of many of the tenets of radical labour process analysis, Coleman and Harris (2008) nevertheless also highlight the effects of similar dynamics in documenting the displacement of direct client service/skills. It is in this context that Baines's (2008) comments on the dynamics of de-skilling may be particularly insightful.

> Along with work practices and philosophies, social work skills have been reformulated under the new learning models of service delivery…. [I]f activities and interactions in the social services do not contribute to cost savings, they are unlikely to be formally recognized or valued and may be denigrated as common sense or personal techniques.

> Although a growing body of literature documents the growth of deskilling …, *little is known about the new skills emerging in the restructured social services.* (Baines, 2008, p. 123; emphasis added)

As I hope to show, myriad relations of *learning-in-activity* swim beneath the surface of the labour process change and the machineries of knowledge construction it depends upon and shapes. The semi-independent skills, knowledge and judgement of Lipsky's "street-level bureaucrats" (1980) are likewise involved. Yet still Taylorization of state welfare work produces other challenges for workers. Ferguson and Lavalette (2004), and before them Gilroy (2000) and Foster and Hogget (1999), find spikes of alienation reaching almost pathological proportions amongst social workers, for example; a sign that bodes poorly for state welfare workers, clients and society, as we will see in this research. Worker alienation – that concept so prematurely consigned to the dustbin by the post-industrialism thesis – has emerged as a research topic of interest yet again. While few have considered state welfare workers specifically, building on it we might still predict that alienation will necessarily entwine with distinctive forms of participation, skill and knowledge formation within labour process activity. Appling a dialogical application of LPT and CHAT traditions we might expect a complex soup of bureaucratic-administrative coping, relative/repressive satisfactions and engrossment, withdrawal, disorientation, and, in some instances, professional dissatisfaction, outrage, disgust giving rise to resistance to existing arrangements, and so on. Understanding how thinking, feeling, knowing, acting people are responsible for each of these, it is argued here, is primarily a matter of occupational experience and, in particular, learning-in-activity.

The Politics and Character of Welfare Work Change in a Canadian Context

As the preceding materials begin to make clear, the present conditions and the resources of occupational consent, accommodation, and resistance within state welfare work did not simply fall from the sky. They were made, over a long period of time. But the situation was not created only from the struggles surrounding professionalism, radicalism or rank-and-file styled activism despite its contribution to the contradictory objects of the family of social work and social work related occupations like state welfare work. Nor can the origins of the situation be attributed only to the phases of management style, or the shifting organizational forms which unfolded from the 1970s to the present. And finally, the present conditions cannot only be understood as simply a reflection of the contradictory nature of the capitalist state sui generis. Rather, the contradictory pressures and limits shaping occupational lives in state welfare work in Canada also emerged out of nationally (as well as provincially and municipally) specific inter-governmental arrangements surrounding administration and financing of welfare services that, along with new technologies, alternative funding schemes, and the application of distinctive labour processes, opened the way for the specific form that neo-liberal austerity initiatives have taken in this context.

In Canada, administration and financing of welfare benefits delivery have been heavily mediated by the wrangling among different levels of government (federal, provincial, municipal). No doubt unique versions of these same dynamics are seen in other countries. In Canada, however, in connection to the state welfare labour process, the story of this wrangling confirms why, and to some degree how, it remains impossible to separate analysis of occupational learning from the broader municipal, provincial, national and even international shifts in political economy. In these terms, here we extend the debates on skill in keeping with the aspirations of contemporary Labour Process Theory generally. The past mediates the present, in this case for example, in terms of such elements as legislation, administration, and finance as related to labour market dynamics and occupational certification/entry requirements. In turn, these shape labour processes as well as changes to the way in which the machineries of knowledge construction unfold and compete for legitimacy and dominance within activity over time.

Different levels of government in Canada have, at different times, been either responsible for and/or in control of delivering forms of welfare services. The shifts in both represent a story of repeated pendulum swings, recognizably similar and yet with distinctive elements associated with each cycle, that in practice have continued to cast the lived experiences, skills, knowledge, and learning of workers and clients to and fro. As Struthers (1994) explains, in the 1930s short term legislation (to deal with the Great Depression) required municipalities to pay 50 per cent of the costs of welfare/unemployment services with the rest from the provincial and federal governments. By 1942, however, in Canada's largest and most industrialized province of Ontario, these arrangements had changed such that the province and municipalities were to bear the costs equally. With the emergence of attempts at the Canadian version of a fully articulated welfare state in the 1950s–1960s, these arrangements shifted yet again. Indeed, the apparent high-water mark of the Canadian welfare state, and welfare service provision specifically, has regularly been tied by many to the establishment of what was called the Canada Assistance Plan (CAP) in 1966.[5] Yet in keeping with the pendulum cycle, in several ways CAP re-established a version of the cost sharing seen in the 1930s with targeted financial transfers from federal to provincial levels of government for welfare services on a 50/50 matching basis. Importantly for us here: in the CAP era these transfers included *guidelines* defining the nature of the services and conditions of benefits under the umbrella rationale of removing arbitrary eligibility restrictions (Struthers 1994, p. 233). Still, less than a decade after CAP's establishment in Canada, it was already being altered to reduce the amount of federal transfer.[6] Global economic crisis, beginning in the early 1970s, in turn, exerted pressures and re-ignited federal-provincial tensions in the area of administration and financing of services (Rice and Prince 2000; Bashevkin 2002).

For my purposes what remains crucial going forward in the book is that, in 1967 and in connection with CAP specifically, Ontario's General Welfare Assistance Act was amended to place municipalities in charge of administration of (as it was then called) services to employable men and their families. In this context, services directed at the remaining people (e.g., disabled, widows, single mothers originally) were made the direct responsibility of the province of Ontario in terms of finance and administration.[7] While generalized pressures toward state austerity continued to grow, in 1994 the province of Ontario assumed responsibility for the *finance* of services directed at those falling under the General Welfare Assistance Act, though at the same time the province did *not* assume sole responsibility for *administration* of these services (e.g., Graham and Phillips 1998).

Here we can begin to see clearly the way that shifting public administration and financing arrangements bear directly on who managed and made policy regarding state welfare work leading up to and including the implementation of the labour process changes affecting the occupational lives of the workers in this research. Building from the types of dynamics just outlined, a key turning point for the purposes of this research was reached. It involved the establishment in 1995 of the Canada Health and Social Transfer (CHST). The CHST collapsed federal transfers dealing with a range of social programs (including welfare services) into one block grant. Importantly, as opposed to the CAP era guidelines, this meant *little to no formal direction* as to how the funds were to be used was provided to the provinces by the federal government. This, in effect, opened the door for more creative experimentation in austerity, notably in terms of forms and scales of de-regulation, privatisation, and public-private partnerships (e.g., Battle and Torjman 1995). In Ontario, for example, immediately in 1995 the former acts governing how welfare benefits were to be delivered were replaced by what was called the *Ontario Works Act*. It was this act that directly set in place the principles (and legislative requirements) regulating service delivery and hence the labour processes at issue here. Moreover (and yet again), the financing of welfare services was altered and in Ontario a complicated trading of responsibilities for various services between levels of government was made. Specifically, the downloading of costly responsibilities including general welfare services now fell to the lower municipal level of government. The province of Ontario would provide temporary grants early in the implementation of a radically different benefits delivery labour process design, for the first time in history fully embedded in legislative regulations, and through the provincial government would manage welfare program finances at a distance vis-à-vis what amounted to a complex piece-rate system (based on Participation Agreements, verification processes, as we will see later in the book).

> In 1997, the Ontario government embarked upon a pioneering joint business venture with Andersen Consulting (now known as Accenture) to redesign the delivery system for social assistance. The 'Business Transformation Project' [BTP] substantially altered the nature of public/private partnerships in the province, allowing the private sector to become more deeply entangled in what were previously deemed to be core government functions. Driven by a desire to cut costs, the BTP sought to comprehensively redesign social assistance programmes, focusing especially upon the introduction of new technologies and practices to support the delivery of Ontario Works (OW) and the Ontario Disability Support Programs (ODSP). The existing delivery system was thought to be too labour intensive, allowing little time for direct staff contact with clients. Moreover, the lack of common technology and information sharing was thought to encourage error and fraud. (Herd and Mitchell 2005, p. 1)

Cost avoidance vis-à-vis heightened control *at the point of production* was, from the very origins of the labour process design, central. Indeed, in a key report by HLB Decision Economics Incorporated entitled *Review and Update of the Business Transformation Project Business Case and Risk Analysis* (HLB Decision Economics Incorporated 2002), commissioned by the Ontario government to provide a financial case for the new labour process in its earliest days of implementation, we see these goals in no uncertain terms. The changes in the general welfare labour process were themselves projected to produce more than $320M in cost avoidance annually, measured in terms of ongoing reductions on a *cost-per-case* basis.[8] Crucially, this depended on establishing *both* a range of new practices of linking eligibility to municipal funding using a far more standardized verification process (named the Consolidated Verification Process or CVP) *and* more extensive third-party information verification capacity. It significantly undermined the possibilities for occupational judgment and intervention by state welfare workers by targeting key task sets central to state welfare workers knowledge production and autonomy.[9] As with austerity measures generally, what became equally clear was that government savings were not in fact the goal (given significant reduction in tax rates, increased pacing of debt re-payment, as well as generous payments to large private sector contractors that were undertaken in the same period).[10] Of course, what resulted was a significant transfer of wealth. What was essential was the mobilization of direct, municipal-level *labour process intervention* in cost avoidance/wealth transfer. This effectively bridged general austerity principles, which were advanced in any case through welfare rate cutting, with a more far-reaching strategy (labour process re-design) for the realization of neo-liberal change.[11]

This background in federal, provincial and municipal dynamics brings us to and helps explain the current arrangements shaping state welfare work in this research. In the arrangement reported on this research, formal responsibilities for finance are managed by contractual agreement between the province and the municipalities. And more importantly, the municipalities have been placed in charge of the local administration while the broader design and control of a now much more uniform labour process – via the *Ontario Works Act* legislation and the province-wide Service Delivery Model Technology (SDMT) – has remained with the province. It is, in fact, a situation ideally suited to work design invented to fight directly, as Taylor put it, a two-front war with workers as well as local management. These are arrangements that produced a type of austerity strategy that could significantly enhance control of the poor as well as lower costs at the point of service production, while seriously undermining capacity for occupational resistance that had historically stood in the way at virtually every turn.

It is inclusive of these multifaceted historical origins that the new labour process and the dynamics of occupational learning will be explored in this book. These origins are embedded in the labour process that workers (as well as clients and local management) face in this research. As we will see in the following chapters, a largely *unified, holistic occupation called*

Case Worker was broken into a series of new, discrete, task-based clusters of jobs (namely, Intake Screening Unit Worker, Case Manager, Employment Services Worker, Eligibility Review, Consolidate Verification Review/ Fraud Inspection, and Clerical Assistance).[12] Whereas a Case Worker used to be responsible for virtually the entire relationship of a client to the welfare system, now intake was to be handled by a separate group of call centre workers; initial eligibility to be reviewed by one set of workers while employment services were planned and arranged by others; maintenance of the case file, in either general or specific populations, to be carried out separately as well; and, regular, consolidated review of all applications for eligibility leading to termination and cost avoidance to remain the purview of still others. Of particular note, this new division of labour resulted in the discontinuation of what workers throughout this text refer to as "life on the road": that is client home visits, more sustained contact with clients and the communities in which clients lived, and so on.

As noted earlier, the new labour process was supported by the introduction of a powerful new intra-net computer technology called SDMT. According to Hier (2003), from the standpoint of workers and clients, this

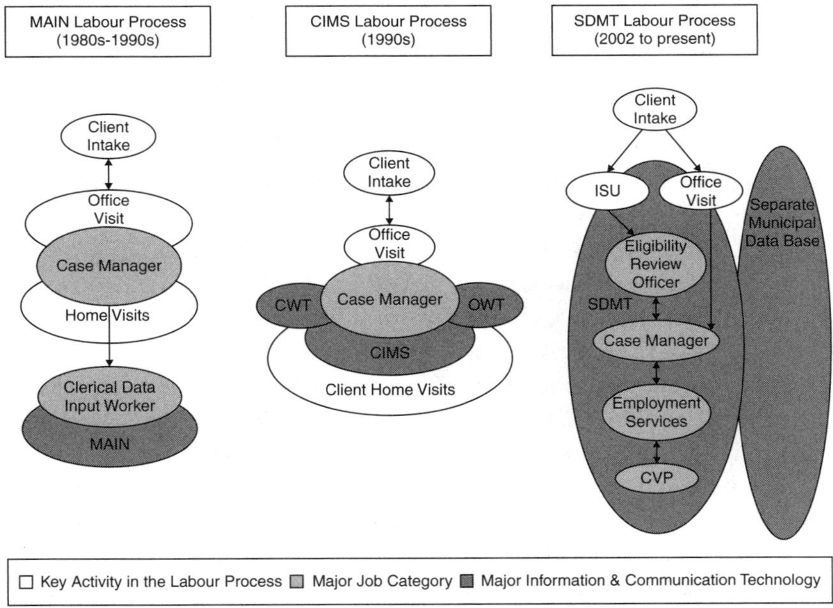

Figure 4.1. Changes in Ontario welfare work labour processes (1970s–2009).

was a technological system experienced as a prototypical *surveillant assemblage*.[13] It was a technology that supported, and was supported by, the new legislation, rules, conventions, purposes, managerial practices, division of labour, and organizational forms. Indeed, in the case of Ontario the current labour process emerges from a series of changes that can be roughly marked by shifts in the central mediating technologies in the occupation. These included the Municipal Assistance Integrated Network (MAIN) system circa the 1980s; Comprehensive Income Maintenance System (CIMS), Case Worker Technology (CWT), Ontario Works Technology (OWT) systems circa the 1990s; and the new Service Delivery Model Technology (SDMT) system as of 2002. In each instance, the shift in technology worked hand-in-glove with broader labour process changes (see Figure 4.1) that, step-by-step, has edged toward what I argue to have been a critical break in occupational knowledge and form.

Conclusions

> When the changes came in, I remember going to meetings [with management] and I remember them presenting about the new work system. They said it would make things a lot easier when the new SDMT system came in. I put my hand up and asked how that would happen? They said it would alleviate a lot of lost time…. What they were talking about was dividing of our jobs. (HJIDAT0404, Case Manager)[14]

Each of these historical and contemporary details will be important as we move forward in the book providing a broader basis for understanding struggles across forms of state welfare worker occupational development. However, in concluding this chapter, it is also worth noting how the resulting labour process parallels closely Aitken's (1960) description of the implementation of Taylorism at the Watertown Arsenal in Chapter 3 as well; eerily similar in fact all the way down to forms of localized deviation from aspects of the work design and governmental debates over financing and inter-governmental relations. It is against this entire historical backdrop that we can better understand how the current Taylorized system was born and continues to be re-born in the lives of workers.

The basic patterns of work, learning, and technological change have been and will continue to be mirrored in historically and nationally specific ways around the world wherever advanced capitalism and neo-liberal austerity flourish. For workers, these patterns have obviously not gone unnoticed. Individual workers like the one quoted at the outset of this conclusion have often paid attention, and so have the unions representing them. In

Canada, the Canadian Union of Public Employees (CUPE-Ontario), the union representing workers in general welfare services in Ontario, for its part released a study citing workplace stress due to downsizing, overwork, and lack of flexibility of work processes (CUPE 2000). Seeing similar changes, the National Union of Public and General Employees, representing many public sector workers at the federal level in Canada, did likewise (NUPGE 2000). Working with the Ontario Public Service Employees Union (OPSEU), Lewchuk (2002) offered detailed documentation of the nature of these concerns in his study of the impact of the new SDMT benefits delivery labour process on workers.[15] Using a standard Karasek Job Demand-Control analysis Lewchuk reported significant increases in managerial control and workload in comparison to other occupational groups. The long and complex process of the *making of Taylorism* in state welfare work, I argue, is central to understanding these concerns.

What Raymond Williams (e.g., 1977) often referred to as *residual elements of history* remain operative in contemporary practices of all kinds. In the approach to skill, work, and learning within the labour process I take in this book, this is generally referred to as the *historicity of activity*: the explanation of how people make history but not as they choose. This approach depends on a recognition of the artefact-mediated nature of human practice. These are artefacts with histories, indeed, artefacts marked by the pleasures, indifference, triumphs and scars of historical struggles. Importantly from this perspective, these residual elements – the cultural and historically patterned constellation of symbolic and material artefacts – are the means by which the state welfare workers in this book learn to make and re-make their work and themselves.

5 Experiencing the De-Skilling Premises of Welfare Work

Introduction

> Have I told you my analogy of Case Workers? We're the SPONGE! ... We have this ability to keep sucking up everything they keep throwing at us. (NF17DB0304, Case Manager)

Earlier I remarked that the labour process change amongst state welfare workers in this research has been as contentious as it has been ongoing and exhausting. However, for workers, the contentious nature of the situation has been interpreted, re-interpreted, and acted upon in a host of distinctive ways. In this chapter I respond to the following question: What are workers experiences, perceptions, and understandings of these changes?

Collectively, the job descriptions for front line state welfare workers in the general welfare system (Ontario Works, or OW) can be summarized as follows. Their tasks are to gather legislatively required information on clients; evaluate eligibility; establish something called a case beginning with what is known as a Participation Agreement (PA); update changes in client's circumstances; and facilitate the delivery of a series of legislatively required benefits to clients (funds and funded services such as counselling, training, and job placement) and, where applicable, their dependents. In several ways, this describes occupational functions that have not changed all that much over several decades. But it also ignores a great deal that is central to shaping worker experiences and perceptions in their new environment. Obscured in this type of description are the key dynamics of the labour process that have in fact changed significantly and have now, for most, established an entirely different character to the work.

100

The evidence that follows initiates the claim that the new labour process represents an attempt at achieving a fundamentally new level of control over state welfare workers and clients vis-à-vis shifts in the practices of learning, skill and knowledge formation in activity. Still, this chapter can only make a contribution toward the broader claims of the book in this regard. It deals primarily with *subjective experience*, and focuses analysis on workers' *perceptions and understandings* of their ongoing encounters with the new work design; their active awareness which includes feeling as well as thought as individuals. That is the term "experience" here is treated as information that is *self-consciously* available to interviewees in the structure of work activity (as well as within the context of a semi-structured interview activity). Thus, recalling the Cultural Historical Activity Theory (CHAT) framework discussed in Chapter 2, we can say that activity as a whole can simply be approximated by the evidence I provide here in this chapter. That is, in CHAT terms, I am addressing accounts of practice that most often link to goal-directed action alone.[1]

Substantiating the types of claims I hope to make overall is impossible, however, without careful attention to the experience and self-conscious perceptions of workers. Exploring these here we begin to understand better how this new labour process produces a series of alternative horizons of concern and struggle within a particular occupation. And to describe these problematic horizons, many interviewees begin with simple but effective statements regarding how, within the new labour process, they are being turned into "factory workers" and "cookie-cutters", and at the same time "telemarketers", "used car salesmen", "bank tellers", or "carpet salesmen". As we will see, many workers now perceive themselves as "tied to the computer", lamenting how earlier they had used their "eyes and ears and judgment [but] now we just type things into the computer". And yet still, workers vary considerably in their positive or negative evaluation of their situation.

In attempting to sort out alternative perceptions we benefit from several, particular objective facts: *the number of sets of hands through which a single client's case now passes has vastly enlarged while worker experiences of clients have, for any one worker, become increasingly narrow.* Indeed, the change in the labour process represents what in traditional work design terms might be described as related to features of both batch and continuous flow production. At times in vague and dis-jointed ways and at other times with remarkable precision, and with differing levels of acceptance, workers nonetheless correctly identify the association of their work with a factory. The most fundamental accomplishments in terms of occupational learning, skill, and knowledge are found, however, in the uneven ways in which new purposes – and we may add here a new object/motive of activity – have descended into their lives. And as was indicated earlier, these changes have been facilitated by a new province-wide intra-net computer software system called Service Delivery Model Technology (SDMT). This multi-dimensional, new master work routing and accounting artefact has been essential in achieving the new division of labour. In fact it embodies many of Braverman's (1974/1998) original concerns and reflects many of Fredrick W. Taylor's original aims. Achieving this division of labour has brought with it not only the potential for new assertions of organizational control, but new occupational identities and new opportunities for the learning of consent and accommodation, as well as resistance. The changes have turned what is arguably a crucial occupation in society – providing support for the rights and needs of the poor – into an open question as to its future function, meaning, and purpose.

Prior to implementation of the new SDMT labour process, state welfare work in Ontario, Canada, could be described as allowing for significant worker discretion, relative autonomy, and with these the development of broader forms of occupational judgement and expertise. In the pre-SDMT era in fact, beyond keeping up with legislative changes, state welfare worker knowledge/skill depended on ongoing, on-the-job professional development through client home visits, coherent strings of client meetings that workers themselves organized, case meetings with co-workers likewise largely organized by workers themselves, and organized mentoring by supervisors who were themselves former welfare workers with expertise in the same labour process. Later on in the book I will discuss how these and other patterns of occupational practice link with the notion of craft work and processes of craft occupational enculturation. However in this chapter, what we find is that the these *prior* patterns of knowledge construction form a central point of reference for workers in their perceptions of the transformations they face today.

While many basic political economic, organizational, and managerial features of the labour process have already been introduced in the book, in the following I report on the dimensions of workers' experiences across several traditional areas of analytical concern within Labour Process Theory (LPT): that is, division of labour, autonomy, control, and workload. Evidence within these theme areas is of interest in its own right. While some basic observations will be provided in relation to cultural historical psychology, it is LPT that provides the structure of the following analysis.

Specifically, we see in this consideration of the *division of labour* how the knowledge base of welfare workers is jeopardized and, in fact, eroding fast. I explore perceptions of how the most basic foundational form of occupational interpretation and knowing in the labour process (i.e., knowing "what is going on"; knowing "what you're doing") has become remarkably challenged. I then turn to investigation of the perceived changes in *autonomy and control*. Here we find pronounced perceptions of loss. Many of these perceptions directly implicate occupational identity. As a variety of approaches to understanding identity suppose, identity is not reducible to pre-existing (let alone merely psycho-biological) expressions of personality. I discuss the ways that occupational identity is a mediated feature of labour process activity specifically. In the next section, I explore the way that workers perceive changes in *workload*. While work intensification is referenced widely by workers in the interview data, the specific perceptions, evaluations and explanations of it vary considerably. Accounts range from those perceiving workload increases as something that has simply "just happened"; others linking the perception of workload increases to worker incompetence; and still others, self-consciously perceiving it as an expression of exploitation, injustice, and possibly ethical and moral failure. These types of perceptions, as we will see going forward in the book, are more than simply complaints and rationalizations. They are important elements of highly differentiated forms of occupational skill and knowledge formation in activity. In the final section, I direct attention to a matter somewhat unique to human services labour processes such as state welfare work: *client relations*. In the prior chapter the significance of client relations, unimpeded engagement with, and knowledge of clients was discussed as a component of professional work and autonomy. Likewise, the role of worker/client relations as a likely target of Taylorist intervention in work design has been noted. In the following, however, we find wide variability in perceptions of the clients and client/worker relations more broadly. This is a matter which will continue to contribute to understandings of the divergence of trajectories of occupational learning in particular ways later on. Most interviewees self-consciously perceive and can easily speak of changes in the pattern of client relations as one of a small number of definitive changes in the labour process. Yet, while some learn outrage and others learn glum resignation, still others learn to go along enthusiastically re-constructing worker-client relations in new (and more limited) ways.

Experiencing Changes in Division of Labour

The critical review of changes in state social work in the previous chapter highlighted some important features of labour process analysis. Research referenced there was, in fact, split on their views on LPT and the application of Braverman's approach specifically however. In any case, to this point we have only obtained a sketch of the core preoccupation in Braverman's work that helped establish the LPT tradition: that is, the vast and powerful implications of the Taylorist division of labour. In point of fact, most welfare workers interviewed in this research voiced explicit concerns about the new division of labour. In most ways it remained an issue that ran like a spine through the entire body of their experiences of change. The workers in the following excerpts (some of whom are formally educated in the field of social work and all of whom have significant work experience in the field) speak to the most common, general perceptions available from the interview data. Together they offer an initial orientation to the new experiences of front-line state welfare workers.[2]

> There are more people with their hands on the file because you could have a fraud investigator, a support worker, a consolidated verification process worker plus a caseworker and an employment worker and an ERO. They've all got a hand on one file. And it's like, important things always get lost. (BDBTH0303, Intake Screening Worker)

> It's terrible. It's a divide and conquer situation. We are so specialized now that I think there is no continuity and I think it's confusing for the clients as well. 'Oh no, I'm not your Case Manager, I'm an Employment Consultant.' 'Oh no, I'm only your CVP Worker.' 'Oh no, I'm your Eligibility Reviewer.' 'Oh no, I'm just going to deal with your intake.' 'Oh no, I'm just doing the Information Session.' So for a client there's such a series of faces, that they're passed off, passed off, passed off, it's like playing hot potato with them and important things always get lost in the shuffle. (HKMAT0404, Employment Worker)

> It's been divided into jobs that really don't make sense either because our jobs do overlap. You really can't divide our jobs and still have it make sense. (HJIDAT0404, Case Manager)

In the forms of labour process activity implied in the preceding excerpts there is an inescapable shift in occupational sense-making; an essential feature of the learning process. The excerpts reference perceptions of loss of a sense of the job, an eroding linkage to a particular knowledge form and with this an eroding capacity for an ongoing development of this particular knowledge form. Unavoidably, these perceptions also reference identity, a sense of occupational personality, and, for veteran welfare workers such those quoted, perceptions are established implicitly in relation to earlier comparative experiences. The organization of perception is fundamental to personal sense-making. However, from the perspective of CHAT analysis sense-making is also distinguishable from the meanings provided/intended by the premises of work design. As we will see moving forward the shifting relations between sense and meaning are continuous with adaptation to and transformation of labour process activity *as well as* workers' distinctive forms of participation in it. Obliquely we find important references to the object of activity which, as we learned from Kaptelinin (2005) in Chapter 2, operates as the "sense-maker".

In the following, a person who was once an Intake Screening Worker but who is now a Case Manager speaks to the newly established relationship between these two positions specifically. In the account we see that these types of divisions have impacted fundamental features of one's ability to learn and engage in occupational knowledge production in activity. That is conscious awareness of "*knowing* what's going on", *knowing* "what you're actually working with" in order that you can "*know* what you're actually doing", and, in turn, *know* who you "are" – all of these are mediated in a highly problematic way by the new division of labour.

I:[3]   So then you wouldn't say you feel now so much that this is your profession as in the sense of a Social Worker but instead you feel more like a clerical type worker? Is that what you're saying?

S: Yes. And more and more we're being told that that's all we are…. And, it's even worse if you're working as a screener [Intake Screening Worker]. Like I worked for a time as a screener and that was an eye-opener. I've seen it from both sides [Intake Screening Worker and Case Manager]. We were specifically told we were only to capture the information, not to even note a lot of it. Meanwhile Case Managers kept saying, 'We need them to give us a good snapshot. We can't just have something sent down to us without seeing the story.' See, the Form 1 information that is produced means nothing without the story. You need the story to back up what's going on and then you know what you're actually working with. You can know what you're actually doing. (HJIDAT0404, Case Manager)

Recognizing how perceptions of experience, particularly as they implicate occupational identity, are highly uneven is critical to this research going forward. Indeed, we will also see that this poses a somewhat deeper challenge to basic presumptions concerning the up-skilling and de-skilling theses examined earlier. Thinking in terms of effects of the new division of labour we can take the experience of the following Employment Worker as an important illustration. Within the new division of labour, Employment Workers would seem to have retained several elements of a formerly more unified job. This next excerpt explains the new labour process, highlighting a slightly different source of contradiction. This contradiction is based on an awareness that, while she personally has been able to retain some autonomy and discretion in her work and aspects of former occupational identity have remained, it has come at a broader expense. Thus, here something in addition to "knowing what's going on" is indicated vis-à-vis perceptions of the division of labour.

> I'm saying that I'm mostly doing what Case Workers, well what really almost all of us used to do. It just doesn't feel right in a lot of ways. What they have done was by [the Employment Services] piece coming over to me now as a specialized Employment Worker that is taking an important aspect of the Case Worker job that we used to grade higher [in the collective agreement] because it was gathered together in one job. The negotiating, conflict resolution, problem solving, dealing with you know, well, those type of issues in a deeper, more sympathetic, empathetic way. Those are job evaluation factors that we have traditionally thought of as being higher. So, that creates a downgrading of their skill when for example you look at the fact that the Intake Worker is supposed to be just capturing the information and never interpreting it. I mean that's part of the legislation now. And then CVP people, they're only supposed to be doing a verification of the information based on information captured at a lower job level. And between [CVP] and people like me as an Employment Worker, what else is left for Case Workers? It becomes all about dealing with the little bits and pieces. They have to work really hard now to string together what's become usually a confusing hodge-podge. (BCBBP0704b, Employment Worker)

The point of these initial, basic reflections is to establish an entry point into understanding the experiences and perceptions of the new division of labour. However, directly stemming from the basic division of labour other divisions emerged as well, some more transient than others. Discussion later in the book picks up on this theme in a more expansive way looking at group formation, but a key example at this point involves the establishment of what were called the Local Business Experts (LBEs) in the initial phases of the implementation process. Their position was established as local trouble-shooting experts with specific skills and abilities, typically focused on using the SDMT computer system. These positions were staffed from among the existing complement of welfare workers. LBEs were often thought to have been crucial for start-up as the new labour process and technology proved to be particularly onerous. However, at the three year mark post implementation (with the loss of special dedicated funding), LBEs had disappeared as a formal job category. Many former LBEs retained a private commitment to doing this work while others were sometimes pestered and cajoled into continuing to do the work informally. It constituted unpaid work atop their assigned tasks. Where they continued, willingly or be-grudgingly, the broader perception of their role remained essentially the same despite the lack of formal recognition. These matters aside, reliance on these LBEs initially helped shape worker capacity and knowledge production activity in a variety of ways, this despite the fact that the LBE position was never constructed as having a role in the training regime as such. Indeed, the training regime, most workers claimed, was woefully inadequate (even if, for a minority, it remained the most important source of information). Extending this point we see that the division of labour, combined with dynamics of the LBE role, produced a particular distribution – or rather concentration – of expertise initially. This was a matter that would produce a variety of implications for the structure of occupational learning over time.

I: I'm very interested to learn about your personal experiences of the feedback and problem-solving processes that have occurred as the new work process and the new technology have been implemented and adjusted. Can you provide some concrete examples of how you've been involved in these types of activities?

S: Well most of the time our LBE, we emailed her if we have particular problems and we got feedback. Usually she just solved the problem and didn't go into complications like for example I was saying before when sometimes the Child Tax Benefit blows out and creates all sorts of overpayments. We were basically just sending her the file information and she looked at it and corrected it. I didn't get to know how it was corrected or what the problem was or anything like that. Not that I really even need to know the bigger reality now or anything, but I didn't even have time to know either, so it's more of we had sort of like a small group of central people where we send our information, and they'd fix it. How or what went wrong we weren't a party to that.

I: That's a good thing?

S: In some ways it's a good thing. Yeah, most of the time it's a good thing just because we don't have to get bogged as to why it happened. Does it matter why or how it happened? Well not really when there's nothing I can do to prevent it from happening in the future, so even if I know why, it's not going to help me, and anyways it's all stuff that just stands in the way of your working with the client in whatever way you can. (HJKAT0404, CVP)

For most workers, meaning and personal sense of the work were signif-icantly challenged by the new division of labour. Furthermore, and with virtually no exceptions in the interviews, until workers began slowly and organically to compose a form of collective response to the decline in their ability to do their jobs, LBEs (first formally and then informally) con-tinued to play a key mediating role helping workers *not* to get "bogged down"; and, as the worker in the preceding excerpt notes, it helped people not to worry about the "bigger reality" and with it questions of "why". In other words, we can begin to recognize how seemingly minor and transient alterations of the division of labour, such as the use of the LBE category, can set in train the potential for deeper and ongoing dynamics of occupa-tional learning in activity. Paradoxically, the lack of effective training and the de facto concentration of expertise in the new division of labour early on also eventually produced capacity among others for a type of defence of the occupation as well, vis-à-vis the emergence of a fully articulated work-around culture, as we shall see.

Experiencing Changes in Autonomy and Control

The preceding series of excerpts on the perceptions of the effects of the new division of labour intertwine deeply with matters of occupational autonomy and control. Workers interviewed clearly perceived radical changes in relations of autonomy and control in the labour process stem-ming from the needs of their employer (the state). And, for its own part, the state must respond to a broad set of needs related to control as well (e.g., the control of workers, the poor, costs, and public perception). I will return again and again to how the nature of the capitalist state is implicated in the analysis. The point here, however, is that these needs of the state are real-ized and taken up vis-à-vis a series of complex mediations *beginning with* the elements over which it feels it exercise the most direct forms of control (systems and workers, as well as benefit rates).

Nowhere were changes in autonomy and control felt as strongly as they were amongst the workers in the Intake Screening Units (ISUs: the system of regional call centres set up to carry out initial client intake). Scrambling interviewee perceptions further, for many in the ISUs, there was no ready point of comparison as this was an entirely new job category. Previously, intake was carried out face-to-face by those who would, in turn, have direct and ongoing relations with the client personally. For state welfare workers who transferred to these jobs, the points of comparison that were avail-able led most to consider their role as downgraded in terms of job skill requirements. Indeed, the transfer of existing workers (and the hiring of new ones) to the ISUs was done on the basis that the work was of a less specialized nature. By virtue of welfare legislation ISU workers were formally *not* permitted to exercise judgments concerning eligibility. They were only to collect the now greatly increased amount of personal information from the client and enter it into the system. It is beginning with the ISU workers that we see the effects on autonomy and control, as functions of work design, at their most pronounced.

Formal determinations of eligibility as well as presumptions based on formal job description and skill requirement, however, do not tell us the whole of the story as regards matters related to either the concrete experiences or the complexities and contradictions of occupational knowledge production. Not unlike findings seen in the literature on call centre workers (e.g., Mirchandani 2012), a closer look at state welfare Intake Screening Workers shows that they cope with a type of highly complex situation and face many of the challenges endemic to call centre work. And as with most other call centre labour processes, the job involves far greater levels of contingency than the formal work design and rules suggest. In the case of state welfare call centre workers, it is contingent and complex work, in part, because of the enormous amount of information, legislatively required, that now has to be collected. It is challenging because workers are dealing with clients who both were unused to the new welfare system and rarely would have at hand the new mass of information required of them. And foundational to each of these things was the fact that clients were frequently exhausted, traumatized, and, in short, busy experiencing the many desperations of poverty. Importantly as a matter of learning (and un-learning) in occupational life: complicating matters were the instances in which the apparently narrow and standardized call centre work triggered prior professional expertise and concerns. In these contexts ISU workers – being either former case workers or educated in a social work related field – would quite naturally construct the exchange as something much more than simply gathering and inputting information. Indeed, in the conclusion of Chapter 3, I quoted the work of Durand (1990), who emphasized the significance of *irregularity* in the *materials of work*. "Irregularity" constantly instigated the need for what he called *break-down work*. The "material" of state welfare work, of course, includes clients who lead complex lives shaded significantly by a wide array of urgencies. Thus what may be particularly important to our analysis here is that these elements of contingency and irregularity are as fundamental to questions of lived autonomy and control as they are inherent to matters of knowledge construction.

In the first of three excerpts that follow we hear from an ISU Worker who provides us with a typical description of the work. He is an eleven-year veteran of state welfare work who was formerly a Case Manager in the system. Here we obtain an introduction to the relations among the labour process, autonomy, and control as workers like him perceived them. In the remaining two excerpts additional, more subtle forms of control and the loss of autonomy experienced by those working in job categories other than the ISU are highlighted. We see the needs for control by the state (vis-à-vis control of workers and clients) woven into these accounts. A major outcome, thus, involves the means by which clients are initially, as Herd and Mitchell (2005) have described it, "discouraged, diverted and disentitled" (p. 1) in relation to their rights as citizens. In terms of the focus in this book specifically, we see that these issues bear on welfare workers' learning lives as well. What begins to come into focus in particular is how occupational commitments – sometimes even those expressing deeper human commitments to the broader social purpose of one's work – do not fall from the sky holus-bolus or simply emerge as expressions of a personality type as such. They are both learned *and* un-learned amid the complex mediations of labour process *activity* over time.

> I don't think the government realizes in many cases, some of the literacy issues of some of our clients, or the needs of some of our clients. Many of these people that are calling are in a very bad way, and some of them are crying when you answer the phone. And there are people with severe psychiatric problems. It's difficult for them to be on the phone. I will also say that in some cases, speaking personally, I will try to make things a bit smoother for them. I will get them calmed down. I will try to get them focused. I want to make sure they understand what they are in for in the second stage, which is the verification interview. I will try to make sure they have the right documents before they go to that interview, and if they don't, I will help them get them. You can help them get some ID if they don't have any, and let's face it lots of people don't have this stuff. Like with my intake work, I do applications for four different regions. So I always told people, that the set up makes the system too cold and impersonal, because all you are doing is dealing with a voice. I was in the field for a long time [as a Case Worker] before I started doing this work. But I can just feel it. I can feel myself finding it so much easier to be cold hearted and say no because I just can't know the person. It's like telemarketing. Like I don't understand why the person is yawning on the phone at 11 am in the morning. It could be that they were up all night because the police were at the place next door, or there was some sort of battle royal on their street the night before, or whatever. So, those are some of the themes that are taken out of the mix, the humanity. (HBBAT0403, Intake Screening Worker)

> They're just statistics and that's the way management seems to be looking at them and I don't like that because to me they're human beings, they're not stats. I felt like I was selling carpets when I was at the Intake Screening Unit. (HIMAT0404, former Intake Screening Worker now CVP Worker)

> We have lost the human touch in there. The computer is so cold and mechanical. We have become a reflection of the technology. We now just regurgitate what SDMT says to us. It's like any sense of professional autonomy is out of the question. I would like to spend a lot of time with the client, like if they're crying at the front desk I'll call them in for a couple minutes and talk to them, but all I'll hear in my head is tick, tick, tick I have to get back to the computer, I have to get back to work … a lot less people who are like me are applying for our positions now, they say 'I don't want to be a bank teller, I don't want to just issue people money, that's not why I got into this'. (HCAAT0303, Case Manager)

The experiences related here are intense. Illustrating the point made in many other accounts provided in the interview data, in exploring the preceding perceptions of experience it seems clear that the work activity changes the worker significantly or, at the very least, has enormous potential to do so. As a totalizing, disciplinary pedagogy, Taylorized work must attempt to teach at many different levels of experience. "Words are like bats," said Marx (Ollman 1976, p. 11), and as we heard from Vygotsky earlier: "ideas readily live in harmony with one another, yet they violently collide in space". Indeed, there is a form of violent collision of perceptions being suggested in these excerpts, but it is violence dependent in the first instance on the *material* re-organization of labour process activity. The first casualty appears to be a worker's sense of autonomy and control. Socio-material re-organizations represent, in this sense, an attempt to ratify an otherwise contested meaning but, more fundamentally and more far-reachingly, ratify otherwise contested trajectories of knowledge construction. They do so using very traditional means.

In the excerpts just presented an important hinge in the analysis of this book is presented. It is a hinge that is illustrated, for example, by the first worker, who tells us he can "just *feel*" the changes coming over him. It is becoming "so much *easier* to be cold hearted and say no". Reminiscent of the dynamics of emotional labour highlighted some time ago in the work of Arlie Hochschild (1979, 1983) and many others since, these express definitive perceptions at a point in time that, in the case of this worker run against years of prior work judgment, knowledge, emotional engagement, and expertise. To be crystal clear: though it is hardly definitive in the data at this point in the book obviously, these are *learning accomplishments* that for some, with time, become elaborated through the re-construction of *personal sense* and *organizational meaning* in trajectories of welfare work learning, skill and knowledge formation. Similarly, in the second of the excerpts we just read, a thirteen-year veteran likewise talks about the shift in her personal sense and feeling concerning the nature of her work. Still another worker has learned to invest her work with the "tick, tick, tick" of the clock in her head. Their stated criticisms appear to suggest an oppositional perspective. However, perceptions of experience – when we listen carefully – suggest a more complex and far more contradictory set of lessons being taught and learned regarding the *eroding autonomy, worker control, and/ or resistance*. And it must be added with particular emphasis, such feelings, orientations – and with them specific forms of skill and knowledge – require an enormous material and socio-cognitive infrastructure to support them.[4]

Others spoke in even more dramatic terms. The increasingly familiar themes of highly contracted client contact and notions of de-professionalization are seen by many workers as fundamental expressions of the new levels of managerial control.

> I think [the labour process] makes me feel like a slave to the computer. Like it doesn't matter who that person is in front of you, if they don't fit into this mould here you're kind of really screwed as a client. Like, you start to think that normal human common sense is out the window and technology rules. And it used to be the computer system was a tool to help you do your job and now the technology is the job. (B3PS0303, Case Manager)

I:	So it sounds like the flexibility to use your own judgment and timing is gone?

S:	Totally gone. It's absolutely structured now, between 8:30 am and 4:30 pm.... I don't have a clue who the client is, or even who was in this morning. I know nothing more than they gave me their income, assets, and living arrangements. (B1PS030, CVP Worker)

> [Before the new labour process] it was very, very different because we did home visits so we went out and we saw the clients, where they lived and stuff like that. We were out on the road, we had our own schedule, we could stop in and see them, especially for young mothers. To see people's circumstances made a big difference.... With this new system, it is kind of like it is out of your control. Someone else is doing things. Now everything is more monitored, plus your work is an open book to the whole province. (SC01DB0303, Employment Services Worker)

I:	In terms of the way you are managed or self-manage your work, how much control do you have over your day or your time?

S:	Myself, personally, I just have to do whatever I can to have some control and I try to ensure that I do. But in the end I will never allow any job, I could be a cashier or working in a kitchen or dishwashing or I could be a store manager, I will never ever allow a job to take total control of me.… But again, I can't stress enough how administration is a large portion of our day if a client isn't in front of us.… I really try hard to make sure that my notes are done because it's the only way we have. (SC02DB0303, Case Manager)

Many of these general reflections are starkly phrased. Still, they are far from uncommon in the interview data. The perception of loss of control, loss of occupational autonomy, and notions of de-professionalization if not proletarianization are clear. Supporting this new awareness of production quotas, the labour process ties workers to their computer through its mediation of a greatly expanded array of more structured and highly accountable tasks: it is in these ways that the "technology rules". The accounts of some suggest they are attempting to rescue some basic level of autonomy. As one worker tells us, "I just have to do whatever I can to have *some control*"; tellingly, one of the newly available pathways to establishing *some control* is through a type of intensive orientation to administrative detail. The spatial and temporal autonomy afforded by life "on the road" that senior workers remain keenly aware of in particular – along with the opportunity to apply what they refer to as social work skills – are generally perceived to have been eviscerated. And once again, for many, there is this central matter of the unfolding loss of personal sense of the client, and hence a personal sense of the work. For many, the perception of the occupation itself had been radically shifted.

The computer can make the decisions for you now, so then all that I am is a glorified clerk. (HIMAT0404, CVP Worker)

I feel like I am a blue-collar working a factory stamping boxes. (O3PS0403, former Intake Screening Worker now Case Manager)

I'm not professional any more, but I used to be that. I feel like I'm in a production line here.… I'm pushing paper. (HJIDAT0404, Case Manager)

Very seldom are you actually going in and using what I would consider social work skills with the participants. (HKMAT0404, Employment Services Worker)

Autonomy has been nearly completely usurped.… Your tasks are set for you, you're booked and you don't even do your own schedule for the most part. You're told who you're going to see, when you're going to see them, what happens next, how long you have available for that client. It's like, 'I'm sorry that you're upset, but the next one's here at the door.' (HKMAT0404, Employment Services Worker)

It's like the computer does so much of the thinking for you. It's not always right, but it still does the thinking for you! (HNMAT0603, CVP Worker)

Of course, we need to qualify these concerns. While these types of expressions of loss of autonomy have relevance to the overall argument in the book, they offer not much more than a rehearsal of the generalized de-professionalization, proletarianization, and de-skilling theses I have discussed already. We encounter here, in other words, depictions of workers as victims. Of course, it is true they have been victimized by the premises of a de-skilled labour process. However, the broader point as we shall see is to place such dynamics in the context of a much more agentive framework of knowledge production through which a series of far more complex and variable practices will be seen to emerge.

Experiencing Changes in Workload

Obviously, workload has an objective dimension (e.g., time use, output, efficiency). Just as obviously, workload has a subjective dimension and thus involves meaning and personal sense-making in relation to notions of efficiency, productivity, standards of performance, perceptions of a fair day's work, its value in relation to and beyond a paycheque, and so on. However, simply recognizing a subjective dimension tells us little about how subjective perceptions are learned, unlearned, or taught.

During the seven years of this study, perceptions of work intensification remained a clear and significant concern, but also an informal and largely private one. Despite either coherent or fragmentary awareness as to the origins of this work intensification, and despite continued attempts at intervention by their union, it was dealt with individually. The types of comments I begin with here were pervasive and spread evenly across different job categories of this new form of state welfare work. Interwoven are a number of conceptual distinctions beginning with the contradictory relations of, yet again, social *meaning* as opposed to *personal sense*, which, as we will see later on in the book, is related to what in Chapter 2 was defined as sense-repair-work/skill. As with experiences of the division of labour and to some degree the relations of autonomy and control already discussed, perceptions of work intensification are again closely linked to the constant need to figure out actively "what's going on", "what you're actually working with", and "what you're actually doing". Personal sense of competence likewise links work intensification to the experience of mistakes in need of repair (and along with it perceptions of control). Each of these reflect the degradation of certain forms of client relations as well, but in this section we also see these links influenced by how workers and management frame production problems. Organizational messaging regarding the nature of the computer and work system (in meetings, memos, daily conversation, and so on) mediated this framing. For example, the persistent assertions by local management that the labour process and the SDMT computer system *do work* (if one only learns effectively) are relevant. Of course, any spoken or unspoken assertions provided by co-workers who, apparently, are doing just fine managing their workload play are relevant as well. How these assertions mediate activity explains, however, whether problems and workload issues either become a *grievance* to be transformed or a *responsibility* to which one must adapt. These and other dynamics of activity are a thinly veiled subtext of the account provided by the following worker who has only a modest amount of prior experience in welfare work. In this account however we also see how notions of work intensification are actively constructed in the most basic sense.

> I think managing time has been much more difficult in the new system. It's hard to compartmentalize what you want to do each morning. When you are in SDMT, the moment you click the button and make a mistake, you just created a half hours work that you have to address right there in order to get it fixed. So that pushes your time table back right away. And also when you are in SDMT you can only be in one case at a time, you can't click in a new case. So if the phone's ringing and a client wants to talk to you, you can't help him right away because you are in a case already. So they have to leave a voice mail, they're anxious, so I think it stacks on the work in that I can't click on a button right away and help them. Where in CWT [the prior Case Worker Technology system replaced by SDMT] I could open multiple cases and work on them all at once. Another change has been the paper flow. Although it's less, it's more. I know that's difficult to understand. Although we get less print-outs, we're getting more paper coming at us. It's creating more work. Every time we click a button it generates a print out to go to the client, so the next morning you're so bamboozled that you forget what the letter was about, you have to go back in the system to see what the letter was about, do you have to shred it, send it to the client. Also, it has generated a lot more work for Case Workers because it is very intense. SDMT is the neediest client we have. It demands info. It demands every ounce of your time. If I have a client, I forget that they're there, it so absorbs you. And making a mistake completely puts you behind the eight ball. It is not user friendly. It's constantly suspending cheques, creating over payments, not only from worker error, but just the system snagging things here and there, this needs to be looked at, that needs to be looked at, it sends you things all the time, it makes you look at so many things…. Workload? Most definitely increased. Increased, absolutely. Management does not see it as more, they barely acknowledge that the system makes mistakes, but they do not acknowledge the increased workload. (HCAAT0303, Case Manager)

It is not coincidental that at points in the excerpt we find SDMT perceived as an active, hungry subject, anthropomorphized, in the worker's life. SDMT is extremely "needy" of both attention and information. And this framing of SDMT tells us something important about the structure of activity that affords these perceptions, the worker's mode of participation, and this worker's standpoint within activity. It is in this context that the preceding worker perceives workload as originating in *repair-work* connected to the computer system which requires new skills and new levels of individual coping and responsibility. On a regular basis, the sheer volume of repair-work disorganizes a sense of what is happening (becoming "so bamboozled you forget…"). And it is the loss of a personal sense of the work that likely contributes most to both the objective – but in particular the subjective perception of – workload intensification. Indeed, we can say that the workload increases objectively because it involves an additional form of *sense-repair-work/skill.*

Beyond this more general dynamic of sense-repair-work, there were also wide-spread, more specific technological design issues that shaped the perceptions of spiking workload amongst workers interviewed. One of the key examples in this regard is related to the SDMT system's *Task List* function. In this situation, there is no easy way to separate out the distinctions between work intensification and themes of control. As we will learn more about in the following chapter, the *Task List* is a SDMT software function that, over the course of the years of the study, in fact grew in importance as a means of work performance evaluation and monitoring. The illustration of the effects of the *Task Lists* in the following also highlights some of the principal ways through which, in this case, the division of labour mediated daily practice for individual workers in relation to perceptions of workload.

S:	From the Case Workers' perspective, the fact that it creates huge *Task Lists* for every change you make in the system on a client's case. That is a huge issue because if you don't go into that *Task List* every day and every client where you've made a change, if you leave that *Task List* even for a day or two, you can end up with a *Task List* that's, like, six or seven pages long. Do you get what this means? The problem with that is you can't go in and check them all off as completed even if you know you've already dealt with them and then just click 'Save.' You have to go into every single task individually and then click them off as completed and then save them each individually. So it, as far as that goes, too, that's very time-consuming. It increases your workload big time. And we have to make it a priority to check our *Task Lists* every morning. If you don't then after even a week or so you literally could spend two whole days cleaning up a *Task List*, and then things wouldn't be fresh in your mind, so we're talking about a lot of extra effort.

I:	Because things aren't fresh in your mind, that's a big source of a lot of extra work then?

S:	It is. It's huge. It's a real problem. (HTHAT0503, Case Manager)

Workers now collect and centralize a much, much greater amount of client information than they ever did before. This serves a number of purposes from the perspective of the state, but in terms of operational management it also supports managerial decision-making and production control, and enhances the managerial tools for worker accountability significantly. Each of these depend upon and require a great deal of additional work on the part of state welfare workers themselves, and yet experiences in this regard depend on how the purposes of the job are perceived. The state welfare worker in the preceding excerpt concludes that the work intensification is a "real problem". Still, we can also see she has begun to learn something important: to make certain issues a priority. Her perceptions of workload change are strongly mediated by the *Task List* function itself. For interviewees like her, in other words, work intensification is edging toward a frame of responsibility rather than grievance.

In many of the excerpts thus far there were different ways of approaching, thinking about and operating at work – in fact, different modes of participation in activity – that one can begin to discern. This is certainly the case in the following excerpt. We see that alternative standpoints in activity allow the construction of essentially the same practices and experiences as not simply a "huge issue" which is extremely "time-consuming" as the worker below describes it, but in addition as something of "a joke". In this sense, different modes of participation have afforded the construction of the new labour process as an *un-workable* system. With the legitimacy of the labour process even partially challenged, as in this case, somewhat different perceptions of workload immediately begin to unfold.

> SDMT gives you a *Task List* that tasks you for everything. It's a joke. Everybody just says the task is done just to get rid of them because if you don't keep on top of your tasks, you'll have 200 of them in a couple of weeks. Management will be all over your ass because it's right there in the system for him to see. I don't know who designed this system but it's a nightmare. It's a joke because nobody is really resolving those tasks. They're just getting rid of them because you have to. I feel like it's an overlord situation. If you don't deal with them, you'd have like a thousand tasks in a month and you'd have no way of having the time to go through and get rid of them. It's a pain in the ass and you're really, I mean really, screwed, if some manager decides they don't like you.... I'll give you a standard example of how much a joke *Task lists* would be if it wasn't for the chance that management could screw you on them. If someone hands in receipts for a child for day care, it will task you again with the kid's name. Like it is saying you're suppose to go to

this kid and get something from him, and this is a kid]whose maybe two years old, obviously the two year old doesn't hand in the day care receipts, their parents do, but it's tasking you on that particular two year old person who you're deducting for the day care for. It's a real joke. It's just one of the stupid things it puts on there for you to deal with. They also task you for something like if someone in Ontario is close in name to someone who's in jail. Holy Christ! What do you think will happen? You get tasked and it's a three part deal to get rid of that task because it's now an ERO complaint so you have to go in and say the ERO complaint is invalid and then you have to take it off the *Task List*. Then there's actually another list you have to take it off of just to say that you've done it. What the hell is that, eh? I guess I could see it if it was the same name but if the name is close, it will task you on it…. Workload is growing for sure. It sucks. But I say that really it begins and ends with how ridiculous this system really is. (HDSAT0404[1], Employment Services Worker)

Across the excerpts I just presented we are seeing different modes of participation in activity implied. Work intensification is recognized in each. However, while perceptions of work intensification edges toward a frame of responsibility earlier, it slides in the opposite direction, toward a frame of grievance, in this latest excerpt. The distinction that is only vaguely discernible at this point pivots on the broader form of participation in activity for each worker.

In yet another variation on perceptions, a significant (though minority) cluster of responses cast a more resigned accent on the experience of work intensification, *even while recognizing the same contradictions within activity*. Asked about workload issues, the following worker registers concerns about the division of labour as well as the loss of significant client contact, *but* does not seem to construct anything like a framing of either responsibility or grievance. And it is no coincidence, I argue, that she does not admit work intensification as such; she merely says the work is "different" despite a range of concerns that for others directly implicated perceptions of increased workload.

I: And all these changes, has it affected expectations of workload?
S: I would just say it's just different. Initially you feel like you're overwhelmed because it's a change, but once you get into actually being comfortable in your own routine then it's intense but manageable. It seems like you're doing a lot more, but I like the old idea of when we had the client all to ourselves except for the specialties such as family support or employment. I liked having them come in and we did the initial interview, we did the case managing part of it and the updates. I'm not really happy with the idea that the verifiers and the case managers are split. I think that still needs

> to be one position because it's just too many people for the client to see. You knew your clients better when you did the initial intake and got to know them at that interview and then you'd continue on with them. You knew them by name, by face. Now nobody knows who they have anymore. Bottom line is that before we knew who [clients] were. You knew their face you knew their name the minute they were calling. Now I myself see them maybe once a year. Case Workers maybe see them maybe two or three times a year.
>
> I: And is that kind of a neutral change or positive or negative?
>
> S: I think that's it's just different. (HDKAT0404[1], CVP Worker)

This worker has learned to become "comfortable" in her new routine – notably, this is despite her misgivings about client service. And in the end, it only "seems like you're doing a lot more".

Unlike LPT research, a search across CHAT research for discussions of workload or work intensification is quite disappointing. With very few exceptions, the issue has not been given treatment. How then might we begin to interpret the role of workload more effectively in relation to skill, learning, and control as a matter of thinking, learning and doing *in activity*? Worthen (2008) provides one of the few starting points in this regard. She directly links the employment contract, worker background characteristics (i.e. age), workload, speed-ups, slow-downs, and so on, as a system of mediations within activity. Central to her analysis of garment factory work is an emphasis on two principal, competing objects and divergent object-relatedness in activity. These objects are realized through a range of mediations, meaning, sense-making, and learning governed by either the piece-rate sheet and incentive plan *or* the collective agreement. It provides us with a series of critical insights that, building on many of the basic themes I have just introduced, will be used again and again in the remainder of the book.

> It may be that at a given point in time, the two activity systems coexist and are not in open conflict: A worker can both get his job done and earn a decent living doing it.… Perhaps the employer's need to stay competitive induces him to set new competitive performance incentives. Workers who complete more orders will be rewarded with a bonus; workers who complete fewer risk losing their jobs. Now, what do the 'operations' mean? A young worker speeds up, not just to do the job but to keep her job. The forklifts travel faster. An older worker pulls a muscle, gets angry, and gets disciplined by his boss. Another worker gathers some people together and cautions them that if they accept the performance incentive competition, new baseline standards will be set by the employer and they will all find themselves working harder and faster for the same pay. They listen, learn, and collectively agree not to compete. Now they work differently. The operations still look the same

> to an outsider: take the order, find the route, pick the boxes, and make the pallet. But the actions are different; instead of competing against each other, the workers are coordinating their pace. Their motive is now to regain control of their work. An outside observer cannot understand what is being learned here without knowing what is actually going on: 'The psychological features of individual consciousness can only be understood through their connection with the social relations in which the individual becomes involved' (Leontiev, 1977, p. 12). Furthermore, this cooperative activity system is directly in conflict with the competitive production activity system of the workplace under the incentive plan. (Worthen 2008, p. 325)

As Worthen's research begins to show from a CHAT perspective on the labour process, workload and perceptions of workload are among several key features shaping and shaped by learning. A worker's perceptions of workload – vague, uneven, ambiguous, inconsistent or otherwise – provide important clues as to the type of object/motive she or he is orienting to within an inherently contradictory labour process activity. Even at this preliminary stage in our analysis we might begin to see that distinctive modes of participation indicated by an overall object-relatedness within activity goes a significant distance toward explaining the highly variable, concrete dynamics of skill and knowledge formation in practice.

Experiencing Changes in Client Relations

> Standardized practices that intensify work and make it less rewarding include the following: shortening the number and length of interactions with clients…. Standardization of the kind of interactions workers can have with clients and the types of interventions they can provide adds a further dimension of alienation to the work. (Baines, 2008, p. 124)

In Chapter 4 the importance of client engagement for professionalized knowledge in human services work was highlighted. A long-standing topic in the research field, Baines (2008) summarizes the literature with regard to the importance of client contact in social work practice specifically. As we will see, many of the same issues apply to state welfare workers as well. The theme of worker/client relations in fact runs through every section discussed in this chapter so far, despite the divergent views expressed on it. In this final section I expand and provide some additional detail on these issues in terms of the labour process and knowledge production. As I explained in Chapter 3, in every Taylorist intervention existing capacities of workers to produce key forms of autonomous knowledge – as linked to key tasks sets – must be targeted. Here we see, as the definitive source of knowledge application and production in the labour process, task sets revolving around worker/client relations in state welfare work present just such a target.

Many workers perceived that the degradation of worker/client relationships was among the most definitive effects of the new labour process. In terms of the disturbance, disorganization and displacement of state welfare workers' knowledge of their clients through changes in the division of labour, changes in relations of autonomy and control, and rising workload, we can ask, Is there further detail to complete a portrait of what exactly the former labour process provided, and the new labour process does not?

> It was like a picture is worth a thousand words. You go into somebody's house you could sort of immediately see how they're living, what's going on you know – if they're living in a state of chaos, all that kind of stuff. As far as assessing employability, personal hygiene, and all the little things you can see and do that might really help people, it's is just there when you're doing a home visit. So in that way, doing the home visit was so much more insightful. Now they come in and they're in front of you and yeah you can tell a little bit about them, certainly you get a gut feeling but then instead of focusing on them and what they're needs are you're focusing on this damn thing here – the computer. (B3PS0303, Case Manager)

> Before, you were seeing the clients in home and so you had a better feel of who they were, what they needed, where they were coming from and there was no computer technology. You would be going out and seeing them and they would be in crisis or whatever. Today it seems more data entry, just the facts. We now know less. (HKMAT0404, Employment Services Worker)

> We don't know our clients. They are voices on a phone or they've become a bunch of notes. We have no idea who they are. I think with SDMT what it did was it reduced the client to a number. And therefore you didn't see them, and not seeing them, and they're really distant, they're far. They're disembodied voices. You don't see them, so you're not communicating with them, so you will never get that rapport, find out what is really going on with them, help them…. [Now] you are working for the system, not for the client. It minimises the individual to an abstraction of being an ID number. Like you're no longer 'John' anymore. You are Benefit Number 1097654 or something. You know what I mean? (HJMAT0903, Eligibility Review Officer)

These excerpts indicate a radical shift in forms of autonomous worker knowledge production capacity vis-à-vis worker-client relations specifically. Implicated here is a pronounced contradiction between organizational meaning and personal-sense-making linked directly to worker-client relations. Wildly different patterns of skill and knowledge formation potentially flow from this situation. Even still, none of this should cover up the challenges that the former welfare labour processes produced from the standpoint of clients. The work of a variety of researchers referenced in the previous chapter, for example, underlines questions of this type in the instance of the current system, but also as an issue of the previous work systems as well. Clients could be made vulnerable in earlier welfare labour processes (i.e., through poor welfare worker practice), and thus we must resist romanticizing prior labour processes. Beyond these cautions however, there are important distinctions to be made: the possibilities for improving and humanizing such services under the auspices of the new labour process have been narrowed considerably. The difference pivots on the recognition that the new labour process itself has placed much greater power in the hands of the state directly.

The following material provides a more contextualized perspective on how the daily work has changed and on the types of skill and knowledge formation practices afforded by the previous work system in terms of worker/client relations. It does so despite the fact that the worker in the following excerpt is relatively young and had only limited experiences within the prior welfare work labour process. She nevertheless is keenly aware of the types of openings for positive intervention as well as the limits and vulnerability of clients that the former labour process produced.

> Before, from point A to Z, meaning first point of contact to granting and becoming an ongoing client, I was it. I was the one who saw that client, gathered all the information, fixed any errors, made them an ongoing client, made sure that the cheque was produced and then started seeing them ongoing for employment counselling and case management, visiting them at their home, getting to know them. I was anticipating what's up ahead: 'Oh boy, their kid's gonna get kicked out of school', 'Okay, she's feeling better these days and wants to think more about what kind of job she wants to do or courses she wants to attend', like that. That's how the flow was. And actually, I like that because anybody could come to me at anytime and ask me a question on that client and I knew exactly what was going on with that person. But now, well, I have the CPO [Case Presenting Officer], the person who does the appeals for clients, come to me and ask me detailed questions about this case and I have to sit there and go 'Can we go and get my old paper files? I had no idea. I just don't know.' I have no idea how to help you help this person because I didn't do the application. (SC02DB0303, Case Manager)

Earlier in the chapter we saw how changes to the division of labour, relations of control and autonomy, and workload were understood differently across workers, we see in the following something similar in terms of the worker-client relationship. This next interviewee is ambivalent about the technology and the labour process as a whole, but the comments suggest an important transformation process underway: that is the learning processes within activity through which an actual person, a *fully biographical client-person*, is transformed into a more deeply commodified *case*, and eventually a *caseload*. Along with this transformation we see a palpable change in her occupational identity and sense of purpose in her work. We should not ignore the fact that mediating the perceptions is her relief in simply having a job. Relationships with clients, however, remain the axis around which her explanation revolves even as she describes how these relationships have become increasingly marginalized in the labour process.

> You're constantly sitting around your computer, in a poorly ventilated office chained to your desk slaving away for your 8 hours in a cubicle smaller than a jail cell, not that I'm complaining. I'm very fortunate to have my job, I love it. We're sadly not in the community or visiting client's homes, seeing what the children are like. Stuff like that. You tend to become detached from all that because of your working conditions. I think your judgement becomes skewed because you're constantly sitting and staring at this computer. When you terminate a client you don't really see what you're terminating. You're really stopping somebody from eating or surviving. It's a white collar job, that's good, I mean that means something, but the collar underneath is really blue. You have a water cooler, you work in an office and all that, but it's quite laborious.... But it's like you start to not really care about the product. It could be a metal tube, a car part, a widget, whatever. Just in the past year or so I've felt a real change in myself. (HCAAT0303, Case Manager)

In still another variation in perception of the changing role of worker/client relations we find a lament for the loss of engagement, coupled with an underlying sense that the new labour process has made the job somewhat more comfortable emotionally. Thus, while workers such as the one just quoted feel "a real change" in their person that presents difficulties, others like the following more fully resign themselves to "how it is":

> We're not able to do any of those of things that most of us really want to be able to do. We can't. Very rarely do I help someone. I'm an administrator, that's what I do. People call me and they say, 'You're my social worker' and I very clearly tell them, 'No, I'm not. Not anymore.' Like, I process your cheque every month,

that's what I do. Those are the facts and that's just how it is. (HABAT0503, Case Manager)

Conclusion

Prior to this chapter I set both the conceptual and historical stage for a better understanding of the implications of the types of processes and perceptions we have just seen. Virtually every interviewee spoke to how work and learning relations that were more unified and holistic under the prior state welfare labour processes have been transformed into relations that are far more fragmented. Although the new labour process was formally premised on the goal of "improved customer service", workers in this research consistently explain that this goal was not supported.[5] On the surface at least, claims based on a classical de-skilling thesis seem difficult to deny. Still, interpretations of the situation by workers themselves vary widely, and to avoid the type of impasse I discussed at length in Chapter 2 the notion of de-skilling needs to be qualified considerably. Indeed, some workers are rapidly becoming resigned. Some are critical of the conversion of client/people to Benefit Numbers, Participation Agreement Numbers, as well as more commodified cases and caseloads. Some workers have either be-grudgingly or willingly helped construct their clients as products that they feel themselves beginning to "not really care about". Only a few workers seem to suggest the need for resistance to the new labour process as such. The situation is far more complex than a generic de-skilling claim would suggest.

Underlying this wide variability in worker response are some objective conditions however; and, among the effects of the new division of labour, the new relations of autonomy and control, and changes in workload, these conditions are felt perhaps most acutely by workers in terms of their relations with clients. In describing contemporary social services work, like Baines earlier, Ferguson and Lavelette (2004) identify a pattern of profound alienation; client relationships increasingly appear to workers "as an 'alien object' – functionally produced by them, but beyond their control and now confronting them as a commodity in the market place" (p. 300). I claim that the interpretations, perceptions, and practices of the workers quoted in this chapter, despite their variation, would seem to each represent a response to something quite similar. And, it is this type of deeper claim that I seek to substantiated further over the course of additional analysis by drawing on CHAT to address the many layers of the labour process, skill, and knowledge production. It is also a type of claim figured generally by Leontiev in his comments on the structure of activity, learning and knowledge construction more broadly.

> The activity of man [*sic*] historically does not change its general structure, its 'macrostructure.' At all stages of historical development it is realized by conscious actions in which a transition of goals into objective products is accomplished and which is subordinated to the motives that elicit it. What is radically changed is the character of the relationships that connect goals and [object/] motives of activity. These relationships are also psychologically decisive. The fact is that for the subject himself, perception and achievement by him of concrete goals, mastery of means and operations, of action is a method of confronting his life, satisfying and developing his material and spiritual needs, which are objectivized and transformed in the [object/] motives of his activity. No matter whether these motives are or are not perceived by the subject, they signal themselves in the form of his experiencing an interest, a desire, or a passion; their function, taken from the aspect of consciousness, is that they 'evaluate' the life significance for the subject of objective circumstances and his actions in these circumstances, giving them *personal sense* that does not directly correspond to their understood objective *meaning*. In given circumstances the lack of correspondence of sense and meaning in individual consciousness may take on the character of a real alienation between them, even their opposition. (Leontiev 1978, p. 91; my emphasis)

I argue that drawing on Leontiev's approach allows us to bring into view a host of additional layers of analysis, though in the case of occupational learning, skill and knowledge this analysis necessarily begins from an understanding of a new division of labour, new forms of control and limitations to autonomy, new levels of work intensification, and the reconstitution of clients as well as worker/client relations.

Indeed, we have just seen that workers begin with the premises surrounding a shared object, as given in the newly designed world of welfare work. They share, communicate, and are offered organizational meanings associated with these premises (sometimes through managerial assertions, as we saw). Indeed, earlier in the book it was argued that Taylorism had to be constantly renewed and re-articulated because of the contradictions of the capitalist labour process itself, and likewise here we see that the object/motive must be persistently re-made in order to function as an effective coordinator or sense-maker in work activity. The reproduction process is complex as well as contradictory. As a whole it can only be approximated here. Thus, by way of transitioning to the forthcoming chapters, it is important to emphasize one last time that in this chapter I have dealt primarily with workers' accounts on the basis of their self-conscious perceptions. This is only one aspect of the story at hand. It does not supply all the information necessary for a minimal meaningful unit of analysis of activity. In fact, while necessary, it is in many ways the most conventional and predictable dimension of this story. Understanding how this is so returns us to the relations between consciousness and activity, and the full meaning of *agentive* machineries of occupational knowledge construction.

6   De-Skilling – Learning Welfare Work and the Mediations of Space, Time, and Distance

Introduction

In the conceptual terminology of Cultural Historical Activity Theory (CHAT) analysis people agentively carry out *operations* in response to the symbolic and material *conditions* of work. Left undisturbed in the course of their everyday lives, operations typically pass with little or no self-conscious awareness. According to a CHAT approach, these dynamics speak to important dimensions of human learning, and as I discussed in Chapter 3 it may be that the *material dimensions* of these conditions of work – including forms of "service work" thought to be liberated from such considerations (e.g., Warhurst, Thompson and Nickson 2008) – play a central role in the struggle over control at work. However, even when recognized, understandings of the crucial role of such operations and material conditions remain under-developed in a great deal of occupational learning research as such. Thus, in this chapter I am primarily concerned with the *seen but unnoticed* practices and in particular the material aspects of these operations within labour process activity.[1] In the analysis of state welfare work, I argue that materialist themes (the mediations of space, time, speed and distance) merge with themes of occupational identity, socio-cognition and even affective dimensions of the practices of skill and knowledge production. In particular, I draw our attention to the significance for occupational learning of what appear on the surface to be mundane, micro-interactions with technology.

In order to support this argument I look to the work of Henri Lefebvre on the production of space (1991). I suggest that Lefebvre's attention to the political economic implications of spatiality – inclusive of his attention to issues of work design and Taylorism specifically – offer several especially useful insights into labour process activity. We will see, for example, how labour process activity relates intimately to Lefebvre's concept of *conceived space* – work space *as designed* – despite the fact that workers are *not* typically an active party in the design process (that is, they are the most often the objects rather than the subjects of design). We will build on several of the observations made in the previous chapter and address Lefebvre's concept of *perceived* space. But perhaps most importantly, building directly on Lefebvre's approach, we will look at the agency, thinking, problem-solving, and learning of workers that come into view clearly when we attend to how space is entered into, used, and re-configured in terms of the practices of *lived space*. I argue here that it is this dimension of spatiality that is perhaps most closely linked to the seen but unnoticed material operations within activity, and the tacit features of occupational learning associated with it.

I begin with a brief discussion of several key concepts from Lefebvre's work on space and I argue this sets the stage for exploring how attention to operations in state welfare work activity helps us understand the way Taylorism and de-skilling shape, but do not fully explain, the learning of the limits of control within the labour process. I go on to outline indicative examples of ways that relations spatio-materiality mediate labour process activity generally. Following this I look at a series of specific functions within the Service Delivery Model Technology (SDMT) computer system that was introduced as an essential part of the new labour process. We see how space, time, speed, and distance afford as well as inhibit certain operations to produce and re-produce particular contradictions in the lives of welfare workers (and their clients). Finally, I look at the alternative operational uses of paper-based (hardcopy) information by workers as an important, easily overlooked, material element within agentive responses to the challenges of spatiality presented by the new labour process.

Returning to First Principles of Materiality: Space and CHAT Analysis

Entertaining the idea of space (as either a focus or a tool of analysis) has proven difficult for many social science researchers. We live in space. Space exists. We move through and across space. Space is where things are. For a long time, for many, it has not been all that difficult to presume that space was a non-issue. For the field(s) of human geography (including cultural, post-structuralist, feminist as well as critical, post-colonial, Marxist, and labour geography), this challenge was met head-on – theorized in terms of concepts such as spatial scale, spatial relations, spatiality, and so on. For others, including sociology of work, organizational studies and labour process theory, a concern for the spatial relations has also been recognizable for some time, though in a different way and (with few exceptions) primarily in the context of a particular set of research themes (e.g. work design, surveillance and control, global production networks, the home/work divide). Across each of these different disciplines and sub-disciplines however, it has remained rare to find sustained treatments of space that at the same time have attended to matters of learning and the practices of skill and knowledge formation in robust ways.

In a book concerned with occupational learning, and now the spatio-material dimensions of conditions/operations within labour process activity specifically – the work of Henri Lefebvre (1991) stands out as a potentially valuable support for deeper interpretation of worker knowledge construction. Indeed, the bases for this type of conceptual integration is not all that difficult to locate. In Lefebvre (1991) he spoke at some length about the labour process, and forged an explicit link between spatial analysis of work and Taylorism. He recognized that Taylorism represented a particularly powerful and widely reproduced exemplar of the practices of that he referred to as "conceived space". In this context he distrusted the human capacity to "read" or perceive the full powers of spatialized control:

> activity in space is restricted by that space; space 'decides' what activity may occur, but even this 'decision' has limits placed upon it. Space lays down the law because it implies a certain *order* – and hence also a certain *disorder* (just as what may be seen defines what is obscene).... Space commands bodies, prescribing or proscribing gestures, routes and distances to be covered. It is produced with this purpose in mind; this is its *raison d'etre*. (Lefebvre 1991, p. 143; emphasis added)

In this sense it is clear that Lefebvre's analysis of conceived space addresses the spatio-material practices of the labour process that most directly materialize the premises of power. Lefebvre went on say: abstract/conceived space "is not homogeneous; it simply has homogeneity as it goal, its orientation, its 'lens'.... It is to lived experience what form itself is to a living organism, and just as intimately bound up with function and structure" (1991, p. 287, p. 94). And it is with these types of conceptual observations, I claim, that Taylorism can be more deeply analyzed.

I argue that Lefebvre's notion of conceived/perceived/lived space complements a CHAT approach to learning and development within the labour process because, in the first instance, it admits the contradictory as well as material nature of activity at a fundamental level. CHAT analyses of occupational learning and the labour process can be said to begin from the premises that define conceived space in so far as the labour process affords, inhibits, and prohibits the mediation of operations, goals, and object/motives of activity. The practices of perceived and lived spatiality parallel closely (though not perfectly) goal-directed action and operations respectively. Indeed, some prior CHAT analyses of work have already opened the door to this type of perspective (e.g., Engeström and Middleton 1996; Nardi 1996; Luff, Hindmarsh, and Heath 2000; Engeström, Lompscher, and Rückriem 2005; Sawchuk, Duarte, and Elhammoumi 2006).[2] Moreover, studies of computer mediation and work design in the CHAT tradition have provided several acute insights regarding how the inscriptions of space in the labour process mediate activity in terms of visibility and re-design specifically (e.g., Nardi 1996; Nardi and Engeström 1999). With sensitivity to the CHAT approach, Bowker and Star (1999) likewise address the links among visibility, space, and classification when they comment: "[a] classification is a spatial, temporal, or spatiotemporal segmentation of the world … a set of boxes, metaphorical or not, into which things can be put in order to then do some kind of work – bureaucratic or knowledge production" (p. 149). Going forward in this book, themes of re-visualization, re-classification, and re-spatialization (of both clients and workers) will become increasingly relevant. The many comments from state welfare workers regarding the significance of "life on the road" within the previous labour process (where they were largely invisible to management) provides but a taste of the important spatial dimensions of occupational knowledge production, and struggle, in activity.

Inherent in the streams of CHAT research on space, the labour process, learning, and development, I suggest, is a conclusion reached by way of a different route by Lefebvre (1991). As Lefebvre notes directly, like the commodity form, conceived space requires human life and human use-value production for its animation (e.g., p. 294). Conceived space must be populated by people responding, in both expected and unexpected ways, to the contradictions of capitalist space. As such conceived space is *not* activity, but rather a mediator of practice (lived spatiality) and perception (perceived spatiality). And it expresses precisely the type of perpetually and necessarily incomplete project that is Taylorism as well.

> the bourgeoisie and the capitalist system thus experience great difficulty in mastering what is at once their product and the tool of their mastery, namely [conceived] space. They find themselves unable to reduce practice (the practico-sensory realm, the body, social-spatial practice) to their abstract space, and hence new, spatial, contradictions arise and make themselves felt. (Lefebvre 1991, p. 63)

Building on these types of observations, as we will see in the analysis in this chapter, practice is mediated by a given configuration of artefacts including software functions, rules, sequences of action, and so on. These play a profound role in shaping activity as a whole beginning from the most minute operation and individual task all the way to the attempts to inscribe an entire division of labour. Specific sequences of action, motion, time, and distance constituting the mechanics of spatiality are central whether these sequences are adhered to or serve as the starting point, or premise, for deviation. We will see the role that specific (conceived, perceived, and lived) spatial practices play in access to information and the direction and shaping of welfare workers' attention, which, in turn, accumulates (largely un-self-consciously) and contributes to wider forms of representations in relation to both meaning as well as personal sense. It is in this context of attention and dis-attention that questions of space/time/distance bear a special relationship to what is actually made physically visible as well as to the cognitive notion of visualizing (e.g., how information allows one to "see" and coherently understand something); visual "distance" also having a unique relationship with passivity (e.g. Lefebvre 1991, 286). What we will find is that spatio-material relationships understood in this way are a site of struggle from the standpoint of the construction of the machinery of worker knowledge construction, and mundane features of this struggle are more definitive than they seem. We will find that workers struggle, for example, with *where* to put what are called system information "note", *where* to find these notes, how to *see* the client's situation *in* these notes, how long it takes to *move between* screens and *enter and leave* screens in search of both these notes and a host of other information, how different client files can no longer be *layered upon* one another, and so on. I argue it is no coincidence that all of the preceding italicized words (in phrases taken directly from interviews) are spatial-visual in nature, and also frequently refer to a subtle but nevertheless tangible spatio-materiality as well. They reference the ways and means by which workers must now see across and travel new *distances*: e.g. how they must "go around … 15 corners before you get to the actual place where you want to be," as one worker later puts it. I argue that mediations by SDMT software, rules and expectations of the labour process, and even the use of paper are *not* simply metaphors for spatio-material relationships. The number of physical movements – whether these are the number of mouse-clicks or key punches accounting for the number of screens or menus that must be traversed – that workers describe in the following materials for example are inarguably matters of concrete, material space, time, and distance. Such things shape practice in ways which are often seen but unnoticed, but which nevertheless are fundamental to understanding the complexities of occupational learning from a mind in political economy approach.

Basic Space, Time, and Distance Mediations
in Welfare Work Activity

Truly effective work design involves careful thinking about the materiality of space and time; it always goes beyond matters of rules, norms, and
conventions. Even in the most basic ways, the arrangement of workspace,
material, tools, people, and so on, shape time and speed, and create distance that either subtly or not-so-subtly afford, inhibit, or prohibit some
practices as opposed to others. Such matters mediate the distribution of
information and thus help to realize, in practice, such things as a particular division of labour. Likewise, proximity to co-workers matters. In the
case of state welfare workers, similarly the form, meaning, and sense of
client engagements depend deeply on the relations of space in which these
engagements unfold. In the field of work design, these and other factors
are seen as the foundations of work flow, efficiency, productivity, accountability, responsibility, discipline, and control.

In themselves, these observations are unoriginal. However, an understanding of the way they are connected to notions of mind in political
economy and occupational knowledge construction in activity is far less
so. As I proceed through the chapter as a whole, I offer illustrations that
tend to grow in detail. As they grow in detail, they begin to support a more
robust interpretation of the construction of the minutiae of the relations of
operations within activity which, I have suggested, we ignore at our peril if
our interest is to delve deeply into the topic of occupational learning. For
now, I begin with some brief and general observations from workers on
spatialized dimensions of practice.

The following worker provides a brief account of practice, and through
it we can begin to note how certain changes in the patterns of mediation
at the operational level of activity are likely to impact skill and knowledge and, in particular, the personal sense of clients, colleagues and the
purposes of their occupation. The spatial effects of the new state welfare
labour process, seen but typically unnoticed, are somehow both vague and
pronounced at the same time.

S: Now we're on three floors. It's very divided. I feel very removed from all my
    co-workers. It's so funny because everything just seemed to happen, the way peo-
    ple interact with one another, the minute SDMT came in. We got different places
    to work, different management, different building, and everybody just seemed to
    change. It's tough to put my finger on how exactly but it did.
I: It sounds like it was a very tumultuous time.
S: It was. It still is. (SC02DB0303, Case Manager)

Important conditions at work changed, and so too did a number of other things for state welfare workers like this one. She cannot explain how the new spatial arrangements changed people, and yet it remains apparent nonetheless that a significant change has taken place. An extended excerpt from a former Case Manager, now an Intake Screening Unit Worker, sheds additional light on the role of space. The comments highlight important mediations of new time management procedures. At the end, he offers some comparative observations on how work was organized previously, emphasizing the effects of changing conditions on co-worker interaction in activity.

> We are tied to that umbilical cord of a phone, so that we don't associate with workers in other departments. There are different offices now, different buildings at different addresses, all with separate departments.... My job now is to answer the phone and screen an application, either they are eligible or not for assistance. The system has us basically on strict time management. We have a little timer which times us to the second.... They say applications can take up to 40 minutes on the phone. And depending on the application, people can do them in 15 minutes, and some take over two hours if the financial situation is complex or an interpreter is involved. So you have to probe into all these things. There are more than 20 types of information items to ask about, and the more they have, the more you have to ask questions to get more info. So you fill out the whole document, you save the info, you do what's called an automated completeness check that makes sure that you asked the right questions, and when the completeness check is satisfied then you run the automated program eligibility, because the system determines right then and there whether or not they have eligibility. So I think, quite honestly, there is so much more time taken right now under the new work system, we're interrogating these clients to the point where – it's unbelievable at times! – because [the ISU] is where it all starts, right. [But] when I first started as a Case Worker 11 years ago, the clients did not come to the office to be interviewed. We went out to their home and interviewed them. So when we were at [the office] we were totally separate from them. Our office was set up in such a way, that we were all basically against walls, seated in a big circle, so there was always communication.... And then usually at team meetings we could catch up on other things. Looking back, it was wonderful. The way things were set up just seemed to make things work very differently. We used to have team get-togethers, pot-lucks, we would go out after work and weekends. It was such a cohesive unit. When we went to the new system, and even when met with the client when they came in, all of a sudden everybody is in a cubicle, or in a separate office, or they're swamped, so the group has really been separated in a lot of different ways, you know? (HBBAT0403, former Case Manager now Intake Screening Unit Worker)

Against the tendency to under-recognize the role of space and time in occupational learning, the preceding excerpts provide a solid, if somewhat basic, glimpse at why activity cannot be understood without careful attention to their inter-relation. Clearly, the vast new patterns of state welfare co-worker interaction that have emerged are dependent on the conditions of spatial arrangement of offices and cubicles. In the ISU a strict time management system shapes how workers interact with co-workers, supervisors, and clients. Important to us here, it is in terms of these new arrangements that "everybody just seemed to change." This is a point drawn into sharp relief by the closing comparative insights of the second excerpt we just read in which the former labour process – arranged around home visits, on the one hand, and teamwork, on the other – constituted very different spatial and temporal mediations.

These preliminary observations open up deeper questions concerning how we understand the premises and conditions of de-skilled work vis-à-vis an analysis of activity. Workers find the re-construction of their relationships, their abilities, and their consciousness initiated by the spatial relations of the new labour process. Basic contradictions of practice at the operational level, in other words, come to play a powerful role vis-à-vis the mediations of what Lefebvre termed conceived space. What we should anticipate, however, is that in conjunction with these premises comes the active construction of broader and more self-conscious practices in course of struggles to re-formulate, cope, and transform, either internally or externally, one's participation in activity. The descriptions of the types of changes in workers' views about clients, decisions about what is and is not relevant in workers' lives – all matters introduced previously in the book – are deeply enmeshed in the emergent operations that respond directly to the conceived spaces of Taylorization as well as the dynamics of perceived and lived space.

Having been introduced to some basic illustrations of the interactive relationships across the types of time/output management, we can now turn to the re-organization of virtual/material space and distance in terms of more specific task sets within labour process activity.[3] In these terms, I focus on the way that the SDMT technology, as linked to the re-design of specific task sets, is a central component of shifts in activity continuously challenging the *relations between goal-directed action and operations*. Specifically, in the three brief excerpts that follow we see how features of the technology – as a direct expression of a type of conceived space – disorganize activity materially *but* that the implications are felt socio-cognitively in the course of the concrete practices of perceived and lived space.

> I can't overemphasize it enough. It takes so long to flip between pages. I might have to change pages fifteen times in one case. So the amount of time that I'm not able to do my work is huge. (HABAT0503, Case Manager)

> It seems like sometimes you have to go, you know, around 15 corners before you get to the actual place where you want to be, so that makes it more difficult. (BKRTH0303, Case Manager)
> There are 500 places you've got to go in order to find what you need. (NF17DB0304, Case Manager)

Recalling the discussion in Chapter 3 we might note how these brief accounts are linked to classic examples of the effects of work routing control exercised at the operational level of activity: important items in their work are no longer being routed to these workers. The design principles, understood as the mediations of conceived space, are not inconsequential. However, here we can begin to see that the accumulation of such practices across the scope of the labour process helps initiate a host of responses that are deeply consequential to trajectories of learning, skill, and knowledge development. These mundane examples instruct us on how aspects of conceived space are brought to life and perceived by workers as uniquely spatialized and temporal challenges. We might be tempted (as so many of the workers interviewed were) to write these off as design faults when in fact they are instead reflective of the necessary contradictions of a Taylorist separation of design from execution. To be realized, task re-design must afford some practices and punish others. But for us here, more than this: the re-arrangement of activity affords a re-organization of thought. Thus, rather than an instance of poor design or inefficient design, the actual root of the issue is the question of for whom the design is poor or inefficient which, for workers, entails conflict between meaning and personal sense as mediated by space/time/distance at the operational level of activity. As the first excerpt in the cluster of three we just examined points out, the new work she does impinges on the opportunity to do *her work*; and as the second and third excerpts indicate, necessarily involved in key work tasks are *actual places* where you do and do not *want* and/or *need* to be. We obtain a glimpse, in other words, of the micro inscription of an alternative nexus of need/motive/object vis-à-vis operational responses to material conditions; and we also see the roots of contestation as a worker's personal sense of her job is challenged by a newly conceived space. I argue each speak to dynamics that shape what skills and knowledge, over time, emerge.

Re-organization of the labour process does not just throw forward problems and barriers. It demand new thinking, feeling and doing in the course of the establishment of new goals, objects, and object-relatedness in activity. In the following illustrations these changes can be seen to unfold from, for example, the need to orient to "*how the computer is understanding the case*". Skill and knowledge suitable to prior labour processes may in fact come to have a contradictory relationship to new skills and knowledge. Thus, while the worker in the first excerpt we see has more than thirteen years of experience which earlier would have confirmed for her that she was not in fact "dumb", now she seriously questions her abilities. For the less experienced worker in the second excerpt, however, we find a similar inability to organize her work "in [her] own mind". In both instances, spatialized operations – the conceived, perceived, and lived space – afforded by work design figure prominently in a system of labour process activity that has seriously disorganized prior forms of occupational skill and knowledge.

> When I have to go back and I have to figure out how I created an overpayment for example, it's not easy because you have to keep flicking back to screens, to screens for each particular month to find out okay, this is where I went wrong but the difference in payment is this much, but why? It's very difficult to maintain a sense of what's happening, how the computer is understanding the case versus just what you're trying to do. Do you understand what I mean? I just can't look at one screen and figure it out, I have to keep flicking, flicking, flicking, flicking. Now it takes forever to find out what it is you want to find out. Either I'm dumb or it's dumb, and I tell you sometimes I just don't know anymore. (HIMAT0404, CVP)

> I think managing time has been much more difficult in the new system. It's hard to organize my work in my own mind to do what you want to do each morning. When you are in SDMT, the moment you click the button and make a mistake, you just created a half hours work that you have to address right there in order to get it fixed. So that pushes your time table back right away. And also when you are in SDMT you can only be in one case at a time, you can't click in a new case. So if the phones ringing and a client really needs to talk to you, you just can't help him right away because you are in a case already. So they have to leave a voice mail, their anxious, so I think it stacks on the work in that I can't click on a button right away and help them. You just start to really lose touch with your clients. Whereas in the old CWT system I could open multiple cases and work on them all at once. That was good, because that's what you actually have to do to do this job right. (HCAAT0303, Case Manager)

Building on observations in the previous chapter regarding the maintenance of a particular form of engagement, knowledge, and personal sense of the *fully biographical client-person*, in the second excerpt we just examined we are of course introduced to an explanation for how the design of the SDMT computer system actually inhibits workers' ability to view multiple client records quickly and effectively. This contradicts what she feels is "what you actually have to do" in the context of a complex, interactive environment with multiple client contacts. In fact, these spatial relations of visibility are actively undermining her abilities to construct and maintain a sense of fully biographical client-persons across her caseload. Distance, and with it the encouragement of passivity in relation to some matters and not others, is playing a role in the reconstruction of client-people. Here the matter of being able to "bounce all over the place" – a mundane but powerful spatial-temporal dimension of the previous labour process – has implications for the dynamics of occupational learning. This is the case, not simply in terms of ease of work or some vague notion of flexibility as such, but rather in terms of the artefact-mediated processes of spatialized thinking and doing, at the operational level of activity, affording engagement with work and clients in some ways rather than others.

Affording Activity with Software: Computer Mediated Space, Time, and Distance in Welfare Work

For the most part, specific SDMT software functions have only been referenced to this point. However, details associated with specific functions are important for an analysis of trajectories of skill and knowledge formation stemming from the operational level of activity. Here I argue that the SDMT's *Notes* function may be an important lever in this regard. I emphasise in particular how, in the new dynamics of the labour process, the *Notes* function plays a key role in the degradation of a contextualized awareness, in occupational thinking, of a fully biographical client-person. In comparison to operations associated with earlier state welfare labour processes, this function mediates thought, learning, and knowledge production in a fundamentally different way in relation to a set of newly designed tasks.

In addition to the loss of elements like home visits and life on the road in communities, to make matters worse, the SDMT technology requires a pre-figuration of the categories of information and results in a disruption of the sequential understanding of client life events vis-à-vis its *Note* system. This chronological ordering of life circumstances and events is of course fundamental to constituting the biographical client-person, and here we begin to see how a coherent narrative of a client-person is, if not entirely abolished, made exceedingly difficult to re-construct. In operations mediated by the *Notes* function workers who attempt such re-constructions must regularly double, triple, or quadruple their work. It is in this sense that the notions of both *repair-work* and *sense-repair-work*, defined earlier in the book, begin to become even more relevant in objective terms. Moreover, the structure of information as well as the type of effort required to re-organize it – that is, to repair it and in so doing repair one's sense of the practices at hand – is bound to the broader object-relatedness of activity. The conceived space of initial work design, in this case vis-à-vis the SDMT *Notes* function specifically, serves as the premise for a series of important contradictions. Each of these points of analysis are illustrated in the comments of the following three Case Managers.

S: In terms of the *Notes* function, it's something that we're now really directed to do by management, whereas before in the old computer system, like I was saying, you go in, make the note right at the bottom where the note ended and that was it. The new one, when you're told to do something and write a note in the file, you've got to find the correct note category, find if there's a previous string of notes that relate to that topic, see if it can go in there. So, you spend a lot of time roaming around the note strings searching through those. A client could call and you'd say, 'OK let me look in the file.' You could look back at one big list of notes as opposed to having to go under 15 different note titles, so they would be definite positives of the old system.

I: So, the looking into the different note categories or titles really complicates your job?

S: Yes, and even knowing where to put the notes, you have to go, 'OK, where are we supposed to put that? Where are we supposed to put that?' And there are so many notes it takes you a long time to go through it as opposed to just say one big screen and scrolling down on the other one. (BKRTH0303, Case Manager)

They've divided [all the notes in the *Notes* function] up into sections and they're very cumbersome. The Eligibility Review Officers, they do fraud investigations, they just complain that you can't print a narrative that has everything in chronological order. Everything is separated into sections. And then you find that what they've done is made a note section for each person in the benefit unit and it transfers with the client. Like if a dependent leaves, all of the notes that are attached to that client were carbon copied into the dad's file. Like, dad's in OW and all his notes automatically copied into the other client's file. It's OK to a point but there's just too much information to look through.... If I really want to see a specific person then I can pull that out but all you get is a list of all the notes and then you have to go into each note. (BDBTH0303, Intake Screening Worker, former Case Manager)

For whatever you do in SDMT you have to make a note and there's been a lot of confusion around notes in terms of what category your note stream should be. For instance, if you send a letter, should you be making a note under a Letters and Forms category, or should you be making a note under an Employment Assistance category? Or say there's a workshop that someone didn't attend. Should you be making a note under Letters and Forms saying you sent a letter to them because they were a no-show so we're re-booking them for another? Or should you be making it under the note string for that workshop? So there's a lot of confusion with the new system. I just don't see any way around it [...] And then, try going in and making sense of

> what's going on with a client based on those note strings and categories. You might as
> well forget about it! … With the different pages and strings and everything you'd go
> into one and say to yourself 'Oh that's the wrong one'. So then you have to get back
> out of that one and then go open another one. (BJGTH0303, Case Manager)

I argue that the preceding excerpts, in fact, provide important elements for an analysis of mind in political economy as well as Taylorism in action. The practice these excerpts have indicated may seem anything but dramatic, but they are addressing the wholesale material re-organization of specific tasks which directly challenge previously autonomous knowledge forms. The re-organization is aimed at affording the selection and accumulation of information and experiences supportive of an alternative knowledge form in fact. Clearly, achieving a coherent object of activity that would bring a fully biographical client-person into view requires a series of operations that are very poorly afforded by the new *Notes* function, and in the instances above we see that space/time/distance are central in this achievement. In the first excerpt, this is accomplished by way of the virtual/material distances that are generated and imposed on movement between functions: that is, *distances* traversed only by typing, mouse-clicking, pulling down menus, "flicking, flicking, flicking", "around 15 corners", and across "500 screens". In the second excerpt, mediated by the *Notes* function we can likewise see that the elements of clients' lives are fragmented, spread widely, and difficult to assemble coherently in one place. The spatial arrangement of information may be ready-made for (effective or ineffective) bureaucratic decision-making, but, for the workers hoping for a view of the biographical client-person, recomposition can only take place by travelling in, out of, and across a large range of note strings/categories. We see a severe inhibition of certain forms of personal sense-making, placing sense-making into a contradictory relationship with certain types of prior meanings of the work. As we will see later on, these dynamics are central to the emergence of divergent trajectories of struggle, coping, and occupational learning. The mediated practices of personal sense-making are sustained or, in the cases discussed in a moment, degraded, by the many specific mediations of the de-skilling premises of conceived space. As yet another Case Manager put it:

> In SDMT you're always going from one category to another in your *Notes* system
> to read the notes. It's all disjointed because it's all done on different dates and some-
> times even by different workers or people who are covering for one another. Or, if
> it's a client that's new to you and you're not familiar with them, the fact that all the
> notes are all categorized and separated is really difficult to get a good handle on

that client. You can basically kiss any hope of knowing who that person is goodbye. (HGWAT0404, Case Manager)

To understand clearly the implications highlighted here we can remind ourselves of the basic fact that meaning-making is indexical (i.e., pieces of information are made meaningful only in context by their relation to other information). Thus, access to and the organization of information themselves mediate the meaning that we can make, affording some forms of meaning-making better than others. Importantly, however, we see the mediations that produce the indexicality here are underpinned by the tangible, material time and effort to move across a type of space. The material sequencing of information is also involved (as a crucial feature of context). That is, as the fields of ethnomethodology and conversation analysis have so consistently demonstrated, practical meaning-making depends on adjacent pairing of communicative points of information: sense constructed out of what came first and what comes next in chains of meaning-making. This is another feature of spatially and temporally mediated activity inherent to many of the preceding excerpts as well. We can fully expect in these situations that recovering, for example, a sense of the biographical client-person (i.e., indexicality and sequencing being particularly central to the very notion of biography) will require an enormous amount of what I refer to as sense-repair-work/skill. The SDMT *Notes* function mediates the abstracting of information and, in the terms of Bowker and Star (2000), re-categorizes it and produces a specific "spatial, temporal, or spatiotemporal segmentation of the world" (p. 149). We see, in fact, that this particular set of operations in activity is enormously effective in challenging the relationship between meaning and personal sense of those interviewed. It is in this way that these essentially seen but unnoticed layers of highly spatialized operations in activity shape the functioning of the broader machineries of knowledge construction unique to a Taylorized state welfare work labour process.

The types of spatialized mediations of operations highlighted here can also be found beyond the *Notes* function. The analysis of the next two interview excerpts, for example, reveals that the SDMT *Task List* function also appears as a key challenge in terms of the object-relatedness of operations within activity as well. It too implicates a hidden underbelly of occupational learning, work intensification, and control vis-à-vis key, re-designed task sets. The SDMT system is, as some workers describe it, an automated manager that prescribes tasks in addition to being a type of materials and work route planner. However, what is distinctive for us here is not the automation of management as such, but rather its re-spatialization. As virtually every careful analysis of workplace control confirms, surveillance (as well as resistance to it) involves a deeply spatialized accomplishment of design. In the new state welfare labour process, managerial control no longer primarily unfolds from a monthly or annual review of work, observation of practice, request for meeting with a supervisor, and so on. Rather, managerial control appears repeatedly, often many times in the course of a single hour, in the *physical work spaces* of computer-mediated activity vis-à-vis the *Task List* function. And, we can also note that while, on the whole, for workers the tasks prescribed by the *Task List* function are rarely useful to *their* work (as distinct from their employment or career), it is this notion of usefulness itself that signals something of analytic interest going forward. An expressed lack of *usefulness* in fact speaks to a powerful contradiction and a clash in fundamental social standpoints within labour process activity – at once personal, occupational, organizational, as well as political economic in nature.

S: I think we have more things to do because of the technology in work now. I don't know if you've heard talk of the *Task List* we have. It's awful. Some mornings I can spend forty-five minutes just working on the *Task List* where I am just literally going through and getting rid of every single task on there. One percent of the tasks would actually be useful to me in terms of actually serving a client. So I'm literally spending up to forty-five minutes a day on absolutely nothing.

I: Describe this *Task List* for me a bit more.

S: It actually is something that can be generated by the system or by workers according to certain rules. So I can generate a task to another worker to tell them to do something on the case, or I can even generate a task for myself to remind me to do something on the case, which would be in itself very helpful in a way. But the problem is the system also automatically creates a whole lot of tasks where really there's no need to follow up on them. But the way it is, we have to get rid of them all because these lists can be monitored and if you don't watch, it looks you're not doing your job, and then presto it becomes a big part of your job or else you've lost your job! Mainly though it's just a huge amount of extra work. (HABAT0503, Case Manager)

S: You know when you stop to think about it, the word "task" has kind of become like a dirty word for us. It's a real negative thing. You'd see the work, and you'd just think, 'Oh, I hate my bloody *Task List*', because it's the system generating stuff for you to do basically.

I: So, what about the way you managed or self-managed your work? Is that involved here in some way then?

S: The computer rules all. Really, the computer rules all. And the priorities, like, it's like in it all there's constantly shifting priorities for management that comes down to you directly through the computer. It's just always there in your face and it's just whatever we can do to feed the almighty dollar. It's whatever's going to generate funding, so like everything it's based on the PA, the Participation Agreement. But like, in my fraud work again too, we have to generate all the statistics and recoup as much money as we can. That's what it's all about now. (HMLAT0303, Eligibility Review Officer)

Through the excerpts that follow I recover a theme that I will continue to build throughout the book, though in this instance we see a distinctly spatio-material dimension as it bears on the nature of activity. This theme revolves around the irregularity of client lives as well as the complexity of multi-client servicing. It is in this context that the SDMT labour process can be seen to produce particular operational contradictions for welfare workers. In fact, with few exceptions workers made it clear that they understood that clients live highly contingent lives even if the way in which this realization oriented their participation in work activity varied. Clients often faced the loss of housing or an empty kitchen cupboard, were on the brink of running out of diapers for their child, and so on. In the context of poverty even basic planning could be subject to urgent contingencies, and this necessarily produced an irregularity within welfare service work also. For many interviewees, though far from all, dealing with such needs was a fundamental part of their interest in the job as a type of "social work". And yet, amidst this contingency, urgency and irregularity, there is a powerful invitation offered by the SDMT system to retreat from engagement with client needs. I argue this pivots significantly on the mediations of space/time/distance as well. As mundane as it may seem at first glance, the time to complete the operations of opening and shutting of client files is our starting point in this regard. We begin to see important implications of the virtual/material spaces and distances that must be travelled (one mouse-click at a time), and how this affords some operations while persistently foreclosing upon or inhibit others.

I: What would you say about the positive and negative aspects about the job before SDMT came online?

S: One of the things I miss most because of SDMT is not having the ability to layer files. So when you go into a file on the current system, SDMT, when you are working on someone's file, if the phone rings, and you go to deal with another person's file, you can't layer them on top of one and other. So you have to exit out of the current file that you are in, open up another file. With the previous technology [CWT],[4] you had the ability to layer files. So for example, if I am working on a file

> in CWT, and somebody called in, I could pick up the phone, and if they inquired about their cheque, I can open up their file on top of the one I already had opened, I could look that up, have another person call in about their file, and I could open up their files on top of the others. The benefit was that you didn't forget. It was better client service in my eyes because I could deal with calls as they came in. Now, because you can't layer, you are just naturally more hesitant to pick up your phone, because you have to finish what you are dealing with because if you close out of it, you are going to lose it. So, if you are in the middle of a note with someone, and the phone rings, you find yourself not wanting to pick up and deal with that person because you are going to lose what you are working on. Now, if you do pick up the phone anyways, you have to make a physical note on paper to go back and finish the previous persons file. Before, you could never forget because the files were layered on the screen, so before you close down at the end of the day, those files would actually pop up at you and ask what you wanted to do, and you could deal with them before leaving for home. (BKSAT0303; Employment Services Worker)

As has been mentioned before, it is very tempting to conclude in accounts such as the one here that we are seeing cumbersome technology and bad design. It is worth repeating, however, that the quality of design can only be judged in terms of its relatedness to the purposes or objects of the activity in which it is embedded. If these objects are contradictory, it might not be so unreasonable to expect that difficulties will ensue. We also see something more subtle and likely more dramatic in terms of the establishment of trajectories of meaning, personal sense, identity and learning: "you are just naturally more *hesitant* to pick up your phone … you find yourself not *wanting* to pick up". Where picking up the phone is an impediment to realizing the objects/motives of design – as it likely is in the context of a cost-per-case funding model, for example (Chapter 4) – it suggests clearly that this design might not be flawed at all. This worker and countless others like her are not, in this sense, merely describing their practice as much as they are describing a broader and fundamentally contradictory machinery of knowledge construction complete with the fears and desires endemic to virtually all important processes of learning. We obtain a snap-shot of learning, in other words, that is silently (were it not for the ringing phones) in the process of unfolding as a slowly advancing, tidal force. As a point of emphasis in this chapter specifically, these dynamics are almost fully divested from what we would conventionally think of as self-conscious intention. Key dynamics of occupational learning are being accomplished *at the operational level* of a reformulated series of space/time/ distance relations: the lived practices of space, the vaguely perceived and mis-perceived practices of space, as mediated by the conceived space of contemporary welfare work.

Paper as a Source of Customization of Spatial Relations of Learning and Control

The excerpt at the close of the previous section mentions something that might reasonably slip detection: the potential significance of paper in the spatio-material practices of activity. By way of the need (at this point in time still unavoidable) for hardcopies of things like personal identification cards and paper file folders for example, an interesting door to variations within activity is left ajar.

I: Are you saying that even with the new SDMT system, you still are working with an actual hard copy file?

S: Uh, yeah we actually make up a new hard copy file so we have the original green file which houses all the information, and then the file I get has a review list which is a two sided list which the person who's actually reviewed it has checked through the physical file and saw, is birth certificate there, is health card there, how many bank records are we missing, what do we need, when was the last time a rent receipt was on file? So we add that as far as that goes and then we create a new file. A new physical file and update the old electronic file.

I: So, a dual system?

S: Yeah, and this yellow file when we're finished with it will have Consents to Disclose and Verify, Rights and Responsibilities if needed, Declaration of Support and Maintenance. It will have a new completed application in it and then every other form that the workers complete. There could be a possibility that if we need to we'll have those in our file. Then that yellow file gets put in the green file, the other physical file. (B2PS0303, CVP Worker)

Quite separate from the stream of paper that is automatically mailed out to clients (over which workers have no control), other paper such as hardcopy files, hand-written notes, binders of SDMT workarounds in many instances, each afford a series of alternative, mediated practices. This is a point that Spinuzzi (2009) has recently summarized insightfully, placing it in the general context of sources of counter-control by workers who, through such practices, often regain elements of autonomy. Despite the rhetorical drive to make the workplace paperless, many workers insist on using it. And for good reason.

We find several points of relevance here in terms of patterns of activity, artefact construction, and mediation at the operational level. While

I highlight the material relationship between things (e.g., paper and computers), once again we find the broader relations of space/time/distance, perception, cognition, and so on, as summarized in the term spatiality, implicated. In lieu of the capacity of SDMT to afford workers' construction of viable accounts of their client's lives and with them a personal sense of their own work practice, workers regularly turn to a modifiable technology with spatial properties that are flexible enough to accommodate alternative object-relatedness and knowledge construction within activity. In the context of the current labour process, paper provides the capacity for workers to exert some measures of counter-control over task sequence and routing of their work. What we begin to see here is how exactly this not-so-new technology offers workers the opportunity of engaging in learning associated with both repair-work and sense-repair-work that are each part of a much larger occupational challenge.

Far from unique in the data, we see in the next excerpt some further, hidden implications of paper. Moreover, we also glimpse how local office management – as has regularly been the case in the history of Taylorism and its two-front war as we saw in Chapter 3 – is often implicated in the support of alternative practices. More specifically, we see how the mediation of activity by paper under earlier labour processes was a point of comparison for a cluster of veteran workers. The question of paper versus computerized artefact mediation takes on additional significance in this context. We see, in fact, the distinctive customizability of work practices vis-à-vis paper, customizable enough to support serious attempts at the re-construction of the personal sense of work that has been subjected to such forces of disorganization. On these issues, the opening line of the following excerpt speaks volumes.

> Originally when we did everything on paper forms it was great because they don't take a lot of space up in their actual file, because it's four sided, folded in half, it had a good flow to it that really made sense. There were lots of spaces for extra things so we go through that application and, well, the only problem was when we did home visits, you couldn't photocopy things, but then again at that time there was not a lot of emphasis on verification. You were a professional, and if you said you verified the social insurance and health card, that was all that was required. You would tick off yes and then when you signed the form you're saying I did see the birth certificate but it didn't mean there was a copy on file, unless clients came to the office, but it was done mostly by home visits. (SC11DB0603; Case Manager)

Beyond its re-illustration of many other earlier points, with this account we see further implications of the nature of the artefact and its mediations: its role, as mundane as it may appear, in helping reproduce a type of professional autonomy vis-à-vis operations. There is no mistaking the relationship among paper, autonomy, and the broader space/time/distance relations in the era of home visits. Paper afforded greater discretionary control by mediating client-based occupational knowledge – in situ – in highly flexible ways which could be, in principle, responsive to contingency.

Variations on several of the earlier points of analysis already discussed appear in the next set of comments as well. As before, the practice described is located clearly at the (seen but unnoticed) operational level of activity. The comments are also useful for highlighting an additional role played by the mediations of the new labour process. Of course, "being tied to your desk more" speaks to a spatialized barrier to working in some ways rather than others. Many workers mentioned this. Likewise common in the interview data were illustrations of how the use of paper files was – and often still is – helpful in affording worker interaction. Opportunities to engage in vibrant learning in various zones of proximal development in occupational life flow from such interaction. Here we begin to see how paper files provide the opportunity to engage more closely with co-workers. Paper is a technology, in other words, that can travel and in this case facilitate co-worker interaction.

I: Is it that there's just more work so there's just less time for just talking about issues at work?

S: Well, yeah I would say that it's just harder now than it was. I can't say exactly why we don't have as much time, but we really don't. And I think that's been the hardest thing for me about the new system. Before, we used to have more time to communicate with each other. See we had the paperwork. Before, a lot of the reports that came off were paper, and we worked on our paper quite a bit more. And now I think because we're on computer all day, because you really are tied to your desk more, you just can't do it as easily. There is just no reason to move files around and talk to other people about a client, or anything else for that matter and now that I'm talking about, it's like, boy that was really important. (HABAT0503, Case Manager)

It is, however, one final illustration that perhaps offers a relevant concluding remark in relation to the basic argument I have outlined in this section regarding the role of paper. The comments are not unusual in the data, and they link directly to the contribution of such practices to the alignment of collective meaning and personal sense that indicates so much about the dynamics of learning, skill and knowledge construction in activity. It is a process within which the concept of the broader object-relatedness of operations (i.e., that to understand operations they must be seen in relation to the object/motives of activity as a whole) is particularly central. It juxtaposes a new sense of reality that is pending with a prior reality that is (or at least was) "supposed to be". Once again, paper would seem to figure prominently.

I: Before the changes, give me a bit of the description of the work process, the positive and negative aspects of how it was before. What you liked and didn't like.

S: Okay, let me think. I think the things I really liked about it was that because it had been around and everyone knew how to get things done the way they were supposed to be. There was much more reliance on the physical items, you know like the paper files and things. So even if you weren't able to understand what the computer system had to tell you, there was a physical file close to hand and you were able to go through that file and could get a real sense of reality.

I: And that was good then?

S: I think so because you could sort of distance yourself a bit more from the system when you needed to somehow. (HLPAT0903, Case Manager)

An easily detectable dynamic of both metaphorical and concrete space/time/distance vis-à-vis the arrangement and use of artefacts in fundamentally distinctive forms of activity is implied.

Conclusions

Unlike in the previous chapter where discussion primarily revolved around self-conscious perceptions of workers that were interviewed, in this chapter I began from a focus on the operations of activity. The implications of basic office design and the role of various artefact mediations involving both specific computer functions and paper were explored. In these terms I claimed there is still much to be understood about spatio-material relationships of learning, skill, and knowledge construction under capitalism and state welfare work specifically. The practices seen here dealt with the important, seen but unnoticed, minutiae of operations in activity, and these are practices that shaped thinking, feeling, and doing in otherwise taken-for-granted ways. I will continue to build on these points going forward in the book. In fact, such observations are crucial components of the process that Szymanski and Whalen (2011) refer to as *making work visible*. Quoting the sociologist (and co-founder of the field of Conversation Analysis) Harvey Sacks, they begin their collection by saying: "we need to see that with some such mundane recurrences we are picking up things which are so overwhelmingly true that if we are to understand that sector of the world, they are something we will have to comes to terms with" (2011, p. 1). In a comparable way, making the *learning* of work more visible has been one of the necessary tasks of this chapter as well as others going forward.

Specifically, in the preceding analysis SDMT's *Note* and *Task List* functions were shown to afford some operations and not others. They presented barriers to the layering of files and the sequencing of information; they mediated the re-spatialization of surveillance; and so on. In part they did some of these things by creating virtual/material distance which takes additional time and effort (as well as interest, attention, skill, and knowledge) to navigate. Indeed, many of the elements outlined in Chapter 5 which sought to introduce the argument that de-skilling as a very real if often misinterpreted phenomenon can be linked to the observations offered in this chapter. That is, workers arrived at the conclusions they did in the previous chapter by way of the types of operational dynamics explored in this one. Bearing on this is the notion that for state welfare workers the *conceived/designed* space is entered into, brought to life, accommodated, and re-configured in terms of the iterative practices that Henri Lefebvre linked to *perceived* and *lived* space.

In fact, Lefebvre (1991) offered a compelling formulation which says a great deal about the relationship among Taylorism, de-skilling, and agentive human practice. He was not so much interested in the details of the learning, knowledge, and skill formation practices that I have begun to explore here. But even still, it is doubtful he would not have recognized that skill formation occurs spatially in latent, under-developed, subtle, and occasionally dramatic forms that regularly re-organize (and occasionally undermine) even the best laid plans of conceived space. Indeed, in speaking to the question of how the logic of capitalist production is to be defined, he responded:

> By the fact, first of all, that it organizes a sequence of actions with a certain 'objective' (i.e. the object to be produced) in view. It imposes a temporal and spatial order upon related operations whose results are coextensive. From the start of an activity so oriented towards an objective, spatial elements – the body, limbs, eyes – are mobilized, including both *materials* (stone, wood, bone, leather, etc.) and *matériel* (tools, arms, language, instructions and agendas). Relations based on an order to be followed – that is to say, on simultaneity and synchronicity – are thus set up, by means of intellectual activity, between the component elements of the action undertaken on the physical plane. All productive activity is defined less by invariable or constraint factors than by the incessant to-and-fro between temporality (success, concatenation) and spatiality (simultaneity, synchronicity). This form is inseparable from orientation toward a goal – and thus also from functionality (the end and meaning of the action, the energy utilized for the satisfaction of a 'need') and from the structure set in motion (know-how, skills, gestures and co-operation in work,

etc.). The formal relationships which allow separate actions to form a coherent whole cannot be detached from the material preconditions of individual and collective activity; and this holds true whether the aim is to move a rock, to hunt game, or to make a simple or complex object. The rationality of space … is itself the origin and source – not distantly but immediately, or rather inherently – of the rationality of activity. (Lefebvre 1991, pp. 71–2)

In the context of both the thought and the terminology used by Lefebvre here, it seems at least somewhat remarkable that nowhere in this work is Vygotsky cited, and yet in my view it would be difficult to locate a more relevant means of extending spatial analysis to the frameworks of either CHAT or LPT. In the myriad mediations of practices – by desks and cubicles, by specific computer functions, by paper files and hand-written notes – a clear but necessarily contradictory logic of space is central to understanding the unfolding logics of activity. These are logics of occupational learning and development that, on the one hand, afford and inhibit, and, on the other hand, occasion unexpected interventions reflecting the mutually defining and mutually undermining interests of the capitalist labour process.

7   Re-Skilling, Consenting, and the Engrossments of Administrative Knowledge

Introduction

As researchers have discovered and re-discovered, workers are not simply appendages of technologies; nor are they ciphers of work design. It was useful to first establish how the various *premises of de-skilling* function in activity, however in the course of doing so agentive responses have tended to take a back seat. On the basis of earlier material alone, we might get the impression that workers are more and less conscious of the situation, but, in the end, offer only fragments of criticism in the course of being victimized, for the most part, by the pre-determinations of a dense system of spatial/temporal mediation. However, even accommodation, acceptance, and consent must be learned. These learning processes are far from straight-forward and they always involve human agency. They are a going concern, and within them are found many opportunities for the unexpected to take shape. In this chapter I seek to explore some of these processes of learning and the dynamics of skill and knowledge production; and here workers are shown always, both individually and collectively, to re-skill in one way or another. It is a point that initiates the first direct substantiation of the argument that de-skilling in one way or another, while regularly mis-conceptualized and misinterpreted, is no myth; nor is re-skilling or the potential for something I will distinguish later in the next chapter as up-skilling. The potential for each is always pending, partially realized, or only intermittently stalled within labour process activity.

Taking into account the distinctions related to job category within the new division of labour in state welfare work and paying particular attention to task sets that often run across job categories, the analysis in this chapter shows that workers under very similar objective conditions learn, unlearn, and re-skill in fundamentally different ways. Moreover, whereas historical mediations (Chapters 3 and 4), conscious perceptions (Chapter 5), and technologically mediated spatial operations (Chapter 6) were the point of departure previously, in this and the following chapter I integrate earlier observations with analysis of the broader dynamics of object/motives and object-relatedness of labour process activity. The basic conditions of activity undergo a process of differentiation – often in subtle, un-self-conscious, and hidden ways – which sets in train certain relations to object/motives of the labour process, and with them specific dynamics of contradiction. Taken together, these begin to define distinctive forms of occupational knowledge production. As understood in Cultural Historical Activity Theory (CHAT) analysis generally, these processes are fully situated and agentive accomplishments. As we know already, they involve artefacts, space, time, personal sense and meaning-making, groups, and individuals. Among other things, these processes explain the accomplishment of professional identity. They also explain affective/emotional dimensions of practice, and the processes of attention/dis-attention and engrossment. Each is a feature of the dynamic (re)structuring of the object-relatedness within activity.

I highlight the origins of a specific trajectory of occupational learning, skill, knowledge, and expertise construction that is deeply *administrative* in nature. It contributes to re-solving real problems, coping with contingencies, and, importantly, fixates upon particular dimensions of contradiction. Through it certain forms of service work are accomplished, and within it people are transforming significant aspects of their own personal working lives. However, I argue that this trajectory represents the agentive reproduction – the *managing and marginalization of core dimensions of contradiction* – rather than the transformation of the labour process. In this case we see empirically how the object-relatedness of welfare worker activity revolves around a *specific form of secondary processing* turning the client/persons into more deeply commodified *cases* and *caseload*. These are issues introduced in a preliminary way earlier. Here I describe them in terms of workers' relationships with object/motives, realized and supported by goal-directed actions oriented toward, for example, the production of "accurate client payment" and the morally infused notions of "full disclosure".[1] In each instance, we discover how distinctive learning and human development processes are afforded by the mediations of the various SDMT functions introduced already (*Note, Task List*, etc.). What these workers encounter, however, is challenging. It requires localized development of object-related operational expertise, clearly expressed in the distinctive forms of rule-bending/breaking (see Glisson and Hemmelgarn 1998; Daniels et al. 2007) and the term I also use, *workarounds* (see also Star

1995; Bowker and Star 1999; Hennessy and Sawchuk 2003). Indeed, what emerges in conditions like these is something akin to a *workaround culture*, a term which describes sustained and embedded practices involving personal as well as broader occupational *struggle*. In this chapter, I speak of the personalized struggles associated with accommodation and consent.

As we will see, rule-bending and breaking, these workarounds, and workaround culture are fundamental in this context to the development of a specific set of occupational identities: identities that are both *at hand* and *in question* as a going concern. In the case of administrative expertise specifically, these workarounds and workaround culture produce and depend upon new skill and knowledge which respond to the peripheral dimensions of contradiction (see Chapter 2) oriented to and oriented by *administrative* object-relatedness within activity. I argue that in this case workarounds not only represent the techniques through which a certain type of service work gets done, but workarounds are also artefacts that these workers construct and use to construct distinctive alignments between organizational meaning and personal sense. These workers develop and come to rely on types of repair-work/skill and sense-repair-work/skill which, in turn, help ratify a particular conception of welfare worker practice; a type of practice that is largely conceived by neo-liberalism and capitalism, vis-à-vis the material application of Taylorism. Importantly, I demonstrate not simply *that* these practices occur, but also *how* and *why* workers learn to become *engrossed* by administrative object-relatedness that afford the occurrence of these practices. These trajectories of knowledge construction establish rich, if deeply contradictory, learning lives marked strongly by *relative/repressive satisfactions* as well as specific forms of emotional investment (and emotional relief). I show, however, that what is perhaps most definitive here is that while complex forms of skill, knowledge, and administrative expertise appear, their trajectory of development is disproportionately pre-occupied (and limited) by *contradictions located amongst the relations of operations and goals of activity*. I argue it is in terms of these specific relations of contradiction in activity that engrossment as I define it here becomes a central feature, or fixture, in the construction of the machineries of administrative knowledge construction.

In the following I begin with an explanation of two important sets of additional conceptual resources. I recover a perspective on consent in terms of the labour process, subjectivity, and games found in the work of Michael Burawoy. And I deepen a theory of games through the use of a theory of engrossment in expert work that builds from the work of Karin Knorr Cetina. I next present analysis of the initial processes of the *channelling* of learning capacities: the nascent construction of games and making-out vis-à-vis engrossment within labour process activity. The initial transitional processes, as we see, are partial and as such fragile. This is followed by an analysis of administrative modes of participation, knowledge, and object-relatedness that are more fully realized and far less fragile *both* as a process *and* as an instance of individual/group participation. Here a clear trajectory is established: the ambiguities of occupational practice begin to decrease, skill and knowledge become more advanced, and as such occupational identities are firmed up. Finally, I report on how (contrary to conventional notions of consent, socialization, and adaptation) administrative knowledge construction can and does involve classic forms of expert performance evident in the distinctive types of rule-bending, rule-breaking, and, in general, the agentive construction and use of workarounds. Throughout this and the following chapter it may be helpful to recall (returning to the notes on method and interpretation I provided in Chapter 1 as necessary), that I have argued for a particular relationship between analysis of talk and analysis of work activity.

On Games, Consent, and Engrossment

Michael Burawoy's early critique of Braverman's initial observations concerning de-skilling and the labour process are useful to the claims I make in this chapter:

> In identifying the separation of conception and execution, the expropriation of skill, or the narrowing of the scope of discretion as the broad tendency in the development of the capitalist labor process, Harry Braverman missed the equally important parallel tendency toward the expansion of choices within those ever narrower limits. It is the latter tendency that constitutes a basis of consent and allows the degradation of work to pursue its course without continuing crisis. (Burawoy 1979, p. 94)

Burawoy initiated a type of Marxist, and at the same time strongly humanist, approach to games, worker culture, identity and the labour process.[2] The theory of games speaks to an orientation to work and coping which helps explain how consent is achieved in an otherwise highly contradictory and antagonistic labour process. Looking carefully at Burawoy's definition of games, however, we see that while they may involve the trappings of sporting fun at times, their dynamics and origins are anything but.[3] It is a concept premised on the broad set of agentive, if highly constrained, choices and investments of energy that workers can, and virtually always do, make (in one way or another).[4] Burawoy used it to identify and explain *why and how* "workers autonomously erect their own cultural and production systems … [which] are usually neither independent of nor in opposition to management" (pp. 79, 80). With this in mind he included in his work a synthesizing excerpt from an even earlier classic in the field of industrial sociology. In reviewing the writings of Donald Roy, Burawoy links directly to the traditional concept of "making out" (i.e., coping, getting-by, making the most of the situation, etc.) under conditions of a matured system of workplace control as follows:

> Could 'making out' be considered an 'end in itself'? It might be suggested that the attainment of 'quota' marked the successful completion of an 'act' or 'task' in which the outcome was largely controllable by the operator; although 'chance factors' were also important determinants. 'Making out' called for the exercise of skill and stamina; it offered opportunities for 'self expression.' The element of uncertainty of outcome provided by ever-present possibilities of 'bad breaks' made 'quota' attainment an 'exciting game' played against the clock on the wall, a 'game' in which the elements of control provided by the application of knowledge, skill, ingenuity, speed and stamina heightened interest and lent to the exhilaration of 'winning' feelings of 'accomplishment.' Although operators constantly shared their piecework experience as a chief item of conversation, and always in terms of 'making money,' they were, in reality, communicating 'game scores' or 'race results,' not financial success or disappointments. (Roy 1952 as quoted in Burawoy 1979, p. 84)

Obviously, there is a range of differences between welfare workers in this book and those workers studied by either Burawoy or Roy: the different sectors (human services versus industrial machining) are likely less important than the fact that the system of production examined by Burawoy and Roy was mature. For state welfare workers here, it is a newly implemented system. Nevertheless, the similarities remain striking.[5] Burawoy remarks,

> Operators at Allied continually complained about 'being screwed' by the company, and initially I associated this with some vague notion of exploitation. Soon I discovered that such anguish referred to the company's failure to provide the necessary conditions to play the game. (1979, p. 82)

It is in this same way that many state welfare workers – over time and unevenly across individuals and groups as we will see – were busy generating the types of relative/repressive satisfactions which were central to the findings that Burawoy's work was among the first to conceptualize adequately in terms of Labour Process Theory (LPT). Indeed, we already saw in Chapter 5 of this book that many welfare workers were offering serious complaints, but, as with Burawoy's research, there is a good deal more to the story. Something beyond the complaints, as he noted, may be fundamental to the reproduction of the labour process on an ongoing basis amid the premises of deskilling and the ever present possibility of crisis.

Also in keeping with earlier studies, we will see that in state welfare work such games are often a co-production of workers and local management (and not infrequently clients). By all estimates in the research, local management circulates and frequently supplies a significant proportion of tricks and fixes that allow workers to work around many of the problems (and some of the procedures) in keeping with local needs (themselves complex and highly contradictory). Perhaps above all, these games are structured by relative/repressive satisfactions that, under the CHAT perspective taken in this book, revolve around transformations and alignments vis-à-vis the object-relatedness of activity. What Burawoy registers, however – a point likely still too often ignored in CHAT research – are the political economic implications of these practices. Such games actively generate not simply energetic participation and consent (as well as expertise), but also the learning that obscures, forecloses, or otherwise marginalizes core dimensions of contradiction within activity that define the capitalist labour process.[6] A particular world of making out and games is constructed in this way and with these implications, through a particular trajectory of occupational learning. This is a level of analysis only gestured at with Burawoy. As will be suggested by an exploration of administrative knowledge-making, this learning involves the *consent* to carry out *conflict* organized in one way rather than another. Specifically, it is consent to deal with some dimensions of *contradiction* rather than others that is the key dynamic defining these distinctive trajectories of learning. Obviously, these processes involve the *channelling* of agency in particular ways. Channelling, in the sense I use the term here, is not a structure that determines practice but a configuration of artefacts and agency that affords some trajectories (of learning, skill and knowledge construction) over others. And, to unfold in this way, channels must entice and invite as well as discipline and punish when necessary. As Foucault remarked, power must say both *yes* to some things as well as *no* to others. Both dimensions of power/knowledge culminate in a *pull* on workers' learning capacities. The consent-making is effective in so far as, as we will see later, making out in the games that workers construct can be sustained as an acceptable – that is, an acceptably diminished – horizon of activity; or as Burawoy understood it, as an end it itself.

While important to the analysis, we can still see that Burawoy (1979) hardly offers a clear articulation of how the practices of skill, knowledge, and expertise construction unfold. CHAT is helpful in this regard, though it can benefit from even further conceptual support when it comes to the learning of consent within the labour process. Thus in turning toward a discussion of occupational knowledge, consent and games, I argue that the work of Karin Knorr Cetina is extremely useful as well. Her focus on expertise in professional work offers a rich resource for exploring what I earlier referenced as the construction of the machineries of knowledge construction. The implications of her observations about professional scientific work, for example (Knorr Cetina 1999), and specifically the practices of detaching and miniaturizing phenomena in order that they can be "brought home" (pp. 27–9) for processing (within a labour process) are significant for us here. Indeed, the dynamics of bringing home and processing phenomena into particular types of objects of knowledge production within state welfare work displays parallels with the transformation of the "bedside science" of doctors (in the early nineteenth century) into the epistemic culture of medical clinics (Knorr Cetina 1999 e.g. pp. 29–31). With the introduction of a new labour process, the state welfare workers too were taken off the road and home visits were formally eliminated as a core component of occupational practice. As we saw earlier, the knowledge production in welfare work relies on responses to highly spatialized dynamics, and the abolishment of "life on the road" was one of the most potent expressions of the changes that the new labour process introduced.

What we will also find in the following is that administrative trajectories of occupational learning within labour process activity fixate disproportionately on *computer-mediated* forms of secondary processing of clients. We will see that administrative learning, expertise and judgement entail the production and maintenance of a new mental distance between the worker and the biographical client-person vis-à-vis the transformation of the latter into more deeply commodified cases and caseloads. Brought home, processed, miniaturized, and detached from the contingencies, biographies, and situatedness of real client-people (who in turn become unfamiliar and difficult to serve directly and are thus largely avoided), the contradictory *relations between object/motive and goal* (see Chapter 2) are *marginalized and made unproblematic*. That is, the contradiction between one's dealings with a biographical client-person as opposed to a case or caseload commodity is transformed in administrative modes of participation in work activity in this way.[7] What becomes clear later is that peripheral dimensions of contradiction are increasingly made *fixtures* of ongoing occupational learning. This secondary processing is organized by a host of mediations, many of which were detailed in the previous chapters. Central to this is the accomplishment of a specific structure of attention and dis-attention. Quoting Tolstoy, Leontiev once remarked, "Notice what you remember and what you do not remember; by these signs you will recognize yourself" (Leontiev 1978, p. 132). It is in this sense that a functioning labour process *affords* a particular structure of attention/dis-attention, a particular structure of remembering and not remembering, and hence particular occupational identities.

In terms of understanding these patterns of awareness and interest, also important to the analysis here and elsewhere in the book is Knorr Cetina's discussion of the dynamics of *engrossment*. This is a concept that likely requires some caution and clarity when integrated with CHAT analysis.[8] However, it is also a concept that has been applied to analysis of professional knowledge production by several CHAT researchers before (e.g., Miettinen and Virkkunen 2005; Jensen 2007), in part, likely due to the fact that the concept is linked to several analytic traditions closely allied with CHAT analysis (e.g. the work of George Herbert Mead and those working in the distributed cognition tradition).[9] It is against this backdrop, with some basic qualifications in mind, that in this analysis I demonstrate how engrossment is rooted in the processes through which individuation "intertwines with ... an increasing orientation towards *objects* as sources of the self, of relational intimacy, of shared subjectivity and of social integration" (Knorr Cetina 1997, p. 9; emphasis added). And implicated here are particular types of knowledge objects (and, potentially, a broader object-centred sociality), that Knorr Cetina describes as open, unfolding indefinitely, constantly being re-defined, and around which practice become configured. These are objects of knowledge-making, that under the correct conditions organize activity, and that insistently call out to be solved (and yet are un-solvable). Her claim is that, taken as a whole, this explains why these particular types of objects have a unique power to bind themselves to a worker's identity-making to instantiate a dynamic of engrossment, for example:

> The assumption we make is that the self as a structure of wanting becomes articulated in work contexts when the subject has agency in relation to objects – when object relations are possible – and when objects are of the kind described, that is when they are unfolding structures of absences. These contexts use, or perhaps we should say take advantage of, the lack-wanting dynamic: they provide an organized

context for giving 'lack' a precise institutional and personal meaning that directs unspecific wants towards clear goals. (Knorr Cetina and Bruegger 2002, pp. 173–4)

And we can add that a fully articulated dynamic of engrossment, as Knorr Cetina and Bruegger later say, also includes elements of "reciprocity" (p. 180) between individuals and objects.

In the analysis in this chapter and elsewhere we will see how particular artefact-mediations within particular trajectories of participation in the labour process produce engrossments amongst state welfare workers that matter a great deal. Clearly, for some workers, at some points, and under certain conditions, the SDMT computer system at their workplace is an object of knowledge and engrossment paralleling the financial traders studied in Knorr Cetina and Bruegger (2002). Related to the use of SDMT, also predicted generally by Knorr Cetina and Bruegger, distinctive forms of workarounds, rule-bending, and rule-breaking become endemic to this engrossment. Likewise, we discover that the division of labour and job performance play important roles in engrossment. It is in these terms that it can be said that certain trajectories of learning, skill, knowledge, and expertise emerge through engrossments (expressed through frustrations, indignation, as well as excitement, fascination, periods of mania, sometimes joy, and frequently a sense of relief) in forms of object-relatedness that partially resolve particular dimensions of contradiction.

Deeply involved in the processes of administrative knowledge construction, games and engrossment are particular forms of human agency involving collective dimensions that are nevertheless organized according to a particular means and ends logic within activity. Specifically, the dynamics of engrossment I explore here involve a narrowing of the horizon of action such that workers achieve and exercise *individuated* human agency (rather than human agency in general) within a contracting system of activity.[10] This depends upon the enticements of realizing a *personal sense* of individuated agency within a particular form of activity. As we will see, the dynamics of achieving individuated agency are recognizable *despite* the collective zones of proximal development, participation in activity, and forms of group cooperation that are necessarily involved. And, a defining feature of learning, skill and knowledge construction vis-à-vis the dynamics of engrossment is the matter of a particular means/end logic within activity. That is the distinction between the collective means of achieving individuated agency and self-expression *as opposed to* collective means of achieving a broader, inherently more collective vision and outcome. Thus, we will discover over the course of this chapter and the next that engrossments do not appear in activity simply because technological objects of knowledge appear to call out to, act reciprocally with, and respond to some form of naturally perpetuated dynamic of lack and wanting inherent to human beings. Rather, engrossments involve entire configurations of artefacts and agency – a labour process activity – to produce distinctive forms of object-relatedness. These configurations are powerful, and their implications are broad. As we will see, they are also vulnerable.

Finally, as a more general point, it is important before moving on to take just a moment more to make sure the implications of the language I am using are as clear as possible. I speak to how workers learn to participate in the same activity, but differently. In itself, this is not a novel observation. It suggests the already well-established general notions of standpoint and multi-voicedness in CHAT research (e.g., Engeström 1987; Wertsch 1991; Holland, Lachicotte, Skinner, and Cain 1998), while LPT researchers like Burawoy and many others since have attended to differences in worker knowledge construction (including differences in consciousness and identity) in their own ways. Yet at the same time, my use of language is meant to emphasize aspects of analysis that have, to my mind, not received the attention they deserve. Specifically, going forward in the book I argue that new forms of *object-relatedness* vis-à-vis particular *modes of participation within activity* are emerging. What we see here is how these differences construct trajectories which are agentive and divergent *as well as* occasions for contentious, political economic struggle for the identity of an occupation in times of change. I use the term *trajectory* to speak to a specific organizing feature of occupational learning, skill and knowledge construction within activity (implicating temporal/sequential dimensions, horizons of action and expectations, and different forms of means/end logic embedded in activity) (Chapter 2). *Trajectories* only suggest and afford certain outcomes. They do not constitute endpoints of developmental activity either for individuals, groups, or occupations. Despite the power of the premises of work design, learning in activity in this case remains significantly open-ended. And thus, as we come to recognize multiple trajectories, we come to see the learning dimensions of a broader struggle for the meaning, purposes, cosmology, or, as I say elsewhere in the book, the soul, of an occupation.

Fragile Transitions toward Administrative Knowledge Production in Activity

In the excerpt that follows we obtain a bit more than a snap-shot of skill formation in activity, in process. Moreover, after discussion of this extended excerpt I briefly juxtapose comments from the same worker seen earlier which helps further emphasize the fragility of her learning. For now, we begin with the fact that she is a veteran Case Manager. The focal point of the excerpt is the very common task-based problem of repairing what are known as "client overpayments". This refers to the situation in which the computer system (SDMT) signals an improper payment (it could be too much or too little) has been issued to a client. In the new labour process, when this occurs a case file is automatically flagged for attention by SDMT, client letters are automatically printed and mailed without the aid of the Case Manager, and a sequence of repair-work practices are triggered. Overpayment related tasks are a key instance in workers' coming to establish a distinctive trajectory of learning. In responding to this repair-work, *prior* work experience, values, morals, ethics, and judgements as well as the learning and application/development of *new* operational skills are all set in motion within activity. With this in mind, the following excerpt begins with a premise that is unstated: the worker has established in her own mind that the client *is qualified* to receive a certain welfare payment, and yet the computer system is suggesting something else. This is not insignificant. Things must be *learned* as well as *unlearned*. In this sense, the premises of conceived space of the new labour process come into direct contradiction with the premises of the prior forms of occupational judgment (now lacking material supports) which must be challenged in the course of the initial phases of the establishment of an administrative trajectory of occupational learning. It is a dynamic that we encountered, for example, in the previous chapter when a worker, be-grudging the extra mouse-clicking she now needed to do, told us that *this* work was getting in the way of *her* work.

The tasks of overpayment work practice described in the following excerpt were more or less typical for workers beginning to engage in administrative trajectories of learning. Sometimes the discrepancy leading to overpayment is obvious to a Case Manager. Its origins can be quickly traced, basic repair-work initiated, and repair-work/skill developed. Frequently, however, the origins of overpayments are not obvious, and a range of judgments linked to or leading toward distinctive forms of occupational expertise are involved in carrying out the repair-work. Specifically, we see how the development of specific forms of expert judgement are initiated through subtle and agentively accomplished shifts in the mode of participation in activity. Importantly, we also begin to see how these may contribute to a specific trajectory of learning. In the moment-to-moment dynamics of activity a worker's attention/dis-attention, skill, knowledge, and expertise formation become oriented by particular dimensions of contradiction. In these instances, the mode of participation and the object-relatedness of welfare work reflect the dominance of contradictions *defined by relations between operations and goals* in activity.

The learning the following Case Manager describes is not only social, it is collective, as we will see in a brief but significant set of statements. In fact, what Vygtosky defined as a zone of proximal development is a collective accomplishment clearly suggested by the account (e.g., when the worker explains how she will "yell over to the person next door" to her cubicle or speaks of the importance of the "help you get" from co-workers). It is just as thoroughly rooted in the new division of labour and technology which deeply shape new limits of worker autonomy and control. The work design (we should recall from discussions in chapters 3 and 4) is an expression of, not simply the mediations of a series of deeply historicized artefacts of Taylorism and occupational culture, but also the need for austerity and the broader political economy of the state. Here we see these mediations are activated within a specific working and learning life.[11]

1   I: What would happen with a new worker then who didn't figure out what
2   happened to that file? The Case Worker would do what?
3   S: The client would either be overpaid or underpaid or that worker would be
4   *ripping their hair* out trying to figure it out and have to probably take it to a
5   supervisor or somebody.
6   I: Can you paint me a picture of that?
7   S: I can give you an instance with overpayments because an overpayment will
8   come on the file and you could have done something, and you have no idea
9   what's even created the overpayment, and a letter comes out and the client calls
10   you and says 'I have this overpayment. It says to call you.' And so, you go
11   'Alrighty then'. You go in and you look, 'Yes, that overpayment was created on
12   such and such a day and I can see that the total is two thousand some odd dollars'.
13   And you look and there it is: February, March, April, May; it's calculated at $511
14   each one of those months. And you go, 'Okay $511', and *it doesn't tell you it's*
15   *the shelter component of that cheque. It just shows the amount* and there's
16   nowhere on that system that you can look to figure that out, to figure out how that
17   overpayment was created. You just *come to know that by looking at that figure.*
18   You look at the *type of number it is, is it an uneven or even type of number, and*
19   *you look at the size, and you start to go 'Yeah, it's got something to do with*
20   *accommodation costs'. So you and look, and you think, and you start to know.* It's
21   like this *detective work* at first, and then eventually *it becomes second nature.*
22   I: So then what do you do? Take me step by step. You'd see the $511 and you'd
23   go, 'Okay, that has to have something to do with accommodation.' But, how does
24   that work? What's next?
25   S: Accommodation cost, yeah, so now you're off and running. You'd go into a
26   different screen and look at accommodation and what date that was changed, and
27   you can't even always figure out why the system did it, but at that point you'd

28   *have some clues* but then you'd probably first think to go looking around the
29   office for an LBE [Local Business Expert], but since they disappeared officially,
30   you would *yell over to the person next door, 'How do you fix such-and-such?*
31   *Ever heard of that?'* I don't think there's many of us who could figure that out *on*
32   *our own.* It gets better and you can go in and fix it with workarounds, but often
33   times there's some that you just have no idea.
34   I: So, how many, one out of 5, one out of 10? How many cases do you need help
35   with on a regular basis?
36   S: It's just the difficult ones, *so maybe 20 percent of the cases* I'd say.
37   I: So it's not just like it happens once in a blue moon?
38   S: No.
39   I: And so there's this *ongoing, sort of long learning curve* part of it that's been
40   going on for a while now since SDMT came in?
41   S: Well, part of it's an initial *learning curve,* if say you were new to the work, but
42   *we're way past that so it's more than just that....* The worst part of this system is
43   that the errors are compound errors. In any other computer system I've worked
44   on, when you do something you didn't mean to do you can always back up a step
45   and then with this one *you can't back up* that step. Well, ninety per cent of the
46   time you can't back up, you just can't take it back. Because you go obviously,
47   'Hey, that wasn't the right thing to do, let me think about what might be the right
48   way'. But you can't do that since *you can't re-trace your steps backward.* So
49   you're in this *crazy situation* where the only way I can describe it is that it's like
50   you have to keep *moving forward in the system, first here, and then here and then*
51   *here until you're way out in left field,* and you can't ever come back to that
52   starting point *where you know that you are where you know.*
53   I: That doesn't sound like a very good situation to be in.
54   S: No, that would be a nice way to put it. It really *plays with your mind,* but you
55   keep trying and trying and things get better with the help you get.
      (B3PS0303, Case Manager)

Difficulties in dealing with overpayments are now ubiquitous in workers'
lives (as well as the lives of clients and managers). Moreover, these are
difficulties that regularly reverberate through the rest of a worker's dealings with a specific client going forward. More serious for clients, they are
nevertheless serious in the lives of workers as well. Choice-making, setting self-conscious goals, and taking action in the context of the broader,
evolving conditions of the welfare office are disproportionately premised
on these specific sets of task-related difficulties. Linked to them is a common series of events. For example, the client does not receive an accurate
cheque, and, following instructions provided in an automatically produced
letter that is mailed, the client makes inquiries. Not infrequently according to workers, the client submits a complaint, and/or the occasional yell-
ing match ensues. For many welfare workers, this is often an occasion

for not simply frustration but the feeling of not knowing the job. These occasions weigh many of them down significantly and play a prominent role within their emerging mode of participation in activity. The accumulation of difficulties also bears on one's career, and on one's formal and informal standing in the office adding additional intensities to the mix. In each instance, all this additional weight implicates what Vygotsky (e.g., 1994, 1998) referred to as *perezhivanie* (emotional experience), what Leontiev (e.g., 1978) wrote about in terms of the *emotional colouring* of activity through contradictions between personal sense and meaning, and what Vasilyuk (1991) likewise associated with a type of internal crisis. All this inherently stands behind, or buried within, the daily practice of state welfare work and learning.

The worker quoted in this first excerpt has more than a decade of experience as a Case Manager. By all accounts, she is considered by co-workers to be an expert Case Manager. She and colleagues are beyond the initial "learning curve" (lines 39, 41–2) of their dealings with the new technology and labour process, as she notes herself. And yet the details of her account illustrate how it is that the emergence of expertise can take many forms and how the labour process activity shapes her thinking and feeling. As she puts it, the work "plays with" her mind (line 54). What we can begin to see is that the skill formation process is engaging for her *despite* its frustrations and *because* of its challenges. Moreover, the account provides a near-classic allusion to the basic mechanics of expert problem-solving. This performance initially demands the conscious attention, but has begun to emerge as expert judgment that culminates in (less self- conscious) intuition and the automaticity of repair-work/skill: a process of "just com[ing] to know … by looking at that figure … the type of number it is", the "clues" it can offer (lines 17–21). Her description of practice as "detective work" (line 28) in a "crazy situation" (line 49) that can inspire people to "start ripping their hair out trying to figure it out" (line 4) is not inconsequential either. It points to a process of *engrossment*. There is, of course, the alarming frequency in which such problem-solving is required (line 36), but this also means that her work is engrossing on a regular basis.

In fact, we see the significance of the unidirectional character of the computer software (lines 48–51) designed with the hopes of dictating work routing, process control and information centralization. In this case, a worker with substantial prior professional experience, can find herself travelling down the one-way rabbit-hole only to end up "way out in left field" (line 51). At first glance, these appear to be dynamics associated with classic de-skilling. Indeed, this is precisely how so many of the workers quoted in Chapter 5 described the labour process themselves, and supporting these perceptions are the types of seen but unnoticed operational mediations examined in Chapter 6. And yet, in listening carefully to this worker, we see that notions of de-skilling remain relevant as a *premise rather than a practice* as such. Re-skilling is unavoidable. In fact, the dynamics of labour process design discipline by playing a uniquely persistent pedagogical role; one which persistently requires active learning and creative problem-solving. Literal interpretations of de-skilling, in this way, are not possible.

Of even greater significance for us here are some additional observations however. Still considering this first excerpt, each suggests processes not simply of engrossment but what we might call the *channelling effects* of engrossment. Channelling may suggest a passive role for workers at first blush. And yet, the worker quoted above is not simply adapting passively to the SDMT computer system and labour process. Rather, she is an *active agent in the channelling of her engrossment*. She derives relative/repressive satisfactions from fixing things and working around problems. There are distinctive reflections of Burawoy's game theory, even if workers like this one enjoy few if any of the trappings of sporting fun. Unlike Burawoy, for us a different question arises. What is the structure of activity, the configurations within the machineries of occupational knowledge construction, involved in this agentive process of channelling?

This first excerpt describes a mode of participation in activity, and a newly emergent nexus of needs/objects/motives in the labour process as a Case Manager. In so doing, it indicates an object-relatedness that shapes this worker's practice in activity in a particular way. While the object of state welfare work remains recognizably *shared amongst different workers*, for each worker, like this worker, the specific relations to the object of activity are becoming specified. A powerfully emergent goal-directed action has become *putting a stop to an overpayment*. The difficulties associated with it engross her on an ongoing basis. The result is that the contradictory relations of this goal-directed action and operational practice are becoming embedded as a key, orienting feature of her learning in activity. Her resolution of these specific contradictory relations produces a greater *personal sense of* individual choice as well as the realization of satisfactions and self-expression within an otherwise difficulty job. Operational contradictions are playing a key role, in other words, as an emerging *fixture* defining (making more and more sense, and gaining greater continuity with) a specific trajectory of learning over time.

The type of re-skilling I have begun to describe is expressed as the process of becoming channelled by specific forms of engrossment. While channelling is a process and an effect, the channel itself involves a series of premises shaped in the first (but not the only) instance by intentions of the designers/state employers. It is a persistent symbolic and material expression of the standpoint of the capitalist state within activity. Notwithstanding, workers must still bring a labour process to life. In doing this, we see creativity and expertise are necessary in the development and use of workarounds. In requiring human engagement, we should note that such practices and the outcomes of activity take on value for their own sake; that is, they have the *use-value* of a very limited form of self-expression, pleasure, and relief. Use-value is, and could never be, entirely absent. Rather it is contracted and hence domesticated. In Burawoy's terms the satisfactions these practices and outcomes provide are relative and repressive. And, at the very heart of the matter is the reconfiguration and transformation of the object-relatedness of one's activity in order to relieve the crisis and contradictory emotional colouring, as Leontiev (1978) says, by re-constructing a stable relation between *personal sense* and the pre-conceived organizational *meaning* provided by labour process design. For workers like the one quoted above, repair-work learning merges with a particular type of sense-repair-work learning as shaped by daily engrossments. Without such agentive labouring/learning, the needs of state are under-realized.

At the general level, at this point it might be easy to simply conclude that a somewhat challenging instance of re-skilling is occurring within an occupation undergoing change. This is true. However, looking closer we might also see that there is a form of expertise emerging through which veteran welfare workers like the one above are finding specific new ways to cope with the fact she can neither see, nor understand what exactly is transpiring in her work. Indeed, for the worker we heard from at the outset of this section, "ninety percent of the time" (lines 45–46) she cannot even "re-trace" (line 48) her steps to obtain an overview of what she may be doing. As such, her learning begins from the premise of a work system – like capitalism as a whole – perpetually in need of attention and repair. *But note*: this is a worker who was quoted earlier in the book (Chapter 5), and earlier in the process of implementation of the new labour process, as describing her work as "punching the time-clock" and "meeting the quota." Moreover, she went on in Chapter 5 to directly contrast her current work with the idea that, under the prior labour process, "doing the home visit was so much more insightful". It allowed her, she said, to really help people. This juxtaposition illustrates the complexity of de-skilling and re-skilling arguments, as well as the importance of recognizing the relationship among conscious perception, framings, and activity as a whole over time. Linking the two excerpts in this way, we begin to see that it may matter less that she held general concerns about the new character of her work initially. This is because, in collaboration with a particular set of co-workers, she is beginning to participate in the channeling of her capacities. She describes, in fact, actively producing engrossment in the object/motive of her work activity in a distinctive way that begins to forefront consent and accommodation despite her earlier concerns, and this provides relative (repressive) satisfactions of its own.

I have taken a good deal of time to consider the first excerpt in detail, and there are a series of relevant insights to be found in it. However, the dynamics I have just explored are far from unique in these data. An additional excerpt from a different Case Manager helps to emphasize and extend many of these points. In the following illustration we see other dimensions of this type of reconfiguration and the emergence of specific forms of object-relatedness in activity. In both the prior and now this next excerpt however, we find workers only just transitioning toward more fully realized forms of administrative knowledge production. In both instances their learning is intense, but the trajectory of this learning – its capacity to generate sustained coherence – remains fragile. If in the first excerpt we looked carefully at the socio-cognitive machinery of administrative engrossments, comments from the next worker tell us more about the ambivalence and struggle that the workings of this machinery entail. Central to this is the creation of new concerns, new points of focus for attention, and newly emerging goals. For the following worker, these new concerns are *not* necessarily more highly valued. These new concerns do *not* speak to how she "wants to live", but the alternative to it is, in her words, "brutal".

S: It seems like the *Task List* is really becoming the most important thing for me. It's a pain in the butt but I have to say it's important. I find it helpful just in that *my job now is about the PA's* [Participation Agreements], and I can search out what PA's are going to be coming up due next month so I can search out that time frame. I can say to myself, '*Okay for the month of March, how many PA's do I have to book so that I'm able to fit them all in throughout my month so they all keep running current?*' *Keeping all your files current is that main thing you have to focus on.* Go through the whole application process. Make sure the assets and everything is still the same. But in the new system, *I have no idea* when the last application might be taken. I have to start searching out notes in order to find out when an application was done on the file or looking at a hard paper file to look for when the last paper application was done.

I: You still have paper files?

S: Because we just can't depend on the technology. Look in my cubicle. I have 140 files in my cubicle. I would say that the time I spend on a computer now is far greater than any time I ever spent on a computer prior to this technology […] But when you compare, when the SDMT work system came in I saw this job turn from what I said was what I considered my *people job has now turned into a desk job* where I'm either on the computer, I'm in a hard file because I can't find the information on the computer in order to be able to find out what I need to do. *Task List, Task List, Notes, Notes, Notes. That's what I do.* (NF17DB0304, Case Manager)

And she continues on by saying the following.

> *It's not the way I want to live but* like you know I can requisition a cheque, it will come off tomorrow morning and I can have it pulled and brought to the office so the client can at least pick it up here instead of waiting three days for Canada Post to drop it in his mail box. You can do it yeah, you can still facilitate it, but it's like *brutal.* And SDMT can throw it on hold on you overnight and *the only way I know is if I check that Task List* everyday to see whose gone on hold and if I was expecting a cheque to come off there's nothing that, there's no method to alert me to the fact that the cheque for whatever reason didn't come off today […] So *if you try to go that way, you feel like an ass lots of days.* And on top of it then you're getting blindsided by a client who calls yelling. I am constantly having to say, 'I'm sorry I don't requisition letters to come off the system. Let me go look and see.' I can't tell you how many times I am having to say that in a day. 'Let me see what's going on because I'm really not sure.' It's hard to keep living that way. (NF17DB0304, Case Manager)

Amongst many other things, in the opening set of comments from this worker, we might take notice of the self-talk and the use of (what I will call) *self-talk-mantras*: e.g., "I can say to myself, 'Okay for the month of March, how many PA's do I have to book so that I'm able to fit them all in throughout my month so they all keep running current?'" I will return again and again to these types of self-talk-mantras as we proceed in the book.[12] What is their significance in terms of the process of beginning to transform one's mode of participation in activity? In the first instance, they represent consequential instances in which the fact that there are "more roles than persons" in talk (Goffman 1981, p. 80; see Chapter 1) indicates a struggle with the multiple possibilities of practice. Beyond being simply an artefact of the interview process, they indicate a type of *artefact production* central to the shifts in one's learning within labour process activity. We can also note (in the second of the two excerpts from this worker) the entire labour process, and specifically the SDMT technology, entices the worker into the world of the *Task List* and *Notes* functions despite her serious reservations: she feels "like an ass lots of days" and "it's hard to keep living that way". We obtain a view of the operations (as in Chapter 6) which are central to undermining prior modes of participation in activity, prior occupational commitments, judgments and purposes, while affording the production of new ones. It "seems like the *Task List* is really becoming *the most important thing*"; it is in fact becoming "*helpful*"; indulging her prior commitments to clients is "brutal"; and, she pragmatically has begun to set to work at building new concerns and new ways of problem-solving and performing. As with comments from the other worker discussed first in this section, intensive forms of sense-repair-work/learning are necessary. Here the appearance of self-talk flags just this type of sense-repair-work learning dynamic in action.

More broadly, we can conclude that the way that workers move toward and begin to become engrossed in a challenging form of occupational learning implicates something traditional industrial sociology recognized long-ago as *making out*. Amid the challenges of a new *game* in which workers may invest their time, energies and learning capacities, there are questions of performance, and, as will see in a moment, accountability, accusations and indignation stemming from the division of labour. In these forms of making out, new types of skill and knowledge are beginning to constitute a trajectory of development shaping attention/dis-attention in the course of building expertise step-by-step. Spiralling outward from the minutiae of operations and the contradictions of the labour process to destinations unknown to (and perhaps even unwanted by) the workers involved, the possibility of an entirely new administrative object-relatedness of activity begins to emerge.

Realization of Trajectories of Administrative Production

I have argued that engrossment begins modestly, even confusingly, but that it could grow successively as part of a transition toward a coherent administrative object-relatedness in activity. Later in the book (Chapter 10) we will learn more about the many sets of factors that support the pathways toward and along different trajectories of occupational learning. However, in the following excerpts we see the result of expanding engrossment that has more fully colonized the broader object-relatedness of activity. This constitutes a more complete realization of the learning of consent. It is a type of consent that is agentively constructed over time by the learning of new patterns of attention/dis-attention, and the construction of skills and knowledge that may constitute a trajectory. It provides a further explanation of what exactly is going on when forms of games and making out are set to the music of practice in the labour process. If one is hesitant to use such terms here, it may be because the "games" of state welfare work deal with the morally and ethically charged business of clients' lives (and not, for example, machining quotas), and yet I argue the underlying dynamics are largely the same.

In the terms and context of the analysis in this chapter, I argue it is virtually impossible to adequately understand learning and skill formation in lieu of administrative object-relatedness and the powers of engrossment in activity. I maintain that ignoring this level of analysis turns the dynamics of occupational skill and knowledge, accommodation, consent and resistance into a mystery. To better understand these powers of engrossment we can turn to the next excerpt. This worker has become fixated on thinking the way the computer does. It is likely not coincidental that he is male (though also see the alternative explanation provided in Chapter 10). There is of course a well developed literature on the relations between gender and computer technology in the labour process that was established some time ago (e.g. Cockburn 1985; Cockburn and Ormrod 1993; Hacker 1990), and gender relations may suggest why his engrossment is so intensely focussed in just such a way. As we will also see later, it is also not coincidental that, despite being 40 years old, he is both completely new to welfare work and has no formal educational background in a social work related field. He has however completed portions of a graduate degree in history. For now we can simply say that his practice seems afforded by an identity and skills that support engrossed participation in work as a kind of accomplished or expert learner generically. Whatever the case exactly, he seems very aware of his own learning process. Indeed, unprompted, he provides a type of pedagogical account of his thinking. However, the key question is, in relation to what objects are his powers of awareness realized, how and why?

I: Since things went live what specifically were the things that you spent the most time on?

S: Trying to figure out how to phrase this so it makes sense. I really had to learn how the system itself thought. How the *information strings worked, how not to break an information string.* I said to myself, 'Gee, *if you don't know the system, the work wouldn't make any sense!*' I'm going to use an example of the accommodation page, alright? It refers to where people have lived, alright? The accommodation page has three separate sections. There is the current address, there is how much they paid for rent and who they live with, alright? That appears as one page, but each of those sections you have to go into a subcategory. You have to change each one of those, at any time, any one of the three changes. But if you don't use effective data changes and change it in the right way, *you could break a string* and suddenly the computer doesn't recognize the accommodation as continuous when it is. They might suddenly break it and see it as a different one, which will totally mess up the accommodation history. And it might mess up rent records and, you know, *the computer might decide* we pay too much or too little. It would cause a lot of money payment problems in the system. Now that's just one page. There's about eight pages like that where *you have to understand how those strings work* and all that. *These strings are paramount to the job.* I realized that *they're at the heart of what you are actually trying to do.* [So] I really had to *dedicate myself to thinking how the system thought.* It's not common sense by any stretch of the imagination. I had to think of the computer as, like, a foreign language. And you know, instead of making it meet my expectations, I had to learn how to meet its expectations. How it thinks. Is that making sense to you?

I: Okay. Still thinking how you learned informally, if you can think of any specific critical incidents that happened that helped you learn something. Maybe you made a huge mistake or maybe something else.

S: Always. There's always huge mistakes. It's all mistake learning. I'd go to someone and say, "Help me fix this." I'd watch what they did, okay, that's fine. More often than not, though, as I said, someone was not available to teach me the system. So I'd get in there and I'd start playing in a circle, alright? So that would be one way I'd learn. Then once I understood, that would be, like, the first month, first month and a half – once I understood a bit of how to fix mistakes, I had started going in on my own and purposely changing something to see what happened. Erasing it afterwards, so the person doesn't have a record of a problem in the system. I did a lot of that, removing spouses, adding spouses, changing accommodation, changing payments, issuing different payments. I did a lot of that on my own, erase it afterwards and that's what really taught me how the system worked. That's where *I really learned how the system thinks and I could think like it. That's the secret.* (HLPAT0903, Case Manager)

As extreme as it may seem, the above example does not represent an outlier case in these data in terms of engrossment; at least not when we attend to object-relatedness within activity.[13] Rather than extreme, this excerpt speaks to set of dynamics common in the data, and moreover it is the logical outcome of the exact struggles discussed in the prior section. In Chapter 5 I noted that, following the initial implementation stage of the new labour process, withdrawal of funding for municipalities resulted in the loss of dedicated Local Business Expert (LBE) positions, and far from slowing down the type of learning described in this excerpt it probably fuelled it. That is, the presence of LBEs (not infrequently poster-children of engrossment themselves) may have dissuaded people from having to know more about computer system initially, but their presence likely stood in the way of a more wide-spread incidence of engrossment. What is pronounced in this worker's comments is the agentive processes of alignment: the purposes of the system are made "paramount [...] at the heart of what you are actually trying to do". And, in abandoning alternatives, one must be "learning how to meet its expectations". Beyond any of the specific skills and knowledge types we might care to investigate, here we find the fruits of intensive repair-work/skill, intertwined with sense-repair-work/skill as definitive of a specific trajectory of learning.

The dynamics just analyzed were hardly the only ones at play in realizing this type of administrative object-relatedness in activity. This next illustration comes from an interview with a worker who has a college diploma in social services, and who had recently dropped out of a Bachelors program at her local university. Prior to becoming a Case Manager she worked in mental health rehabilitation for six years, and arrived only a few months prior to the new SDMT labour process being implemented. Whereas so many other workers struggled with repairing a personal sense of their work, this worker's concerns – while in substance otherwise identical to the struggles of others – are almost completely marginal to her account. So too, we find further warrant to conclude that there are likely processes of marginalization of particular dimensions of contradiction vis-à-vis specific modes of participation in activity. The machineries of her own knowledge construction have established a trajectory of occupational learning that, to her, is largely identical to how she functioned in her prior social services work and the way she functioned, more briefly, in welfare work prior to the new labour process. It partially accounts for her framing of the increasingly negative experiences of clients in the new welfare labour process that have been so powerfully documented elsewhere (e.g., Eaton Mosher, Evans, and Little 2004; Lightman et al 2006; Chunn and Gavigan 2004, 2010). Specifically, these types of client experiences, while recognized by this worker, have become irrelevant to her actual mode of participation in activity and hence her occupational learning. Like many others in this section, she experiences a type of *autonomy* supporting and supported by a series of *relative/repressive satisfactions* under the object-relatedness of activity she has constructed. In light of what we already know from the research, the excerpt begins with a remarkable characterization of the work. For her at least, nothing has changed.

I: I'd like to focus on the new way that work is organized in your job. Can you provide some concrete examples of how your work has changed in terms of the following areas: the way you are managed or self-manage your work.

S: *I manage it great.* Like I said, I don't structure my days differently. *I don't do anything differently under the new work system.*

I: Have there been any changes that have affected professional relations in terms of communication with clients?

S: I'd say no.

I: What about in terms of the positives and negatives of SDMT technology?

S: Positives and negatives? SDMT would be a great system if it worked the way it was supposed to work. It's a nightmare to work with sometimes. I would say the things that I work on the most are related to overpayments, definitely overpayments, cancelling cheques and not having them reproduced, *removing cases from one budget and adding them to another budget.* Just *maintaining the caseload files* really. It's very date sensitive so it's not very logical in the real world. It goes by month so mid-month changes really screw it up.

I: Do the clients get a sense of whether it's a good or a bad thing?

S: You know like I said, there was some good and bad things with the old system and there's some good and bad things with the new system. In the end I think it just evens out with regard to the service the clients are receiving. *I think the service is actually a lot better now*, not because of SDMT technology but because of the whole application process, going through ISU. I think it's better. There's a three or four day turnaround, they get seen right away, they know what's going on right away. Case Managers are able to tell them what their cheque is going to be right away with a great deal of accuracy. (SC08DB0303, Case Manager)

The way in which challenges, frustrations and "nightmares" have become positioned within activity speaks to the framing of her work in terms of her goal-directed actions and in terms of the overall administrative object-relatedness she has been able to achieve. Understood in this way, the situation, in some ways, immediately becomes somewhat less extraordinary. The relations of self-consciousness and activity, organized in this way, makes the system subjectively better and lowers the personal sense of difficulty as well as work intensification. Central to this is the type of "secondary processing" that I mentioned at the outset of this chapter. It is pronounced in the case of this worker. Her work has become "removing cases from one budget and adding them to another budget. Just maintaining the caseload files really". Unlike the workers we heard from in the prior section, it speaks to a series of learning and skill accomplishments based on a type of sense-repair-work/skill in which a specifically *administrative* object-relatedness in activity has been coherently realized.

Building further on these initial illustrations, another worker, this time with a significant amount of welfare work experience in addition to an educational background in theology and prior work experience in counselling, sums up the way he participates in the new labour process activity in this way.[14]

> I: Please give me a description of the previous work process. As you do so, can you also provide some indications of the positive and negative aspects of this process from your own perspective, based on your own personal experience.
>
> S: Actually, other than learning the new system in the computer, things have just evolved. When I started with CWT, OW, CIMS, it wasn't a whole lot different than what we're doing now. It's just a new tool.
>
> I: Okay, now can you provide some concrete examples of how your work has changed in terms of, but not exclusive to, the following areas: the way tasks are divided?
>
> S: No.
>
> I: How about the way you are managed or self-manage your work?
>
> S: I'd have to say no again only because *they hired me as a Case Manager and I will manage my case files. In the end that's my job*, and I've always felt that way and I've been given support that way. (SC07DB0303, Case Manager)

This worker's substantial levels of welfare work experience did not deter him in the least from constructing his job as administrative in nature. In fact, the radical restructuring of the labour processes – given this form of object-relatedness – becomes largely invisible. The changes at work are dis-attended as is the plight of clients; client concerns are made marginal to how activity comes to be organized. The clues to how activity is made this way, what skills and knowledge help construct this type of trajectory of learning, are found in his concise responses in his final two sentences which offers a full ratification of *client-people as a caseload* commodity. Agentive learning practices of this type unfold through this defining form of artefact construction in state welfare work. And based on these types of illustrations, we already can begin to see that work experience obviously does not necessarily mediate activity in the same way for every worker. Equally relevant is the fact that we *cannot* conclude that resistance, for example, flows simply from either a generalized rejection of change or some type of naturalized defence of one's prior occupational identity. Indeed, as I did earlier in the chapter, we could easily juxtapose earlier comments from the workers quoted here to show fundamental changes in their orientations have taken place over time.[15]

Taking the point further, in a final illustration for this section I focus on another experienced Case Manager (14 years experience). She holds a Bachelor degree, though it is not in the field of Social Work. Taken together with the types of examples I have just discussed, her comments can be seen as broadly representative of the dynamic achievements of an administrative trajectory of occupational knowledge production. We see woven into the account are virtually all of the problems and the mundane problem-solving practices we have seen before. This time, however, we obtain a clear sense of the relationship of these to a fully realized trajectory of administrative learning inclusive of the mediating role of management surveillance specifically. This of course involves an issue raised in the prior chapter regarding the monitoring of workers vis-à-vis the SDMT *Task List* function. Like others heard from in this section, this worker has largely resolved the struggle to construct sufficient personal sense in order to cope with the dimensions of contradiction in activity that stem from, for example, the new division of labour. The details are challenging to follow in the account (the list of abbreviations provided at the front of the book may be helpful). This in fact underscores the specialized terms, experience and knowledge base of these workers in many ways. However, while the meaning of the task set associated with the *Support Page*, for example, is a stable and shared one in the labour process generally, I argue we see that the personal sense of it can become highly differentiated and explicable only by reference to the specific object-relatedness in activity as a whole. I note that the following excerpt is a continuous conversation. Because it is lengthy, as I do elsewhere, I present it in three parts in order to both illustrate better the different dimensions of activity within the account, and to support a more detailed analysis.

[Part A]
1   I: So tell me what you do.
2   S: *I see my work as being part of a system.* The ISU takes the call from the client.
3   They put it all into the computer, then it is assigned to one of our Verifiers, and
4   then they do the actual intake, making sure all the answers that they gave on the
5   application to the ISU are correct. They verify all the ID and then determine if
6   someone is eligible or not, and then it come to one of us [and then] we *manage*
7   *the file in SDMT.*
8   I: From your perspective, what are the positive and negative aspects of SDMT?
9   S: I've got *three positives.* It's a current time frame and it's linked with the whole
10   Province and I can see all the file notes. I never had access to that before. I can
11   see everything, and that's positive.

[Part B]
1   I: And any negatives?
2   S: Negative is you can't go backward to fix things.
3   I: Do you need to *fudge things* sometimes?
4   S: Yeah, well if there's a problem with the *Support Page*. If they're going to get
5   support starting on the first of June and I want it to come off their June cheque I

6   have to say it started the 15th of May even though it doesn't start until the first of
7   June. *But my problem is now my name is associated with everything.* You know,
8   you put in this information and that's not the information you want to, but you
9   have to find a way to *make it work right according to the legislation.* I mean *the*
10 *legislation, that's my job.*
11 I: Is it also because it's the only way the eligibility engine will start?
12 S: Right, it's by changing that date, support only, like that's a big one for me.
13 That's the only one that's bad in my view. That date has to be linked with the
14 support list, the *Support Page* and the *IRS support* is a *pain in the butt.* With this
15 system we're supposed to be able to track information, but it has to be the first of
16 the month. *That's not reality, but that's not the point.* I can't do a change of
17 address half way through the month either. It has to be the first of the month on
18 this system. So again you're *fudging just to follow the legislation properly.* If
19 there's an incarceration, with SDMT I have to go in there and actually adjust it
20 myself on the program eligibility list to say they were incarcerated six days, so
21 deduct six times how much they get a day and adjust it. I can't go into that thing
22 and say they're incarcerated this date or it just won't work.
23 I: But aren't those dates important, say in a fraud case, or maybe even a criminal
24 court case or something?
25 S: Yeah and that's important. Those dates aren't matching, but your notes should.
26 That's *the thing about notes that's most important.* They're there to *protect you.*
27 *Does everybody do them? No!* You have to append every single *note* that you
28 made plus you have to put it in three different spots. So if I remove a spouse, I
29 have to put that under *Benefit Unit* saying, 'Remove spouse'. If it causes an
30 overpayment, I have to put it under payments/overpayments. You know, like
31 there's so many different sections I have to put the same *note*, and *a lot of people*
32 *don't append notes*, they make a new one every single time. You're going
33 through pages and pages trying to find something just so you can *make sure the*
34 *job is being done correctly, [and] my name is on that!* And even if I make a
35 change somewhere else, suddenly somewhere else where *I didn't make a change*
36 *my name is on the bottom of the page, and I didn't even touch that page!* And
37 *management is saying like, 'No that doesn't happen'.* Trust me it happens.

[Part C]
1   I: And that is significant in terms of your personal accountability?
2   S: That's right. So now it's showing *I made the change on the Income Page when*
3   *I didn't.* Somebody else who may be a Case Worker or may be in Employment or
4   somebody who's a Verifier, whatever, it brings information over. I don't know
5   how because none of us have been able to figure it out and *we swear up and down*
6   *we didn't do it.*
7   I: Well everybody makes mistakes.
8   S: *But I didn't make a mistake! When you know you didn't do it and nobody*
9   *believes you because your name's on it, that's not right. There's this overpayment*
10 *but I'm telling them, 'It wasn't me!'* The system brought that over from someplace
11 else! It's harder *to defend yourself* when your name is on it. But I think you must be
12 *accountable.* I take that very seriously, but getting to the point where people
13 are *accountable* that's the hard thing […] So you're constantly, *you can't accuse*

14   *people but you know it wasn't you.* You try to get *some level of control* of it and
15   like I said, in the beginning, *I don't have any control* in the beginning. I don't
16   make that eligibility decision, like a weird case, and I'm not supposed to go back
17   and ever question anybody else's decision so I'm supposed to just focus on the
18   PA and then it comes up six months later that they never lived at that address.
19   Well I don't know because I've taken somebody else's word. They've taken
20   somebody else's word and that person took the client's word! Where's the
21   *accountability?* (SC11DB0603, Case Manager)

Workers have their capacities captured and channelled, in part, by their own agentive engrossment in particular aspects of an unfolding activity. In it they play a particular role in a particular way. Generalized notions of either de-skilling or re-skilling (or up-skilling for that matter) simply will not suffice in this context. As we see in this excerpt, Part A introduces this worker's overall positive evaluation of the new labour process (lines A2, 9–11). As we move forward, she doggedly re-frames her experience in relation to distinct practices and purposes (lines A6–7; B10). I argue that the administrative object-relatedness of activity can be understood to be organizing a specific mode of participation in activity. In order to function she must "fudge" dates: she must engage in rule-bending, rule-breaking and workarounds (lines B3–7, 8–9, 12, 16–22). In turn, this emerging object-relatedness accounts for her reliance upon (and endorsement of) the SDMT *Notes* function for example (lines A10–11; B25–26). This is a function which many other workers see as ineffectual, counter-intuitive and which very likely degrades their occupational capacities. For her and others like her, it has become a crucial tool that is made to fit with, and afford newly realized goals of service to the welfare legislation and her case-load management/maintenance. Through these practices she has repaired potential contradictions between personal sense and organizational meaning. This has resulted in the experience of individuated control and a satisfying form of self-expression. What stands out, of course, is the fixation on administrative accountability: "My name is on that!"; "I think you should be accountable"; others should take seriously that they too "should be accountable" (e.g., lines B7–8, 33–36; C2–6, 8–10, 12–13, 15–16, 20–21). These are statements that generously pepper the account. Concerns over the lack of control are, in turn, expressed in terms of performance as well as the need to "protect" (line B26) and "defend" (line C11) oneself. Overall, it is made clear in the excerpt that the new object-relatedness of her extensive learning – her re-skilling in the face of the premises of de-skilling – is administrative accountability, a prominent element of administrative knowledge and expertise.

As an example of an advanced administrative learning trajectory, far from criticizing the *Notes* function, by Parts B and C in the excerpt, she is noticeably indignant towards other workers who were not orienting sufficiently to it.[16] The language of accusation suggests something more than simply a generic concern for performance however. Introduced is an interpretation of a particular occupational ethics, and this provides evidence for the successful production of a powerful new mediating artefact (lines B27, 31–32; C3–5, 14, 17–18, 19–20). In this sense, practical ethics obviously cannot be considered the purview of only some trajectories of occupational learning. Practical ethics can be, and perhaps always are, central to many forms of practice, *but* here we see they likely gain additional force *once a particular object has been siezed*. Especially important, in the course of these now established patterns of attention, dis-attention, learning and skill development the division of labour is made *less contradictory* (line A2–7). She remains critical of the fact that management will not admit that they ignore what she feels is a breach of administrative accountability (lines B36–37). She bristles at their lack of admission in fact. And, as we cross from Part B into Part C her point is finalized.

What accounts for the dynamics illustrated in this extended excerpt overall is not some vague notion of occupational personality as such. Rather, we find dynamics, such as those seen in the previous section, becoming finalized in the course of the way the worker has come to learn to work. The structuring of operational practices in activity are vital. I emphasize that it is no coincidence that the SDMT *Notes* function serves as a key thread in the account. Over time, workers like this one have become expert at using this function *because*, *not despite*, its inability to allow the construction of the biographical client-person. She both recognizes and at the same time dismisses the contradiction in no uncertain terms, i.e., what she is doing is "not *reality*, but that's not *the point*" (line B16).

The Curious Case of Workarounds in Administrative Expertise

Today it is still too often thought that administrative knowledge development revolves primarily around bureaucratic rule-following, this despite the many sources of evidence that show rules simply do not work in this way. The fixation by professional regulatory bodies (along with so many practitioners and researchers of professionalized occupations) on formalized standards of practice subtly endorses this mis-conception. Superficially, the notion of accountability that appeared so centrally at the close of the previous section may even suggests this as well. However, in the interview excerpts thus far it likely has become clear that rules are artefacts that mediate, rather than determine, practice. Fudging, rule-bending and breaking are clearly part of administrative object-relatedness in activity. These are processes deeply implicated in the way workers struggle to generate personal sense of the organizational meaning provided by pre-conceived rules of the labour process. However, these processes also help us understand how equally expert performances (as opposed to what I will define as genuinely up-skilled practice in the next chapter) may be equally represented in entirely different trajectories of occupational learning.

Across many of the excerpts in this chapter workers explicitly and pragmatically expressed the ways in which their performance came to be understood in their organizational lives under the new SDMT labour process. They described their performance (good, bad or otherwise) as linked directly to a series of key task-related elements such as the following: the look of coherence in one's caseload; dealing effectively with voice-mail; low rates of client complaint through tightly controlled (and limited) worker/client interaction; keeping the number of active tasks in the *Task List* low; keeping the number of overpayments to a minimum including limiting the amount of managerial or supervisor assistance with overpayments; assuring that system notes were organized so as to respond effectively to co-worker and managerial inquiry; and finally, personal accountability in the case of a potential fraud review process. Again, on the surface, we might be tempted to associate this type of performance with an intense dedication to formal requirements and rules. And, workers themselves frequently perceive and speak of rules in this way. However, in each instance, much if not all of these forms of performance are actually dependent on forms of rule-bending, rule-breaking, and workarounds as opposed to rule-following per se. In the analysis in this chapter, workarounds break and bend some rules in order that others can mediate certain types of practice more effectively. What we are talking about is, primarily, a process of *contention over the ordering, or prioritization, of rule-mediations*. Indeed, this is a contradictory experience for those developing administrative knowledge.

I: So tell me, what don't you like about the work system now?
S: The notes. I don't like the amount of fixes that we have to do. I don't like the work-arounds. You shouldn't have to work around things to do your job.
I: How would you define a workaround?

S: Sometimes, like right now there's an instance where if I have a case with a pregnancy involved, and I want to put a benefit in for six months and what the system should do, is after six months it should close off that benefit. It should stop issuing cheques. What is occurring now however, because logistically with SDMT each page doesn't run the program eligibility in the same way, what is now occurring is that six months after that benefit was supposed to end, a cheque is still going out and then all of a sudden, say I go and I change the address, I hit a screen that impacts on program eligibility and all of a sudden the system goes, 'You were supposed to clear that off', and it creates an overpayment.

I: So this is a situation where a client that has to pay that money back?

S: Exactly. And I don't think that that's unfair. *That's the rule.* They weren't entitled to the money. The legislation is very clear. They don't deserve that money obviously. But now you've got this person in front of you, and you have to tell them that they've done nothing wrong, it's just the system. So there's a *workaround I developed where I have to task myself.* So those kinds of things are very tiresome, but my beef is that you take it for granted that [the government] invested in this system. It's a fairly simple concept that it should be grabbing these things and yet it's not.

I: And it creates stress on the client I take it, but does it also create stress on you?

S: Well I have to spend this time to explain to all of them. Those are some of the negatives of SDMT. And the fact that they haven't effectively trained us, I think it kind of sucks. In understanding CIMS, you understood the logic of how the system was going to read the action that we were trying to do to create a benefit. Each page on SDMT, for years now, we're still learning the logic of how it impacts on program eligibility and how often the engine is running. *My job is to process cases.* SDMT is stopping me from doing this effectively. It looks bad on me. I have to watch my *Task List* really carefully so I don't look like I don't know what I'm doing. That's something that's really frustrating. (SC03DB0303, Case Manager)

In thinking through this and other excerpts in this setion it is worthwhile recalling that a trajectory of learning is partially defined by the specific forms of skill and knowledge that can help turn what is contradictory and beyond control into something over which one can (more or less; in reality or imagination) exercise some level of autonomy and control. In this context, these forms of skill and knowledge include workarounds. For the preceding worker, workarounds, and using otherwise additional steps (e.g. using the *Task List* function to "task" oneself) to carry them out, are a means to "process cases" effectively. She is concerned that one "shouldn't have to work around things to do your job", *but* in concrete practice to observe some rules she must prioritize and work around others creatively. For those engaged in administrative knowledge production, rules embedded in legislation and job performance review policy appear to consistently *over-rule*, as it were, and mediate the use of many other procedural rules. Such practices are functionally necessary within a highly contradictory labour process activity, and they provide further evidence for our understanding of the nature of administrative object-relatedness. Workers must make extensive use of the *Task List*, but keep it cleared out so you don't *look* – and here we might add *feel* – "like you don't know". Like other workers we have heard from in this research, we see her capacities have largely been captured by the relations between operational practices and goal-directed action in SDMT labour process activity. What is also clear is that she has secured a personal sense of her work ("my job is to process cases"), her *repair-work* can be focused, as it is, on achieving the broader object/motives provided by the work design.

The first excerpt in this section recalls many of the issues surrounding the general relationship between engrossment and administrative object-relatedness in activity that I discussed earlier in the chapter. However, workarounds play an important role in sustaining and perpetuating this relationship between engrossment and object-relatedness. To understand this, it is important to make a preliminary observation regarding why (given that this research took place over seven years) workarounds have remained so prevalent thus allowing them to become so central, albeit in distinctive ways, to the daily learning lives of state welfare workers. It is not all that difficult to understand: over the course of this study the system was constantly being upgraded. Virtually all workers spoke of a seemingly endless series of new versions of the software and the seemingly unlimited number of system patches. Of course, the result was an ongoing need for established workarounds, the need for many new workarounds in response to software changes, and hence a perpetually renewed channelling of skill, knowledge and expertise vis-à-vis the dynamics of engrossment. In other words, we see in this instance how conceived space (Chapter 6) is effective in supporting the building of specific trajectories of learning in part because it establishes a workaround culture that engrosses permanently.

The following excerpt bears on these issues, and whereas earlier in the chapter workers most often spoke about task-related learning, here we see more specifically that learning workarounds is particularly important. We are also introduced to a range of additional mediating artefacts. These include not simply additional paper file artefacts constructed to help resolve the type of operational/goal-action contradiction, but also a separate municipal computerized finance system (an expression of the inter-governmental relations we took the time to review in Chapter 4). In the course of these mediations we see the familiar role of everyday cooperation of workers. We also begin to see more clearly the cooperative role of local management in these workarounds.

1   I: But what is the process of problem-solving when these new problems come up?
2   What do you do then?
3   S: What happens then is we try to take a look at it and see if we can figure it out
4   on our own. That's important because it really *doesn't look good if you're running*
5   *to management all the time.* But in our case, if we can't, we can send it to a
6   trouble-shooter and she can review it. She *doesn't get paid to do it anymore*, but
7   she still does it god love her! Then she might do a note and e-mail the Case
8   Manager back. We have a lot of workarounds. Like I said, I'm dealing mostly
9   with the overpayments in my work. That's probably the biggest one that I deal
10 with on a day-to-day basis, is that kind of scenario.
11 I: Okay, can you tell me more about a specific problem that's come up recently
12 during your work and how you went about solving it?
13 S: Well, I guess it is the reimbursement. Again, this is more specific to
14 overpayment. But under the reimbursement page, again, we can't always post
15 everything that we get back. Because for whatever reason, say the client is a
16 single person, it will let us postdate the money he got for August but it won't let
17 us post against the *community start-up* of three hundred dollars that he also got at
18 that time. So like me, the main thing is just trying to get the job done and *not*
19 *cause a whole hullabaloo.* So our workaround, what our solution has been is to
20 basically put in a *very comprehensive note* so that hopefully when the *client calls*
21 *in screaming* at you that you can scream at them right back and say, 'Hey, I
22 actually paid you back X number of dollars!' You know in our municipality we
23 also have a *back-up system* where we, like, we post it, we report the income to
24 Finance [in the municipality]. So we also have a *back-up way of showing*, of
25 giving to the client to show the government to prove, 'Yeah, they did pay back.
26 We did get back the eight hundred and twenty and not the five twenty.' Like that.
27 Another major workaround is CPP [Canadian Pension Plan payment]. We make
28 our claims on our CPP assignment. Someone is pending CPP. We have to do the
29 assignment. We get notified that we're going to get paid back our money. And
30 then again, as soon as somebody is eligible for Canada Pension Disability say,
31 they're automatically eligible for Ontario Disability. So the way Ontario
32 Disability works is they find out the CPP is giving seven hundred dollars a month
33 starting April 2005. We've already claimed it. So what they do is they have to, in
34 order for them to do their *retro calculations, they have to put the start date of*
35 *2005*, which *creates an overpayment* on money that we've already claimed and
36 are getting reimbursed for. So we had to work it out. It's been a struggle but
37 we've finally got our *supervisors working with us* where they will create the
38 overpayment for us but they make it *temporary uncollectable* to keep it off the
39 system. And then when we get the money back, instead of *bumping up against the*
40 *reimbursement [function], it bumps up against the overpayment [function]* and we

41   can handle it that way. Every day we solve problems by creating a new problem
42   that we can actually solve. (HMLAT0303, Eligibility Review Officer)

This worker outlines the complexities of a particular example of advanced administrative performance implicating many of the elements of performance listed at the start of this section. The stresses of worker/client conflict, likewise, mediate this performance, its skill and knowledge development processes as well as outcomes (lines 20–21). However, much more central to the structure of the account and providing important clues as to the structure of the activity itself, is how the worker must cope with other forms of accountability whether they involve an individual worker's performance (i.e. looking good by not making a "hullabaloo": line 19), or the reporting of municipalities to higher levels of government (lines 24–25). What are the key resources affording and advancing the trajectory of learning and expertise in this mode of participation? Unpaid labour of local experts (lines 6–8) and a cooperative work group (lines 3–4, 36–39) are two important ones. Local (municipal office) managerial cooperation (lines 23–24, 36–39) is another. Notably, the means of dealing with an operational contradiction has produced new applications for "temporary uncollectable" overpayments along with the use of a local back-up system are likewise crucial.[17]

Amidst the account we also find an example of the type of channelling of skill development that poses distinctive questions regarding the relationship between de-skilling and conventional notions of consent. We encounter activity that produces, what in the literature on expertise appears as a standard example: solving an unsolvable problem by creating a problem that is solvable (lines 37–42). In these ways, we can see how it would be mis-leading to say that administrative knowledge and skill is rooted simply in servile and uninspired bureaucratic rule-following. Administrative knowledge relies on ongoing, collective communication, intuition, creativity and *a feel* for the fundamental identity of a problem at hand. Importantly in the case of the practices of administrative knowledge construction, an unhappy client does not motivate this expertise [indeed, the worker talks about the tools that allow her to yell right back at the client (lines 21–22)]. Rather, this is a form of expertise in activity that is motivated by, and that intimately understands, that avoiding any "bump up against the reimbursement [function]" (lines 39–41) in the system is the way you avoid being seen as "running to management all the time" (line 4) and making "a whole hullabaloo" (line 19). As CHAT suggests, all of these accomplishments rely on the alignments between personal sense and organizational meaning in relation to labour process activity as a whole. Making out, games and engrossment are key elements helping to explain why and how, in the course of distinctive modes of participation in activity, new skills, knowledge and expertise develop, and, in turn, facilitate advancement along an administrative trajectory of learning. Much if not all of these forms of performance are deeply dependent on creative forms of rule-bending, rule-breaking and workarounds.

Turned into to objects of dis-attention, in this trajectory of administrative knowledge production, it remains important to again raise the matter of how the contingencies of client's lives come to figure in activity. There are clients who are pregnant. There are others who require community start-up funds to get their lives going again. There are those who find themselves in screaming matches with their welfare workers. Others have or develop disabilities, and state retirement income becomes a complex matter intertwined with other benefits. And finally, there are an inordinate number of clients who are forced to quickly reorganize their tenuous household finances because an overpayment they had received must be suddenly paid back. I take all of these examples of contingency simply from the one account we have just discussed to make a point. The complex contingencies of a real client-person's life, and the contradictions it implies in relation to economic life under capitalism, all must be brought home, in Knorr Cetina's words, for substantial secondary processing for this trajectory of knowledge development to exist. The agentive mind in political economy – shaped by highly differentiated engagements in the relations of contradiction in activity – remains central to this achievement.

Conclusions

This chapter has focused on the learning of consent. I address it in terms of an administrative trajectory of occupational learning within labour process activity. In the first analytic section I explored transitions toward this type of learning and we discovered the agentive processes involved in engrossment that, as I put it, begins to capture and channel human energies and the potential for certain types of expertise. The participation in an administrative trajectory of learning in activity could be fragile. In fact, we can sense clearly that, for some, it was capable of collapsing with little notice leaving a worker to flounder significantly. I next provided analysis of administrative object-relatedness in more fully realized and coherent forms. Finally, against the still too frequent presumption that these types of administrative learning could be understood as instances of conventional rule-following,

I focused on rule-bending, rule-breaking and workarounds. Implicitly, I have argued that it is a mistake to draw a generalized association between the challenging and re-working of rules on one hand, and the practices of resistance on the other. Indeed, we see that the "street-level bureaucracy" I spoke of earlier in the book may come in many forms. Here we see clearly that certain forms of workaround are fundamental to the process of administrative knowledge production and consent.[18] Thus, while there are almost no indications that state welfare workers are engaged in sport, there is plenty of evidence pointing towards the creative use of rules in which human agency figures prominently. Games, in this sense, are not defined at all by competition or fun, but by the production of a range of relative/repressive satisfactions that can engross. And in the context of the energetic, contradictory, and often challenging construction and pursuit of these types of satisfactions, we can say that these workers were learning a variation of the arts of making out.

Across the analysis we find a portrait of a particular mode of participation in activity. It is one of three types that I discuss in this book, two of which, I argue, are particularly central to the struggle of defining an occupation in times of change. I intended to highlight how specific forms of complexity, autonomy, and skill formation intertwine in distinctive ways, despite the same objective task-based conditions of work and technological design, management structure, and broader political economic context. In the case of administrative knowledge production specifically, the processes of making a *fixture* of contradictions between operations and goals are definitive. These relations of contradictions offer a particular challenge to sense-making in its earliest and most fragile phases of development. Indeed, these early phases are fragile *because* of the substantial amount of sense-repair-work/skill involved, required, and to be mastered. The minutiae of the operations involved is important, however there is no way to understand why and how this is so in isolation from the types of goal-directed actions which eventually dominate this specific mode of participation in labour process activity as a whole. As such, this distinctive form of object-relatedness has been *learned* in the course of situated practice. This learning produces an often tenuously constructed, and not altogether straight-forward, concern to satisfy the needs of the system: to "think like it" and be recognizably accountable to it. Thus, for the workers we have met in this chapter, the mastery of their work life and the possibility for forms of self-expression, control and *individuated agency*, become the mastery of forms of administrative knowledge in activity; an example of what McDermott and Lave (2006) described so incisively as "the social practices of alienated learning" (p. 89).[19] Occupational identity is, drawing on Leontiev, "the movement of the systems of objective social relations into which [one's] activity is drawn. [Identity] thus no longer seems to be the result of a direct layering of external influences; it appears as something that man [*sic*] makes of himself, confirming his human life" (1978, p. 136). While we will see that there are alternative, more expansive ways of confirming one's working life in the following chapters, here at least we can say on the basis of detailed evidence that the notions of *consent* must be understood as a somewhat more richly loaded learning achievement.

It is not particularly original to have observed that both initial and ongoing engagements in workarounds engross workers. LPT research is rife with examples, and framed in a somewhat different way they can be found in CHAT studies of work as well. However, I argue that this type of empirical support for an understanding of the learning of consent and resistance at work, and an understanding of how these processes unfold as a matter of the dynamics of mind in political economy specifically is less common. Taylorized labour process, work design and conceived space do not give birth to these processes of consent alone. Consent must be agentively learned. And, building on the work of Knorr Cetina, as the term engrossment begins to specify, emotion, intuition, feel, the reciprocal relation of occupational identity and objects are fundamental to this achievement. Equally instructive, these are issues that Leontiev (1978) discussed in relation to activity and personality in connection to the repair of disjunctions between *personal sense* and *meaning*. As we will see in the following chapter, understanding these dynamics of activity is useful for appreciating learning of a very different kind as well.

8 Up-Skilling, Resisting, and Re-Keying for Craft Knowledge

Introduction

> Officially what we do is dictated by others. We are to just follow what we are told. And according to our own compassions or just that kind of commitment that you're dedicated to, if I want to make a decision and it does not fit the system, it is simply, no. In this field I think it must be made flexible. I mean that's worth fighting for I'd say. (HMBAT0404, Case Manager)

The new welfare labour process in this research was designed with austerity in mind. Quite apart from either direct cuts in welfare rates or the outsourcing of design work to the private sector, to firmly secure its interests the state sought to discipline the poor by disciplining those charged with administering their rights. It did this with tried and tested methods: through radical labour process re-design. Having reviewed the materials thus far, we see better now how changing the way workers worked – channelling the investment of talents, learning and energy, and securing consent – became central to the needs of the capitalist state. However, not all workers became invested in the dynamics of administrative knowledge production that the complex mediations of this new labour process design recommended. The practices, skills and knowledge of consenting sometimes went unlearned.

While there has long been a recognition amongst researchers that an occupation can be composed of many different purposes, forms of skill and knowledge, and identities (concerning welfare/employment services, cf. Blau 1955/1963), in this chapter I clarify the dynamics that give rise to these differences. I chart a distinctive trajectory of learning that is both resistant to technological and labour process design as well as fundamentaly more transformative than the one seen in the prior chapter. Here we see *how* the machineries of knowledge construction themselves can be constructed to produce something quite different. We find analysis of the struggles to resist channelling and types of engrossment specifically. In turn, we see how the design of work was challenged by a host of agentive occupational learning dynamics revolving around recovering and creating (what I refer to as) a form of state welfare work *craft knowledge*.[1] As we will see, this term "craft knowledge" is meant to designate an expansive development of skill/knowledge *forms* in activity in the context of a mind in political economy approach. It speaks to the production of trajectories of learning through which contradictory relations across *all dimensions of activity* (operations, goal, object/motive) are subjected to self-conscious concern *and agentive intervention* in both thought and action.

The analysis in this chapter has a special link to the theoretical synthesis I provide in the closing chapter of the book because the occupational learning discussed here addresses how workers can be seen to struggle to de-alienate their practice and construct their work and the client as expressions of *use-value*. In this sense, their mode of participation in activity comes to be *governed* by a distinctive dynamic. This type of value orientation mediates and is realized by the accomplishment of distinctive, daily, goal-directed actions and operations in opposition to the designed structure and technology of the new welfare labour process. In contrast to the practices seen in the prior chapter, overlapping but distinct operational skills – a form of work-around that more literally seeks to work *around* the principles of the new labour process – are developed to cope with, for example, the various SDMT functions (*Note*, *Task List*, etc.). Indeed, picking up from analyses provided in Chapter 6, a vast shadow system of paper files that mediate the construction and reconstruction of the biographical client-person partially explain the dynamic of goals, operations and object-relatedness as it unfolds with active intervention by workers. Unlike the types of learning processes seen earlier, the trajectory of craft learning is defined by contradictions across operations, goals *as well as* object/motive levels of activity. While hardly eschewing administrative competencies as such, the workers in this chapter exhibit additional forms of advanced expertise. I will argue that these workers are engaged in a genuinely *up-skilled* mode of participation in labour process activity.

With these introductory comments as the backdrop, I begin the chapter with a discussion of conceptual tools that will allow us to more clearly articulate the types of differences within activity that help define divergent trajectories of occupational learning. Specifically, I draw on ideas linked to Erving Goffman's concept of *re-keying*. This is followed by a section exploring the fragile, initial development of the trajectories of state welfare work craft knowledge development, and then an examination of more fully realized forms of this distinctive type of occupational learning.

On the Re-Keying of Activity

Making visible the variability and divergence of trajectories of occupational learning, skill and knowledge development is not always easy. Afterall, the rules, structure of management, divisions of labour, technologies – in objective terms and by design – are widely shared and, in terms of individual job categories and specific task sets identical. There are, in other words, vast layers of similarity with which the analysis variability and divergence must contend. In the previous chapter workers developed a customized form of object-relatedness that depended upon engrossment, channelling, making-out and a type of work performance game. It was a situation that required and afforded new skills and knowledge. However, while these concepts have been helpful in moving us to this point, they are not adequate for characterizing the additional complexity of activity that is the focus of this chapter. In short, some additional conceptual assistance is needed in order to grapple with, on the one hand, the similarities, and on the other, the distinctive features of practices in terms of resistance and the unfolding of oppositional transformations. This assistance is found in the work of Erving Goffman, his concept of frames and, in particular, the fluidity, the ambiguities, and the multiple, co-existing realities that can be explained by his concept of the *re-keying* of activity.

There can be little doubt that Goffman discovered things about social cognition that Vygotsky, Leontiev and others in the Cultural Historical Activity Theory (CHAT) tradition had discovered earlier by way of a very different path. In fact, Goffman was familiar with Vygotsky's work.[2] But, in pursuing different paths in the way they did, we find the opportunity of discovering distinctive contributions that may be complementary and uniquely suited to analysis here. It is very likely in my view that at least some of Goffman's work is intuitively recognizable to students of CHAT.[3] In *Frame Analysis* (1974) he begins with a concern that revolves around the process of knowing, sensing and socially resolving answers to the question: *what is going on here?* Of course, this same question emerged as an important point of analysis in the prior chapter as well. But here Goffman's work is necessary, I argue, because of what he does with this question in addition to the types of dynamics we have already seen. He was among the most adept analysts of the interactive processes through which people may shift their modes of experience. Specifically, Goffman's work will attune us to unique dimensions and dynamics of variability within activity that are typically only hinted at in either CHAT research or the diverse streams of the contemporary Labour Process Theory (LPT) tradition.

Eccentricities were characteristic of Goffman's style, but we might imagine that these were at least partially responsible for giving rise to new openings that, in the case of this research, may be central to the co-constructed co-existence of differences within labour process activity, and the way distinctive occupational skill and knowledge unfold. First, however, it makes sense to begin from a brief summary of what I claim is a shared *conception of mind* found across Goffman and CHAT research. In this regard, Goffman explains how *frames* are "not merely a matter of mind, but correspond in some sense to the way in which an aspect of the *activity itself is organized* [...] These organizational premises – sustained both in the *mind and in activity –* I call the *frame of activity*" (Goffman 1974, p. 247; emphasis added). These premises in fact define what Goffman refers to as the *primary framework*. Indeed, the primary framework of state welfare work is described in earlier chapters of this book where I addressed labour process design and conceived space. As in CHAT, Goffman also recognizes that the self-conscious and un-self-conscious dimensions of primary frames vary wildly in their degree of organization, but that they nevertheless offer actors important means of engaging in meaningful activity.

> Some are neatly presentable as a system of entities, postulates, and rules; others – indeed, most others – appear to have no apparent articulated shape, providing only a lore of understanding, an approach, a perspective. Whatever the degree of organization, however, each primary framework allows its user to *locate, perceive, identify, and label a seemingly infinite number of concrete occurrences defined in its terms.* He [*sic*] is likely to be *unaware* of such organized features as the framework has and unable to describe the framework with any completeness if asked, yet these handicaps are *no bar to his easily and fully applying it.* (1974, p. 21; emphasis added)

What is particularly clear in Goffman's work is an understanding of the significance of artefacts – both those internal to the person (e.g., cognitive or emotional schema, affect, etc.) and those external to the person, whether they are symbolic or material (e.g., a discourse, a space, a tool, etc.). Likewise, for Goffman each artefact had a *biography* that had significance to the on-going production of frames/activity: "Each artefact and person involved in a framed activity has a continuing biography, that is, a traceable life (or remains of one) before and after the event, and each biography ensures a continuity of absolute distinguishableness, that is self-sameness"

(1974, p. 287). In other words, he recognized deeply that *mind* was cultural *and* historical.

In CHAT and Goffman's work neither frames nor activity are structures in the conventional sense of being simply limiting, external and/or constraining, however. They enable and afford as well as restrict. They are mediating resources for personal sense and meaning-making. In these terms, again, Goffman is particularly clear that the *process of framing* is a source of variation; a practice through which the primary frame may be altered.

> [F]raming does not so much introduce restrictions on what can be meaningful as it does open up variability. Differently put, persons seem to have a very fundamental capacity to accept changes in organizational premises which, once made, render a *whole strip of activity different from what it is modeled on and yet somehow meaningful, in the sense that these systematic differences can be corrected for and kept from disorganizing perception, while at the same time involvement in the story line is maintained.* (Goffman 1974, p. 238; emphasis added)

What we find here in other words is an important means of further distinguishing the subtle variations in the learning trajectories, as well as the subtle variations in skill, knowledge and expertise necessary for these trajectories. It speaks to the means by which a sufficient meaningfulness of activity is maintained even amid the making of subtle and not-so-subtle differences that do not necessarily disorganize involvement in a recognizable "story line". The simultaneous accomplishment of recognisability and difference in modes of participation in activity are primarily understood by Goffman as a process of *keying*. As he puts it, "keying represents a basic way in which activity is *vulnerable*" (p. 83; emphasis added). In its basic form, it is defined as follows: "the set of conventions by which a given activity, one already meaningful in terms of some primary framework, is transformed into something patterned on this activity [...] The process of transcription can be called keying. A rough musical analogy is intended" (1974, pp. 43–44).

In this context we can note that in the previous chapter I explored how it was that the conceived labour process activity, while agentively achieved and subject to forms of rule-bending and workarounds, was *not* in the end made vulnerable (i.e., it was instead realized, albeit in creative ways). We will see that this is an important difference. Indeed, linking material across several of the previous chapters we can say that the primary frame provided by *conceived space* (of Taylorist design) for example, was confirmed, extended and deepened as it was *perceived* and *lived* in the course of administrative knowledge development. Applying Goffman's terminology to the argument in Chapter 7 specifically, we might say that making-out, games and the types of engrossments that produced "channelling" can be understood as a series of *key sustaining* processes rooted firmly in the new primary framework provided by work design. I argue this contrasts in a fundamental way with what we see below. Here, I analyze the processes through which the key of the primary framework activity is *not* sustained. The primary framework is *re-keyed* in the course of generating alternative modes of participation, alternative object-relatedness in the labour process, and alternative trajectories of occupational knowledge development, each related to something I defined earlier as *object-work/skill*.

One final implication for a conception of primary frames, their keying and re-keying, can be mentioned by way of concluding this section however. It concerns the future status of the state welfare work occupation as a whole.

> [t]aken all together, the primary frameworks of a particular social group constitute a central element of its culture, especially insofar as understandings emerge concerning principal classes of schemata, the relations of these classes to one another, and the sum total of forces and agents that these interpretive designs acknowledge to be loose in the world. One must try to form an image of a group's framework of frameworks – its belief system, its 'cosmology' [...] (Goffman 1974, p. 27)

Despite the historical clues gathered together earlier in the book, the fact is we cannot know the exact "cosmology" of the occupation of state welfare work in the past. What we can see, however, is that in the present the re-organization of the labour process has initiated a struggle for its future. In fact, Goffman went on to speak about framing, keying and re-keying as involving a struggle over the "realm of being" (1974, p. 57).[4] Thus, from the vantage point of this book, we might say that such a struggle involves the question of which of the diverging trajectories of practice, identity, skill, knowledge and learning within activity will ultimately re-constitute the primary frame of the occupation.

Fragile Transitions toward Craft Knowledge Production in Activity

As I did in the previous chapter, I begin with a section devoted to recognizing both the constant *pull* of the Taylorized labour process and state austerity, as well as the tenuous and sometimes fragile responses of workers to it. Across this and the previous chapter we find similarities in terms of many of the task-related practices that workers undertake in relation to this pull. However, the analysis that follows sheds light on how and why some of these processes are distinctive from those seen earlier as well.

The following set of two excerpts are taken from an interview with the same young woman. She started the job just after the implementation of the new state welfare labour process, as a Case Manager. She has a bachelor's degree in psychology. As we learn in the second part of the extended excerpt, prior to this she had worked for six years in a group home for troubled youth. Importantly, we see here a newcomer's initial experience of the channelling of her attention, energies and learning capacities. This channelling is linked to a suddenly expanded workload not uncommon in the new labour process (as we saw earlier in Chapter 5), and with it a fragmentation of a personal sense of her clients. It emphasizes yet again the relevance of operations in activity. Likewise, it is an example that helps reject the claim that resistance emerges simply from some type of naturalized, automatic defence of prior practices and occupational identity. She has just begun her career.

> When I first started I was given a 'hard to place' caseload. Then I went from the 'hard to place' which was capped at 50 and then all of a sudden went into a 'general caseload'. I kept my 50 which were hard to place, but then there were all of a sudden another 110 people I never met before. They all got letters sent out to them, 'This is your new case manager. If you have any questions, call her' [...] and now thinking back I really noticed *a change in everything*. I was *all of a sudden three days behind in my voice mail*. I was answering messages from 3 days ago. I had to change my voice mail to say, 'Leave me only one message' because my other 50 were used to me picking up my phone and not even having to leave a message. And I remember too at that time it was like, 'Surprise, surprise, you picked up your phone!' and I was like, 'Well yeah, as long as I was not in an appointment and I can'. I *found myself*, like leave a message, retrieve a message, call them back, they're not home, leave them another message, play phone tag. And then it *got to a point where I didn't answer my phone all day*, I would just *let it go. I got so far behind*. Plus you need, income statements have to be done, emergencies have to be looked after, and I'd always be saying 'I'm sorry you have this overpayment, it's going to take some time for me to dig into it, like that.' [...] It was just so much. *I tried to stop and think*: do you have enough money, do you have enough food, do you have enough diapers? But it was, 'I'll get back to you', leave them a message and then people were like 'I called you yesterday and you didn't return my call.' I said 'Yes, I have your message from the third and I'm still working on messages from the first'. So, there was a backlog of that and it was like *I just couldn't think anymore*. (SC06DB0303, Case Manager)

Paying attention to the ways that the pieces of concrete description provided in the account (as well as aspects of the structure of the account itself) address important features defining the character of her work activity, we see a distressing series of challenges. Many workers experience these same challenges. They appear first as concerns about performance and workload. She is backlogged. Without necessarily intending to, she *finds* herself *deciding* not to answer her phone. She describes the sensation of not being able to *think* and perform. In all this we might say that she was being invited – cognitively, emotionally, materially, culturally and in a sense historically – to take up an administrative mode of participation in activity. We can see clearly the early makings of a type of administrative orientation amid the uncomfortable experiences of overwork, confusion and withdrawal. Her initial response to withdraw from work is something associated later on in the book with a trajectory of floundering (see Chapter 10), but here it underlines the fragility of a distinctive, emerging trajectory, and how, under certain circumstances this trajectory could collapse or be re-directed. Floundering about, for this worker at this point, is a transitional moment in her thinking, feeling and knowing within activity (i.e., it has not yet become a trajectory of floundering as such). A partial warrant for these conclusions is that she goes on to quickly indicate a specific set of efforts – far more self-conscious – through which she attempts to repair a personal sense of the client-person despite the potentially overpowering whirlwind: "It was just so much. *I tried to stop and think.*" She tells us how she would consciously ask herself: did the client have money, food and diapers?

Elsewhere in the interview she tells us more about the thoughts she struggled intentionally to think – and *use to mediate practice* – across alternative trajectories of learning. Combined in these efforts is a strenuous and emotionally coloured reassertion of the role of the life, and in fact the use-value, of the client-person. It is this type of social/cognitive/affective dynamic that speaks to how different trajectories of attention, dis-attention, skill and expertise are implicated, particularly in the case of these tenuous periods of crisis and change (*perezhivanie*). She goes on.

> But then I remember so clearly the first time I had a client that told me she had a child that was not in her care. *I remember her story really well.* I mean I heard about people taking children away from people, but I had never met someone or thought it was common, which was very *frightening*. [...] I started out wanting to save the world but between my job at the group home and then this one though, I realized if I can make little impacts here and there, they all add up and I've served my *purpose*. I've done what I've set out to do. I want to be able to *maintain the integrity of my*

relationship with the client. Before, I used to blame things in the system. You know, that's when I was saying things like 'Hey, it's not my fault. There was a technical error.' But now I think I have a bit more confidence, and *I feel I know how I can find a way* to be committed to the client. (SC06DB0303, Case Manager)

We see here a difficult and effortful challenge. It speaks to defining features of occupational learning without which understandings of skill and knowledge in the labour process quickly degenerate. And, I claim it is a challenge that only makes proper sense when read in light of the details of the labour process activity established over the prior chapters. Through specific types of interventions, workers like this one are in fact attempting to resist the channelling of their capacities. A central element of this resistance is the establishment and maintenance of the biographical client-person within activity as having real, fully humanized needs (like the worker herself). Likewise, it is important to note the power of the operational level of activity presented in the account: it produces a constant pull toward the reorganization of a very large set of symbolic and material practices involving the relations among personal sense, meaning, and consciousness in activity. Here we obtain our first glimpse at efforts to fundamentally *re-key activity*; a practice intended to refuse the ready invitation to administrative trajectories of knowledge development and its relative/repressive satisfactions.

The re-keying of activity is attempted vis-à-vis the re-organization of the mediation of practice and thought inclusive of the construction and recovery of alternative artefacts. Recalling again my introductory comments in Chapter 1 regarding interpretation of the data, across this first pair of excerpts artefact construction is marked, in particular, by the reports of self-talk in work activity (as well as the use of self-talk in the account).[5] However, in the sequence that is defining the trajectory of development, the first attempt (the use of a type of self-talk mantra: "do you have enough money, do you have enough food, do you have enough diapers?") is only moderately effective in re-keying the object-relatedness of the activity. Left here, we might anticipate that either continued floundering or engagement in an administrative trajectory of learning would emerge. The power of the myriad mediations of labour process activity – including the summary powers of conceived space – is assaulting not simply her ability to think and feel in general, but her ability to construct a sense, a purpose, and ultimately a trajectory of learning of one type rather than another. Significant difficulties remain in the course of her practice until her second attempt at artefact construction/recovery which is more successful (described in the second excerpt). Why is this the case? This second attempt is based on the production of a self-talk mantra as well; one that is equally concrete, but according to the account one that is likely more emotionally charged (i.e., the "frightening" story of the removal of a child from a specific client-person she came to know well), and more strongly mediated by a broader object/motive in her life. The effect is significant. It mediates a new "confidence" in her being "committed to the client". The excerpt provides a grounded account of an initial, albeit still extremely vulnerable, transition towards a distinctive third type of work and skill: a form of skill, knowledge and work practice I refer to as *object-work/skill*. This worker demonstrates a good example of how a distinctive, alternative mode of participation and object-relatedness of activity can be produced, and specifically how leading activities are potentially re-keyed. These achievements depend upon artefact production to re-key participation amid the whirlwind of operations that otherwise threaten to change both her "purpose" and her sense of self significantly. She adapts, but just as clearly she also struggles and begins to transform the object-relatedness of her participation in occupational activity.

The point of this section is to begin to explore the processes of resisting – partially, tenuously, more and less successfully – the pull of the administratively-oriented key of the primary framework of state welfare labour process activity. While the worker we heard from in the first pair of excerpts appeared to initiate a transition towards a type of craft trajectory of occupational learning, others were less successful although even in these instances the process generates a self-conscious awareness of alternative possibilities. Unsuccessful transitions to craft learning, as in the following case, seem to regularly conclude with points of critique about the work system, but, importantly, in these instances the concerns remain dispersed and unfocused. It is vital to note overall how such processes unfold, mediated by concrete arrangements within labour process activity, such that a distinctive series of occupational learning experiences, skills and knowledge is progressively accumulated and further refined as a fully indexical, situated achievement (see Chapter 2).

S: I have to be honest though, I don't want to go back on the road. *I worried about clients then. I don't anymore.* I didn't worry about my safety ever though and I had a couple scary times, but I would worry if someone didn't have enough money that month like much more personal things. Like now at 4:30, I'm walking down those stairs, I don't *give it another thought* until I'm walking back up them the next day.

I: Is the social purpose of the job being eroded a bit? Like the idea that you're really
       doing something for your community.

S: That's gone definitely. I have no doubt. I think I could say, I mean, the powers
       that be, wherever it comes from, you hear about power and corporations now
       and [welfare services] are run like a corporation. And, it's like the *domino effect*.
       They don't care about us and we care less about the client and that isn't right at
       all. I do have a problem because we were much more effective when we cared
       and when they cared about us. We have lost so much being, becoming a corpo-
       ration. We as employees have lost a lot of the benefits of the job. It's just not
       personal. You just don't feel like anybody cares. Just get your job done and go
       home and shut up.

I: And you said this has a domino effect in terms of clients' attitudes.

S: Well yeah, I think it has to. So why should we care? It's not what the powers that
       be above us are doing to us. I don't think that's how it should be, but we have such
       a lot, the Case Workers particularly, have such a lot to do *we don't have time to care*.
       (B1PS0303, CVP Worker)

In this excerpt, elements of the concept of a *trajectory* of learning accomplishments are implied by the very notion of a "domino effect". We see
indications of how the broader activity, in terms of organizational management as well as worker-client relations, is inherent to an accumulating sequence of accomplishments. It illustrates in yet another way why, in
the context of a new labour process which has radically altered these relations, resisting an administrative (primary framework) keying of activity
is so difficult. Indeed, in the following chapter I discuss further evidence
in terms of inter-worker relations and the dynamics of group formation
which further mediate these processes. What is most relevant at this point
is less the recognition that state welfare workers have "lost so much", or
that the worker has "a problem" with it, but rather that *despite* these types
of generic critiques and concerns a transition to a stable, alternative trajectory of craft learning is far from guaranteed. For the time being at least,
this worker struggles and yet continues to learn to "not worry anymore",
to "feel" different, to forego having the "time to care", and to "go home
and shut up".

Something both similar and yet distinctive is expressed in the following excerpt. As we see, there is a series of fundamental criticisms of the
labour process that may be necessary for the potential re-keying of activity
in relation to craft knowledge, but which are nevertheless insufficient –
particularly as isolated concerns – to fully establish a robust and coherent
new trajectory of learning on their own. Critique, in other words, is not
enough.

> SDMT is not a very friendly [computer] system. I don't see it as being a very
> friendly system. I know what they were trying to do when they developed SDMT
> and I know they wanted something that could go province wide and where we
> could see and that's something I do like about it. I also know its Internet driven and
> it's very slow. It has to be very slow, because so many people are using it. I under-
> stand they thought they could invent a system where the worker didn't have to
> think. You put in information and the system is supposed to tell you if the client is
> eligible or not eligible. But, I'll tell you, maybe 80% of the time it will be incorrect
> in issuing or in helping clients they way they need to be helped. Plus these are peo-
> ple. So it becomes *finding a way where the worker can manipulate the system to make it
> do what we want it to do* because really if the system could do it, they really wouldn't
> need us. I find it a very *black and white system for a very colorful kind of a job*. In my
> view it just doesn't mix. [...] And it's taking longer to do things that I need it to do.
> To make a hydro payment, to save somebody, like to keep their lights and heat on,
> just yesterday I had a fight with the Hydro Company and I think they, well they did
> it, they called my manager to complain. That's the first time that that's ever hap-
> pened, but I was really upset, just to make a hydro payment, so that my client with
> little children, so the hydro is not disconnected. It took me approximately an hour
> of all the things I have to do, jump through hoops just to pay that bill. Not only
> that, to note it all on SDMT and touch all the different parts. You see with SDMT
> when you're issuing now it's not just one area where you go in and you issue. You've
> got to touch like a whole lot of different places in the system. When you're creating
> a cheque you have to go to the notes. The notes have different sections where you
> should be writing. If it's something to do with benefit unit and it's something to do
> with arrears, you're in the income section, just in the notes, you're in the benefit
> unit summary part of the notes and you're making a change and you're flicking
> on a lot of different pages just to pay one, one small thing so to do this job right
> you need a lot of steps and a lot of workers I find are skipping those steps because
> there's just not enough time in the day to do all those steps. (HJIDAT0404, Case
> Manager)

As with so many like her, the preceding worker, though critical of aspects
of the technology and labour process, still entertains considerable ambivalence. She thus remains open to engagement in the engrossments and
channelling of administrative object-relatedness of activity. Albeit reluc-
tantly, the operations – in particular those linked to the dense networked
information requirements of SDMT and its *Notes* function, the enormous
amount of "flicking on a lot of different pages" and so on – continually
press in on, and mediate, the distribution of attention and dis-attention in
the course of activity for this worker. For her, workers paying less attention to the *Notes* function are "skipping" steps; a relevant indication of a
particular object-relatedness that is persisting. However, she points to the
inherent contradictions of a "black and white system for a very colourful
kind of job". She is sensitive to the urgent contingencies and irregularity

of lives of clients, but these remain still too marginal to the unfolding of her mode of participation in activity. Moreover, a possible attempt to generate a type of craft orientation is disciplined further with a complaint to her manager from the electric company. Again, we see the tenuousness, but also latent potential, of transitions to trajectories of craft knowledge construction.

The following illustration provides additional detail, involving a longer period of time, concerning how the process of the channelling of expertise may be partially resisted within activity. Here I take some additional care to summarize a broader set of points. In terms of the dynamics of interest in this section of the chapter, it offers a clear and comprehensive account representative of the practices of many of those interviewed in this research. At 56 years old, and with 18 years experience on the job, this Case Manager is one of the workers who, unlike a significant proportion of others, does not describe any periods of poverty in her own past life. She grew up the daughter of a unionized electrician though, like the majority of interviewees, identifies herself as middle-class. She is quite active in her local union. She is white but refers to herself simply as Canadian. While having recently begun to take some university courses part-time, she holds a college diploma related to social work. Each of these demographic/biographic indicators will become increasingly relevant as we complete the analysis in the book. I note once again that the following is a continuous section of discussion broken up into parts in order to facilitate analysis. Parts A and C explicitly illustrate issues central to state welfare workers who see, and continue to struggle to create, their job in the mould of some type of *social work ideal*. But, I argue this struggle is predicated on the makings of a specific form of craft knowledge. It is a struggle which requires a constant effort to re-key labour process activity in a particular way.

[Part A]
1 I: Can you tell me your thoughts on the way your tasks are divided up?
2 S: Well I mean this job by its nature isn't always conducive to keep it in a
3 manageable *little square box because you're dealing with the people.* For me, I
4 mean there are Case Managers who like to operate in a *very structured*
5 *environment.* It's like they'll sacrifice everything to just get that structure. They
6 really get into that. I'm really not one of them. I'm more *loose ended.* I guess I'm
7 kind of not as organized as I should be. I really shouldn't say that because I am
8 organized in a lot of other ways. You can be super organized and you would not
9 survive in this job for a week if you didn't have some organizational skills
10 because it's become too big of a job. *There's your phone, your messages, your*

11 *walk-ins, you know, all the support that you give other staff, and your*
12 *supervisor's demands, and your manager's demands,* the community demands for
13 the rapport and referrals we have and like you know you couldn't possibly not be
14 organized at some level or you'd flounder. In a month you'd be like, 'Oh shit', so
15 I think my organizational skills, I leave them *kind of loose ended* because *now I'm*
16 *thinking about it* I actually kind of think that's really important to the way I
17 actually deal with clients. I don't want a *structured little box* where I say 'Okay
18 15 or 20 minutes,' and then go 'Next', kind of thing. And I've been really kind of
19 *afraid*, especially coming into the *office and the cubicle scenario* that we've
20 become like that, like this *cattle herding of clients. Lots of us, we* are all *afraid* of
21 that. So I've sort of intentionally left it that so okay, this might pile up but I'm
22 *prioritizing my time face-to-face with a client or telephone calls* or whatever.
23 *Client contact, that's the thing. Knowing what's really going on with people.* So,
24 *it might look like I'm disorganized because I've got this load over here* but on this
25 other side I'm *very organized as far as meeting client needs.* I'm not saying I'm a
26 super Case Manager and all my clients are super happy because we all have our
27 complaints but that's just sort of the way I organize.

[Part B]
1 I: And what about the workarounds?
2 S: Oh I *hate the workarounds*.
3 I: Don't they make it easier for you?
4 S: Yeah, but *we've got a million of them.* Try to remember them all. I've said to
5 myself again and again that I *won't even try because you know that's not what it's*
6 *all about.* But oh my god, we've got workarounds for everything. It's you know,
7 you have to know the system well enough half the time to even do the
8 workarounds because the system is so unreliable. We're always pulling out
9 sheets, we just got a list of new workarounds the other day with about eight or
10 nine, what *we call 'The way SDMT should work'* scenario. We're *constantly*
11 *getting them coming our way.*
12 I: So who gives them to you? Do your supervisors and everybody supply you with
13 the workarounds? What do you mean you got a list?
14 S: Supervisors won't admit it really. I mean that's just their management role, to
15 sort of keep it on the low-down because they know some people would be just so
16 much more disgruntled at the idea.
17 I: So are these survival skills or what?
18 S: They are but it's just that there's too many problems within the system that the
19 *workarounds get to be a problem too.* I mean we're just too busy to be constantly
20 figuring them out, and just again the nature of the job, I mean you could have a
21 case today that would present almost every foreseeable form that you're going to
22 have in your cabinets to use and then you might not have that form for that
23 situation for 5 or 6 or 7 weeks or longer in a lot of cases so in others words if you
24 run into some little SDMT glitch that you have to use a workaround solution to
25 deal with, like I've decided *I'm not going to keep them in my mind every day.* It's
26 just *not even a practical thing that you can do.* You know *you learn them just*
27 *because.* It's one of those workarounds, or whatever. So *you could spend time*
28 *flying through your manuals* to see what the workaround is for this or that. Or,

29   what memo did we get on that, or what are we supposed to do in this situation.
30   Well the way I look at it, that's not very time effective to be having to do that
31   stuff *given what we need to do in reality*. And it's not only that, it frustrating, it's
32   extremely frustrating in your work day when you've got client after client back to
33   back you know, demands of meetings and whatever else that management puts on
34   you and then you've got to look up a workaround for the most recent glitch that
35   SDMT is throwing at you which is constant and continual.

[Part C]
1   S: I mean *if you interviewed everyone here I think they'd say the same thing*. I
2   mean I'm ticked at the system and I'm probably voicing that pretty noticeably and
3   I go to the supervisors too. I tell them. If they could get the glitches out of it, and
4   if it were a little more friendly just for Case Managers then it probably would be
5   not a bad system but we've been waiting for years for them to get some glitches
6   out of it that are well, and I don't see anything but more glitches [...] I mean *you*
7   *walk out of here most nights I think, I'm really buzzing*. I tell you, a lot of us *go*
8   *home and wake up through the night* and go, 'Oh my god, that cheque is not going
9   to go out!', or, 'I forgot to pull that! The client was told to come in and pick up
10   the cheque tomorrow and I forgot to pull it!' The fact is you're constantly multi-
11   tasking on the computer and the phone and the paperwork. There's *a real pull to*
12   *make it like you're just shuffling papers*, you're just constantly shoving a piece of
13   paper in a file and *clearing out your Task List*. Like that's so *unprofessional as far*
14   *as getting to the grips with your client's issues. It's not me*. (NF18DB0304, Case
15   Manager)

This final illustration of the section speaks in very specific ways to the agentive means of re-structuring one's mode of participation in activity. It speaks to the re-keying of the object-relatedness of participation in activity that successfully resists the channelling of expertise in one direction while affording and permiting it to begin to expand and develop in another. We see that this depends significantly on this worker's active construction, and partial recovery and use, of particular symbolic artefacts. Many of these artefacts relate to a social work ideal and a professional identity, the origins and contradictions of which we took time to explore historically in Chapter 4. In CHAT this process can be referenced generically in terms of the dynamic of historicized internalizations, externalizations and transformations.

Discursive artefacts (like the self-talk mantras we have already seen) are regularly rehearsed in the worker's mind. The prevalence of these rehearsals offers some warrant for claims about the character of activity, but there are other discursive constructions that also assist in realizing alternative forms of mediation as well. They can be categorized in two ways. First, there are artefacts that are created/used to produce a target of resistance. In this latest series of excerpts, these include the notions of a "very structured environment", a "little square box" (line A3), a "structured little box" (line A17) as well the "cattle herding of clients" (lines A19–20). And second, there are artefacts that are created/used to specifically resist these newly formulated targets. These include the "The way SDMT should work scenario" (lines B9–10), and the style of organization of one's work that she calls "loose ended" organization (line A6). *Together* they are effective in the re-keying a particularly important set of mediations in activity that would otherwise lead to the type of channelling addressed earlier in terms of administrative performance: e.g., "it might look like I'm disorganized because I've got this load over here but on this other side I'm very organized" (lines A23–25). We might say, in G. H. Mead's terms (1934/1967, e.g., pp. 173–178), that the "I" is producing the artefact-mediated practices for the "me".[6] The basic notion of self-talk in this sense aligns with Mead's formulation in several ways. However, it is a process perhaps even more fundamentally addressed in relation to a much broader object-relatedness in activity by Vygotsky, Leontiev and CHAT tradition in terms of the generation of personal sense vis-à-vis the *social-in-thought*.

Specifically, for these instances of the social-in-thought to generate significant change the types of artefacts mentioned earlier benefit from being *collectively externalized* in activity. Self-talk in the account is important for understanding this process. But more relevant still, we also see the potential for these new artefacts to be used in daily conversation to re-organize social relations through which they can be collectively externalized. In this regard, we can note this worker's multiple references to shared meaning-making: e.g., "lots of us" (line A20); the regular use of "we" (lines A13, 20, 26; B8, 9, 29, 31) which includes reference to the "way SDMT should work scenario" (lines B9–10). As I will discuss at length in the next section, *self-talk mantras* have the potential to become externalized as powerful *we-talk mantra* artefacts.[7] In re-keying for craft trajectories of occupational learning they offer an alternative pathway toward a personal sense of collective (rather than individuated) control, though, in the end, they have the potential to do much more. Equally supportive of this type of observation, however, is her comment that "if you interviewed everyone here I think they'd say the same thing" (line C1). In fact, virtually wherever interviewees in this research began to establish coherent trajectories of occupational learning (of whatever type) these same types of comments can be seen. As I show in the next chapter, this is related to group formation, and limited to specific communicative spheres, such comments are essentially accurate. The point here is that, in this specific trajectory of learning, *we-talk mantras* provide evidence for the significance of *collective internalization/externalization* of mediations supporting the achievement of unique forms of object-relatedness within activity.

Activity is, in this context, a thoroughly cultural, historical, and political economic affair. It is also a socio-cognitive battle ground. There is, as she states at the close of the excerpt, "a real pull to make it like you're just shuffling papers, you're just constantly shoving a piece of paper in a file and clearing out your *Task List*" (lines C11–13). This is the constant pull to dance to an activity of *certain key*. It is also the pull of the premises of de-skilling without which we could not hope to understand either instances of re-skilling or up-skilling or the distinctions between them. It is relevant to our understanding of activity that she explicitly says, "now I'm thinking about it" (lines A15–16). This helps to confirm the notion that at crucial points – in the account *and* in her work practice itself – she is clearly referencing either un-self-conscious operations or object/motives (which are being actively surfaced to self-consciousness in the course of the interview). In terms of operations specifically, the "pull" appears to workers like this one as "your phone, your messages, your walk-ins" (lines A10–11) as well as the spatio-material arrangements of activity, e.g., "office and cubicle scenario" (line A19). Compared to my earlier analysis of engrossment in Chapter 7, in fact we discover a critical instance of re-keying of operations specifically in relation to the treatment of workarounds. That is, in Part B we see how, vis-à-vis this mode of participation in activity, a certain class of workarounds can and must be *actively made un-engrossing*. It is both an effortful and agentive practice of transformation. Not only are the operations described unavoidable in the new labour process, but, as she says, lists of them are constantly "coming our way" (line B10–11) and "there's too many problems within the system that the workarounds get to be a problem too" (line B18–19). So, she tells of how she self-consciously repeats to herself "I won't even try" to remember the workarounds (line B5). They are simply "constant and continual" (line B35). In so doing, she actively defends specific goals and forms of object-relatedness from them; she keeps operations from becoming an object of problem-solving that may engross. In fact, she vigorously undertakes a form of *object-work*, and learns new skills and knowledge suitable to it. Helpful to this process is the collective construction of, in essence, a container for these particular invitations to engrossment. This is another function, in activity, of the "way SDMT should work scenario" artefact. Building from the many, many things that constitute her occupational learning in this way, in the end the account begins to provide important evidence of the partial resolution of certain *relations of contradiction* in activity. This is a process summarized by the emergent capacity to *re-key* and *re-solve* the contradiction among the pull of the operations, her goal-directed actions, *and* a potential client-centred object/motive in state welfare work. As she points out, "you *could* spend time flying through your manuals" (lines B27–28), but it is "not very time effective to be having to do that stuff given what we need to do *in reality*" (lines B30–31). This is a version of "reality" which, unlike the alternative versions explored in the previous chapter, could be recognized, *retained and activated*, rather than dismissed.

In analysing this excerpt we can also begin to map a process of transition across *repair-work/skill, sense-repair-work/skill* and *object-work/skill*. Warrant for the claim that this type of successful sense-repair-work and object-work was being initiated can also be found in the emotional colouring, at key points, in the account. Following Leontiev (1978, e.g., p. 121), we would expect that intense emotional colouring of participation in activity would surface in instances of active contradictions between organizational meaning and personal sense, again associated with a type of crisis and the concept of *perezhivanie*. In this regard, we can take seriously the choices this worker makes in the account as telling us something about the organization of her work activity itself. In fact, several times she refers to fear (lines A19, 20) for example. In Part C, she also refers to panic as serious worries invade her sleep (lines C8–10). Here we see the intimate dimensions of the struggle among the potentially engrossing operations of activity (and the relations of contradiction it entails), personal-sense-making, and the broader object-work she is now attempting to carry out. Indeed, closely linked to this question, there are also a range of value-laden expressions peppered throughout the account. We see the frequent use of the words "should" (rather than could, might or would) and "shouldn't"; we see the pejorative framing of the "little square boxes" (A3). Each of these suggests something more than simply a pragmatic view of practice. They suggest the emergence of distinctive affective and value-based dimensions of her mode of participation, as well as the (re)construction of a specific type of craft identity.

Finally, it is important to note for a moment one further implication of how artefacts are created within activity. The value-laden dimensions of activity I have suggested, and the way that new artefacts become internally related within the structure of activity raises the question of the construction of *relations of legitimacy/illegitimacy*. That is, the occupational learning process illustrated in the preceding excerpt (and many others in the book) also describes a process through which collective externalization results in an *expanding legitimation of alternative practices*. Whereas in the prior chapter, a type of legitimacy was creatively refined and in some cases sharpened to a fine point in terms of administrative accountability, here we find something different. Re-keying in this way implicates an emerging coherence that extends from difficulties in everyday coping, questions and critique, *through to* new patterns of object-relatedness beyond those presumed in the primary framework of labour process design. These alternative patterns fore-front, rather than marginalize, important dimensions of contradiction in the course of laying distinctive claims to occupational identity. Clues as to the dynamics involved in this trajectory of development specifically are found in the worker's remarks about the role of "client contact" (line A22), the centrality of knowing "what's really going on with people" (line A23), as well as in such statements as, "that's so unprofessional as far as getting to the grips with your client's issues. It's not me" (lines C13–14). Across the analysis in this book we see the term "professional" as something of a floating signifier taking on a host of different meanings in terms of practical occupational ethics. Indeed, its contradictory historical origins allow for this. Thus, it is likely more important to note how we are seeing an object-relatedness that admits the contingencies of clients' lives are reflected in contingency in workers' lives, and in turn how this reflects a fundamentally more expansive possibility for occupational knowledge production. In fact, we are seeing everyday political acts of working life in motion (Haug 2010).[8] Indeed, as I will return to in the final chapter of book, what is increasingly being legitimized in craft trajectories of occupational learning is an orientation to the use-value essential to, but often systematically marginalized, within, labour process activity.

Realization of Trajectories of Craft Knowledge Production

In drawing distinctions regarding the establishment of trajectories of either administrative or craft knowledge production within activity, I am making claims linked to what (respectively) Leontiev refers to as "fractionation" and "consolidation".

> The *mobility* of separate 'forming' systems of activity is expressed … in the fact that each of them may become a smaller fraction or, conversely, may incorporate in itself

> units that were formerly relatively independent. Thus, in the course of achieving an isolated general goal there may occur a separation of intermediate goals as a result of which the whole action is *divided into a series of separate sequential actions*; this is especially characteristic for cases where the action takes place *under conditions that inhibit its being carried out by means of already formulated operations. The opposite process consists of consolidating isolated units of activity.* This is the case when objectively attained intermediate results flow one into another and the subject loses conscious awareness of them. In a corresponding manner there is a *fractionation or, conversely, a consolidation* also of "units" of psychic images.... Before the naked eye the process of fractionation or consolidation of units of activity and psychic reflection – in external observation as well as introspectively – is hardly distinguishable. (Leontiev 1978, p. 67; emphasis added)

As Leontiev says, to the naked eye the differences between "fractionation" and "consolidation" are "hardly distinguishable". As we see, with careful analysis of the process, objective distinctions can be made between a type of agentive, expert coping/re-skilling, on the one hand, and an agentive, expert up-skilling that is linked here to resistance, on the other. One of the bases for this distinction is that up-skilling implicates more encompassing, and more far-reaching trajectories of engagement in society and political economy *in activity*. This is what Engeström (e.g. 1987) likely would refer to as learning by expansion, and, in the terms of Marx, might be called historical (versus epochal) practice (Sawchuk 2003a). It is in this type of consolidating mode of participation in activity that operational engrossments of the kind we identified in Chapter 7 can be rejected by workers; making-out and games associated with a "fractionation" of activity can be partially or entirely resisted; and, the "primary framework" of Taylorist work design, and the conceived space of the new labour process re-keyed.

To build on the point we can turn to the following excerpt. The Case Manager we hear from next has been doing her job for 15 years. She is 39 years old, holds a Bachelor degree in psychology, and a college diploma in early childhood education. She identifies as having a disability. She is highly active in her local union. Her account begins with the type of description of workarounds ("fudging") that are by now very familiar. Her brief description provides evidence of dexterity in these terms. Yet, most types of workarounds hold little fascination for her. In terms of the argument in this chapter, this is not insignificant. Equally relevant are her frank and firm comments that give evidence of the object-relatedness of her practice within activity. It suggests subtle but definitive differences in comparison to what we saw in the previous section of this chapter where we encountered workers engaged only in the fragile, early phases of transition toward a type of craft learning trajectory. Here is an excerpt that begins to describe a more fully realized craft knowledge, a stabilized, alternative object-relatedness in activity, as well as a clearer and more confident craft knowledge based occupational identity.

I: Describe for me how you solved an overpayment problem. Walk me through that process.

S: Sometimes it is just based on dates that the computer is going back to – RBC's [Re-Budget Calculation]. I think of it actually as a CIMS thing, so it was a RBC. Because the computer is so date sensitive, if you don't get the dates right you create an overpayment very easily. So you go in and you change the rent, or you pull the rent out, or you add a spouse, or you take a spouse out.

I: Do you fudge?

S: Do I fudge? Of course! Sometimes I have to.

I: Do you create workarounds?

S: Yeah for sure. *But I do it for one reason* because I was always trained that, like I mean a hundred years ago when I started, I learned it's better to always fault on behalf of the client. So that you know, if you make a mistake, if it is going to be a mistake, then it's going to be a mistake on the behalf of the client rather being punitive. I don't care what happens, *I refuse to create undue hardship for people* because you know if they're at this point in their life, requesting this help, I mean listen to their stories, you've got to be pretty low. They're still some people out there scamming the system, but by far it's genuine people, and it's the genuine people that I'm going to error for every time. And *if they're going to fault me on that, then fault me on that – I'll deal with it!* (SC12DB0603, Case Manager)

The types of partial attempts and early, more unstable re-keyings, equivocations, ambivalence and contradictions detectable in many of the accounts/activity described in the previous section have melted away. A firm, confident and sustained re-keying of participation in activity is described. She is aware of both the contradictions and, indeed, the penalties of her practices. Her activity is oriented by "one reason" that aligns tightly and explicitly with the biographical client-person (people complete with "stories" and a "life"). She makes it clear that a new logic of thinking, action and learning has been set in train. As we now know, it is one which, whether it was learned "a hundred years ago" or not, must be actively recovered and sustained if it is to effectively govern her participation in activity on an ongoing basis. As I mentioned, the brief statement summarizes an expertise in repair-work ("Do I fudge? Of course!"), but this repair-work lies *in service to* a specific and coherent personal sense of what the work is about that is quite different from what we encountered in the previous chapter. Involving a wide array of the specific skill types conventionally defined in the literature on work skill, I argue that the overall learning accomplishment must also be understood as a function of successful and skilled repair-work, sense-repair-work *and* object-work. It represents a trajectory of successive accomplishments through which the primary framework has been resisted and re-keyed. Evidence of these dynamics is easily identified, for example, in her rejection of legitimated performances of accountability: "fault me on that – I'll deal with it!" What appears as an individual stance, in other words, is in fact a reflection of the many hidden accomplishments of the (individual and collective) re-keying of activity over time.

However, this brief excerpt serves only to provide us with a relatively narrow window into a re-keyed mode of participation in labour process activity. Without further information, what Leontiev would refer to as a consolidation appears as either a personality trait or alternatively a remarkable leap in the face of the pressures and changes in learning we investigated in Chapter 7. A more detailed illustration provides us additional insights. The next excerpt begins to offer answers to the question concerning different mediating artefacts that were created and legitimized, and which, in turn, helped to solidify these types of re-keying of activity. In a paired interview with a Case Manager (highschool diploma; white; level of union involvement unknown) and an Employment Services Worker (college diploma; white; high level of union involvement) who together had over 36 years of experience we learn more about this process.[9]

1   S[b]: Listen, you've got to get cheques out. You've got to get them out at a certain
2   time. None of that has changed. But basically what they did before is they kept
3   building on old technologies and just expanding your capacity to do your job,
4   making you able to see more of what you're doing and have more control over
5   every aspect.
6   I: OK, so SDMT [computer system] is suddenly done with a different use in
7   mind?
8   S[b]: Based on our experience the only way it makes sense to describe it is that it
9   was *designed for the purposes of reporting to prove that Accenture has saved the*
10   *province money.* [...] So, that's built right into the computer program, and if you
11   look at the data capture that's done, there is extensive data capture around
12   capturing that information. New clerical support positions have been created in
13   every municipality to ensure that that information is appropriately captured. And
14   it's about five or six screens. It's more than employment support.
15   I: So this is definitely a change in focus? Like people spend their whole work day
16   just trying to get stats for reporting purposes?
17   S[b]: Yeah, to make sure that it is properly captured, that people are getting cut off
18   or having their benefits reduced as a result of this process. I mean that is one of

19   the things that this program definitely captures. [...]
20   I: So, it's basically a fancy way of keeping statistics so the main thing becomes
21   that stats box?
22   S[b]: Exactly.
23   I: I mean you're saying its purpose is to feed the stats box, but that the system is
24   not a help to you, for your purpose, to do your job?
25   S [b] & S[a]: No!
26   S [a]: Not to us it's not. Why do I know that? Because you have to lie to it and you
27   have to trick it. You have to trick it to work right in some areas. And I don't agree
28   with that philosophy.
29   S[b]: Sure, to do my job I have to get cheques out to people. But a lot of times you
30   just can't tell that machine the truth if you want to get a cheque.
31   S [a]: Yeah, you have to lie to it. You're not lying to it about people's incomes or
32   their shelter rates or anything like that. Not that. But, which box am I thinking
33   about that drives me just insane? Oh yeah, the box that asks them: do you have
34   any past employment? And, I'm thinking do you or don't you? If you put yes, it
35   won't do it. You won't get a cheque to somebody. You have to put no.
36   S[b]: That's right, you've always got to pretend that nobody works, ever. But then
37   again I do not rely on SDMT for me to do that work action planning. As an
38   Employment Worker *I start from scratch on a paper. It's really important. I get*
39   *out of SDMT completely.* That's the only way to do it [...] See the employment
40   part ties automatically to income calculations. So if you put information in about
41   employment, it ties to the income piece, which creates problems after in getting a
42   cheque out. We don't want to go there. We just say to the client: 'No, never
43   worked, right?' 'Right.' (BCBBP0704[a], Case Manager; BCBBP0704[b],
44   Employment Services Worker)[10]

There is of course a great deal of discussion of operations in this excerpt. Particularly prominent are those mediated by the SDMT computer system. Like virtually all interviewees, these workers acknowledge the operational realities of the new welfare work labour process repeatedly: e.g., "You've got to get cheques out" (lines 1–2, 29–30, 35). Cheques are obviously fundamental to the lives of clients as well as one of the most tangible outcomes of the work of many of these workers and a common idiom. However, successfully issuing cheques is positioned in the account as an otherwise *un-engrossing means to an end* that appears in relation to more expansive practice. This is distinctive from the dynamic we saw in the prior chapter where the successful issuing of cheques devolved rapidly in accordance with personal accountability, managing caseloads for minimum "hullabaloo", and in general good administrative performance. Even still, it is important to note that we can see (lines 39–43) a virtually identical description of the operational problems and peripheral dimensions of contradiction of the work is provided (a fact that might obscure crucial differences for many other approaches to work skill analysis). Moreover, the account does *not* suggest that these workers have resolved the contradictions associated with these operations any more or any less than workers we heard from in the prior chapter. In the case of the employment information input, however, they collaborate with clients in each instance to cope with these problems (lines 33–5, 40–3). In general terms, forms of cooperation are endemic to the labour/learning process even in the context of the emergence of oppositional perspectives in the workplace. In this case, it is cooperation that involves workers and clients (and undoubtedly local management as well though it is not mentioned here explicitly). In the prior chapter cooperation involving clients is virtually impossible to detect. The main point here, however, is that we can also see that the structure of the mode of participation of these workers in activity depends significantly upon the process through which they *do not* become invested and engrossed, as such, in their mastery of such techniques.

Looking more closely still, now we can ask: How is engrossment resisted in the practices of these workers? One answer to this question involves paper, that important artefact that I took time to discuss in Chapter 6. "I start from scratch on a paper. It's really important. I get out of SDMT completely" (lines 38–9). Referencing not simply working off-line somehow but rather actively countering a particular primary framing of activity vis-à-vis a shift in artefact mediation (the use of paper), this refers to a type of important operational practice that helps to materially embed the re-keying in activity. Also introduced earlier we see evidence of particular types of collective externalization essential for the elaboration of the trajectory of occupational learning. Examining this excerpt carefully, we can see it addressed in a number of ways. Plural personal pronouns ("we", "us", and "our") are selected in the account at significant junctures and each are linked to practices that tend to resist the primary framing of the new labour process activity specifically (lines 8, 26, 42). In the context of this more fully realized craft trajectory of learning, such indications suggest something crucial about the structure of thought and perception in activity. Also suggested is how collective externalization may be particularly helpful in defining an oppositional standpoint within activity. The alternative *self-talk mantras* that we saw – vis-à-vis forms of *collective* internalization/externalization specifically – are converted to powerful forms of *we-talk-mantras/ artefacts* in this sense.

The account allows us to warrant several relevant claims. These claims revolve around the way that distinctive modes of participation and object-relatedness within activity come to be structured. This involves the means by which workers are learning and generating distinctive skills and knowledge, and in turn new levels of occupational expertise in the course of everyday work practice. The workers offer a particular construction of the work technologies that were used prior to the new SDMT-based labour process. According to these (and other) workers, the prior work technologies built progressively, in the course of their use, on worker skill, knowledge, goals, purposes and personal sense of the work at hand. These are the former technologies that they preferred specifically because they felt it allowed them to "see more", and have greater autonomy and control over their work (lines 2–5) in terms of a specific object-relatedness. These technologies allowed them to join personal sense with occupational meaning of particular kinds. They go so far as acknowledging alternative, conflicting standpoints in the designed purposes of SDMT specifically in relation to forms of meaning and sense-making in fact (e.g., "I don't agree with that philosophy", lines 27–8). Connected with this are observations regarding state welfare work as embedded in provincial politics, financing and specifically public-private sector partnership consulting that produced SDMT and the labour process design (lines 8–13, 17–26). These workers remark that welfare work and SDMT specifically have been designed to keep statistics ("to feed the stats box", line 23), eventually for use in cost avoidance through the process of CVP tracking. And so, what is important to note is how they have come to see the screens of SDMT in a fundamentally different way, on a daily basis in activity, as having been "designed for the purpose of reporting that Accenture has saved the province money" (lines 9–10). By contrast, while matters of autonomy and control (as well as "seeing more") discussed in the prior chapter are also mediated by the same reporting, statistics, and stats boxes, the purpose and overall object-relatedness of the activity seen here are fundamentally different. In this way, the comments of these workers suggest something much more than just critical observations, although their critique is expansive and coherently unified. The account suggests what Leontiev refers to as a process of "consolidation" in activity, and this necessarily implicates the establishment of a trajectory of learning (and questioning) that helps explain ongoing attention to some matters and not others. Activity is consolidated, in cases such as these, through a re-keying process.

From a CHAT perspective, this draws our attention to the mediating role of what can be called *eligibility artefacts and objects* (including, for example, the Participatory Agreement counts, or "production quotas", that workers elsewhere in the book remarked on). Specifically, this draws our attention to the role of these types of artefacts in establishing the bases for financial transfers to municipal administrations, the funding for the private sector consultancy contract, cost avoidance for the provincial government, and, in general, the administration of an austerity program in welfare services. Such artefact mediations are anything but inconsequential if we are seeking to understand the practical instrumentation of austerity within the occupational learning of state welfare workers. And, in this regard we can recall a crucial document discussed in Chapter 4 (HLB Decision Economics Incorporated 2002), and through this see the relations of important dimensions of contradiction at a particular level of generality in activity. That is, among a host of other features, a defining element of the SDMT software in this regard was the type of "stats box" to which the two workers in the preceding excerpt refer. As an important mediation in workers lives and the labour process, here we see the shaping of the object-relatedness of practices, activity, and highly contradictory forms of skill/knowledge development. This excerpt is indicative in terms of understanding the intersection of the minutiae of occupational learning, neo-liberal austerity, and, in fact, the pressures of monopoly-finance capitalism. Those charged with managing the poor are learning at the conjuncture of both hyper-irregularities of the lives of impoverished clients and attempts at hyper-regulation vis-à-vis a new labour process.

The following excerpt provides a continuation of the interview with the same pair of workers. I argue we see further expressions of the processes of object-work/skill and its outcomes. Unsurprisingly, these processes centre on the familiar theme of recovery of the biographical client-person as well as the use-value of state welfare craft knowledge. It is a point that underscores my earlier discussions regarding professional human services knowledge and access to direct and sustained relationships with fully biographical client-people as a critical source of occupational control (Chapter 4). It is worth pointing out that that neither worker is formally trained in the field of social work. In terms of a CHAT analysis of craft trajectories of learning, I argue that the excerpt illustrates the processes through which the contradictions between operations and goal-directed actions that so firmly undergirded administrative knowledge production are firmly marginalized. And finally, also by way of comparison, we can recall those workers who we met in Chapter 7 who were ambivalent about how clients perceived the changes in welfare as well those workers who believed that, for the client, conditions were neither better nor worse but "just different". Again, in the following excerpt we see something quite different.

I: And from the client perspective, how do you think clients experience the new work system?

S[a]:   *It's a slap in the face!*

I: But it wasn't always this way? The way work was organized before, you were more engaged with clients?

S[a]:   [sighs] How to explain. I mean *that was your job*. It was you and the client. You made your visits and a lot of people would find work within the month or get back with their husbands.

I: So there was a more humanized aspect to it?

S[a]:   Oh yeah.

S[b]:   There was a whole bunch of, like Rhonda[11] over there used to have her trunk full of groceries, products out of her own garden if it was needed. Yeah, and I would say as recently as '95 when we were still doing lots of home visits I can recall cases where Case Workers would come into town and get food and take it out. There was no ability, I mean the voucher did no good because the person had no ability to get to the grocery store, particularly in the rural areas. There was a lot of that.

S[a]:   And a lot of people didn't know about handicapped child allowance, they didn't know Canada Pension, and you were in the home, you had time, I mean if they were on crutches or, I don't know, they just came through chemo-therapy you could suggest different pensions and things to them. *There was just a lot more.*

I: Did you like that part of the job?

S[a]:   Yes I did.

S[b]:   But now it's far more business-like…. It's not social work….

S[a]   I mean years ago you were a *mother, a doctor, a lawyer, a physician, a nurse. You took on all those aspects.* I mean you were referring people here, referring people there. They were phoning you, you were sending them to a shelter, to the doctor for this, for that, bringing them up to hospital […]

S[b]:   First thing I would look at is are they living safely and is their family safe? Are they healthy? Are they totally well emotionally and physically? If not, what do they need? …

I: So that was social work.

S[b]:   Yes. And we're still trying to do it. (BCBBP0704[a], Case Manager; BCBBP0704[b], Employment Services Worker)

It is not hard to draw the conclusion that a distinct and fundamentally more expansive, consolidating form of occupational knowledge production was a possibility within the former labour process even as we admit that it was a form of occupational activity racked with contradictions of its own. It was a labour process through which learning to be a "a mother, a doctor, a lawyer, a physician, a nurse" was more readily afforded as an inherent part of carrying out state welfare work, as these workers attest. And, according to this excerpt, it is a form of practice that many workers are "still trying to [learn how to] do".

The pair of workers in the preceding two excerpts are veterans of state welfare work. As we will learn in the chapters to come, this is not unrelated to the analysis. However, we should not forget that workers with similar levels of experience were encountered in discussion of administrative learning as well. Indeed, younger and less experienced workers also appear as indicative illustrations from the data in both this and the prior chapter. As we will see in Chapter 10, taken separately, neither age, work experience, race, disability, union participation, nor education levels nor a host of other demographic factors adequately explains the dynamics we are seeing. Nevertheless, the Case Manager in the following excerpt is also a veteran (seventeen-year welfare work experience). She describes herself as white and disabled, is moderately active in her local union, and has a bachelor's degree in sociology and psychology. Her account allows us to discern in a particularly clear way the nature of the structure, object-relatedness, and mode of participation in this type of trajectory of craft knowledge production. In it we see a series of culminating references to a great many observations already offered in the book to this point.

S: For instance if their circumstances change, they move to a new address, or they are in jail, or an institution which effects their eligibility, you've got to work hard to try to set them up with housing. It happens all the time. For instance today, it was actually not my case, but somebody else's, we had a client that had been staying at the shelter, but she and I together we made a few phone calls. Over the years you make connections with different landlords, right? With the SDMT system you can't produce a cheque immediately. It's an overnight process. So, I made arrangements with the landlord for him to stay the night, and he could pick up the cheque tomorrow to pay the rent, and based on my word the landlord let him in with no money. So you kind of *develop your own style, and your own method of case management.* But SDMT has certainly made this type of thing more difficult to do. As I said, I have been around for a while and have experienced a lot of changes over the years. *We used to do our job primarily by going out to the client's home.* We would see the client, take the application, come in, deal with the info. We would hand it to a clerk. The clerk would input the details. We would make our decisions, issue the cheque, do a follow up contact with the client, and regular updates in that manner. *Now, 95% of the clients come into the office.* We have *little cubicles, where we're all blocked together, which makes the privacy aspect very difficult.* But the client comes in, they bring in the docs, we input the info directly ourselves, through SDMT, and do the necessary paperwork. Just to go back a bit. That's basically what my job is now; today as a case manager. Prior to coming to this job, I'm actually from another province, I spent five and half years working as an officer with adult correctional services, and previous to that, I did my university and a year for my thesis. I have an honours degree in Sociology and Psychology and no [laughing], this wasn't the line of work I had in mind, but I was a single parent when I went to university, and due to the circumstances I felt that I needed some time off. This job came along, then the house mortgage, and so on. And I feel like *I actually made the job into something I like.* Because with many problems that we have with the computer systems, with the clients, with whatever, if you don't like your job, or you're not in it because you want to help people, you're going to find it very unsatisfying. And for me, being able to do something for that one or two people, I mean you're going to be burned sometimes, but not as often as that and anyways its actually not you that gets burned but the system. But if it's one person, that you help, *that gives the intrinsic value.*

I: And so you're motivated by the human component? Doing the work for its own purpose?

S: Well, yeah. That's why I'm still at the city in this job. And also one of the reasons I returned to case management. I still do SIR [System Investigation Report] case management during back up or absences. The reason I gave that job up is that it was always hard luck cases, always problems. I just felt that it's easier to deal with regular case load, and you can accomplish much more. *I sometimes think of it as a contribution to the city* in a way. With the new work changes, their dividing up of the tasks, I had the chance to choose, and I chose to continue with case management because I feel that it gives you *more hands on contact with your client.* If you take it, like lots of people don't, you get a chance at least to know them, and it's not just a matter of inputting info into the system. (HCWAT0303, Case Manager)

The biographical client-person is made central to this worker's practices. The mention of privacy issues implicitly supports the notion that her daily work involves matters that *are* private and unique to the client. On this point, the structures of activity seen in the prior chapter are made all the more distinct in comparison. There, client privacy never was seen as a mediating issue in this way. Moreover, in this chapter we see a substantial set of state welfare workers in this research who described their interests in terms of what we might call (and what they often called as well) a tradition of "social work". Just how large or small this set of workers may be will be explored in Chapter 10, but the importance of mediations associated with this type of social work ideal is just one of the many reasons we took the time to explore the relationship between state welfare work and social work earlier in the book. For now, we can note that this excerpt provides a text-book example of the notion of social work ideals in her concluding thoughts. I argue, however, that these comments offer an illustration of, and depend in the first instance upon, a particularly clear realization of object-work/skill and successful re-keying of labour process activity. Furthermore, it is crucial to also recognize that the contradictions rooted in relations between operations and goal – those stemming from ongoing problems in operations and the attempt both to repair them and to repair the relations between meaning and personal sense of work in terms of administrative object-relatedness – are yet again almost entirely marginalized. That is, the account provides evidence that they are made marginal in the course of learning within a particular trajectory of occupational development within activity. She is not following a standardized case management path as defined in the new labour process. There is a flat rejection of concern for the fact that the type of performance she undertakes will likely work against her in the context of administrative accountability and career progression. She undertakes several of the definitive tasks of her work collectively with another like-minded welfare worker, and her learning trajectory incorporates an expansive, established network of contacts in the community whose help she secures by giving her word.

Despite its prominence at this point, my concern in this analysis is not for professional/occupational (or personal) ethics as such. They cannot be ignored, but ethics and the types of moral injunctions implicated in what we have seen across Chapters 7 and 8 have proven rather flexible and, I argue, fully dependent on a range of other dynamics. Rather, I speak of these dynamics primarily as relations of legitimacy and increasingly (going forward) as the dynamics of use-value within activity. In these terms, the focus is on what warranted claims can be made in terms of the structure of activity giving rise to a particular trajectory of occupational learning. Here the evidence suggests an example, within the cluster of examples of analysis in this section, of a not-to-be-dismissed mediational achievement of activity, learning, knowledge, and expertise. The worker in this final excerpt explicitly speaks of the intrinsic use-value of this work despite recognizing the systemic challenges she faces. Essential to her learning is the legitimization of a trajectory of occupational development. She is explicitly asked about whether or not she feels doing the work is of value in itself. Beneath her positive response, unfolded and developed through the course of re-keying of activity, is the social and material realization of specific interests in an effortful building of a structure of attention (and dis-attention) that shapes her investment of time and energy.

Conclusions

This chapter is closely linked to the prior chapter as a parallel, comparative analysis of a type, and in both we see that workers were not simply describing their practices but the dynamics of change in their practices. In the prior chapter, I described administrative state welfare work object-relatedness that involved a type of the secondary processing (Knorr Cetina 1999) through which, in a complex series of emotional, cognitive and socio-material adaptations and transformations, workers learned to construct biographical client-people as client files, cases, and eventually aggregated caseloads/commodities. In turn, as caseloads, state welfare work was managed, afforded, mediated, and developed in terms of a distinct trajectory of more advanced skill, knowledge, expertise and judgment. Central to the analysis in Chapter 7 was the notion that some dimensions of contradiction in activity were clearly marginalized while others were made more central. Retreating to ever smaller spheres of engagement, in essence, increased one's capacity to exercise individuated forms of agency within a specific trajectory of administrative learning. In Chapter 7, we heard echoes of Burawoy (1979) but also learned a good deal more about how the dynamics he addressed can be linked to the construction of the machineries of knowledge construction. In the current chapter, we have turned our attention to a very different mode of participation in activity. We found how, in Knorr Cetina's terms, the *bringing home of a phenomenon* for processing – and one's engrossment in it – is something that some workers *attempt* to resist and others *do* resist effectively such that Stetsenko's (2010) concept of "collaborative transformative practice" is easily discerned. Among other things, the biographical client-person is allowed to retain prominence. In both instances the same recognizable melody of state welfare work is played, but in a different key. The cogs of the machineries of occupational knowledge construction could be made to turn in a different direction.

Beyond the specific, agentive dynamics of participation in labour process activity I have analyzed here, what is particularly significant to defining administrative re-skilling or craft up-skilling is the individual and collective generation of distinctive relations among operations, goals, and object/motives in terms of systemic contradictions. Administrative *re-skilling* centres one's energies – and specifically one's capacities for repair-work/skill and sense-repair-work/skill – predominantly on contradictions linked to the *relation between operations and goals* within labour process activity. In contrast, as the focus of this chapter, *up-skilling* involves the centring of workers' energies – their effortful and expansive sense-repair-work/skill and object-work/skill – on contradictions across the *relations among operation, goal, and object/motive* more broadly. As we have just seen, involved in these practices are occupational artefact creation and the transformation of occupational artefacts. This includes the production of specific forms of self-talk mantras that, when subject to forms of collective internalization/externalization, can be converted to specific types of we-talk mantras that lead to expansive, collective outcomes of knowledge building. Indeed, it is worth repeating the point that there were, necessarily, collective dimensions of administrative trajectories of learning seen in the prior chapter, and certainly the use of the word "we" is hardly the sole domain of the workers we see in this chapter. However, in Chapter 7 the uses of "we" (e.g., pp. 181-82) disproportionately were linked to administrative workarounds. What is definitive in understanding the differences are the specific forms of indexicality involved: not simply the places it appears in their accounts, but in turn the way the we-talk is embedded in activity, the function it serves for these workers, the sequences of practice, the when, where and how it is activated in their occupational learning lives, and so on. Among all the differences we must note that allow us to speak confidently about the nature of learning, skill and knowledge construction, we can see that the we-talk mantras/artefacts in this chapter have a very different means-end relationship. Their relationships with core (as opposed to peripheral) dimensions of contradiction suggest that the *we* used by workers in this chapter is a *we* that leads to a much broader *we*. It is a *we*, in other words, that includes client-people and the labour process more broadly, and, potentially, the dynamics of community, economies, and societies as well.

This analysis is far from the first to observe that the definition of up-skilling need not rely on (as it still too often does in the literature) judgments linked to the supply, demand and value on a labour market, and/or the normative valuing of one set of skills and knowledge over another. This analysis sought to begin with the practices of skill and knowledge construction in relation to the dynamics of the labour process itself. Specifically, I look to the structure of activity and its realization, in diverse ways, through the situated practices of learners themselves. In this context, up-skilling refers to a distinctive mode of participation in activity within which the trajectory of occupational learning is consolidating and broadening *rather than* becoming fixated (or engrossed) in mere fractions of activity as a whole. I maintain that up-skilling is an accomplishment that marks the transition to the specific skills, knowledge, and expertise involved in the openness, ambiguity, and expansiveness of *object-work*. In contrast, re-skilling describes a narrowing of the field of engagement in activity through which a worker may establish or enhance a personal sense of individuated control and agency only. It is a point that Leontiev (1978) elaborated upon in terms of the unique capacities realized through an awareness of one's embeddedness in the broader relations of activity, and indeed society.

V. I. Lenin wrote about what distinguishes "simply a slave" from a slave who is reconciled to his position and from a slave who has rebelled. This difference lies not in knowing one's own individual traits but in perceiving oneself in a system of social

> relations.… It is only necessary to emphasize here that inclusion in the system does
> not at all mean being dissolved in it but, on the contrary, means finding and disclos-
> ing in it the force of one's action. (Leontiev 1978, p. 139)

As will be addressed in the closing chapter, in this context I am speaking increasingly of a recognition of embeddedness in a much broader system of social relations that allows the "finding and disclosing in it the force of one's action". I argue this is defined by attempts at the resolution of dimensions of contradiction revolving around the struggle to legitimize use-value in activity: that is, the use-value not simply of one's own life as a state welfare worker, but the use-value of living, breathing, biographical client-persons, the community being served, the type of political economy we might yet realize, and so on. In this regard, I am not talking about the realization of individuated autonomy in a successively reduced scope of participation as was described in Chapter 7, but practice oriented to ever more elaborated and wider circles of intervention. These wider circles of intervention are defined by trajectories that cannot be understood in isolation from the premises of de-skilling, and they subsume forms of re-skilling. I argue these are trajectories of occupational learning and practice within activity that are referenced clearly in many of the most realized forms of what I have been calling state welfare worker craft knowledge production in this chapter.

These comments lead me to one final point. In moving forward, despite intermittent efforts in the text, the way I have organized the analysis might invite a certain mistake in interpretation. The mistake would be that there exists several entirely separate worlds of state welfare work in this research. This is only half true. In the context of the seven years of data gathering (which was also the first seven years of this organizational change initiative), what we see is that the different modes of participation in activity are *still* more *nascent* rather than they are *mature*. In this research, at this point, individual workers can occupy, move across, and even straddle different trajectories of occupational learning. For the majority, the transition to a coherent, stable trajectory of learning (of any kind) remains tenuous. In the face of a radical change, workers quite literally changed, and many turned around and changed again. They changed the way they worked, and hence the type of worker that they were. It is likely a type of academic conceit to think it would be any other way. Notwithstanding, my point remains that the limitations (that is, the plasticity of human beings) do not prevent us entertaining the claim that these multiple trajectories *do* speak to, and allow us to understand better, a vital dynamic: how these specific changes in the labour process have occasioned a struggle for the meaning and soul (or, what Erving Goffman would have referred to as the "cosmology") of an occupation.

9 Divisions of Knowledge Production, Group Formation, and Occupational Enculturation

Introduction

In exploring the construction of the machineries of occupational knowledge construction I have referenced general background characteristics of state welfare workers, but only intermittently have I woven points of discussion relating to these characteristics into analysis. I have done this primarily in order to facilitate interpretations of the survey data in Chapter 10 (allowing easier linkage to the qualitative analysis that precedes it). However, in this and the following chapter, I focus in greater detail on these and how they affect and are affected by emerging trajectories of learning in activity. Throughout much of this chapter, I specifically deal with the dynamics of an occupation in transition in terms of the experiences of veterans and newcomers.

On the surface, there is a somewhat familiar story of generational cohorts in this chapter. But it is a story that in the end is about the mutual and interactive formation of cohort differences in the course of participation in activity, and not simply about the characteristics of the cohorts themselves. We see that many veteran state welfare workers (those who began in the mid-1970s through to the early 1990s: cf. Figure 4.1) struggle to reconcile the types of organizational and personal occupational transitions now shaping their work life. This is hardly unexpected. However, as we will see, it is a situation in which extensive occupational knowledge of the past can be made both a burden as well as a resource for dealing with the present and future. The past produces particular difficulties as well as potentiality in the learning lives of veteran state welfare workers, and the dynamics of activity that help explain how and why this is so come clearly into view when we pay careful attention to their accounts. They are a cohort that entered the occupation in an era in which home visits, life on the road, relative autonomy, and particular forms of collegial relations in the offices produced a much more coherent sense of work activity. This was an era in which work was managed by more experienced welfare benefits social workers, primarily men, who were promoted into supervisory roles, but who could speak at the very least from direct (albeit gendered) experience of the same labour process that they managed. According to workers we hear from in this chapter, it was an era in which job-shadowing and close senior-novice apprenticeship models of occupational enculturation were wide-spread organizational practices. Between the 1970s and early 1990s most of the classic features of a bureau-professional regime were prominent. Particularly important for us here, this was an era that included a key period in which formal entry requirements for the job referenced social work or social service education explicitly. For many workers, as we will see, this held great significance (even if it was unevenly applied). Not surprisingly, at this time a concern for computer literacy was first absent and then simply peripheral to occupational entry.

For their own part, the newcomer cohort – lacking the lived experience of the prior eras of state welfare work – carried far fewer of the burdens (and resources) of institutional memory, skill, and knowledge. Often less secure in both their employment and their identities as state welfare workers, *younger* newcomers specifically also had the added trepidation tied to their life-stage (e.g. establishing a home, raising a young family, as well as establishing a new career with little union seniority). With their more limited access to the resources of comparison and with preoccupations that increased a sense of insecurity, we see how in some instances being a newcomer offered distinctive supports for embracing the new labour process and technology in terms of trajectories of administrative learning in activity. Still, newcomers were hardly alone in doing this. Many veteran workers also continued or came to embrace such trajectories, and as we have seen newcomers could be found among those examples of workers who struggled to engage in forms of state welfare craft learning as well.

The central point in this chapter, however, is that the veteran cohorts we see here are not only products of past labour processes with immutable occupational identities. Newcomer cohorts (old and young) are not simply the products of the unique challenges they face revolving around lack of experience, labour market insecurity, and so on. Rather, both cohorts, and with them the evolving character of the occupation and occupational knowledge, continue to be defined and re-defined by the ongoing relational dynamics *between* cohorts. Linked to this, in chapters 9 and 10 I confirm the distinction between the technical and social divisions of labour of Taylorized welfare work. Tasks can be divided technically in this way or that, but the new roles created still have to be populated with certain types of people and where there is some systematic pattern in how this is done, as in this case, we can see the effects of a social division of labour as well. The dynamics of learning and development in activity are related to both of these dimensions of the division of labour. In the analysis here, I explore how certain aspects of the social divisions of labour produce important social divisions of knowledge production as well.

Patterns of entry into the occupations of state welfare work are an important initial point of departure for an investigation of the social division of labour/knowledge production, as well as dynamics between cohorts. However, the construction of *beliefs* about occupational entry among workers (accurate or inaccurate) may be particularly important in the case of this research. That is, beyond changes in qualifications and the formal occupational entry process, we find a series of additional processes of meaning and sense-making within labour process activity itself that are equally important. Formal policies and rules, informal practices, and conventions (in particular those shaping the formation of work groups) also play a vital role in understanding the hidden relations of the social divisions of labour/knowledge production. I demonstrate that under conditions of labour process change the (real and imagined) shift in entry level requirements affects how workers actively construct, mediate, and initiate occupational learning trajectories. In this chapter it will become increasingly relevant to note in this context how integration of newcomer and veteran cohorts – and with it *inter-generational occupational enculturation* – is now far more problematic. The organizationally supported forms of occupational apprenticeship, job-shadowing, and collegial office culture that were mixed with welfare work life in the different pre-SDMT eras are gone, and new relations are being negotiated, made-up on the spot, managed, and co-produced. As we will see, the increased homogeneity of work groups in terms of occupational experience (i.e. newcomers grouped with newcomers, veterans grouped with veterans) has become an important emerging property of activity and, I claim, the machineries of knowledge construction. In these terms, a still-too-often-ignored under-belly of occupational learning continues to involve the complex dynamics participatory of *membership* (e.g., Lave and Wenger 1991; Orr 1996; Sawchuk 2003a). I argue this too speaks to an overall pattern of emerging isolation of newcomers from veterans (and vice versa) which, in turn, plays an important role in shaping the struggle over the nature of the occupation going forward.

I begin this chapter with a brief recovery of the relevant literature on learning, work, labour markets, and careers. I show that there remains a gap in considerations of the dynamics raised across the book as a whole regarding complexity, diversity, as well as divergence in occupational life vis-à-vis modes of career entry and progression. I indicate that only a relatively small cluster of studies have meaningfully registered these dynamics in robust, empirically informed ways, that relate to skill, knowledge and occupational learning in the labour process. Following this, in Part 1 of the chapter, I turn our attention to the state welfare worker interview data revolving around themes of beliefs about cohort differences and group formation practices. In Part 2, I explore related findings from the welfare worker survey (for a description of this survey see Chapter 1). Here we see the effects of prior education and computer literacy as well as orientations to training, informal on-the-job learning, and practices of co-worker helping. In this way, we see how differences in these areas likely have a strong effect on workers' views of the current labour process in the aggregate.

Implications of Occupational Entry Processes, Labour Markets, and Careers

Contemporary mainstream labour market theory has often oriented to occupational entry by arguing that narrow, occupationally specific knowledge and skill sets have become less important. Replacing them, it is argued, are abilities related to critical evaluation, conflict resolution, flexibility, and team-work. These concerns reflect those taken up by what has been called the *new vocationalism* perspective. Analyzed, debated, re-made over the last two decades, it is a perspective that remains a powerful theme in the research on relations among labour markets, education, vocational training, and skill analysis to this day (cf. Symes and McIntyre 2000; Rojewski 2002). At the core of this perspective are the largely unquestioned needs of capital and the meeting of these needs through the individual development of *human capital* (cf. Livingstone 2004). This perspective has as its intellectual roots the post-industrialism thesis that was discussed earlier and in which we find the consistent presumption of the need for increasingly high levels of formal, post-secondary education for occupational and life course success. Similar presumptions have come to embrace a concern for on-the-job and informal learning as well. It is predominantly from this vantage point that changing skill requirements in the workplace caused by new technologies and advanced labour processes are said to more and more require effective symbolic analysts, knowledge workers, or members of the creative class in some way (e.g., Zuboff 1988; Reich 1991; Frenkel, Korczynski, Shire, and Tam 1999; Florida 2002). The contradictions that underlie many aspects of the post-industrial thesis, human capital theory, and new vocationalism are, according to the argument in this book, largely shared. However, as Lehmann and Taylor (2003), among others (e.g., Kincheloe 1999; Lehmann 2000; Livingstone 2004; Livingstone and Sawchuk 2004), have pointed out:

> The reality behind this rhetoric, however, reveals a couple of problems. First, while such a knowledge worker would be characterised by initiative, flexibility and the ability and courage to question the status quo, most vocational education, according to Kincheloe (1999), is still designed to 'instil compliance and facilitate social control' (p. 148). Second, the majority of workplaces continues to be organized around Taylorist principles of control, or are engaged in various forms of re-Taylorisation in response to market deregulation (Bosch, 2000). Therefore, the extent to which [...] new-found skills are likely to be actually utilised in the workplace is questionable. (p. 63)

This last point is one well worth considering. When we do, however, we find in this study of the lives of state welfare workers that, in distinct ways, new found skills and knowledge *are* being generated even while the questions about autonomy and control continue unabated, and the exact nature of these skills must be explored more deeply. Furthermore, in this research many workers (old and young, newcomer and veteran) *do* question the status quo. Here, however, what we also see is that this questioning is regularly subject to channelling and engrossment in ways that both discipline and reward. And moreover, we also see clearly that critique of one's work does not necessarily mean differences in terms of concrete practices. Thus, the accuracy of new vocationalism perspectives suggesting the legitimacy and importance of new knowledge work skills that are replacing older, more specialized ones becomes opened for inquiry, while the standing critique of this new vocationalism perspective can benefit from additional clarification.

Amid the ambiguities I note here, there are in fact a variety of other questions that the post-industrial, human capital, and now the new vocationalism perspectives do not seem to answer as well. In the case of the introduction of an advanced, web-based computer system (such as SDMT) which is still too often treated as the sine qua non of the knowledge economy we need to ask the following. How and under what conditions of work activity itself do either generalized or specialized knowledge forms of an occupation become applied, developed, or changed? What explains the fact that a relatively sophisticated form of human services work, like state welfare benefits delivery, has actually appeared to have lowered its formal educational entry requirements? Why do state welfare workers, as we saw earlier in the book, suggest their job is becoming de-skilled, even while they learn a vast array of new skills?

The theories of post-industrialism, human capital and new vocationalism are not the only ones that have some bearing on the answers to these types of questions. There are also approaches that focus on career theory and career transitions specifically. And thus to understand better the relevance of the dialogic approach that I apply in this book it is important to note that career theory has been a staple in Human Resource Development and Organizational Behaviour literature going back at least fifty years. Wilensky (1961, 1964) summarized the state of the art at that time as being rooted deeply in the economic optimism, cooperation, and highly bureaucratized organizational conditions that characterize so much of the first quarter-century following World War II in the West. Since Wilensky, though not without significant exceptions, it is still arguable that the field has tended to become increasingly organized by the mating of traditional cognitive psychology and rational choice theory on the one hand, with mainstream studies of management and organizational development on the other. In this context, a review of contributions to the several handbook-style collections in the area over the last two decades (e.g., Arthur, Hall, and Lawrence 1989; Kummerow 2000; Feldman 2002) confirms that, since Wilensky's analysis a variety of changes have emerged. We can note, for example, a general split between more optimistic visions oriented by what are called boundary-less careers and occupations unencumbered by restrictive bureaucracy (e.g., Arthur and Rousseau, 1996), on the one hand, and those seeking to recognize many of the negative changes in career patterns based on the degradation of occupational laddering (e.g., Osterman 1996), on the other. Recent developments in the literature, however, seem to indicate that the nature of organizational change itself may be particularly central to how people construct and understand their occupations and careers, and in a recent, extended review of the career theory literature Baruch (2006) outlines the impact of relations of individual responses and organizational contexts.

Among the changes that have shaped contemporary career systems are developments in the social and economical realms, as well as in individual identities. Global *macro-economic and social forces* provided impetus for a growing number of global careers, for introduction of females and minorities to the full range of roles (albeit discrimination still clearly prevails), for major *restructuring of organizations, and generally a less stable business environment*. At the micro-level, they are coupled by a development in *norms, values and attitudes to life and work*, which are manifested in new behaviours of individuals.... On the one hand, the career is the *'property' of the individual*, who may be inspired by new social norms, but on the other hand, for employed people, it is *planned and managed to a large extent by their organizations*. (p. 126; emphasis added)

This is far from unhelpful, and the bulk of Baruch's review, like several of the contributions to the Symes and McIntyre (2000) collection, goes on to challenge dichotomies that characterize the field of career studies as a whole: organizational order versus chaos, boundary-less versus traditionally structured careers, organizational versus individual origins of development, and, so on. Indeed, there is a strong argument concerning why it is important to challenge any dichotomous lines between such issues. However, what may be most relevant to us here is Baruch's discussion of the linkages between macro-economics and socio-political change. In it he suggests the role of restructuring, as well as the inherent relations between *individual careers and their management vis-à-vis the inner workings of organizational life* may be crucial. While analyses emerging from either the new vocationalism perspective or career theory will need to further grapple with the processes through which organizational change shapes the reconstruction and potential divergence of occupational learning and careers within the labour process, their identification of relevant questions provides us with a partial starting point for analysis.

Part 1: Worker Beliefs and the Practices of Division across Veterans and Newcomers

I begin the analysis in Part 1 at the point of occupational entry of state welfare work. As we saw earlier in the book, there is information that may be cobbled together regarding the history of charity work, professionalization, radicalization, welfare policy, shifts in labour process, and other issues shaping the nature of the state welfare work occupation today. However, research on changing qualifications, entry requirements, and labour market conditions for state welfare work is simply not available in the existing literature.

In order to move forward in this context, we can recall that in Chapter 4 of the book I also established the character of important shifts in inter-governmental relations and responsibilities for welfare services in Canada. Among other things, these are shifts that defined who made and now makes decisions about qualifications and requirements, and, in turn, the labour market conditions related to these decisions. The formal separation between the occupations of state welfare work and social work that I likewise noted have in fact contributed to these shifting dynamics as well. Here I argue, however, that these shifts have important implications for occupational enculturation, skill and knowledge development over time. We can recall from Chapter 4 that, for example, the administrative and financial control of welfare services during the Canada Assistance Plan (CAP) era (1966–73) helped initiate a particular occupational trend in state welfare work, in part related to the powers of federal guidelines. Moreover, we also learned that the push for professionalization was a powerful force in social work leading through to this period, and, for a significant time, it reverberated through to state welfare work despite the loose ties. Here we might add that general labour market conditions in Canada likely also played a role in shaping these changes. The increase in credentialization in state welfare work was also likely influenced by the rapidly increasing levels of educational attainment in the country generally (Livingstone 2004).

Thus, in Ontario from the late 1970s through to the first half of 1990s the formal requirements for entry into state welfare work, by a combination of forces, tended to grow. Further supporting (and complicating) this, again as we saw in Chapter 4, the Ontario's General Welfare Assistance Act had been amended placing municipalities in charge of administration services. It was in this context that the basic forms of "social work ideals" (for a time referencing social work qualifications explicitly), built up historically, took on a more elaborated and more codified character in state welfare work. Linked to these changes, a particular type of autonomous occupational culture emerged, supported by the expansive processes of informal relations of learning as well as in-house training referenced at the outset of this chapter. These supports included not only monitored probationary periods, but organized mentoring, job shadowing, and, in many (though not all) cases, developmental testing in the first year of employment. Due to de-centralized administrative control, local practices varied. However, a distinct, effective, and comparatively intense, formal and informal, as well as more professionalized enculturation process became established over this roughly twenty year period.

Accounts provided in this research suggest that these trends orienting toward formal qualification began to slow significantly in the 1990s, and it was at this time that a decline in emphasis on social science and particularly social service related (college-based) and social work (university-based) credentials likely began. However, far less gradual changes then emerged, associated with the implementation of the new SDMT labour process in 2002. A distinct and much more uniform shift in *formal* occupational quali-fication was quickly set in place, and accompanying it new dynamics of enculturation rooted in labour process design, as we will see here, were set in motion. While aspects of municipal administrative control still accounted for some persistent differences across clusters of offices and regions in this research, in the first phase of implementation the new labour process, formal entry qualifications immediately became more generalized. The *formal* emphasis on related social services experience, social work and social work related educational requirements was supplanted. Computer literacy and data processing experience grew in importance.

As we will see going forward, the formal changes in entry requirements have had effects that were not so much direct as they were mediated by a variety of practices and dynamics in labour process activity itself. Even so, by the conclusion of this research in 2009, we see that for newcomers successful transition into the occupation (often, but not at all exclusively, beginning in the Case Manager job category) had been facilitated by computer literacy and data processing skills significantly. The accounts provided by both key informants and rank-and-file interviewees (as well as findings from the survey administered in this research) on the basic shifts in occupational culture substantiate the changes quite clearly.

Worker Perspectives on the Changes to Initial Qualification: Beliefs-in-Action

Most workers interviewed in this research spoke at some length about changes in entry requirements over the years. Even most newcomers, while not having experienced the changes directly, expressed a clear awareness of them. The following excerpt, however, is provided by an eighteen year veteran of welfare work. In the course of addressing the topic of entry level requirements the excerpt links together a range of research themes seen already in the book. Moreover, there is reference to discussions and information sharing through participation in local union activity, an important theme that will be considered again as we proceed toward the concluding chapter.

S: I've been in social services since 1985. It was my beginning. I was a Case Worker until 1996. From there I was what we called an Overpayment Recovery Officer, from there I was an Employment Services Worker, as well as I have done most other positions for short periods of time.

I: So you've been involved in welfare services for a pretty long time then eh?

S: I would say I'm well-rounded.

I: Okay, now the formal qualifications required for this specific job, that's both your paper qualifications and practical qualifications, what are they?

S: Well, the paper qualification when I started was a BA in either the social sciences, social work or psychology. Social Work was considered very highly but for me, I only have a BA in sociology. Secondly, the requirements, I have augmented myself. I took computer courses at the community college to learn how to use a computer because back when I started none of us were using computers. So we really did not have those skills then. So, I have taken a number of computer courses. Also, in this particular position, I had to understand all the regulations and the Act in order to do this particular position that I'm in. I obviously have to know all the basics like Microsoft Word. I use Excel a lot. I like using spreadsheets. I have taken a course in Access though we don't have that here. So these are the qualifications. And as well as it was standard in my day that you had to have a driver's license because we used to do home visits, but we do not do them now, not on any regular basis.

I: Okay. And let me just ask you, you said when you started you required a BA. Are those qualifications the same now?

S: Well, that's the thing. There is a debate at present time within the union structure that we've noticed that the qualifications have been removed by management. We believe this is an effort to downgrade the position to more of a clerical function than it was previously, okay? In my day it was a bit different. I was a Case Worker, I was on the road, I controlled things, I had my own district, a geographical area that I was the Case Worker to. That does not happen anymore.

I: Okay. What are the formal qualifications now, if not a BA today?

S: You know what? In the last posting, there weren't any. I did not notice any formal qualifications at all, to be truthful with you. So I don't know what that actually means. (HJMAT0903, Eligibility Review Officer)

We find in this excerpt a concrete introduction to the focus of the analysis, and, in terms of these data generally it offers an indicative description of veteran workers' experiences and perceptions. It provides a grounded example of the computer literacy learning process, the type of broad experiential base that many of the veteran workers have developed by working in different types of jobs across different welfare labour processes and technologies. It references the former qualifications, including those in social work education. It concludes with concerns over the present direction in entry level requirements. Among veteran workers such as this one, it was commonly understood that qualifications had been lowered. Examining accounts across the interview data, the source of their information was most often other workers, or their own glances at the description provided in current job postings.

In fact, the interview schedule used in this research asked specifically about issues of qualification past and present. Other veteran workers such as the one who follows (eleven years experience; high level of union participation) contextualized the changes in entry requirements in greater detail.

I: Okay. When you first applied, what were the formal qualifications that they asked for?

S: You had to have a college or university degree or diploma. Preferably in college they would accept *a Social Service Worker Diploma; otherwise it had to be a university degree in Social Work.* That was, I think, the primary one, preferably a background in social services, training in the types of social issues we deal with and interpersonal skills.... They've since changed the qualifications and that's what they emphasize more.

I: They emphasize the interpersonal?

S: *Well I mean more the administrative, interpersonal things, getting along with people at work, and certainly technical things....* [In terms of my own background] other than the fact that I was pretty comfortable using a computer, I had taken key – about that time it was called "Typing" in high school, that kind of thing. That definitely was a benefit when the changes came in. And the fact that I was fairly comfortable with computers, they didn't scare me. And I had a computer at home. So I was able – even, like, there were some people who had never literally never touched a mouse before SDMT. So the fact that I knew my way around a computer and was comfortable, that was probably one of the biggest things, and the fact that I had really good interviewing skills. It wasn't like I had to learn, like, *in the case of the new people,* they're learning how to interview, especially because they've changed the requirements. They have people who are, like right now, clerks becoming workers. *They don't have the background* necessarily in interviewing, and in case work and in all that kind of – in case fields and writing up summaries and that kind of thing that I did. *So you see, I have a BSW [Bachelors of Social Work]. So I had a lot of that training that was pretty intense. It was just the technology that I had to learn versus the job [...] But right now, like I said, mostly it's feeding the information into the computer. I have a Social Work degree but I don't need social work to be doing overpayment work, right?* So even as a Case Manager, all of these people – and *you can see it in the notes [i.e., the SDMT Notes function] of the newer workers* – it's putting the information on the computer, clients say they haven't worked in eight years. That's it. That's all you see. (HMLAT0303, Eligibility Review Worker)

It is of course somewhat ironic, given the concerns about performance monitoring and managerial surveillance, that some of the most important information that this worker has used to form her view of newcomers is found through her access to their work through the *Notes* function of SDMT. But further confirming discussions earlier in the book, she makes it clear that she feels that she herself is no longer doing a form of state welfare *social work*.

While the worker in the preceding excerpt does not seem particularly aggrieved, in fact, a majority of the veteran workers interviewed did express feelings of deeper frustration, and sometimes anger, linked to their perception of changes in entry requirements. The workers in the next two excerpts, for example (both with thirteen years seniority and post-secondary credentials in social work but varying levels of union participation), commented as follows:

> *The qualification of our job description, it is now I guess grade 12 minimum, I'm very angry about that.* People in the office, they've gone through college and university courses and they've had to take out OSAP loans because it was a requirement and I myself just think that you really need some sort of professional training in order to do the job properly. What's been happening is *they've been taking clerical staff and making them into workers and I'm very angry about that.* (HIMAT0404, CVP Worker)

> I: So these practical skills, is it fair to say they stressed more of a social work type of thing more than technical skills back when you started?
>
> S: Oh absolutely right it is, yes, because you would be going out and seeing [clients] and they would be in crisis or whatever. *This is more data entry. Just the facts you know. I mean though that really pisses me off.*
>
> I: They stress those types of things more now when they hire people, than the social work?
>
> S: For sure! Most of them *just have the computer skills!* I mean that was just never asked when we started…. Now, *I just don't know where the future is going.* (HKMAT0404, Employment Services Worker)

The bases for a divide between veteran workers and newcomers is implied. Labour process change including a new technological system is perceived by veteran workers to have facilitated a re-structuring of entry level requirements in the pursuit of a new type of state welfare work. Formally, entry level requirements have been changed considerably. The job postings that were viewed by researchers in the course of carrying out this study, for example, did indeed exclude a listing of the types of qualifications that veteran workers referenced, replacing them with computer-related requirements. However, even the apparent facts do not tell the whole story.

Labour process and technological change have continued to shape entry requirements over the course of several cohorts of state welfare workers, but it would be a mistake to draw any rigid lines across several decades in these terms. Moreover, the interaction between workers who entered under different requirements, labour processes, and practices of enculturation has produced a host of other mediating effects as well. Building on the types of insights found in prior chapters, the issue of entry requirements is only one piece of the puzzle explaining how distinctive and divergent forms of occupational development emerge. In principle, given the transformation of the entire labour process for all workers, newcomers and veterans might be expected to be on somewhat more equal footing. What we see, however, is something quite different: there is a differentiation that revolves around specific management practices *as well as* informal patterns of coping amongst workers in the course of group formation within the labour process activity.

Group Formation and Its Role in Divergent Knowledge Production

What has become clearer in this research is that in the face of the efforts to Taylorize the labour process of state welfare work, a new workaround culture has necessarily emerged. The new technical division of labour has produced a range of different types of jobs, whereas before the vast bulk of the state welfare workers carried out essentially the same tasks. Likewise, gone are virtually all of the types of organizationally supported forms of enculturation associated with prior eras. Formal training has not filled the gap well, and for a significant proportion of workers, not at all. In this situation, forms of on-the-job, informal learning in activity become particularly important to the dynamics of trajectories of occupational knowledge development, and what we hear from veterans and newcomers on this topic is quite distinctive. Earlier I raised the matter of the relationship between not simply the technical and social division of labour, but divisions of knowledge production as well. Here we see the emerging social division of labour *and* an unfolding division of knowledge production. By and large, the latter is an unintended consequence rooted in overlapping, and sometimes conflicting, inter-worker relations within activity. The origins of the dynamic cannot be laid at the feet of the formal labour process design alone. Central to understanding this are a series of combined effects. These include the way the change in the labour process encouraged a workaround culture, a culture of expanded on-the-job group learning-in-doing, and specifically the development of networks for occupational development that repeatedly activated particular zones of proximal development in activity. Workers with nineteen and eleven years of experience in their positions (with similar levels of union participation and reporting no disability, but self-identifying as white and Aboriginal) respectively, explain it this way.

> I can see a lot of *the informal like water cooler talking*, and you know it happens like if I had a case, for example, and I don't know how to do something I would ask somebody: 'Have you ever had this before?' And they'd say: 'Oh yes, this is

> what I did'. I've learned a lot more short cuts, so here I am doing it the long way all this time and then *somebody just happens to see me and says*, 'What are you doing it that way for? Just press this button'. I've had a lot of those. (SC01DB0303, Employment Services Worker)
>
> *Between each other*, we in our office, we have a *buddy system* where we kind of cover for each other and take care of each other quite often. Like in my *little group* there are four of us and we work really well together because we're in our own little huddle over there. (NF17DB0304, Case Manager)

Scratching beneath the surface of group formation provided in these accounts, in the following excerpt we can begin to see several sources of the unintended results of new social divisions of labour/knowledge production. In the first instance, unsurprisingly, these sources are linked to the new technical division of labour as well as work intensification. However, as we see in greater detail later on in the chapter, these job categories tend to be related to levels of experience and seniority in the local bargaining unit as well. For now the point is that there is a relatively pronounced clustering of workers together in terms of job categories. This veteran worker (Eastern European, medium union participation and reporting no disability) explains:

> We've had such a dividing up of work that now *one area believes that they're being put upon more than other areas* so, 'Oh yeah well I'm in this department and I have to do this, this and this. We have it so bad.' *Before, everybody was doing the same job. We were all Case Workers.* We all dealt with the employment, we all dealt with yearly updates, everybody was doing the same job, and so like somebody said and if you were having a bad day or whatever, you could say them, 'You know what, my bad day was last week so I could help you today'. Now it's much harder to do that. People have different jobs and only a small number of us have experience in it all. *People hive off.* And, it's also just hard to help anybody when *you're swamped, so sometimes you have to be selective.* (HTHAT0503, Case Manager)

Prior labour processes involved work teams as well, but they were embedded in a fundamentally different labour process and dynamic of occupational enculturation. Now, with the basis for shared experience provided by doing the same job (and a host of other supports) gone, what we begin to see here are new patterns of group formation. On the one hand, the challenges of work intensification and problem-solving drew people together as a coping response. At the same time, as the account we just read illustrates, the challenges of workload encouraged a type of *selectiveness* in helping others. This selectiveness is shaped by the range of separate job categories provided by the new division of labour, and, although there was little direct evidence of it in the interview data specifically (see Chapter 10), broader social differences more than likely played a role as well. It is for these reasons that we can begin to explain the origins of both more isolated and more homogeneous group formations *within* job categories as well as across the labour process. Intensifying these effects in many ways, given their lack of direct experience with the new computer system, local managers rarely had personal expertise to share. This also played a role in undermining support for more broadly inclusive occupational enculturation. Thus, we find even further pressures, in the form of specific mediations, affording the establishment of a potentially divergent, on-the-job group learning dynamic in activity. Interconnection across groups, possibly involving what Edwards (e.g., 2005, 2007a) refers to as *relational agency*, appears to elude most. Indeed, relational agency is said to depend upon "joint action with others ... learning how to access the interpretations and support of others and importantly how to offer interpretations and support to others" (2007a, p. 258), and here the types of alignment of purposes that Edwards describes are quite narrow. We find instead constrained and contained agency in the course of object/motives of activity under contention.[1]

In part these groups developed in isolation from managerial prerogative, as several of the preceding excerpts indicate. However, it becomes clear that group formation was not simply a product of worker-initiated "selectiveness" in response to constraint, work intensification, and the technical division of labour as such. Nor was it simply an indirect effect of shifts in occupational entry. Rather, beyond their inability to serve as a support for spreading occupational enculturation vis-à-vis their own working knowledge, management influenced these formations in the course of their response to increasing workload, financial pressures, and the need to address vacation coverage. Like most everywhere today, workers are required to fill in for each other during vacation. However, in this case, there were important implication of these practices for the structure of activity and learning. The Case Manager in the following excerpt puts her finger on a specific example of how group formations were shaped by management in these terms. What is crucial is the concentration of individuals within small, more homogeneous groups. I argue this offers yet another relevant mediation shaping the trajectories of everything from the patterns of the distribution of information to collective sense-making and the sustainment of particular beliefs in activity.

I: So how do you cope with all the challenges at work?

S: *You have buddies.* So I have three other buddies *for coverage* when we're off on vacation. We cover each other's work.

I: And so is it the case that sometimes you're not familiar with the clients you're dealing with because they're not yours?

S: That's right, I mean I'm lucky because of *how we sit. We're in like a quadrant.* There's four desks and we're all buddies, so I can at least hear a little bit from the conversations that they do have with their clients, so I know some of the specific needs, which ones need certain stuff and which ones don't so that really helps. (SC11DB0603, Case Manager)

Referenced earlier in the book, discussions of the operation of zones of proximal development now might be understood in a new light, as dynamics that can support forms of exclusion. That is, building from the example provided by this account, we get a glimpse at an additional way that forms of activity are often shaped by human resource practice, in this case the way management responds to vacation rights against a backdrop of state austerity. Under conditions of growing public-sector austerity, cash-strapped municipalities charged with administering welfare services (but restricted in their ability as well as their willingness to raise taxes) run into unique difficulties coping with such basic matters as vacation coverage. In this context, local municipal management in this research regularly constituted these types of work groups to cope with financial constraints as a practical human resource policy. Workers indicated this was also deemed an inexpensive way to train on-the-job, given the ongoing problem-solving needs associated with the challenges of the SDMT technology. Moreover, interviewees explained that people who were "personally compatible" were placed together, a vague enough statement, but one that very likely implicates a range of social differences. More importantly in terms of the structuring of activity as it regards either newcomer or veteran worker status, pragmatically, managerial-initiated work group formation also placed together those with similar levels of vacation rights (e.g., two, three, four weeks, etc.) as established by seniority levels directly. Thus, workers already sharing the same job categories, and now also levels of work experience, and very likely social backgrounds, were clustered into more intensive, sustained contact with one another, essentially, as a matter of policy. I argue that factors such as these play a serious role in the ongoing construction of particular trajectories of object-relatedness in activity, and hence alternative perspectives, perceptions, consciousness, as well as skill, knowledge, and expertise.

Comments from newcomers give us additional insight into how these dynamics relate to occupational enculturation. Each of the following workers had less than two and half years on the job (they were twenty-six and twenty-seven years old, respectively but both described themselves as white, reported no disability and low union participation). In the case of the first excerpt it is worthwhile noting that across all job categories, Case Managers exhibited the greatest diversity in terms of levels of experience. As such, it was this job category which involved increased opportunity for tensions between veteran and newcomers, *and* it was also here that in principle we might expect inter-generational occupational enculturation to remain the strongest. The results, however, were highly uneven, and in one instance speaks to how the homogenizing tendency of group formation was achieved by other means.

I: How does the system affect the way that co-workers work/communicate together?

S: My experience, I was *hired at the same time as 8 other people, we were put in the same job basically and I sort of became friends* with those other people but our experiences were different depending on the team we were assigned to. I was assigned to a team that was very cliquey, a very unfriendly team, which is known through the entire organization. This other group of friends though was super helpful. I owe them a lot, but in terms of team work, *I would ask a lot of questions and not get a lot of help.* In terms of the software SDMT, *most people were so busy they just didn't have the time to help out somebody that was new,* never mind fix the problems that I created, which was very easy to do with SDMT, not that I couldn't issue a cheques.... So it terms of teamwork it's very cliquey and depends on the team. (HCAAT0303, Case Manager)

S: *I learned I have to resource myself.*

I: What do you mean you have to resource yourself?

S: Well if I have to speak to someone I will go find my information while if you're a younger person and more shy, maybe it might be more difficult.... But for me it doesn't make any difference. I'm very social and outgoing so *I'll go and talk to anybody, whether they're on my team or not.* I know that there have been some people that have *resentment between a person having this type of work compared to the other work or who are in this team or that one. It seems to have divided some people.*

I: When you say resentment toward people that have this kind of work, what do you mean?

S: Well like some people are in verification so they feel that they, they might feel that their job is not quite as important as case managing or a Case Worker might feel that the person doing verification has an easier time with the job. (HNMAT0603, CVP Worker)

The interview data reveal a clear, if not absolute, pattern. Many newcomers, as in the second excerpt, were forced to find their way into occupational networks beyond their work group. Many newcomers had difficulty gaining a toe-hold in those work groups that contained more veteran workers, in part due to workload and the pragmatically "selective" nature of these learning relationships, as a senior worker earlier put it. The concentration of workers of a similar age and level of experience in particular job categories further ratified the divisions as workers most frequently collaborated with those holding the same job. A point I will return to in the discussion of the survey results in Part 2, most newcomers, as in the first of the two excerpts, appeared to gravitate to other newcomers.

While notions of personal compatibility likely intensified the homogenization effect in a variety of different ways (implicating gender, race, and other social differences as we will see), a particular strong dynamic emerged directly out of the fact that management necessarily used vacation rights in group formation as a means of assuring a level of equity in the face of rising workload. Amid this complexity, veteran workers, not infrequently mis-directing their frustration at the entry level requirements, regularly seemed to find less in common with newcomers. Thus, in tending toward greater homogenization within work groups, and having broken the prior supports for inter-generational occupational enculturation in broader terms, the dynamics of divergent occupational development within activity have been supported in taking hold.

Part 2: Newcomers and Veterans in the Survey Data

In order to test and extend our understanding of certain differences explored both in Part 1 of this chapter and indeed earlier in the book, in Part 2 we turn to data analysis based on a representative survey of the population of state welfare worker conducted in the course of this research.[2] Having established a series of important dynamics of practice, learning, skill and knowledge construction in labour process activity already, here we begin to see how fine-grained qualitative analysis relates to the aggregate picture. The goal is to expand an understanding of the dynamics of different experiences, viewpoints, practices, and trajectories of knowledge construction looking at the things that mediate and which are mediated by the many divisions of labour and learning.

As in the chapter as a whole, distinctions related to state welfare work *experience* and *age* variables are the primary points of departure for a series comparisons over the following sections.[3] A much larger range of variables (including the full set of demographic indicators) is taken up in the next chapter. As we will see in both chapters 9 and 10, survey respondent views on the positive or negative effects of different aspects of the labour process are particularly important. I begin here with an exploration of how welfare work experience and age relate to job categories and computer literacy, and, later, variables such as prior education, training, and informal on-the-job learning.

Job Categories, Age, Work Experience, and Views on the Labour Process

Several of the basic dynamics impacting on the emergence of more homogenous work group structures under the new SDMT-based labour process were raised in Part 1 of this chapter. There I indicated that both job categories and seniority-based vacation rights were particularly relevant. These features of employment relations, I argued, produced mechanisms that mediated processes through which the divisions between veterans and newcomers in the new labour process were accentuated with implications for occupational enculturation.

To begin to explore and expand on these points, I turn to an assessment of whether or not there is a basis for supporting the claim of homogeneity in work groups in survey findings dealing with job category and work experience variables. If there is support for this claim of homogeneity in the survey day, then in the very first instance we would expect to see the more senior workers concentrated in particular job categories. Looking at the survey data we see that this is the case. Approximately 10 per cent of current welfare workers were hired post implementation of the new labour process in 2002. Twenty-two per cent of workers sampled were less than thirty-five years old, with very few below the age of twenty-five years old (1% of the sample). As suggested in the qualitative analysis, Case Managers tended to be moderately younger compared to the sample as a whole. And importantly, the survey confirms that Case Management was the job category where workers with the least welfare work experience were concentrated but also where a mix of newcomers and veterans was most prominent. By contrast, both older and more experienced welfare workers were significantly over-represented in the Consolidated Verification Process Worker, Eligibility Review Worker, and Employment Worker job categories in the survey data (all differences at the $p < 0.001$ level) (see Figure 9.1).[4] According to the interview data, the latter two of these are the job categories that appear to have retained the greatest amounts of autonomy with the Employment Worker perhaps most closely approximating the more holistic Case Worker job of the pre-SDMT era. It is worth noting as well that the vast majority of veterans in every job category had typically done Case Management work.

The relationship between work experience and job categories, and in turn the relationship of work experience with other variables, provide an important element to the argument. Thus we can ask, What kind of viewpoints and perspectives were actually associated with newcomers and

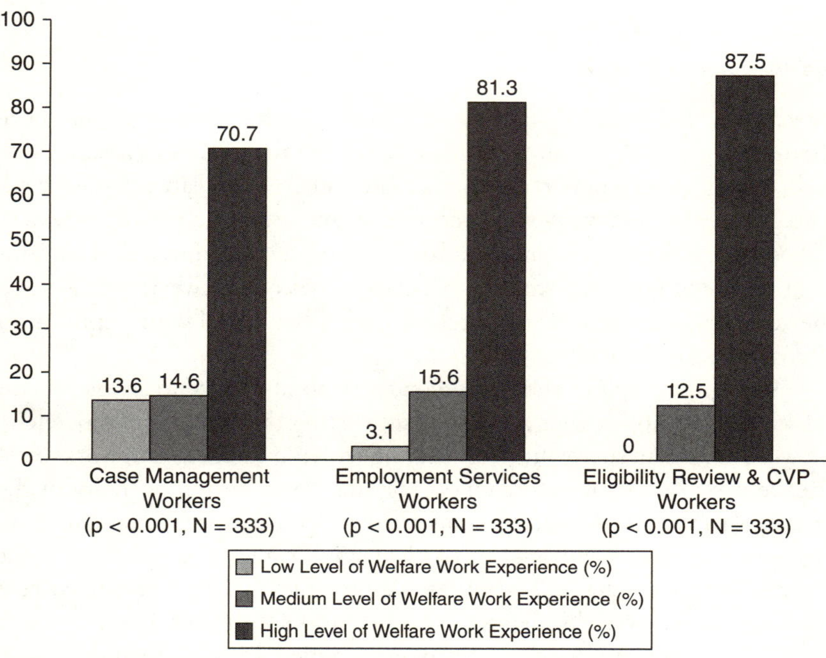

Figure 9.1. Distribution of welfare work experience across job categories.

veterans? Across the survey results we can see that less experienced workers tended to rate the labour process more positively when compared to
more experienced workers. Specifically, the survey asked about many different aspects of the labour process, and by initial observations we can see
that the more experienced workers stand out in terms of being more critical of the work system and the SDMT technology (see Figure 9.2). On
virtually all measures of views on the effectiveness of the labour process,
veteran workers register more serious concerns. These concerns include
viewing the labour process as negatively affecting clients' lives, reducing
the opportunity to apply their skills and knowledge on the job, and lower-
ing workers' sense of control and autonomy while at the same time veteran
workers more often rated the work system overall as ineffective. However,
it is equally important to note that in all scores related to views on the
SDMT technology and the work system *both* older *as well* as more experienced workers have significantly higher levels of ambivalence (e.g., in a
Likert-type scale question they are far more likely to select the less extreme
responses). The qualitative data are helpful in understanding why this is
and what it means. As many of these workers explained, this was related

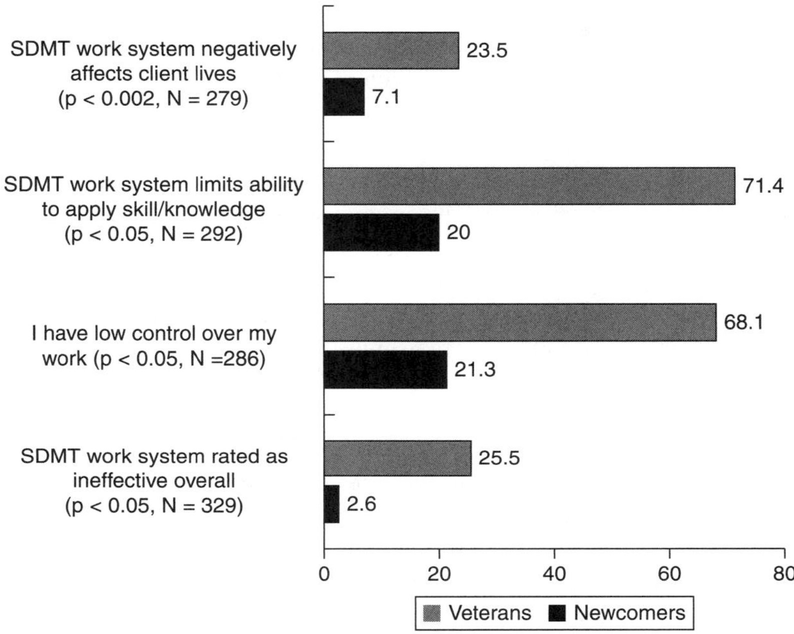

Figure 9.2. Ratings of SDMT/labour process by work experience.

in part to the fact that they have seen changes before in welfare work (or for older workers who are new to welfare work they had often seen similar changes in their prior employment). In this context, likely we are seeing greater confidence in an ability to cope as well as a somewhat greater sense of security overall. Of course, in one way, many of these findings are unsurprising. Older and more experienced workers have made significant investments of effort, skill, knowledge development and learning linked to the prior labour processes, and could be expected to be critical of changes undermining these investments, even if they are not easily rattled by work re-organization. More experienced workers of course have the added security of union seniority. At the same time, I note that, in light of this ambivalence and/or worldliness, the estimations of the *strength* of criticisms of the new labour process by older/more experienced workers are very likely conservative: that is, where criticism is registered, it is less likely to represent a vague, fleeting or uninformed dissatisfaction.

Linking the observations emerging from these two sets of preliminary comparisons, we find some additional bases in the survey data analysis for understanding that there are very likely learning dynamics that relate closely to work experience, age and also job category. However, I also argue these findings point toward several explanations for homogeneity in work groups, possibly serving as a barrier to engagement, exchanges and learning across newcomers and veterans. And, I claim that (building on earlier analysis of distinctive trajectories of occupational learning as well) the capacities for re-keying modes of participation in activity are likely at least partially affected in this way. The dynamics suggested by these survey findings do not, obviously, tell the whole story. Indeed, Chapter 10 describes a much more complex picture overall. But, we do find here some basic materials informing claims related to a distinctive distribution of critique of the labour process across different work groups.

Prior Education and Views on the Labour Process

Of course, a point that I started with in Part 1 of this chapter was the matter of entry level requirements and prior educational attainment across different workers and groups of workers. Drawing on the survey data, the status of these in relation to the occupation more broadly can be clarified further. In this survey, newcomers with post-secondary (college or university) education were typical (Figure 9.3). However, this profile of educational background in the population is striking in two principal ways. First, the majority view of veteran workers during the interviews that newcomers tended to have *less* education is simply *not* borne out. Post-secondary educational attainment is virtually indistinguishable in relation to welfare work experience levels. And yet, there is also some modest evidence of slightly increased hiring of those with simply high school education immediately prior to and since the new labour process was implemented. Thus, instead of a blanket trend toward decreasing entry level requirements, the findings here suggest something more complex that possibly speaks to an emerging bifurcation (between those hired with lower educational attainment and those with higher educational attainment); a relatively small but not unimportant affect most likely linked to role clarifications associated with the new division of labour.

Exploring these data more deeply, we can also look at the subject area of post-secondary educational attainment as opposed to the general level of attainment. As we have seen, certainly the working idiom amongst veterans held that younger and less experienced workers were less likely to orient to a type of "social work ideal" with many of these veterans linking this explicitly to the notion that schooling in social work or social work related areas was now no longer formally required. Thus, we can ask, Has

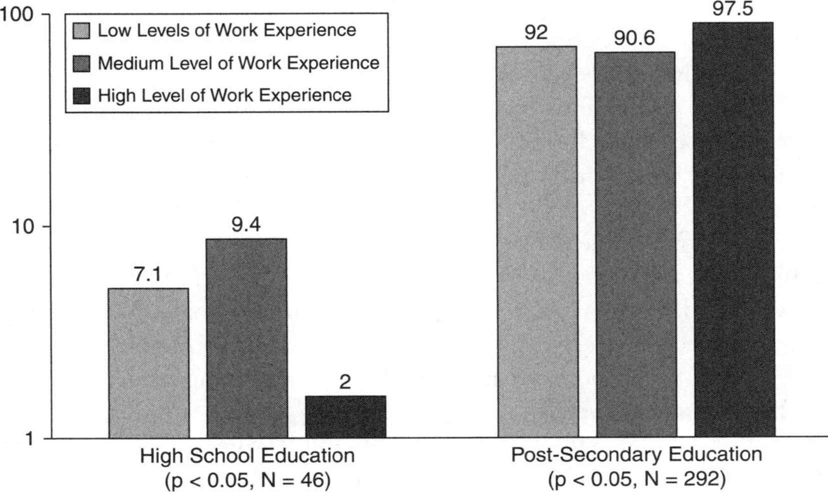

Figure 9.3. Educational attainment by work experience.

the prevalence of social work or social work related education changed since the implementation of the new labour process beyond formal entry requirements? While many workers held college diplomas in social work related fields, the emblematic educational attainment among workers remained the Bachelor degree in Social Work (BSW).[5] In fact, among both veterans and newcomers, statistically speaking, holding a BSW remained rare. The survey indicated that just fewer than 10 per cent of respondents overall held a BSW.[6] Central to my point here, however: similar to the findings which tended to debunk the perspective of many veterans that newcomers are less educated generally, newcomers were just as likely to hold BSW degrees as veterans (in fact, marginally more likely) despite the fact that social work related education and experience had been removed as an entry requirement. Among the most pertinent points this suggests is the fact that, quite separate from formal requirements, beliefs-in-action and the construction of views amongst particular groups of workers within the labour process itself must be attended to carefully in this case.

Pursuing this issue further, earlier in the book I took time to explore links between professional social work and state welfare work. As we saw in Chapter 4, the construction of various notions of a "social work ideal" (either professionalized or more radicalized forms) had been a hard-won object of struggle for social workers in Canada. And indeed, for state welfare workers interviewed in this research it was very common to find that (whether holding a professional social work degree, or not) a significant number of workers understood themselves to be engaged in something they explicitly referred as a type of "social work". Despite this it remains a challenge to clearly understand the links between social and state welfare work in these terms. Beyond the extremely weak forms of recognition of state welfare work within the field of social work (by social worker associations) that we saw earlier in the book, specific differences in skill and knowledge undermine the link between the two occupations as well. While in the past state welfare work incorporated a type of "case work" that partially echoed social work practice, with the implementation of the new labour process coherent notions of case work had disappeared. Moreover, state welfare work had never incorporated other defining aspects of social work (e.g. clinical practice).

In this context (and amidst this ambiguity), what becomes clear in this research is that holding a BSW degree and the disciplinary knowledge it entails is likely *not* the primary way in which the ideals of social work bear on the lives of state welfare workers. From the perspective of a CHAT analysis of the labour process, social work ideals are most effectively understood as a powerful symbolic artefact, almost exclusively appropriated, reconstructed, and applied in state welfare work *within the labour process itself* in such a way as to mediate certain types of learning. Supporting this claim further, in the survey findings we see that holding a BSW degree *did not* appear to consistently relate to as many of the core measures within the survey as one might have expected. In fact, welfare workers surveyed who held a BSW were among the least likely to support the perspectives we might otherwise associate with the ideals of social work. For example, far more workers holding a BSW indicated that the SDMT labour process allowed them to control their work and make decisions effectively (85.7% versus 50.6%; $p < 0.02$). This at least partially suggests an orientation to administrative learning that, as we saw earlier, resulted in workers tending to reject the idea that the new labour process had brought about any particular change. In fact, on its own, holding a BSW degree did not appear to do the type of mediational work associated with the development of welfare work craft knowledge. Indeed, 83.3 per cent of those respondents *holding a BSW* indicated that the work system made a *positive* contribution to their client's lives while only 55.6 per cent of respondents *without a BSW* said the same thing) ($p < 0.05$). It is in this context that the expectation that formal education in social work or social work related fields are a key source of social work ideals for state welfare workers (and possibly an important source of resistance to the changes to the labour process) is seriously under-mined.

Overall, I argue, we are forced to consider even more seriously how it is that the structure of work practice, occupational culture, the formation of groups of learners, and enculturation within the welfare labour process activity itself has evolved. These types of findings begin to confirm the powerful but otherwise hidden effects of the gradual constitution of the occupational culture of state welfare work historically which, as I argued earlier and in Chapter 4, likely took a critical turn during the otherwise short-lived CAP era (the late 1960 to the 1970s) before facing the types of challenges we see today. The findings of this research support this claim in a somewhat unconventional way however. Specifically, the empirical evidence begins to undermine any strict argument regarding the direct effects of prior educational attainment and formal policies surrounding occupational entry even in the instance where these involve university-based social work (or other social work related) education. It begins to suggest that, rather than a direct effect, we are well served to consider how the formal dictates of occupational entry and educational training play highly mediated roles in the broader dynamics of cultural activity within the labour process itself. And moreover, it is very likely that it is the contradictory processes of mediated practice within activity that both gives rise to and sustain – at least partially, among some, at this point in time – residual elements of the occupation in the context of radical change.

Training, Informal Learning, and Computer Literacy

We have now seen some important additional sources of information across newcomers and veterans that shed light on differences that, in turn, help characterize the dynamics of group formation and its potential role in labour process activity. In this section I turn to survey findings that relate to the work-based training and learning processes more directly. I begin discussion with survey questions concerning whether workers found learning the SDMT computer system and work system difficult or not.[7] On their own such findings are less than satisfying. Interpreted alongside the qualitative analysis and through selected bivariate comparisons, however, I argue they aid us considerably.

A key dynamic that emerges from these data is that workers with *more* welfare work experience and greater occupational knowledge actually found learning on the job to be *more* difficult. The types of post-industrial, human capital, and new vocationalism perspectives I outlined at the outset explicitly offer essentially only one explanation for this fact: some types of skills and human capital can become obsolete. Here we find a more complicated story once again. Necessarily this is so, in the first instance, because changing labour processes virtually always involve the complex effects related to integration of both new and existing cohorts. Relations between prior and emerging knowledge forms is ever present, and where we consider the actual dynamics of organizations we quickly see that the explanatory power of the notion of obsolescence is limited to say the least. In fact, in aligning the discussion of certain variables here with the analysis found in Chapters 7 and 8, an explanation characterized simply as a matter of obsolete skill and knowledge being supplanted begins to look especially hollow.

Findings in the survey specifically showed that 37.7 per cent of veteran workers and only 12.2 per cent of newcomers ($p < 0.01$) indicated that on the job learning in the new labour process was "hard". And, when this was checked on the basis of age we see the pattern repeated. Here 50 per cent of respondents between twenty-five and thirty-four reported learning the system as "easy" compared to slightly more than one-third (38%) of those between thirty-five and forty-four and less than one-quarter (23%) of those between the ages of forty-five and fifty-four ($p < 0.01$). However, while work-related learning was deemed more difficult by both older and more experienced workers, one immediate question which this raises concerns the issue of computer literacy levels as partially (or perhaps wholly) responsible for these differences. Were divisions between veterans and newcomers fomented somehow by distinctions in terms of computer literacy levels? Clearly, computer literacy has now taken a central role in both the formal and the practical requirements of the state welfare work occupation. Unsurprisingly, generational differences have granted (younger) newcomers higher levels of computer literacy. The survey data bear this out though the difference is perhaps not quite as large as might be expected. The survey shows that 61 per cent of veteran workers and 82 per cent of newcomers had either medium or high levels of computer literacy ($p < 0.01$).[8] In part, as both the survey and interview data revealed (nicely illustrated by an excerpt from a veteran Eligibility Review Worker [HJMAT0903] in Part 1 of this chapter in fact), the differences have likely been attenuated by veteran workers supplementing their learning with additional computer courses at the local high school or community college.[9] No newcomers in the survey indicated additional course-taking of this type. There is something even more important to note here however. In terms of reported computer literacy levels across respondents we see that computer literacy levels *did not*, in fact, affect workers' indications that learning in their job was either easy or hard. That is, about 28 per cent of those with low computer literacy indicated the

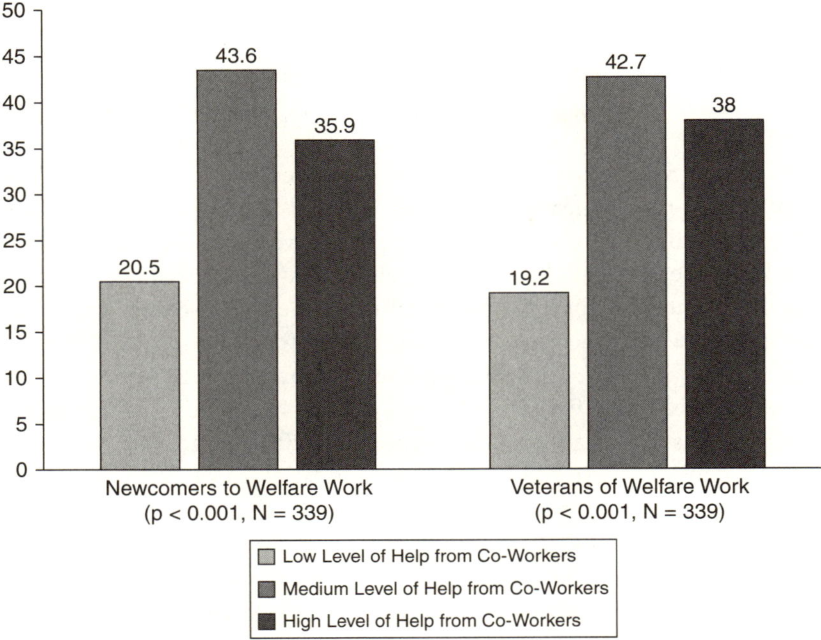

Figure 9.4. Level of help received from co-workers by level of welfare work experience.

work system was easy to learn versus 31 per cent of those with high levels of computer literacy ($p < 0.001$). This is a statistically significant finding and obviously not a very large difference, and it should give pause. Moreover, it can be added that general education level and attainment in terms of educational field did not show any systematic effects on whether learning was either considered easy or hard whatsoever.

If not dependent on prior education, prior education type, or computer literacy levels, surely ratings of ease or difficulty of learning the new work system might be expected to be dependent upon informal on-the-job learning and specifically the amount of help respondents reported receiving on the job from co-workers. Indeed, the discussion of group formation earlier points out that informal and specifically group learning dynamics are central to workers' everyday coping and learning. However, in terms of this survey of state welfare workers whether workers perceived themselves to have had greater or lesser amounts of assistance from co-workers on the job *did not* depend upon work experience (see Figure 9.4). Both newcomers and veterans reported receiving virtually identical levels of help from co-workers ($p < 0.001$).

We are left, in other words, with few obvious answers explaining the differences between newcomers and veterans in terms of their rating of the ease or difficulty of learning under the new labour process. For this reason I turn instead to the sources of information and learning that were considered most valued by respondents. Specifically, the survey asked respondents to rate the importance of either "organized workplace training" or "informal on-the-job learning" to their work.[10] When we cross-tabulate and test the findings on these two questions with welfare work experience levels we see that the most dominant individual variable associated with those who thought informal learning on-the-job was most important was level of work experience. Overall, almost four-fifths (79.7%) of the respondents who valued informal on-the-job learning were veteran workers. Remarkably, only 9.4 per cent of newcomers said the same thing (p < 0.001). This is a strong statistical relationship with a large difference, and when we consider these types of findings in relation to views on the labour process we see something even more important. That is, cross-tabulating views on the most important sources of information/learning for respondents with their views on the labour process, we see that across the different measures of labour process effectiveness, consistently those who valued organized workplace training the most were much more positive about the new SDMT labour process and technology (Figure 9.5).

By way of concluding Part 2 of this chapter, we see that the survey data largely confirmed the concentration of veteran workers in particular job categories, and, as we saw in Part 1, job categories were an important element of group formation. But what exactly happens in such groups? What are the most relevant outcomes of this grouping process? Part of the answer appears to be that some groups of workers develop critical perspectives on the SDMT labour process and technology. And welfare work experience is associated, statistically and otherwise, with significant spikes in these critical perspectives. What we need to consider here is that critical perspectives do not emerge simply from a worker's head but rather from discussion and shared sense-making: that is, a particular type of zone of proximal development, a significant mediator of which is group formation. And so, amongst these final points of discussion in this sub-section we see something more. Critical discussions, giving rise in a variety of ways to orientations to occupational learning, are mediated by preferred sources of information and learning. Here we see that those who appear most critical of the new labour process tend to privilege informal on-the-job learning rather than organized training.

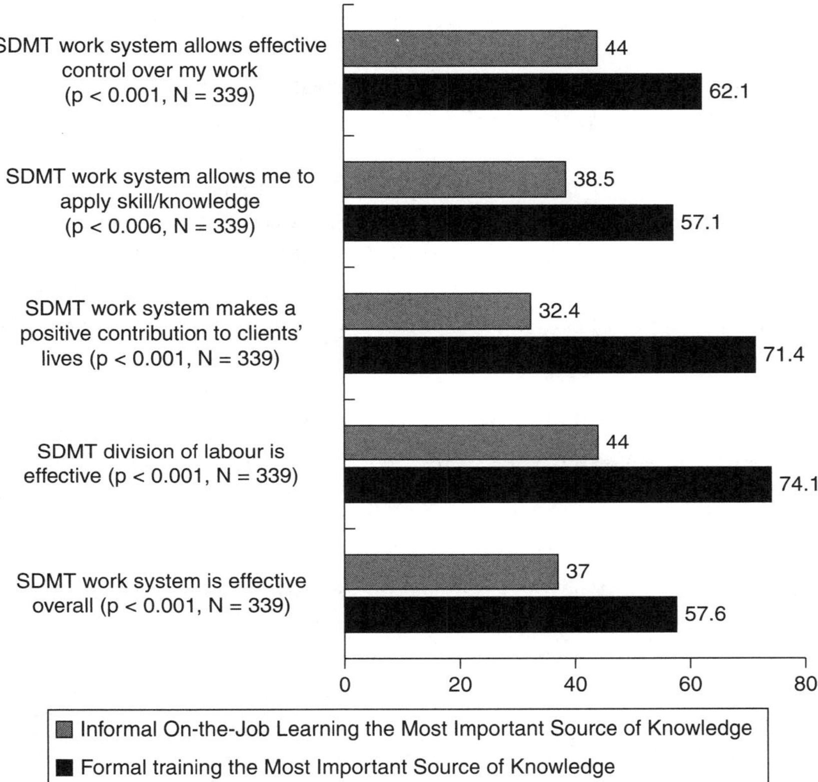

Figure 9.5. Valuing workplace training versus learning from experience informally by ratings of SDMT/labour process.

Building from the type of analysis seen earlier in the book, from the perspective of artefact mediation (its historicity, the designed purposes embedded within artefacts, and so on), these findings are not unimportant. Organized workplace training is constructed in parallel with the original design principles of the labour process. Organized training is in fact a key artefact of conceived space. It is in this sense that trajectories of learning mediated by artefacts derived from this organized training can be expected to establish orientations more favourable to the labour process as designed even while mediating otherwise creative forms of administrative learning overall (Chapter 7). This training appears to afford, in other words, the maintenance of some dimensions of contradiction while supporting the resolution of others in activity. Informal on-the-job learning is of course widely present across the labour process as we have already seen. Its prevalence is, in part, an expression of a workaround culture. At the same time, however, the *privileging* of informal on-the-job learning speaks to another dynamic altogether. In fact it speaks to an entirely different way of participating in labour process activity, and thus has broader ramifications. In this research, the priviledging of informal on-the-job learning appears to afford the engagement of the otherwise hidden core dimensions of contradiction inherent to the new labour process (Chapter 8). In contrast to even the best practices of organized training, informal on-the-job learning and the privileging of experiences related to it leaves the messy contingencies of ongoing organizational life and the face-to-face realities of the fully biographical client-person unbleached and more prominent. And in this sense, the valuing of informal on-the-job learning is very likely both an outcome and resource mediating a particular trajectory of occupational development.

Conclusions

There have been some important changes to the entry requirements of state welfare work. However, building on the qualitative analysis and in turn inferring from the findings of the survey, it seems clear that the *direct effects* of these changes have not been as radical as many of the veteran workers interviewed seem to believe. Still, the facts do not stop a functioning mythology about newcomers (as less educated, in social work or generally) from emerging and mediating forms of cohort dynamics within labour process activity. Interestingly, we saw that there is virtually no evidence that such entry requirements speak to the production of the types of *social work ideals* implied by these concerns in the first place. What the evidence does tell us is that in the face of serious learning/workload challenges veteran workers in particular are likely to have become "selective" in terms of those with whom they problem-solve and exchange help, and there is a more elaborate structuring of activity implied by this selectiveness than likely meets the eye. As absurd as it may seem at first blush, the petty realities and unintended consequences of vacation coverage, the managerial practice of putting people of like mind together in a group, informal (worker generated) cliques, and so on, are important. Such things multiply the effects of the division of labour, concentrating work experience while supporting the development of diverging practices, view points and expertise in the new labour process. Newcomers, it seems, are more likely now than in earlier eras of welfare work to be left to informally seek out other newcomers, and/or cope, problem-solve, learn, and develop occupational knowledge in more isolated ways. When placed within either managerially established groups or when alienated by informal cliques, these newcomers respond in kind and cluster with those like them. As we have seen in the earlier analysis in the book, newcomer or veteran status *does not determine* occupational learning trajectories, but here we can see that it can and does play an important mediating role in work activity. Perhaps most importantly, newcomers are frequently being deprived of the cultural artefacts of inter-generational occupational enculturation. In this way, what I have referred to as the ideals of social work in state welfare work are more than likely one of the many mounting casualties of the new labour process for newcomers. Through tendencies of concentration and homogenization, the rapid blurring of these social work ideals – and with it the fully biographical client-person – speaks to at least one of the key supports helping trajectories of administrative knowledge development to flourish.

The general goal of this chapter has been to test and extend the argument that the (formal and informal) concentration of veterans and newcomers into separate groups suggested in Part 1 is linked to some potentially important differences between these two groups. The survey data helped trouble a variety of conventional notions regarding how computer literacy, general educational attainment, education program (i.e., social work), and formal occupational requirements play a role in the workplace. In this way several presumptions associated with post-industrial and/or human capital perspectives were challenged. Moreover, the chapter has emphasized the degree to which many mainstream studies of careers and labour market entry (and new vocationalism) have under-appreciated and in some instances mis-understood the important, concrete, everyday dynamics of working and learning life activity.

The analysis has also added fuel to the argument regarding how the distinct and divergent trajectories of state welfare worker knowledge development are in each instance an occasion of struggle that belies the easy characterizations of de-skilling, re-skilling, or up-skilling. What is more, the shifts in trajectories can also re-shift. Trajectories are not a finalized project simply waiting to conclude over time. They are not to be necessarily associated simply with any individual worker her- or himself. Rather, these trajectories are the result of complex mediations that, now can be seen to include mutually defining forms of group formation. Even the identification of the homogenizing tendencies – despite the evidence of their existence – does not defend against the fragility of these trajectories. This is because of the inherent contradictions embedded in agentive participation in activity. All workers in this context are desperately, searchingly, pragmatically, successfully, or less successfully seeking a resolution to the contradictions of alienation as well as control. In so doing, they are tracing both the power and the limits of alienation and control at each step. It is difficult to deny that younger and less experienced workers reported much less difficulty in proceeding within new labour process arrangements. Without a functioning dynamic of inter-generational enculturation, these are, after all, arrangements against which they typically have little or no basis of meaningful comparison. But younger, inexperienced workers are neither young nor inexperienced forever. The process of occupational enculturation amongst newcomers, unavoidably and by attrition, cannot help but play a powerful role in the future definition of the occupation.

10 Understanding Prevalence, Roots, and Factors of Trajectories of Knowledge Production

Introduction

Some time ago, the sociologist Michael Burawoy (1979) turned a critical eye toward survey research on workers. His conclusions, and those of many others since, challenged how surveys about work and workers relate to general societal attitudes on the one hand, and the perceptions and concrete practices of workers on the other.

> When [survey responses] are divorced from their context, how can one interpret the enumeration of a set of attitudes? To what reality do these attitudes refer? They appear to reflect a general attitude toward work in capitalist society, to a reluctance to engage in meaning-less, boring, and coercive routines. Inevitably they miss the adaptations workers make to compensate for the deprivations they endure. (1979, p. 138)

Indeed, Burawoy likewise noted, "even the attitudes expressed while on the job do not necessarily correspond to behaviour there.... The idiom in which workers couch and rationalize their behaviour is no necessary guide to the patterns of their actual behaviour" (1979, p. 138). Referring often to the way people talk of their activity through the idiom of economic gain or the cash nexus, for example, he makes it clear that analysis of how idioms mediate worker experience (and their reporting of this experience) requires great care. The type of historical, political, and institutional context and detailed qualitative analysis which I have provided are interpretational supports for exercising this type of care in the study of state welfare workers' learning.

With Burawoy's cautions and these interpretational supports in place, I argue we are now in a position to provide a more extended review of the findings from the survey of the provincial welfare worker population that builds on what we learned in Chapter 9.[1] I do this to try to deepen our understanding of the dynamic differences in activity that have been highlighted to this point. I try to make sense of the complex *configurations* of mediation that shape *administrative* and *craft* modes of participation/object-relatedness, as well as those related to a third trajectory of learning (only dealt with generally until now) which I call *floundering*.

In this chapter I provide three main sections of empirical analysis. The first two of these are rooted in discussion of what I have identified as especially important "litmus test" questions in the state welfare worker survey: questions which produce consistent and coherent patterns closely linked to dynamics that have emerged in the course of qualitative analysis in prior chapters. Specifically, first I address an issue that, for the workers in this research, appears as emblematic of the new labour process. It involves workers' assessment of the positive or negative effect that closure of the centralized Intake Screen Unit (ISU) call centre system would have on their personal work-life. As I show, views on this question offer particularly clear indications as to how different workers are orienting to the new labour process, and how, in very pragmatic terms, they either accept or reject the new division of labour. I claim that the distribution of responses that emerge offers one of the best opportunities to infer the prevalence of different trajectories of occupational learning. Next I turn to another litmus test question in the survey which deals with resources for resistance within the new labour process. Here I explore levels of union participation that, I argue, help us better understand an important mediation in trajectories of craft learning within state welfare work activity. I claim union participation provides a crucial, additional sphere of information-sharing, communication, and learning that, it seems, is strongly associated with what I refer to as an "amalgamated critique of the labour process" that mediates the machineries of occupational knowledge production. This is a critique that appears to play a special role in trajectories of craft learning by unifying otherwise disparate and often fragmentary concerns in thought and action. Within each of these sections of analysis additional dynamics of the object-relatedness of activity within a population of workers as a whole are suggested, implicating a range of social differences directly.

I conclude this chapter with two factor analyses. In certain respects, these analyses represent an attempt to parallel Burawoy's (1979) use of regression analysis in his study of industrial machinists. Like Burawoy, I explore the relationship between effects of practices at the point of production and those linked to broader demographic differences. In doing this

I offer a layer of argument that claims, amid the issues of broader social identity, the dynamics of work itself are not to be ignored.[2] Distinct from Burawoy, however, the focus here is on the details of occupational learning, and specifically the divergent, competing trajectories of knowledge construction. Moreover, whereas Burawoy offered analysis of dynamics in a single factory, here inference to a much broader occupational population is offered based on a province-wide survey. The first factor analysis explores the structure of different labour process-based variables in relation to what emerge as distinct factors that are interpreted as administrative, craft, and floundering trajectories of learning. This integrates and furthers the argument developed earlier. In the second factor analysis however, I go on to show how the survey data can further illuminate and substantiate the existence of multiple *pathways into and along* these different trajectories of learning based on broader experiences, attitudes, and demographic differences amongst workers rooted, in part, beyond the workplace itself. Here, I argue, we find a distinctive contribution to debates about the relative autonomy of the labour process *in relation* to learning and knowledge construction dynamics within activity.

Exploring Views on the Division of Labour and Approximating the Prevalence of Learning Trajectories

As we learned beginning in Chapter 4, the transformation of state welfare work in this research included the establishment of seven regional Intake Screening Units (ISUs) initially. Three years after implementation of the new labour process, however – in part because these call centres were felt by provincial/municipal administration *not* to support financial management (austerity) goals – these centres were slated for closure.[3] The timing I am describing here matters a good deal to interpretation of the findings. This is because announcements of the intention to close the ISU system began to circulate in the summer of 2005 *just as the survey research reported in this book was being conducted.* Importantly, respondents had *not yet experienced* the effects of the closures, and at the time no decision had been announced indicating how intake would be reorganized. Confirmed in worker interviews and key informant consultation, the wide-spread presumption among workers (as they picked up their pencils to complete the survey) was clearly that with the closing of the ISU system there would be a return to a more unified intake and case work process.[4]

On first glance, paying close attention to the results of a survey question related to views on how the closure of the ISU system would affect people's work may seem to be a peculiar point of interest.[5] However, on closer inspection we see that it is not peculiar at all. More than many others, responses to this question involved an important idiom that was clearly decipherable as well as highly consistent with open-ended responses (as well as the interview data). That is, responses in the survey, in fixed-choice questions confirmed in open-ended response options, consistently tied the role of the ISU call centre system to workers' broader outlooks and orientations to the SDMT labour process overall. In contrast with the negotiations, interpretations, and accommodations that unfolded on a daily basis within a complex labour process, the prospect of ISU closures seemed to stand out at this particular point in time as a direct referendum on the new division of labour. It is not hard to imagine why. The establishment of the regional ISU system entailed the concentration of the work of first contact with clients in a completely new series of tasks carried out by an entirely new category of work (Intake Workers). Not only was ISU intake work initiated by an automated response system, but task design emphasized particularly intensive control in terms of talking script, time and output management (chapters 4 and 5). More than the reorganization of work across the many other new job categories, intake work was largely seen as definitive of the collapse of case work. That is, alongside the cessation of home visits and life on the road, for virtually all workers, the establishment of the ISU system seemed emblematic of, if not Taylorism explicitly, the fact that the continuity and direct engagement in client-focused case work were no more.

What is crucial to note here is that despite a shared understanding of what was at stake, the findings on workers' views on the closure of the ISU system clearly suggest that state welfare workers orient themselves (as well as experience and learn) differently within the labour process. And in this context we might expect that at least two distinctive sets of welfare workers would orient *negatively* to the closure of the ISUs and re-unification, in whole or part, of the division of labour. First, we might expect that those workers floundering and performing poorly amidst the tidal wave of challenges could respond negatively to the prospect of additional changes and, more than likely, additional responsibilities for clients. Such things were this groups' most immediate challenges. Second and perhaps more confidently, we might expect that those whose efforts, skill, and knowledge development had already become (or already were) more oriented to a type of administrative object-relatedness in activity would not welcome the potential re-unification of the division of labour. That is, having already established a clear trajectory of learning and expertise in the new labour process over the three years leading up to the survey, these workers would not welcome a shift back to a more unified division of labour. Moreover, as we already saw in Chapter 7, we might anticipate this second set of workers simply to have fewer concerns about the new division of labour itself, having established levels of personal accountability, new capacities for legitimate performance in the existing arrangements, and so on. Indeed, for these workers, more engaged client-person contact might be particularly unwanted or at least unsettling. A third and final set of workers, however, might be expected to orient *positively* to the prospect of closure of the ISU system. We might expect that these would be workers who welcome the change enthusiastically as it would put them in more direct and sustained contact with clients, re-invigorating for them a defining element of occupational knowledge and control, and allowing them to pursue their interests in "social work ideals" while supporting forms of state welfare work craft learning.

Most of these expectations begin to bear out in the research when we explore the open-ended responses on views concerning the ISU closure in the survey (Table 10.1). Distinctive interpretations of workload and client engagement, as well as divergent visions of the nature of the job, are all strong themes in these open-ended responses. Specifically, Table 10.1 offers a representative sample of the most common verbatim explanations given regarding why a worker responded to the fixed-choice portion of the question in the way she or he did. Extending our earlier qualitative analyses, these open-ended responses begin to demonstrate that workers who indicated that the closure of the ISU would *negatively* affect their future practices felt strongly that it would increase their workload and take time away from administrative work like processing files and mail. Importantly, one of the most common concerns voiced by these workers was that the closure of the ISU would force them to deal more often with clients, a practice which many of these workers actually said was a "waste of time" because it would get in the way of completing their work. Workers indicating that the closure of the ISU system would *positively* affect their future work practices provided very different open-ended responses. They indicated that the closures would allow them to do such things as increase their autonomy on the job, gather more complete client information, prepare clients to deal with the welfare system and the challenges of poverty better, carry out higher quality case planning, apply their training and local knowledge of the community, help them reduce crises in clients' lives, and so on. Obviously, distinct sets of interests, goals, purposes, and motives are reflected.

Table 10.1. *Open-ended survey responses on effects of the closure of the ISU*

Closure of the ISU Will *Negatively* Affect My Work Because … (i.e., Preference for Maintaining the Current Division of Labour)	Closure of the ISU Will *Positively* Affect My Work Because … (i.e., Preference for Reducing the Current Division of Labour)
• higher work load • SDMT screens will not be populated … more work for me! • increase those not eligible making it through to the worker creating more work • more appointments with ineligible clients • more time wasted with ineligible clients • more time required to complete application process • client will not be screened therefore more screening work for me • I'll have increased phone calls • burnout • more general inquiries about eligibility • client may not qualify, which is a waste of time for Case Worker • interviewing non-eligible or inappropriate clients • ISU provided valuable info to clients • more irate clients coming into the office • less time to process mail • longer appointment times; won't be able to complete my work • it will just cause more confusion • more changes … blah!	• currently client not prepared for interview • will allow more time to do better case plan • client will spend shorter time in crisis • applicants will be speaking to local qualified social staff • client centered – not feeling lost in technology • I can address support issues from the beginning • gives me greater decision making ability • more credibility in the eyes of the client • better communication when it is done locally • more accurately informing clients what benefits they are eligible for • it will be easier for clients to apply and for me to make referral • intake worker familiar with community geographic resources • client service improved • clients will only have to explain their story once • better communication that is clear and timely • more of a personal approach to the interview

Bearing in mind its limitations, the cross-tabulation of the fixed-response ISU closure variable with a series of other variables can be used to begin to tell us more about why workers oriented to the labour process so differently. In this way, I argue that we can begin to extend the profile of the most important mediations shaping the different trajectories of occupational learning in activity already examined by using the survey data.

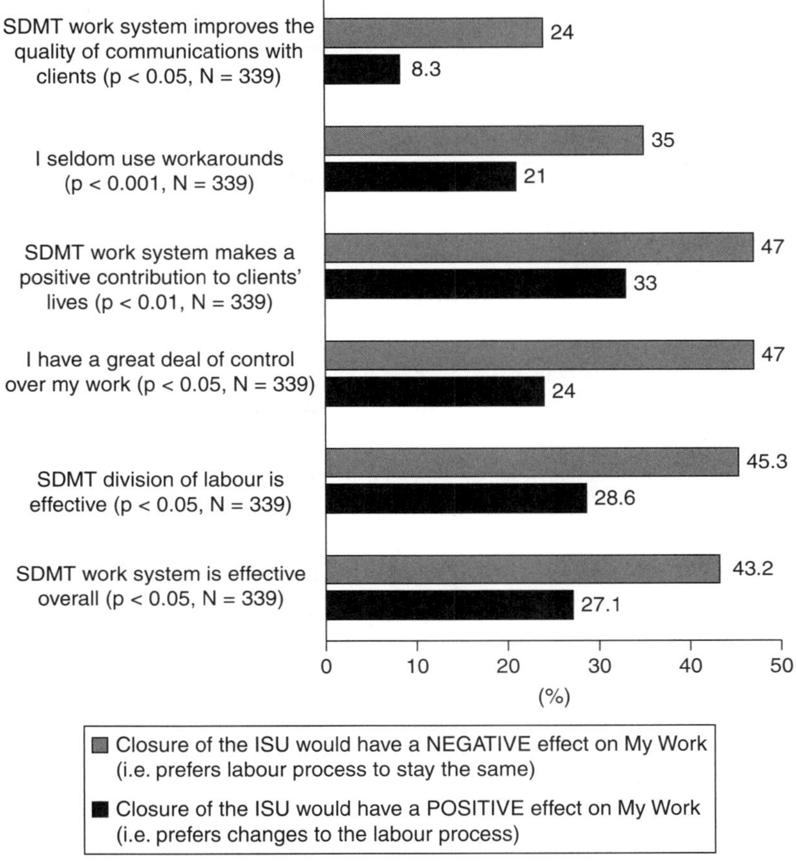

Figure 10.1. Ratings of SDMT/labour process by views on effect of ISU closure.

Some of the most relevant correlations in this regard are summarized in Figure 10.1. I discuss them as well as a few other additional relationships not appearing in this figure.

In looking at the data with regard to questions relating views on ISU closure and those concerning evaluation of the SDMT labour process including respondents' perspectives on the broader purposes of work, as Figure 10.1 shows, we find several statistically significant relationships. Interestingly, taking the findings in this section as a whole what we see is that the ISU closure variable proved very powerful in supporting an overall analysis. More powerful even than any individual variable within the set of variables designed to capture views on the labour process as such.[6] As per

Burawoy's comments at the outset, the effects of respondent idiom matters. To begin with, we see that when respondents felt that the new SDMT labour process was *effective overall*, they also tended to believe the elimination of the ISU would *negatively* affect their work (43.2% versus 27.1%; p < 0.05). This begins to establish an important linkage. Likewise, we see that those who felt specifically that the new division of labour was *effective* also tended to believe the elimination of the ISU would *negatively* affect their work (45.3% versus 28.6%; p < 0.05). Testing the pattern in another way, we see that workers who expressed concerns over a *lack of control* over their work tended to see the closure of ISU as more likely to make a *positive* contribution to their future work practices (47% versus 24%; p < 0.05).

Another key indication relating the survey data more directly to distinctive modes of participation in activity and the trajectories of knowledge construction can be derived from a look at the relationship between the ISU closure variable and the variables relating to how respondents rate the quality of various outcomes of the labour process. Again, the qualitative data serve as an important guide to interpretation here. Specifically, knowing about the decline in the quality of direct worker/client relations within the new labour process based on analysis earlier in the book, responses to these questions provide some insights into what workers likely value most about their work and their way of working. In this context we see that three times as many respondents who felt the new labour process actually *improved* the quality of communication with clients also felt that the closure of the ISU would have a *negative* effect on their work (24% versus 8.3%; p < 0.05). Respondents who felt the new SDMT labour process had a *positive* effect on clients' lives were also more likely to believe the closure of ISU would make a *negative* contribution to their work (47% versus 33%; p < 0.05). While the size and statistical strength of the differences vary across these correlations, nevertheless a clear pattern emerges: respondents who felt the new labour process was *effective* and served clients well wished to have the current division of labour (as symbolized in a very tangible way by the regional ISU call centre system) *maintained*. And conversely, workers who were more critical of the new labour process, its treatment of clients, and the quality of communication with clients anticipated closing of the ISU as having a *positive* effect in their work lives.

Finally, we should note that earlier in the book we established "workarounds" as having multiple uses and meanings amongst workers. Workarounds were ubiquitous in both administrative and craft trajectories of occupational learning within labour process activity. In this context, where a respondent indicates *not* using workarounds I argue that we find reason to suspect something significant may be at play, and we can hypothesize these respondents are most likely *not* effectively engaged in either administrative or craft trajectories of occupational learning. When we test this expectation we see that in fact there is a sizeable proportion of respondents who felt the closure of the ISU system would have a *negative* effect on their work who also were *much less likely* to indicate using work-arounds frequently if at all: 37.9 per cent versus 62.1 per cent (p < 0.001).

Of those variables *not* featured in Figure 10.1 there are a range of instances where no direct, statistically significant correlations were found, but which, in their absence, raise another series of useful points about the nature of the influences on trajectories of occupational learning. I return to a broader discussion of these later, but for now we can note for example that survey analysis indicated having a Bachelor of Social Work (BSW) *did not* affect views on ISU closure in any systematic way. Presumably, formal social work education would have some relationship as a source of the "social work ideal" which figured so prominently in the prior analysis, but as we saw in Chapter 9 it did not, while here we confirm its marginal effects in another way. Likewise surprising, given the types of other effects we observed in Chapter 9, a worker's level of welfare work experience also *did not* affect ISU closure variable responses, and *nor did* either class or racial/ethnic self-descriptions.[7]

To summarize and draw some additional implications, in the first place, we saw that the open-ended survey responses to the ISU closure question suggested divergent sets of interests, goals, purposes, and motives in work practices among state welfare workers. Following this, in a series of cross-tabulations involving the relationship between responses to the ISU closure question and those relating to views about the labour process more broadly, we saw many additional types of differences supportive of the argument for divergent learning trajectories. The results were clear and statistically significant. Moreover, on the bases of this series of tests one further conclusion can be suggested. The ISU closure variable – clarifying an otherwise more complex array of statistical associations – provides us a means of approximating the proportions of workers in the sample engaged in at least three different modes of participation and learning in labour process activity. Admitting the type of fragility of trajectories and fluidity in worker practices discussed in Chapters 7 and 8, the data suggest that state welfare workers who view the closure of the ISU as positively affecting their work – that is, those *critical of Taylorization* of the labour process – account for *approximately a third* of the overall survey sample. And, in relation to the qualitative analysis, we find a warrant for the claim that these workers are the respondents most likely to be engaged in trajectories of *craft knowledge production*. In contrast, *a different third* of this sample is generally both more positive about the new labour process and negative about the prospect of ISU closures, and with the additional support of the qualitative analysis we can conclude that these are workers more likely to be engaged in *administrative trajectories of learning*. And yet, in the preceding discussion we are also provided with additional information regarding a remaining *third* of the sample. This refers to workers who responded that the closure of the ISU would have a negative effect on their work, but who appear to do so for distinctive reasons that *do not* match the profile of either administrative trajectories of learning. This was the set of respondents who indicated they did not tend to use workarounds or use them very infrequently. On the basis of these preliminary cross-tabulations (as well as the qualitative findings), I suggest that this remaining third in fact represents those who at the time of the survey were experiencing significant difficulties coping with the challenges of both re-skilling and up-skilling. They may be engaging in practices of social withdrawal (as we will see in a moment), or they may simply be finding themselves engaged in a particularly fragile transition toward one of the two other trajectories of learning and development. More clearly, these workers are likely those who have become, temporarily or in an ongoing manner, dominated by the effects of de-skilling. As I referred to earlier in the book and shall discuss further, they are *floundering*.

Understanding a Key Mediation of Welfare Work
Craft Learning

In terms of both the qualitative and the quantitative analysis, there are a range of dynamics, relations, as well as key variables that provide a deeper appreciation for the complexity of occupational skill, knowledge, and learning practices. In this section I focus on the matter of union participation which seemed to be suggested as a relevant issue at certain points in the qualitative findings. In general terms, in this section we see some strong correlations between level of union participation and a host of other measures in the survey. I argue these provide evidence that may speak to a series of broader mediations affecting modes of participation in labour process activity.

The potential effects of unions in workplace learning have not been addressed to this point in the book. Thus, to place this brief section against a somewhat broader backdrop I note that in Livingstone and

Sawchuk (2004) it was argued that union culture shapes and is shaped by occupational learning, relations of power and the legitimacy of knowledge forms. Comparing case studies across several different economic sectors and organizational forms, unions were found to be an important resource explaining a range of learning dynamics. Applying CHAT specifically, elsewhere I examined the way that, amongst manufacturing workers, a crucial dimension of these power/legitimacy/knowledge relations was rooted in the production of additional public spheres of communication, often involving local unions. And, the dynamics of informal membership in groups/networks (i.e. the processes through which people came to be either included or excluded), and the production of unique language artefacts can combine to form different patterns of working-class learning (e.g., Sawchuk 2003a, 2003b, 2006a). On the bases of these types of studies we might anticipate that unions and the distinctive communicative spheres they establish locally would be relevant to state welfare worker learning as well. However, what we find is that the role of union participation is somewhat less clear than we might otherwise have expected.

In fact, in the welfare worker survey union participation was assessed in terms of many different types of concrete practices: talking about union issues, reading union materials, attending meetings either regularly or sporadically, holding appointed or elected positions on committees within and beyond the union local.[8] This approximated different levels of union participation. Figure 10.2 summarizes findings that reveal differences between those who indicated higher or lower levels of participation in union activity. When analyzed in terms of level of union participation, we see a consistent series of differences (with moderate to strong statistical significance) in terms of level of critical concern across nearly all major elements of the labour process. Views on the effects of the new labour process on workload, clients' lives, worker/client communication, the ability to apply one's skill and knowledge on the job, as well as overall ratings of the work system and its division of labour are all perceived more negatively amongst those with higher levels of union participation. As with responses to the ISU closure question, these are findings that will figure in the interpretation of the factor analysis later on. Based on results from bivariate analysis however, I can claim that – as one of a limited set of variables in the survey linked strongly with attitudes about work – as union participation rises, so too does a critique of the labour process.

On its own, the link between attitudes toward work and union participation is not particularly surprising.[9] Unions commonly help workers

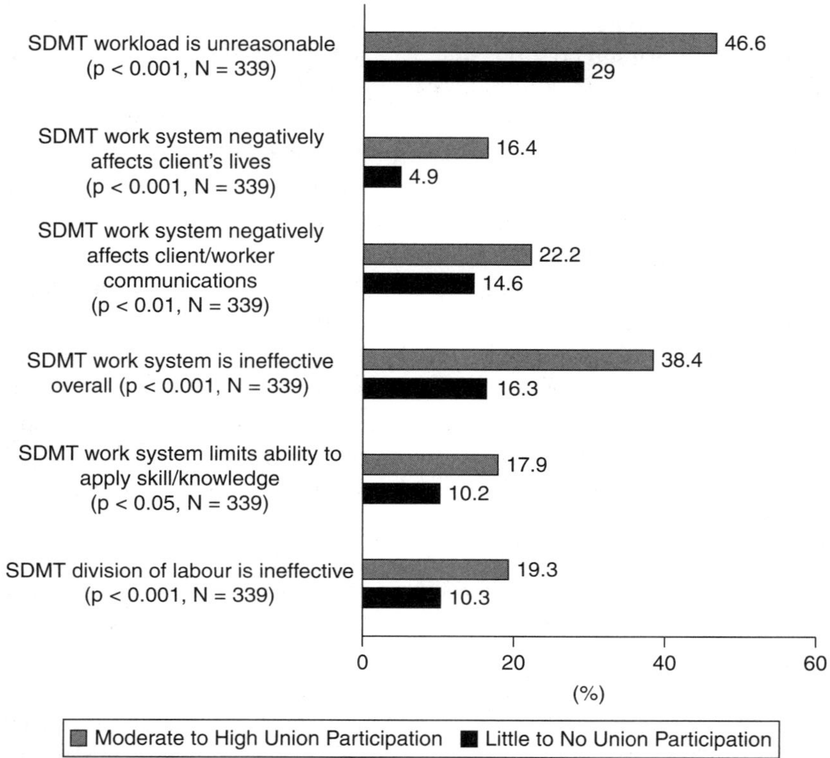

Figure 10.2. Ratings of SDMT/labour process by level of union participation.

learn more about the challenges they face, a process which in this case seems to lead to specific levels of concern about the new labour process. However, included within a broader CHAT analysis of the labour process, findings like these emphasize the level of union participation, along with age/work experience that we explored earlier, as relevant sources of mediation. My claim here is that it is very likely that something more than simply criticism and concerns are being generated. That is, union participation level shapes not simply workers' orientation to and critique of the labour process, but plays a role in workers' ongoing practices and learning within labour process activity. Specifically, I argue that occupational development relates to workers' engagement in additional spheres of communication, meaning, and sense-making opportunities that unionization can provide. Importantly, the additional meditational resources that union participation offer seem to produce what I refer to going forward as an *amalgamated critique of the labour process* (i.e., a combination of multiple concerns that seems to indicate something more than the sum of its parts).

In the findings in the previous section we saw a similar *amalgamation of critique effect* associated with positive views on the closure of the ISU call centres. I linked this to craft knowledge production. We might be tempted to see something similar here: a more or less direct relationship between union participation and craft knowledge production. I caution against this interpretation. In fact, what becomes clear as we move forward is that we are dealing with a variety of complex configurations of mediational effects, and some relevant observations toward this point include the following. Based on the survey results, the statistical relationship between levels of union participation and views on effects of the ISU closures is *not* statistically significant. Moreover, age, gender, and educational attainment do not show any significant bivariate statistical association with level of union participation either. There were, however, two variables that were statistically associated with participation in union-related activities that are worthwhile considering as we move forward. Those indicating higher levels of union participation in the survey were disproportionately white (23.9% versus 5.9%; p < 0.02). And, returning to an issue raised in the prior chapter, newcomers (based on work experience as opposed to age) in the survey sample show virtually no union participation (p < 0.001). These and several other findings support the suggestion that the different trajectories of occupational learning already identified are very likely established in *a number of different ways* by a much more complex set of effects than might otherwise have been anticipated. From a CHAT perspective on the labour process we might say that there are distinct configurations of mediations that workers assemble in unique ways, and these processes involve combinations of work-based practices, attitudes, and broader social differences. I suggested the approximation of prevalence in the preceding section offered a special, and likely fleeting, snap-shot in time of the workforce on the basis of the unique internal consistencies across a set of variables. Vis-à-vis the production of an amalgamated critique, union participation very likely plays a role in these learning dynamics as well, however what is equally clear is that the resources that participation in these particular spheres of communication provide are not evenly distributed. Beyond this, however, we can conclude simply that there are a range of interaction effects amongst the variables, and a series of bivariate analyses can take us only so far. It is for this reason I turn to one final pair of analyses.

Combined Influences and Pathways of Divergence in Occupational Knowledge Production

In this type of survey analysis we are often tempted to think that statistical associations speak to concrete groups of similar people actually clustering together in reality. This of course is a mistake. Even the evidence I provided for the existence of three streams of learning in the survey sample earlier must be interpreted with great caution. At the level of concrete reality of thinking, knowing, feeling acting people (that is real people) the story is much more complex indeed. I argue proxies have an important place in analysis, but they must be kept in this place and used to serve analysis of far more fluid, overdetermined series of active learning processes.

This dynamic, overdetermined learning process was a feature I emphasized at several junctures in the interview analysis where I noted, for example, how comments from the same worker, at different times, could sometimes appear in discussions of de-skilling, re-skilling, and up-skilling. In both Chapters 7 and 8 where the main argument was presented for the existence of distinct trajectories of occupational learning, I included sections detailing the uneven and fragile processes of *transition toward* each trajectory. The uneven and fragile nature of these types of transitions themselves suggests how individuals were struggling, and that individuals were more than capable of reversing course and switching to an alternative trajectory. We must avoid, in other words, reifying the learning of workers into any strict series of ideal types, and instead use these categories as a resource for understanding workers' learning in motion, as in a constant process of becoming. While there are clear tendencies within labour process activity – explained in this research in terms of identifiable configurations of mediations and object-relatedness in particular – this is not to say that the trajectories of knowledge construction are unchanging in the lives of any specific welfare worker, or by extension in concrete groups of workers. Different claims I make, in other words, deal with different levels of generality (Chapter 2). Thus, while it can be argued that the different *modes of participation and object-relatedness in activity are analytically stable*, the engagement of *concrete individuals within these dynamics is assuredly much less so*. Occupational learning is a *going concern*. Drawing on the French Regulationist approach, Demazière, Horn, and Zune (2007), for example, capture this well. For them, "going concerns" involve

> collective actions with some stability and continuity, achieving results approved by the users and based on relationships characterized by a *mix of dependency and conflict*.

> But, for these 'going concerns' to function, no matter what their characteristics, a minimum of order and common, shared, social rules are necessary. This *order itself is generated by collective action*, and is *elaborated and transformed* during exchanges and transactions between members. In other words, these projects are *highly processual*: they are characterized by negotiations *and* permanent adjustments. They are organized actions in which rules are *interpreted and adjusted*, and *individual motivations and preferences altered*. (Demazière, Horn, and Zune, 2007, p. 36; emphasis added)

And yet, these authors go on also to recognize types of differences that emerge between workers in which "[a] closer look at the crossroads between control and autonomous regulation modes is necessary to understand how the *organized construction of heterogeneity* takes place" (2007, p. 45; emphasis added).

In aspiring to use the state welfare worker survey data in the ways I have just described we can discern that there are not only *distinctive trajectories of learning* and that certain variables speak to particular impacts on these trajectories, but that there may also be a variety of *different pathways* into and along these otherwise patterned modes of participation in activity. There is, in other words, a contested as well as an organized "construction of heterogeneity" unfolding in terms of occupational learning. The individual sets of comparisons between variables seen earlier (bivariate analysis using cross-tabulations and chi square testing) served the purpose of offering some useful insights that complemented the qualitative analysis. Indeed, I draw on many of these points again in the remaining discussion. However, as we have also begun to see clearly, there are a great many correlations and interaction effects to consider. Given this complexity and the possibility of multiple interactions between variables, in order to explore this issue of different trajectories of skill and learning as well as different supports for the pathways into and along these trajectories, I turn to the multivariate technique of factor analysis. As we will see, factor analysis is useful for offering insights on the possible existence, strength, and groupings of variables through which a series of statistically derived themes (factors) are suggested. It is a technique through which a series of new variables, themselves not part of the original survey instrument, can be considered.[10]

Two factor analyses were carried out on the survey data in order to assess whether or not groups of variables could be related to different trajectories of learning and knowledge construction. This first set of variables I tested was composed of measures that relate more or less strictly to experiences on the job. I refer to them as the *labour process set* and they relate to the dynamics of practice in the workplace, at the point of production, specifically. Second, I tested for factors in terms of workers' social background and broader experiences, variables that are less directly connected to the labour process, though still relevant to how trajectories of learning and knowledge construction unfold. Many of the variables in this second analysis were demographic in nature, however some related to broader experiences and attitudes. Arguably, two (union participation; participation in implementing the new work design) could have been included in either factor analysis. However, I included them in the second set on the basis of the presumption that neither was a formally required element of the work process (e.g., workers are/were free to choose to participate in either union activity or the work design implementation process). Moreover, union participation has been regularly and persuasively linked to broader social attitudes as well as demographics.[11] Taken together, I refer to this second set of variables later as the *broader experiences, attitudes, and demographics set*. Finally, it should be noted that factor analysis is a statistical procedure that requires us to *eliminate* those variables that do not load onto and explain variation systematically across the emergent factors while we *extract* (retain) those variables that do. As we will see, in interpretation of the results it still remains important to pay attention to how the variables that are excluded may be just as relevant to our thinking as those which end up being included. Throughout the discussion of these two factor analyses, findings from the previous section of this chapter (and elsewhere in the book) are integrated as necessary.

Factor Analysis of the Labour Process Set

In the course of discussion in Chapter 9 and the first half of this chapter we can see that a number of variables have seemed to emerge as particularly relevant. Nevertheless, to explore further and elaborate on these findings I began this first factor analysis with nineteen of the core variables addressing worker responses on questions included in the labour process set defined earlier.[12] The extraction process revealed that eleven of these variables loaded on three factors. The specific phrasing used for each initial variable in the left-hand column of Table 10.2 recognizes the directionality of the relationships (i.e., it speaks to what would otherwise be reported as positive or negative correlations) in order to help emphasize the meaning of the particular result. The identified factors are interpreted and labelled based on the content of variables and the strength of factor loadings. In this first factor analysis we find what can be considered strong statistical significance.[13] The three factors explain 56 per cent of the total variance. As I have mentioned before, cautious treatment is in order and careful attention

Table 10.2. *Labour-process-based factor analysis*[a]

Variables	Factors		
	Factor 1 Craft Knowledge Trajectory	Factor 2 Administrative Knowledge Trajectory	Factor 3 Floundering Worker Knowledge Trajectory
SDMT Division of Labour Ineffectiveness	.822		
SDMT Overall Ineffectiveness	.791		
SDMT Does Not Allow Use of Skill & Knowledge	.773		
SDMT Does Not Support Decision-making and Control at Work	.746		
SDMT Negative Contribution to Clients' Lives	.681		
SDMT Does Not Support Worker/Client Communication	.667		
SDMT Inflexibility	.610		
Importance of Producing Accurate and Timely Client Payment		.742	
Importance of Communicating Effectively with Client		.739	
ISU Closure Will Have Negative Effect on My Work			.798
Infrequent of Use of Workarounds			.663

[a]Extraction method: principal component analysis. Rotation method: varimax with Kaiser normalization.

to the qualitative findings will be used in the interpretation. With this in mind I turn to a brief discussion of each of the three factors that emerged from analysis.

Factor 1: "The Craft Knowledge Trajectory". In terms of the first factor in Table 10.2, we see confirmed here that – despite all the differences and fluidity that swirl around complex, agentive activity *and* despite wide-spread fragments of criticism offered by workers – a defining feature for the processes highlighted in this factor is an *amalgamated critique* of the current labour process. As we saw earlier in this chapter, this type of amalgamated critique was linked closely to both union participation, and in a separate analysis (vis-à-vis workers' views on the ISU closure) *craft trajectories of learning* specifically. Indeed, the qualitative analysis in Chapter 8 provides evidence of both an amalgamated critique and an expansive up-skilling as well. We will also recall, however, that union participation and ISU closure variables did not correlate with one another directly, and in fact a small web of variables (e.g., age and work experience) featured correlations that, likewise, seem related to craft learning but again not directly. I will take up these other variables in the second factor analysis, but for now we can note that herein lies the unique role and importance of the construction of an amalgamated critique. The central point here is that the factor analysis links the tight grouping of separate criticisms into a more coherent amalgamation – that is, the production of a distinctive and powerful mediating artefact – to trajectories of craft (as opposed to administrative) learning in a way that separate, contributing variables do not. Thus the suggestion here is that while it may be achieved in a host of different ways, the road to craft trajectories of learning likely need to go through the construction of an amalgamated critique of the labour process.

Factor 2: "The Administrative Knowledge Trajectory". As we will see, it is important to interpret the three factors comparatively to understand them adequately. So, in the case of claiming that factor 2 represents administrative knowledge trajectories we can begin by confirming that the dominant set of variables has little to do with the type of amalgamated critique we see in the first factor. Rather, the administrative knowledge trajectory factor is composed of output-related (producing accurate and timely client payments) and process-related (communicating effectively with clients) variables, the latter being a variable that may be particularly vulnerable to multiple interpretation (i.e., "effective" communications with clients depend on the goals and purpose the worker has in mind; cf. Table 10.1). That is, building on insights from Chapter 7, we can confirm in the aggregate that administrative knowledge construction likely breathes life into the labour process in a particular way, primarily through attention to (administrative) outputs and processes. Of course, we should also recall that these are dimensions of the labour process that link directly to the particular types of job performance I described in Chapter 7 as well. Yet, just as we can find some (albeit more fragmented) criticism of the labour process amongst administrative modes of participation in activity, likewise those engaged in craft knowledge production also pay attention to matters of output and process as we saw in Chapter 8. We see evidence of these dynamics in the survey data. However, in identifying this second factor as related to administrative knowledge trajectories we can note that amongst those engaged in craft knowledge production, the concern for work output, process, and performance is made subordinate to and organized within activity by a broader and more far-reaching amalgamated critique leading to more expansive, up-skilled practice.

Factor 3: "The Floundering Worker Knowledge Trajectory". Having received only intermittent attention prior to this chapter, the factor analysis contributes to the claim that a significant proportion of respondents in the survey were likely *not* effectively pursuing *either* craft or administrative trajectories of skill and knowledge development in activity (at least not at the time of the survey). The survey captured responses approximately three and half years after the implementation of the new SDMT labour process, and there was in fact no shortage of indications that many workers were still struggling to cope (as distinct from those who were coping in different ways). In other words, while some embarked on different trajectories involving re-skilling or up-skilling, still others experienced difficulties that were, at times it seems, virtually immobilizing. In these instances there is evidence in the interview data (though, not surprisingly, it is largely provided in reference to *other* workers) that some were in a process of withdrawal from work life in the welfare offices. The term "floundering", in fact, was offered by one of the workers quoted earlier in the book describing this exact type of process. These floundering workers were often described as experiencing sustained crises, typically culminating in recognizably poor job performance. Many interviewees noted that workers and management would typically only become aware of a truly floundering worker after some time, often by virtue of some event or complaint brought the situation to light.[14] Interpretation of this factor echoes the findings presented in the first half of the chapter, where we saw responses on the survey that indicated a set of workers who felt the ISU closure would *negatively* affect their work *and* who at the same time reported *infrequent* use of workarounds. Rejecting a return to a more unified division of labour (suggested initially by the possibility of the closure of the ISU) it was likely these workers had significant concerns about the possibility of having to assume additional responsibilities within a labour process in which they were already decidedly overloaded. The suggestion of overload is linked in this case to findings indicating that these same workers *rarely or never* use workarounds. In this regard, qualitative analysis earlier in the book is definitive: adequate work performance – *of any type* – would be virtually impossible without workarounds.

In light of the limited direct attention to floundering in the qualitative analysis, prior to continuing it may be relevant to pause for a moment to offer a brief illustration to concretize these findings. As I mentioned, there are a variety of dispersed remarks that appear in the interview data that relate either directly or indirectly to the type of process I am describing here. The following worker, for example, talks briefly about a typical instance of floundering. In it many of the basic themes seen in the interview data more broadly are likewise detectable.

> S: We had a worker who just couldn't do it. It's not that unusual really but like she had all the training. She'd been recruited from within, she had the qualification, like she'd gone back to do some schooling and posted into a Case Manager position from within, was good at what she was doing before, but now just couldn't do the Case Management work, couldn't keep up with the volume of the work. Management said they supported her in her work and they honestly did in my view, but she finally went into a cocoon in her office and eventually it was discovered she had 6 months of uncompleted work in her office.… I kind of expected this person to have limited ability, but that wasn't the case at all. She had such a quick mind, but for whatever reason what was being done by management to teach her the job was just not there. The formal processes were in place, but they just were not working.… And of course the system is so cumbersome, over time the informal support from co-workers began to disappear because co-workers felt they were doing her work for her. Carrying her.
>
> I: So these informal networks can be fragile and since there are personalities that come into it, it might not work so well all the time.
>
> S: Yes. I mean it's a social network and if you're not part of that network then you don't have access, so if this kind of thing is necessary to do your job, then it's a real problem. (BPSBP1009, Employment Services Worker)

In the case of floundering, factors such as group formation and the development of informal networks within activity discussed in Chapter 9 are more than likely pivotal. That is, in their absence, they produce very different learning dynamics. We saw that group formation and informal networks were key sources of co-worker helping and workaround learning, critical to shaping the direction of coping, thinking, and choice-making. Overwhelmed and going "into a cocoon", we can begin to imagine all the more why the prospect of further changes to the division of labour (i.e., through the closure of the ISU) would be unwelcome. And finally, we might also recall from earlier material how the struggle to transition into one of the other two trajectories of occupational learning may also be involved. That is, floundering trajectories of learning almost undoubtedly begin very much as a fragile (but ultimately failed) transition that over time, for a significant number of workers, takes on a distinctive life of their own. The factor analysis of the labour process set suggests features of just these types of mediations in activity.

Factor Analysis of the Broader Experiences, Attitudes, and Demographics Set

The point of using factor analysis is to help support more encompassing interpretations of complexity. To a limited degree, it does so for us again here in terms of the identification of the statistically significant contributions to what I call *pathways* toward and along different trajectories of occupational learning amongst state welfare workers in activity. Broader experiences, attitudes, and demographics – in fact, issues of identity – live a double life. They are, of course, implicated in the dynamics of work life itself as well as having origins and dynamics beyond the workplace. As I noted at the beginning of this chapter, this was an interest taken up by Burawoy (1979), and related to this, here I give these variables focused treatment. All the same, as in the first factor analysis, the goal is to see how practices and mediations relating to a specific set of variables relate to one another, and in turn may relate to the main set of occupational learning trajectories that have been discussed.

Procedurally this second analysis began with all the relevant variables in this category of general demographics, broader attitudes, and experiences. In the survey there were a total of thirteen variables of this kind.[15] The factor analysis process led to the exclusion of roughly half these variables. We see, for example, that despite the frequent mention of the "social work ideals" of state welfare work in the interviews, holding a Bachelor of Social Work did not survive the extraction process. This further confirms the findings surrounding its lack of relationship with many of the other variables as discussed earlier. General computer literacy was also not retained, and again this confirms some earlier findings (Chapter 9). Other variables of lesser interest, in part, because they correlated either very highly or not at all well with other more robust indicators were excluded as well (e.g., union seniority, prior involvement in the initial work design consultation process). In the end, the extraction process loaded remaining variables onto four factors that, I will argue, speak to multiple pathways toward and along the different trajectories I have been discussing. As earlier, findings from the qualitative analysis as well as additional cross-tabulations are used to guide interpretation. The factors identified in the analysis account for more than 61 per cent of the variance (see Table 10.3).[16]

Before proceeding further, several points are important to note. In comparison to the first factor analysis, the following analysis is necessarily more exploratory in nature, and in point of fact it is somewhat unconventional in ways that I will address in a moment (e.g., the inclusion of a factor composed of one variable). The scope of mediations being considered

Table 10.3. *Broader experiences, attitudes, and demographics factor analysis*[a]

Variables	Factor			
	Factor 1 Pathway to Craft Knowledge Trajectories	Factor 2 Pathway to Administrative Knowledge Trajectories	Factor 3 Pathway to Craft Knowledge Trajectories	Factor 4 Pathway to Administrative Trajectories
Educational Attainment				.919
Orientation to Union	.758			
Social Class		.743		
Race	.557			
Age			.737	
Gender			−.775	
Disability		.675		
Welfare Work Experience	.597			

[a]Rotation converged in six iterations. Only factors with loadings above 0.45 reported. Extraction method: principal component analysis. Rotation method: varimax with Kaiser normalization.

here has been expanded considerably (having effects within and beyond the workplace). At the same time, the discussion of the qualitative research earlier in the book could not adequately forefront all the broader demographic, attitudinal, and experiential differences being dealt with here. Interviewees rarely, if at all, mentioned several of the variables in this set. It is also important to note how in this analysis the notion of *pathways* is meant to imply a series of supports, most stemming from broader social life, social differences, and biography, which in part mediate movement *toward* engagements in the different types of knowledge production as well as *along* trajectories. This attention to the process of movement toward types of knowledge production helps to explain, for example, that while in the first factor analysis we were able to identify what I called a trajectory of floundering in activity, in this second analysis a specific pathway toward a floundering knowledge trajectory is not distinguishable. This is perhaps not completely surprising. Floundering, after all, is largely defined here as a lack of, or stalled, attachment to the occupational learning trajectories with which the original research design was primarily concerned. Whatever the exact case, discussion in the following material draws on the first factor analysis, but as we will see for a variety of reasons, interpretation here is more challenging and conclusions necessarily more tentative (a finding in itself in many ways).

Factor 1: "Pathway to Craft Knowledge Building (Orientation to Union, Welfare Work Experience, and Race)". In terms of the first factor, we see some earlier claims confirmed. Two variables loading on this factor can be thought of as approximating key mediational resources contributing to craft knowledge production in state welfare work. Where they are absent, it is suggested here, one of the two major pathways towards craft knowledge construction is much less likely to be initiated or continued. As we saw in the prior factor analysis, positive orientation to the union vis-à-vis higher levels of participation is associated, though indirectly, with craft knowledge trajectories. In part this was because such attitudes supported access to and engagement with information resources, opportunity for certain types of exchanges, and social relationships that appear, in the end, to support the development of the dynamics of amalgamated critique artefact mediation within the labour process. The types of mediations that were analyzed in detail in Chapter 8 as a type up-skilling process seem to support the pathway being described here in a variety of ways.

In terms of greater background in welfare work, I argue that reserves of welfare work-based skill, knowledge, and institutional memory as well as established work relationships provide the potential to mediate a more expansive critique and, in turn, opposition to the new objects of welfare work as designed. Central, but by no means guaranteed to lead to these patterns of mediation, are the memories of earlier labour processes: for instance, experiences of closer engagement with the clients (as biographical client-persons) through practices such as home visits and the development and use of expertise and judgment associated with life "on the road". As was suggested earlier in both our basic bivariate and interview data analyses, the resources of work experience must likely be considered effective only in combination with other sources of mediation.

A more complex explanation is needed to address the last of the three variables which contributed to this pathway factor. In this survey, on the basis of individual pairs of cross-tabulation, the race of welfare workers was statistically associated with many variables quite poorly (e.g., job categories, amount of help received from co-workers, age, welfare work experience, educational attainment, holding of a BSW). However, confirming the broader observations of Galabuzi (2006) and others regarding the relationship between race and employment in the Canadian public sector, Baines (2008), for example, notes that "in many parts of [Canada], First Nations workers and workers of color were excluded from the better mainstream social services jobs until fairly recently" (p. 126). In research exploring issues of race and skill in Canadian social work professions, Baines (2004c, 2008) documents the unique forms of up-skilling and resistance by racialized social services workers, as well as their concentration in what she calls "ethnically specific services and programs" (2008, p. 123). Although state welfare work is a generalized service program, there remain some relevant overlaps between it and the social work professions that Baines is speaking about. In part this is because of the practice in state welfare work of assigning certain client populations to particular workers in the course of case management. Baines specifically notes in fact that amongst the social workers of colour she interviewed there was "mild surprise at the notion of deskilling" (p. 126). Though the dynamics across social workers and state welfare workers must be considered distinctive, this suggests some potential explanations for why race may co-vary with pathways toward and along trajectories of craft knowledge production.

Confirming our interpretation of this factor further we also find some evidence that, in comparison to others, state welfare workers of colour are *not* very likely to be floundering. That is, in comparison to welfare workers identifying as white, workers of colour report significantly higher levels of use of workarounds (51.8% versus 37.1%; $p < 0.05$), which, as we saw earlier, are associated with either administrative or craft trajectories (and not floundering as such). Perhaps the most challenging element of explanation involves a finding briefly mentioned earlier: welfare workers of colour were significantly less likely to participate in union activities (5.9% versus 23.9%; $p < 0.01$). What this likely suggests is that for those who *did* become involved in their union, a significant combined effect was seen between variables supporting movement toward and along trajectories of craft learning. Overall, as suggested by the stickiness of these particular variables it appears likely that a general oppositional perspective operating across these variables is the defining dynamic. That is, once again the construction of and affordances provided by an amalgamate critique is central, and the sources of this critique are multiple. Though it is only one of the two major pathways toward and along craft knowledge learning, this factor describes interacting features that open the door to this trajectory for some state welfare workers, including specifically (though not exclusively) those who are racialized, experienced in welfare work, and positively disposed to (or not otherwise dissuaded from) participation in their union.

Factor 2: "Pathway to Administrative Knowledge Building (Class and Disability)". Making sense of this factor also requires some explorations not fully undertaken elsewhere in the book. In the first instance, this factor is loaded on most strongly by the respondent's selection of a middle-class self-description. The middle-class response was the modal selection in the survey. In fact, three-quarters of the respondents chose this response. It is worth noting, however, that the middle-class response does not correlate with educational attainment in the survey findings.[17] Also important is the fact that these responses do not correlate (positively or negatively) with union participation level.[18] Perhaps most important of all, however, is the fact that the middle-class response *did not* correlate at all with the type of amalgamated critique we saw linked so tightly with trajectories of craft knowledge production earlier. Finally, though we do find some indications that those workers describing themselves as middle-class reported using workarounds at lower levels in comparison to those selecting other class identifications (36.6% versus 53.4%; $p < 0.05$), there was also *no* statistical relationship between respondents selecting middle-class descriptions and views on the closure of the ISU, which, taken together, were findings linked to our identification of those workers that were floundering. Thus, across these separate cross-tabulations, hand in glove with observations from the qualitative analysis and by a process of elimination, we find warrant for the interpretation that this particular set of variables supports entry into and along trajectories of administrative rather than either craft or floundering learning in the state welfare work occupation.

Also included in this second pathway factor were indications of disability. In terms of the way the variable was coded, the positive loading indicates that we are referring here to workers who responded that they did *not* have a disability. As with the middle-class response, those indicating not having a disability were the majority (91% of the sample), but there are no indications in the survey data that the types of jobs, level of welfare work experience, or level of educational attainment correlated in any systematic way with indications of disability/lack of disability. Moreover, there were no discernible patterns of statistical relationships among disability and social class, race, or gender variables. Other indicators that were important in terms of disability status which we can note in an interpretation of this factor include the following. First, we find *no connection* to the type of *amalgamated critique* that is so strongly associated with craft knowledge production despite the fact that, on the question asking about general effectiveness of the labour process, 46.4 per cent of disabled workers (versus only 19% of non-disabled workers) did offer criticism ($p < 0.002$), and workload was a concern (i.e., 50% of disabled workers versus 31% of non-disabled workers said the workload was unreasonable; $p < 0.05$). That is, those without disability tended *not* to offer criticism of the division of labour or the effect of the new labour process on clients' lives or worker/client communication. In addition, workers without a disability were slightly more likely to be focused on timely and accurate payments to client (84% versus 72%; p < 0.02), a focus which, as we saw previously, is generally linked to administrative concerns. What is more, there is strong statistical support indicating that those workers *without a disability* were less likely to participate in union activities in comparison to workers *with a disability* (20% versus 41%; p < 0.01). While as we saw earlier much the same could be said about racialized workers, here again we focus on a configuration of effects, and this tells us something relevant in terms of links to administrative as opposed craft knowledge trajectories. Overall, we see that a particular class identification (i.e., middle-class self-designation) along with a *lack* of disability tend to mediate forms of consent to the new labour process, which, in turn, help mediate the movement of state welfare workers toward and along trajectories of administrative skill and knowledge learning.

Factor 3: "Pathway to Craft Knowledge Building (Age and Gender)". The third factor found in Table 10.3 shows loading on the age and gender variables. Dealing with each in turn I begin by recalling that the qualitative research suggested how with age comes work experience that often, though not exclusively, included work in welfare services. Moreover, as some older interviewees noted specifically, they frequently knew and identified more closely with their community from having lived there longer as well. These were matters that emerged from time to time in the qualitative analysis and when they did we saw that this type of community identification was not an insignificant mediator of activity. This begins to suggest a link to trajectories of craft knowledge production. Age on its own, however, shows *no* statistical relationship with job category, level of help from co-workers, educational attainment, level of union participation, class self-designation, or race. However, age *does show* a statistically significant pattern of correlations with what I have been referring to as an *amalgamated critique* of the labour process that proved so important in the first factor analysis as well as discussion earlier in the chapter and book as a whole. Still, while consistent, the statistical significance and size of the age effect are clearly weaker in comparison to those seen in the pathway factor 1 earlier. Specifically, we find the following (all comparisons are based on chi-square tests for *older versus younger workers, respectively*): rating of overall ineffectiveness of the labour process (17.6% versus 14.9%; p < 0.05); the labour process makes a negative contribution to clients' lives (28.6% versus 17.4%; p < 0.05); the division of labour is ineffective (14.9% versus 8.3%; p < 0.05); the labour process has a negative effect on decision-making and control over work

(15.6% versus 14%; p < 0.001); the workload is unreasonable (39.8% versus 26.5%; p < 0.05). Equally important is the fact that there is also *no relation* to the view that producing payments in a timely and accurate manner is necessarily important to older workers (and as we saw this was a variable strongly associated with administrative learning trajectories). Finally, in terms of the age variable in the survey, we find evidence that undermines the idea that older workers are floundering. There were *no differences* in frequency of use of workarounds based on age, and moreover, it was younger workers who tended to view the closure of the ISU as likely to have a *negative* effect on their future work practice (55.1% of younger workers versus 28.6% of older workers; p < 0.001).

In terms of the way the gender variable was coded in the survey research, the negative loading indicates that in Table 10.3 we are referring here to *male* workers. Male welfare workers make up only 10 per cent of the sample. In this rudimentary way the traditional observation that social work is a feminized occupation is sustained. There is no shortage of detailed studies and discussion of feminist approaches to social work professional practice (e.g., Kirst-Ashman 1992; Dominelli 2002; White 2006; Lazzari, Colarossi, and Collins, 2009). Stalker, Mandell, Frensch, Harvery, and Wright (2007) for example have linked a highly gendered ethic of care to social workers who were both burnt-out by excess workload, but emotionally satisfied and extremely committed to their work. Their focus was not state welfare workers, but nevertheless the findings suggests that we might anticipate some notable gendered differences in terms of responses to labour process change, skill, and knowledge. Likewise, the research of Baines and colleagues (e.g., Baines, Evans, and Neysmith 1998; Baines 2004a) highlights how in the context of work organization change in social work "the gendered nature of the workforce is crucial to the whole story" (Baines 2004b, p. 276). The literature on gender and caring work more broadly is of course even more established. Despite all these points, from the perspective of occupational learning in the state welfare labour process, gendered relations seem to play out in complex ways that elude simple characterization. To understand how this is so, we can again draw on a series of bivariate analyses.

Why the gender variable ends up included in this factor specifically is not easily discerned. Beyond the low number of male respondents (which, as elsewhere in the analysis, challenges the effectiveness of statistical comparisons), on the basis of additional review of the data the best estimation here is that it relates to the matter of amalgamated critique of the SDMT labour process. In most measures women and men are essentially identical in terms of their concerns about the new labour process. There is, however, one exception (counter-intuitive given the literature just summarized). Male state welfare workers in this survey sample responded with a somewhat greater concern over how the labour process was negatively affecting clients' lives (27.8% versus 20.9%; $p < 0.02$). Moreover, though not statistically significant (i.e., $p < 0.1$), the results indicate that male respondents are *less satisfied* than female respondents with the level of control and decision-making ability they have in the labour process (only 32% of men were satisfied with these conditions versus 51% of women). Following Baines (2004b), here we simply cannot leave aside the effects of gendered expectations of control (emerging from gendered privilege). Nevertheless, on the basis of these data alone it may not be as easy as it seems to separate out the two craft knowledge pathway factors. For example, there are very few male respondents in the sample who had been hired since the implementation of the new labour process and they were disproportionately older generally, and this speaks to a particularly type of relationship between gender and age in this survey. In turn, there is also a strong correlation between welfare work experience and craft knowledge production. Age is not entirely separable from this either, and thus it raises questions regarding welfare work experience as an intervening variable perhaps. To complicate matters further, women are twice as likely to be workers of colour in the survey sample. Interpreting a particularly clear difference between pathway factors 1 and 3 is thus made all the more difficult.

Factor 4: "Pathway to Administrative Knowledge Building (Educational Attainment)". Under normal circumstances factor analysis does not recommend retaining a factor composed of a single variable (for obvious reasons). However, I include it here for the sake of the broader discussion in the book as a whole and because it provides a good opportunity to further address the relations between prior education and occupational knowledge raised elsewhere. In speaking about educational attainment here as a "factor" (as opposed to simply examining the variable's correlations with other variables in the data generally), I mean also to embed the discussion in considerations of both the pathways and the trajectories of knowledge production. Understanding the meaning of the finding will require, once again, a process of elimination of a series of competing interpretations.

The first thing we notice in these data is that there is no statistically significant relationship of findings on the educational attainment variable in terms of either levels of union attitudes/participation or levels of state welfare work experience. This offers some preliminary support for the claim that we are likely *not* dealing with a pathway linked to craft knowledge production. After all, both union participation and welfare work experience were closely, albeit indirectly, associated with the craft trajectory in a host of ways, as we have seen. Second, while we find that as educational attainment rises workers respond more often that their work is inflexible ($p < 0.02$), beyond this we fail to find a statistical relationship between educational attainment and the type of amalgamated critique of the labour process which was so strongly associated with trajectories of craft knowledge production. Third, we find that as educational attainment rises so too does one's use of workarounds: for example, among college educated respondents 44 per cent use workarounds frequently and among university educated respondents 57.1 per cent use workarounds frequently ($p < 0.002$). Drawing on the earlier discussion of the importance of workarounds, workers associated with this fourth pathway, in other words, are not likely floundering. Thus, taken as a whole and having undermined possible alternative interpretations, we find some support for claiming that this variable/factor is linked to administrative rather than craft trajectories of knowledge development in activity.

Conclusions

The argument in this book revolves around the process and significance of conceptualizing the struggle for the identity of an occupation in times of change vis-à-vis divergent and competing trajectories of occupational learning. These are trajectories that remain still too opaque in the literature in terms of contingencies, agency, and most of all structures of knowledge construction specifically. The qualitative research formed a base to these arguments. Over the prior chapter and, in particular, this chapter, I have expanded beyond and complemented this base with the use of the survey research. However, as all survey researchers know, some of their best laid plans (e.g., question design) do not function in the way that they hoped (and occasionally they do not meaningfully function at all). There are several examples of this in the research. As I pointed out at the start of the chapter, survey research must attempt to deal with the idiomatic nature of responses, and the meaning and personal sense that workers produce from the various discourses they have at hand. In this context, survey researchers must establish a coherent means of penetrating these barriers to interpretation as best they can if they are to develop warranted claims that go beyond statistical significance. However, stemming from the qualitative research in particular, several litmus test questions in the survey were identifiable. These were questions that were useful for interpretation, displayed coherence as well as consistency with findings from the qualitative analysis (and thus some measure of external validity). In the first half of the chapter I took time to review data that clustered around two important examples in this regard. The first was the question of how workers anticipated that the closure of the ISU call centre system would affect their future work practice. I argued that although it is a seemingly obscure variable at first glance, outside the cessation of home visits and life on the road (that so many identified with a more unified division of labour, and about which the survey failed inquire), the responses to the ISU closure question had important implications. One of these implications was that it likely provided one of the best snap-shots possible of the prevalence of different trajectories of knowledge production, modes of participation, and object-relatedness within labour process activity. Prevalence is a question that quite reasonably arises in research like this, and on the question of prevalence the qualitative analysis could only make gestures. However, the question about the ISU closures also placed front and centre, yet again, the critical importance – to both power relations and learning – of the division of labour. Going further, the results from the ISU survey question were not seen here as simply a means to generate claims about prevalence however. Rather, I argued these responses were linked to subtle but definitive expressions of different standpoints within activity that contribute to the overall analysis of labour process activity.

The second litmus test question (union orientation/participation) served a slightly different function in the analysis. It was not capable of providing indications of prevalence, in part because a range of intervening variables were discovered to be at play (including matters of class, race, age, and disability). I offered a brief discussion of the significance of orientation/participation in union life and the potential role of union culture as an additional communicative sphere for workers. In the end we saw that state welfare workers oriented to and more deeply engaged in union life were supported in the construction of what I called an *amalgamated critique*: critique that was less fragmented, more unified and internally coherent, and, as a mediating artefact, capable of supporting a specific trajectory of occupational learning within labour process activity.

The last half of the chapter offered two examples of factor analysis. I argued that the complexity that emerged out of the qualitative analysis, and then the complexity of interactions between survey variables that emerged out of the bivariate analyses earlier, recommended this type of technique. The first analysis was based on variables that reflected experiences and practices most directly rooted in the state welfare work process itself. I demonstrated how craft knowledge trajectories and the dynamics of the construction of the machinery of occupational knowledge associated with it were mediated by an amalgamated critique, itself largely (though hardly exclusively) associated with additional spheres of communication, information exchange, and learning provided by higher levels of union participation. Both those who were engaged in craft and administrative trajectories of knowledge shared a more intensive use of workarounds which distinguished them from those who, for a variety of reasons, were floundering in some way. At the same time, administrative trajectories of learning were seen to be associated with concerns such as worker accountability and output-related practices (producing accurate and timely client payments) and so on (a theme raised in the qualitative analysis and further confirmed here). In sum, an understanding of the complex mediations of the trajectories of learning detailed in Chapters 7, 8, and 9 was both expanded and further supported.

Though it was not the primary purpose of this chapter, it bears mentioning again that in some ways this analysis both confirms and disconfirms a long-standing discussion in the Labour Process Theory tradition. The argument for the relative autonomy of the labour process suggests that the practices and experiences of the labour process itself are more or less autonomous from factors rooted primarily outside the labour process. The level of clarity of the results of the first factor analysis as opposed to the second offers some modest evidence bearing on this relative autonomy thesis. However, understood as mediations within the labour process, the so-called external variables cannot be discounted. In the second of the two factor analyses we saw, for example, that race, disability, gender, age, prior work experience, educational attainment, and orientations to unions clearly mattered as supports for pathways toward/along different trajectories of occupational learning. How they mattered was complex. Generalized notions of social exclusion in occupational life, in this sense, are broadened further to include processes of the channelling of the expertise, consent, as well as learning of resistance. Racialized identity, for example, was linked empirically with a form of occupational learning that tends to resist the designed objects of the labour process, but likely most effectively under certain conditions. Alternatively, *not* having a disability and describing oneself as middle-class (and the many mediations that concretize such features of identity in the course of activity) suggest supports for entering into forms of administrative trajectories of learning according to the survey research here. Gender may have been associated with craft knowledge formation, but in a somewhat ambiguous way. And the mediations flowing from educational attainment were likewise discussed throwing open several questions about the dynamics of learning at work. Each of these findings, I argue, contributed to an explanation of how occupations might become dominated by knowledge production that, as Leontiev (1978) put it earlier in the book, is either "fractionalized" or "consolidated".

11 Mind in Political Economy and the Labour Process – A Use-Value Thesis

Introduction

To repeat two phrases used from the outset, this book has been focused on the *construction of the machineries of knowledge construction* (Knorr Cetina 1999). It has been less about conventional occupational skills and knowledge than it has been about the *processes that realize them and make them possible* in activity (Leontiev 1978). I have tried to show how a dialogic use of Labour Process Theory (LPT) and Cultural Historical Activity Theory (CHAT) helps us to come to grips with a more fully situated – and more deeply humanized – perspective vis-à-vis state welfare work activity. Each tradition posed important questions and in some instances filled important gaps in the other. I argued that together they suggested the substance of a mind in political economy approach which offered a contribution to breaking the impasse of contemporary research on skill and the labour process, among several other things. The dialogue that flowed from these pages was with researchers of both the labour process and learning.

Through this research I have oriented to the following question: Why and how is it that workers come to make choices and find themselves investing their considerable learning capacities differently over time? In my various responses to this question I argued that we discover additional ways to appreciate how occupations might be transformed from within, how resistance is generated, as well as how consent permits "the degradation of work to pursue its course without continuing crisis" (Burawoy 1979, p. 94). And make no mistake, the development of ability, skill, knowledge, judgment and expertise, attention, dis-attention, personal sense, and meaning fundamentally shape, are shaped by, and are inextricable from, the production of consent, accommodation, and resistance. This is certainly true in the workplace (and very likely elsewhere).

Distinctive trajectories of occupational learning in activity emerged as fundamental points of analysis, and *each* trajectory engendered forms of struggle to adapt and transform one's self *and* the surrounding world. However, in each trajectory of occupational learning – in the processes that defined the divergent constructions of the machineries of knowledge construction – we discovered in my view that the shifting relations of *contradiction* was a persistently overarching feature. The notions of the contradictions of capitalism, the capitalist state, and the capitalist labour process, on the one hand, and the notions of contradictions as an inherent dimension of human learning and development in activity, on the other – represented a key terrain of overlap between CHAT and LPT.

Furthermore, I claimed at the outset that the study of public sector human services work presents a particularly useful opportunity to explore these contradictions. In part, this was because the questions that surround these occupations seem to demand a particularly attentive consideration of learning as it implicates matters of human purpose and need, price, and worth. More and less directly, these considerations are central to the forms of state austerity that are on the march in advanced capitalist countries around the globe today, and the concrete realities of public sector occupations like state welfare work may have an uniquely clarifying role to play in our understanding. For in such occupations, the relations of use-value and exchange-value in occupational life take on an immediately tangible, extended, and (almost) impossible-to-ignore quality. That is, in the case of state welfare work, economic vulnerability is fundamental to the business at hand. Lives are recovered or broken on a worker's watch virtually every day. As the history of debate about the meaning and purposes of the broader field of social work showed so clearly, in these types of occupations the human face of the contradictions of economic life within advanced capitalism is inseparable from the daily work. Indeed, what a study of welfare work like this emphasizes perhaps the most are the extraordinary efforts, resources, and socio-technological arrangements that are necessary to suppress, or otherwise channel, what I take to be an inherent human concern for the use-value of workers, their work, *as well as* the lives of clients, families, and communities.

This notion of *use-value*, as lying at the foundation of the type of dynamics I have examined, emerges out of a broad perspective on human learning as well as work.

> Human labour has rarely been of a fulfilling kind. For one thing, it has always been coerced … it has been carried on in class-society, and thus not as an end in itself but

as a means to the power and profit of others. For Marx, as for his mentor Aristotle, the good life consists of activities engaged in for their own sake.... When we do so, however, we are realizing a vital capacity of our "species being." And this in Marx's view is as much a form of production as planting potatoes. Human solidarity is essential for the purposes of political change; but in the end it serves as its own reason.... Production for Marx, then, means realizing one's essential powers in the act of transforming reality. True wealth, he claims in the *Grundrisse*, is "the absolute working-out of human creative potentialities ... i.e. the development of all human powers as an end in itself, not as measured on a predetermined yardstick." (Eagleton 2009, pp. 124–5)

Eagleton alerts us as directly as anyone in recent times to the distinctions between activities *governed by* either exchange-value or use-value. More important still is the fact that he also alerts us to the motor of human engagement found in the often ignored broadness of Marx's conceptualization of *production*. Production, in the workplace as well as beyond it, always pivots on the things we *do* – and the things we *learn – for their own sake*, for their use-value. It is in this sense that occupational learning lives are in a state of sustained and unavoidable contradiction under capitalism, and analyses that avoid this fact are perpetually disadvantaged. With these overview comments in mind, in this chapter I offer a theoretical synthesis of core themes and empirical findings of the book as a whole: a synthesis that results in an alternative thesis. This alternative is something I refer to as a *Use-Value Thesis*, and it begins with an extension of the commentary on dialectical materialist contradictions and human learning initiated in Chapter 2.

Principles of a Use-Value Thesis – Contradictions in the Labour/Learning Process Revisited

Along with colleagues such as Leontiev, Vygotsky co-founded the CHAT approach to learning I sought to apply in this book. And in the introduction to Vygotsky's *Mind in Society* (1978), Cole and Scribner write:

Marx's theory of society (known as historical materialism) also played a fundamental role in Vygotsky's thinking. According to Marx, historical changes in society and material life produced changes in 'human nature' (conscious and behavior). Although this general proposition had been echoed by others, Vygotsky was the first to attempt to relate it to concrete psychological questions. In this effort he creatively elaborated on Engels' concept of human labor and tool use as the means by which man changes nature and, in so doing, transforms himself.... Thus for Vygotsky, in the tradition of Marx and Engels, the mechanism of individual developmental change is rooted in society and culture.… Vygotsky generalizes his conception of the origin of higher psychological functions in a way that reveals the close relationship between fundamentally mediated nature and the dialectical, materialist conception of historical change. (Vygotsky 1978, pp. 7–8)

Quoting from Vygotsky's unpublished notebooks, Cole and Scribner (cf. Elhammoumi 2006) go on to show in his own words how Vygotsky had hoped to build an approach to *the study of the mind* based on *Marx's method*.

> The whole of *Capital* is written according to the following method: Marx analyzes a single living 'cell' of capitalist society – for example, the nature of value. Within this cell he discovers the structure of the entire system and all of its economic institutions. He says that to a layman this analysis may seem a murky tangle of tiny details. Indeed, there may be tiny details, but they are exactly those which are essential to "micro-anatomy." (p. 8)

Thus, from its very start – in its enfolding of Marx as well as Engels on the nature of human beings and the nature of work, in its championing of the relevance of the "tangle of tiny details", or what I referred to as learning made of a "billion things" – a perspective on CHAT echoing from Vygotsky's *Mind in Society* came to be embedded as one of several vital resources for an analysis of mind in political economy in this book. Through the work of Vygotsky, and in particular in the work of his colleague Leontiev, a distinctive path forward was opened for the analysis of occupational learning and knowledge construction as a thoroughly contradictory process of realizing distinctive dimensions of value in the world, and with it the humanities and inhumanities of the labour process.

It is in these terms that I begin my closing remarks in this chapter by briefly recovering a set of implicit principles of the labour/learning process that have been operative throughout the book. That is, the idea that central to understanding the functioning of (past, present, or future) society is that people are both the fully agentive human subjects as well as the objects of history. Over time, societies make and change people, and people actively make and change societies. On the surface, this is uncontroversial. However the implication for the analysis here is that it is through this broad production process that people satisfy their individual and collective (cultural, psychological, and material) needs. And, in capitalist societies, this dialectic of needs/objects/motives takes on two general and necessarily intertwining forms: i) trajectories of human learning and development that construct the satisfaction of needs *directly* as *governed* by the mediations of use-value production; and ii) trajectories of human learning and development that construct the satisfaction of needs *indirectly* as *governed* by the mediations of exchange-value production, market relations, and capitalist accumulation. These forms are necessarily intertwined because use-value necessarily provides the basis for commodity production (in that ultimately consumers buy things that they need or want to use in and for themselves). And, in addition use-value (e.g., intrinsic satisfactions, social relationships, meaning, identity, personal commitment to the quality of a product or service, etc.) continues to be produced at work even if only some of it is assigned market (i.e., exchange) value. In other words, use-value production is both the basis for market relations and also central to the experience of work itself. As Hampson and Junor (2005) put it,

> 'Work' does not mean only 'hard labour' ('ponos'), since work can sometimes become 'play'. Equally, a diversity of forms of action like play, games, casual conversation, expressive action, emotional action and symbolic action (like the devotional, the sacrificial, the sacred) is, at times, at least partially constituted by 'work'. (2005, p. 168)

At their core, however, the purposes of use-value are found in *doing*: the doing of consumption and the doing of production. And in the latter, we find the persistent, radical potential of de-alienation and transformation that I argue matters a great deal.

In all this, as Marx observed, a defining feature of capitalism is that it must challenge and master this core human principle of human need and use-value production. As it expands and matures, more and more of our use-value production becomes *governed* by the principles of exchange-value production. Life perpetually bubbles away, people learn, re-learn, cope, struggle and re-define themselves as well as the world around them, but activities are increasingly commodified, fetishized, estranged, and alienated. At a broad level of generality, this expresses the basic contradiction between the forces of production and relations of production. And this contradiction implicates but is not only defined by either conflict or repression. Indeed, it is these types of contradictions that undermine any simple dichotomy of *good* and *bad* work. At work, workers find and play a role in producing meaning, joy, engagement, as well as encounter conflict, stress, frustration and exploitation. It is the contradictory "micro-anatomy" (as Vygotsky called it) of value production in labour process activity that makes for a lively but often fragile social order.

Chapter 2 offered a set of introductory comments on contradiction in human learning and activity. There we saw that according to one of the most prominent contemporary voices in the CHAT tradition, Yrjö Engeström, contradiction in activity is inherently related to value generation and the commodity form. His work goes on to define what he called secondary, tertiary, and quaternary contradictions (i.e., dynamics expressed in such ways as role conflict in organizations, attempts to introduce new objects, the inter-relations of different systems of activity, and so on). These more peripheral expressions of contradiction, it is important to say, are deeply interwoven with but *not* necessarily unique to paid work or capitalism however. Unique to capitalism are the primary, or rather *core*, dimensions of contradiction in activity. Thus, throughout this analysis I sought to carefully avoid the fetishization of peripheral dimensions of contradiction in labour process activity. In this book I argue these core dimensions of contradiction play a role mediating, orienting and governing each and every expression of what are otherwise termed peripheral contradictions of the labour process. And, as I indicated in Chapter 2, this can be clearly understood when we make use of dialectical materialist thought attending carefully to such matters as the level of generality in analysis.

It is through theoretically and empirically elaborating on these core dimensions of contradiction and their many peripheral dimensions within occupational activity that a synthesis across concepts and findings is offered here. This is what I call a *Use-Value Thesis*. A Use-Value Thesis orients us to a broader, more unified analysis in several specific ways beginning with the use of the basic techniques of dialectical materialist thought in terms of the core dimensions of contradiction. A consistent orientation to dialectical thinking is important to sustain an analysis of the inherent motion, change and mutuality of various dimensions of contradiction that constitute human learning and development within concrete activity. At the centre of the approach are the persistent humanizing and potentially de-alienating powers of use-value production.

As I wrote in Chapter 2, the aspiration to apply a more thoroughly dialectical materialist analysis to occupational learning within labour process activity benefits from more specified points of departure. Chapter 2 provided examples of such points of departure. I returned to them at a variety of critical junctures in the book as means of perceiving more clearly the interrelations across capitalism, indeed global financial-monopoly capitalism specifically, the state, neo-liberalism, austerity, work re-organization and the learning lives of state welfare workers in the empirical analysis. These examples of research directly traced different dimensions and movements of contradiction at different levels of generality. The dynamics they addressed included the following: the *relations between the socialization of the forces of production and capitalist relations of production*, their repressive, exploitative, as well as emancipatory potential in terms of workers' knowledge (e.g., Adler 2005, 2006, 2007a); the importance of the way dominant notions of skill are constructed in vocational training and the labour process through the *de-humanization of the knowing/acting subject as well as the persistent disturbance and disorganization* of the lives of workers (e.g., Jackson 1994; Seddon, Henriksson, and Niemeyer 2010); and, the mutual constitution of *labour-power and personhood* (e.g., Rikowski 2002a, 2002b).

My approach in the book made a direct resource of these observations in order to effectively support the more general aspirations of analysis. Likewise, I drew on the traditions of LPT research on skill, the argument initiated by Vygotsky, Leontiev, and the CHAT tradition (vis-à-vis Marx and Engels), and, the recovery of the language of dialectical contradiction from Engeström through to the critical refinements offered by Avis and others. Indeed, linked inherently to my approach was the concept of *collaborative transformative practice* as emphasized by Stetsenko (e.g., 2010) in Chapter 2 as well. I claim it is through the application of these types of resources primarily, that a Use-Value Thesis on occupational learning can be realized. Through it, I argue, several new opportunities for understanding skill, learning and the labour process come into view. Each resource this Use-Value Thesis draws on contributes to the substance of something that might reasonably be called a *mind in political economy approach to the labour process*. They represent separate, and in some cases otherwise un-related, conceptualizations. Yet, I claim they each can be brought to bear on an understanding of not simply the contradictions of capitalism as such, but, as the earlier excerpt from Eagleton highlighted, the recognition of the role of the vital capacities of our "species being". That is the persistent, agentive, humanizing life force of use-value in people's working lives.

A Use-Value Thesis on State Welfare Work

With a particular set of empirical materials, in this book I have attempted to trace the movement of the realities of state welfare workers over a specific period of time. With special attention to accumulating instances of what the philosopher Evald Ilyenkov refers to as the "relative resolution" of contradictions, the analysis discovered and attempted to explain divergent learning and working in times of change.

> The dialectical materialist method of resolution of contradiction in theoretical definitions thus consists in tracing the process by which the movement of reality itself resolves them in a new form of expression. Expressed objectively, the goal lies in tracing, through analysis of new empirical materials, the emergence of reality in which an earlier established contradiction finds its relative resolution in a new objective form of its realization. (Ilyenkov 1982, p. 263)

In these terms, the core sets of evidence addressed the following: i) the history of a particular, and particularly powerful, form of work design (Taylorism); ii) the complex and uneven history of the occupation of state welfare work including the historical shifts of related labour processes; iii) workers' self-conscious perceptions across major analytic categories of the labour process (division of labour, autonomy/control, work intensification, complexity, etc.); iv) the technological and spatial mediations of practice; v) learning interventions in the course of the establishment of divergent trajectories of occupational knowledge construction; vi) the significance of changing occupational entry, group formation dynamics, and occupational enculturation; and vii) worker perspectives on the labour process and the many mediations of work practice by broader demographic features shaping pathways toward and along different trajectories of occupational learning in the aggregate. Taken together, we saw an emerging portrait of an occupation both in motion and facing an uncertain future.

In order to review the findings adequately *and* to synthesize them in terms of a Use-Value Thesis on mind in political economy and the labour process, I offer three thematic sketches to conclude the book. These deal with divergent learning trajectories, the seen but unnoticed mediations of activity, as well as occupational activity in relation to the capitalist state, political economy and social change processes more broadly. In each sub-section I work from evidence already presented and claims already argued. In each case I emphasize how expressions of the core dimensions of contradiction within activity help to explain the contemporary construction of the machineries of knowledge construction in state welfare work. Through this, I argue, we can see more clearly the emerging *new objective forms* (of occupational learning life) suggested by Ilyenkov.

The Divergences of Occupational Learning – Contradictions and Trajectories of Knowledge Construction

Chapters 7 and 8 were focused on trajectories of *administrative* and *craft* knowledge construction and learning, respectively. The differential patterns of engagement with contradiction distinguished the character of these different trajectories. That is, differentiated and differentiating patterns of active engagement by workers with the contradictory relations *between operations and goal-directed action* (administrative trajectories of learning) on the one hand, and those including the *broader object/motive* of activity (craft trajectories of learning) on the other, were defining features. How was this so?

The learning of *engrossments* discussed in Chapter 7 was seen to narrow the scope/horizon of intervention in activity to isolating forms of goal-directed action. These actions were seen to link ever more tightly over time to forms of relative/repressive satisfactions vis-à-vis the reciprocities offered by particular computer and organizationally mediated operations in particular (i.e., mediated by SDMT software realizing the promience of specific constructions of accountability, performance, career-making, and so on). These types of processes, it was argued, helped accomplish a *personal sense* of *individuated agency/control*, even while they depended upon group efforts and specific types of zones of proximal development. These processes included what I referred to as instances of (and emerging expertise in) *repair-work* as well as the work of altering one's personal sense of *self and work* aligning each with the organizational meanings provided by the premises of labour process design (i.e., a specific form of *sense-repair-work/skill*). These minutiae of occupational learning expressed something significant. Through them, we saw how the *contradictory relations between operation and goal-direction in activity* were, over time, made a key *fixture* in work practice. In turn, this helped further explain the character of *administrative* trajectories of occupational knowledge construction. Here, activity was defined by the dynamic suppression (and repression) of collaborative transformative practice in relation to the core dimensions of contradiction. Using Leontiev's terms, this mode of participation and emergent object-relatedness of activity was found to be *fractionated and fractionating*. This was used to warrant my use of the concept of *re-skilling*, an often under-specified by widely used term derived from sociology of work and LPT traditions.

By contrast, in Chapter 8 we saw the importance of the practices, means, and mediations of *re-keying* in activity. The concept of re-keying described very different modes of participation and object-relatedness within activity that were made distinctive through, in the first instance, successful forms of *resistance to administrative engrossments*. These processes involved specific forms of artefact-creation, sub-vocalizations, and vocalizations of distinctive *self-talk* mantras that, within equally specific processes of *collective internalization and externalization*, were converted to powerful forms of mediating *we-talk* mantras in the course of collaborative transformative practice. The combination of artefact production in activity played a distinct role in re-keying practices. Building on this, I charted growing expertise in repair-work/skill and sense-repair-work/skill and demonstrated the emergence of a third work/skill type as well: *object-work/skill*. In Chapter 8 this culminated in the processes through which the *contradictory relations across operation, goal-direction, and object/motive in activity* were, over time, made a defining *fixture* of *craft trajectories of occupational knowledge construction*. In other words, the core dimensions of contradictions in activity were made central in and through this learning. Using Leontiev's terms, this mode of participation and emergent object-relatedness within labour process activity was found to be *consolidated and consolidating*. This, I argued, offered a genuine warrant for the use of the label of *up-skilling*.

It is in light of these many dynamics and the recognizable distinctions between patterns of occupational learning that the contradiction between use-value and exchange-value could be seen to play a crucial role overall. In the course of accumulating occupational learning achievements, *administrative trajectories of occupational knowledge production* became increasingly shaped by, and increasingly contributed to, a particular nexus of object/motive/need that affirms the *governance* of labour process activity by *exchange-value over use-value generation* in these workers' lives. This also involved the squeezing of the opportunities for the meeting of individual and collective needs directly (i.e., use-values generation) into ever narrower regions of work life practice. In this sense, a state welfare worker resolved the contradictions of capitalism for and within herself. Carried out *socially* and *collectively* only in the most limited forms of means/end transaction – we discovered the complex process of learning to narrow the scope of engagement in occupational life to the most peripheral dimensions of the contradiction of labour process activity as defined by austerity goals represented in work design.

In the course of a very different set of accumulating occupational learning achievements, *craft trajectories of occupational knowledge production* were the result of the construction of an alternative nexus of object/motive/need. Here the trajectory of development was characterized by the increasing governance of participation in labour process activity by *use-value generation over exchange-value generation*. This helped to explain expanding instances of transformative engagement with manifestations of the *core dimensions of contradiction*. Here the particular form of object-relatedness in activity resulted in a growing influence of a nexus of object/motive/need in which the direct satisfaction of individual and collective needs (of workers, clients, and community) penetrated into ever larger regions of work practice. A personal sense of socialized, rather than individuated, autonomy began to prevail as a feature of learning for these workers. Again, what Leontiev referred to as a consolidating rather than a fractionating mode of participation in activity was identified. Workers learned new technical skills and knowledge. They creatively worked *around* rather than creatively within the machinations of the labour process as designed. Unavoidably, they learned the kinds of politicized lessons that Baines (in a set of observations I will return to again in a moment) refers to as "a humanizing force and a force for resistance and change [that] extend beyond the workplace". This, Baines argued, was akin to the dynamics that Gramsci called "trench warfare" (2008, pp. 129–30).

Thought of in a slightly different way by borrowing from Lave and Wenger (1991), in drawing peripheral dimensions of contradiction more and more tightly into the orbit of the agentive engagement with central dimensions of contraction, it might be said that trajectories of craft learning express a *centripetal* dynamic. And in administrative trajectories of occupational learning we see the opposite: a *centrifugal* dynamic which forces human attention and investment of energies to the periphery, further from the core dimensions of contradiction. Whether we use these types of terms or those offered by Leontiev, the fact is that Chapters 7 and 8 put the agentive, human face on forms of consent, accommodation, and resistance *as forms of occupational skill, knowledge, and learning practice*. What I identify as *floundering* was not inconsequential but, in terms of the focus here, secondary. Where floundering did not refer to the learning and practices of hiding poor job performance or social withdrawal, it addressed workers actively negotiating a clear entry point into one of the two principal modes of participation within activity that were identified. Thus, we can say that state welfare workers – moving *toward, along and between* administrative and craft trajectories of learning – were engaged in a constant negotiation of *labour-power within and against relations of control* that deeply implicated *personhood*. It was a struggle that I argue can only be recognized properly in terms of the *socialization of the forces of production and the capitalist relations of production*. And it is set against the presumptions of skill, the objectifying relations of work design, and their *disorganizing* effect on the production of working knowledge.

These are the precise types of observations that a Use-Value Thesis is meant to generate. It is a thesis on occupational learning in capitalist society aimed at exposing how *difference* becomes *divergence*, divergence may result in broader change, and I argue it provides new opportunities for assessing the struggle for the *meaning, price,* and *worth* of vital occupations like state welfare work in times of change. Perhaps foremost, it is a thesis meant to highlight how such struggles are always ultimately fuelled by the use-value generation of workers that must always bring the otherwise alienating machineries of work design to life and in so doing express what Marx referred to as our "species being". Occupational change as well as social change are the result of many things, but, in this way, are likewise traceable in the accumulated, memorable, half-remembered, and un-remembered learning accomplishments that define the full character of different diverging trajectories of knowledge construction in working lives. A Use-Value Thesis aims to integrate the centrality of the core dimensions of contradiction between use-value and exchange-value that define capitalism: it speaks to the reasons for their marginalization in thought and action. It seeks to address the messy humanity at play within the changing conditions of contemporary work life, as well as the experiences, choices, emotions, knowing, and acting summarized in the terms repair-work/skill, sense-repair-work/ skill, and object-work/skill. As I wrote in Chapter 2, the book is addressing occupational learning in *times of change*. The *times* I speak about here are those linked with austerity, re-organization, de-skilling, and the arts of knowing and not knowing in a system of fragmented knowledge. And, throughout rests the claim that the production of occupational knowledge – the struggle over the development of the content, tools, sense, meaning and purposes of jobs themselves – speaks to and may yet be re-discovered as a crucial companion to other forms of political economic participation.

The 'Seen but Unnoticed' Dimension of Occupational Learning – Contradictions and the Relations of Spatiality, Group Formation, and Broader Social Differences

Within the analysis of this book are claims that an entire world of *seen but unnoticed* dimensions of learning and activity are as intensely political and economic as they are cultural and historical. Used in a variety of places in the book, this notion of the *seen but unnoticed* is a phrase drawn from the ethnomethodological research tradition. As noted, I use it to refer to the thoroughly interactive and agentive structuring of attention/dis-attention, and the object-relatedness of self-conscious and un-self-conscious practices. From the perspective of CHAT, operations remained a crucial example of instances of practices that were seen but went unnoticed. And we have seen that the mediations of operations in distinct task sets by minute computer functions, by spatiality, by group formation, as well as by broader dynamics of identity (including age, race, gender, disability, and educational attainment, for example) each played an important role in occupational learning. Again, the relations between peripheral and core dimensions of contradiction in activity were implicated. On what bases do I make this claim?

The significance of operations and the distinctive relations of contradiction of divergent trajectories of occupational knowledge production were highlighted earlier. What has not been reviewed in terms of relations of contradictions is the matter of spatiality that was analyzed at a variety of points, but in particular in Chapter 6. The application of Lefebvre's approach to the production of space supported the interpretation of occupational activity and specific forms of spatiality as fully contradictory, material dynamics endemic to capitalism. The contradictions of the mode of production were implicated. That is the mutually defining and mutually undermining relations between the state employer and state labour emerged and mediated occupational learning in the course of the implementation of the new SDMT-based labour process. Supported by the overview of the principles of work change and the intentions of the state highlighted in Chapters 3 and 4, in Chapter 6 we saw in detail how the requirements of neo-liberal austerity were embedded in *conceived space* of the labour process *as designed*. And yet likewise, we also saw the contradictions of learning in activity as workers populated this space, *perceived*, and, in particular, *lived* within and sometimes against the limits of conceived space. Specific attention was given to the operational functions of the SDMT software: software which mediated, afforded, inhibited, and prohibited a range of operations that workers registered self-consciously only in times of crisis. The true power of these mediations, however, was found when routine was reasserted and in the course of carrying out operations in activity workers "just felt a change" coming over them as we saw. The frequently taken-for-granted relations of *space/time/distance* I examined in Chapter 6 supported an additional layer of interpretation for the notion of the *de-skilled premises* of the labour process. That is, we explored how the contradictions between the realization of exchange-value and use-value across the premises of the conceived space of design and the uneven dynamics of perceived and lived space were a powerful mediating force in occupational learning.

Many workers lamented the change in their relationships with clients in the new labour process. However, what went largely seen but unnoticed by the vast majority (even many of those highly critical of the re-organization of their work) was how the de-humanization of the client in occupational learning unfolded from the dynamics of *secondary processing* (Knorr Cetina 1999). Here, at the level of operations, an important contradiction between the human use-value of a *biographical client-person* and the exchange-value of *case and caseload* commodification was seen to play out. As we saw, the conversion of people into cases mediated (and was mediated by) perceptions of legitimized work performance and in many instances the achievement of careers as well (Chapter 7). We also saw how this secondary processing was based on the principle of cost-per-case administration/financing embedded within work design (Chapters 4 and 8). In each of these cases, the production of highly contradictory patterns of *dis-attention* was central. However, we can observe also that under certain circumstances dis-attention could play an entirely different role. That is, for workers successfully engaged in a craft trajectory of occupational learning their *dis-attention to administrative engrossments* was a pivotal accomplishment. Moreover, in this research we even encountred distinctive forms of workarounds that were circulated widely (often aided by local management). The differences between them that emerge within different forms of participation in activity were rarely, if ever, noticed self-consciously. They too were essential to the ratification of orientations to either meeting the needs of the designed system of work and exchange-value generation, or rejecting these needs in favour of various forms of use-value generation.

While in Chapter 9 attention was paid to the contradictory dynamics of workers' perceptions (and mis-perceptions) of each other vis-à-vis group formation, interwoven with this argument was also a range of mediations that were seen but unnoticed. Few, if any, workers self-consciously recognized how such things as the arrangement of cubicles (also discussed in Chapter 6) or managerial practices of forming teams were a significant feature of their own shifting occupational identity, learning, skill, and knowledge development. However, amidst the concerns of veteran state welfare workers about changing entry requirements, these seen but unnoticed mediations may have been crucial. Indeed, the influence of union participation (Chapters 9 and 10) – generating an additional sphere of communication, information exchange, and occupational learning – was seen to shape activity in ways that typically went unnoticed as well. Each of these un-self-conscious dimensions of operations within activity sharpened contradictions not just in the learning lives of individual workers, but within the learning lives between groups of workers. These observations contributed to broader claims regarding the decline of inter-generational occupational enculturation. I argue, vis-à-vis a range of hidden learning dynamics, this decline is inseparable from the shifting nature of use-value and exchange-value governance in activity.

As one final example of an interpretation of the analysis in terms of a Use Value Thesis we can turn to the many hidden dimensions of occupational learning addressed in the second half of Chapter 10. There I explored the mediating effects of broader social differences. The way in which the contradictory relations of occupation and social class were shaped by and implicated many other aspects of identity was explicitly tested. No doubt limited by the initial design of the interview protocol, few interviewees spoke directly about the full range of social differences in the workplace and how these differences shaped occupational learning. Indeed, almost certainly pivoting on multiple forms of privilege, for workers either some or all of such mediations were seen but unnoticed. The survey data, however, revealed something different, if not always definitive. Gender, disability, race, age, and a host of other dynamics were found to be implicated in the achievement of different trajectories of occupational learning. The establishment of a craft trajectory of occupational development in activity, for example, was supported by a set of distinctive pathways toward and along it. Racialized workers appeared to draw on different, and differently configured, resources than did non-racialized workers, as they embarked upon and realized craft learning in state welfare work. Male workers seemed to engage in this trajectory of craft learning differently than female workers. While identifying as a disabled worker did not seem to co-vary with craft learning as such, reporting no disability in the survey seemed to be associated with a pathway toward and along trajectories of administrative occupational development. The types of interactions across social difference that we saw, and their bearing on how occupational learning itself unfolds, were not typically available to workers in a self-conscious way, but they were nonetheless important. A Use-Value Thesis, in this sense, emerges as an important means to recognize analytically not simply the self-conscious and un-self-conscious dimensions of something that we might call *occupational class struggle*. Rather, in attending carefully to the seen but unnoticed, a Use-Value Thesis offers an opportunity to pursue an understanding of a broader range of mediating dynamics (originating both within and beyond the relatively autonomous relations of production). The analysis necessarily raises almost as many questions as it answers in these terms. However, it confirms in a distinctive way that the contradictions of use-value and exchange-value that define the production, reproduction, and transformation of class relations cannot be considered in isolation.

The Contradictions of the State, Neo-Liberalism, and Monopoly-Finance Capitalism in Occupational Learning

As I argued from the outset, state welfare work is propped uncomfortably at the fault-line of economy and civil society. Beyond the work of those referenced in my discussion of the nature of the state as well as state welfare and social work labour processes in Chapter 4, several of the basic preoccupations of a Use-Value Thesis are already identifiable within the existing, critically-minded literature (cf. Lavalette 2011). In Canada specifically, Baines (2008) suggests important links among notions of social work skill, resistance, and broader political economic contention under capitalism. The excerpt that follows is rooted in the dynamics of social work and its relationship to social change as well as the hidden resources of broader social mobilization. It is, however, invaluable in terms of observations concerning a Use-Value Thesis as it applies to state welfare workers as well. She describes dynamics of activity that

> reveal a gradualism that expands the opportunities of others (clients and workers) to survive and possibly to retain dignity and energy within an often unwelcoming and uncaring society. Some may argue that the actions described herein are not skills, rather they are techniques or everyday behavior.… [T]hese skills not only extended social caring beyond narrow agency resources and mandates, but also suggested new ways of understanding social work practice as a humanizing force and a force for resistance and change.… They are part of an overall strategy to manage and negotiate power relations that extend beyond the workplace. This kind of multisite, often commonplace, resistance contributes to a process that Gramsci (1971) called *trench warfare* – a form of struggle in which noncompliance with social institutions undermines rather than overthrows the control of dominant groups and in the process builds new social relations and institutions. (Baines 2008, pp. 129–30; emphasis in original)

The analysis offered in this book attempts to draw these types of observations into a more detailed discussion of the dynamics of occupational learning through the use of concepts derived from LPT and CHAT primarily. The observations are remarkably consistent with the types of approach described earlier by, for example, Adler (e.g., 2006, 2007a), who sees the seeds of social change even in the alienations and exploitations of advanced labour process designs. In the research in this book we have been able to recognize new levels of state employer control *and* the limits of this control through a mind in political economy approach to the activity of state welfare workers. The general *contradictions of control* in this case are the contradictions of use-value and exchange-value realized within the new forms of labour process activity initiated by the austerity measures of the neo-liberal state under capitalism. Thus, recalling further the analysis in this book, we can ask, In what way is this so?

I began by recognizing that the current wave of neo-liberalism and public sector austerity has emerged out of a contemporary system of global financial pressures that are attributable to a debt crisis ultimately brought on by what Bellamy Foster and Magdoff (2009) and others have referred to as *monopoly-finance capitalism*.[1] However, in terms of a broader relationship between political economic relations, on the one hand, and the changes in state welfare work labour/learning processes, on the other, I noted in Chapter 4 several prior phases of change including those that, in North America, also pre-dated the twentieth century (e.g., the administration of volunteer charity work). I argued these broader historical observations provided several points worth considering in discussion of the contemporary changes in work organization as well as workers response to it. Even still, in contemporary Canada, neo-liberal austerity and global monopoly-finance capitalism, as we saw, entered the learning lives of state welfare workers in fits and starts including, but not limited to, the overtures represented by New Public Management. The impacts of these shifts were realized in the contemporary context, through the new political freedoms experienced by conservative government (vis-à-vis a long series of changes in federal and provincial funding and administration responsibilities), the use of private sector partnerships as well as the availability of new technologies. I argued that it was through these changes that the state could finally enact the familiar turn toward a sweeping application of Taylorism to state welfare work. In fact, in Chapter 3 we saw a re-framing of Taylorism (reassessing its unique powers in terms of a material approach to learning and task design in a two-front war specifically). In Chapter 4 we encountered the historical reasons and evidence for its application today. In the light of a broader synthesis, in this chapter we can now recognize the dynamics of the contradictions of use-value and exchange-value at a much broader level of generality as well as by dialectical extension, but which nevertheless a Use Value Thesis finds traceable to the minutiae of the occupational lives of workers in this research.

In fact, Chapter 3 was meant specifically to reinvigorate an awareness of particular principles of capitalist labour process design (Taylorism) as an enduring force rather than a fossil. Emphasizing the origins, commitments, and powers of Taylorism in its attempts to achieve the ongoing goals of capitalist production stresses all the more that the SDMT labour process in state welfare work (despite being part of the public sector) was now more intimately revolving around the contradictory relations of use-value and exchange-value. In outlining its application in some detail (beginning with analysis of de-skilling in Chapter 5 and Chapter 6) I suggested the eerie familiarity of Taylorism as a particular type of (two front) war over surplus value and control which solidified the role of contradictions in the analysis further. At the same time, Chapter 4 also historically traced the evolution of several key mediating resources of both resistance (in this case, the struggles of social workers in Canada to legitimize the more radical purposes of their work) and consent (i.e., the establishment of professional occupational status in the context of bureau-professional regimes).

Against this backdrop, a Use-Value Thesis recommends that few if any of the dynamics I identified in the book could be readily understood outside the mediations of neo-liberal austerity, or global monopoly-finance capitalism as embodied in the familiar turn toward a type of Taylorism. It was in relation to these premises that the new labour process in question here were established. Specifically, as I sought to demonstrate across several chapters this involved the contradictory nature and role of the capitalist state. This role requires that, on the one hand, it must maintain a semblance of legitimacy. In the case of this research, at present in Canada, it must continue to be seen to deliver some minimal form of service to the poor. On the other hand, the state continually comes face to face with the intensifying tasks of social control within the confines of a turbulent system of capitalist accumulation.[2] In basic form, the situation is one that has not changed in some time (cf. Gramsci 1971; Miliband 1973). However, it is the context through which the state's need to control and manage clients coincides with austerity and, in turn, the need to exercise greater control over welfare workers themselves. This re-organization of the labour process and management of workers is thus ultimately rooted in, as Piven and Cloward (1971) noted, the regulation of the poor.[3] To some, perhaps, these are externalities of the learning/labour process. However, in this book we saw important mediations in the lives of state welfare workers rooted in political economy of the state expressing these dynamics precisely. Again, the discussion of "level of generality" in Chapter 2 identified the general framework (i.e., dialectical materialist thought) for understanding how this was so. These mediations of labour process activity emerged in the form of the contradictory features of occupational learning in which work design and the SDMT technology were central. This, as we saw, resulted in increasingly contentious interactions between worker and client; a site of interaction which lies at the heart of the knowledge form that Taylorism, as defined here, sought to disturb, disorganize, and, if successful, eventually displace. The dynamics of learning that were explored stemmed directly from mediations of everyday practices by premises of austerity and de-skilling in the labour process (Chapters 2 and 3). These premises took the form of specific artefacts and configurations of artefacts which afforded a specific object-relatedness within activity. These premises were central constituents of a particular form of conceived space in production (Chapter 6). Together they represented a key link among political economy, the contradictions of the capitalist state, and contentious dynamics of occupational learning.

These *times of change* draw increasingly stark battle-lines between worker and client, sets of workers, as well as across workers, local management, and the state employer. The lesson provided by Lipsky (1980) should not be ignored however: "street bureaucracy" in the lives of state welfare workers is alive and well. Amongst workers, local management and, not infrequently clients, these times of change also produce forms of cooperation under specific circumstances and around specific points of shared concern. Even still, workers bear misgivings about their work, their clients, and possibly their occupation, while the distrust and suspicion of clients themselves are increasingly pronounced as well (Herd and Mitchell 2005). Indeed, the new levels of vulnerability of the biographical client-person as well as meaningful worker-client relations should not cover up the challenges that the former welfare labour processes produced from the standpoint of clients in particular. Research on social work and state welfare work referenced throughout the book persistently underlined important questions of this type, and they clearly bear on the broader dynamics of occupational learning. Clearly, clients were made vulnerable in earlier welfare labour processes, but in an entirely different way. Thus, while guarding against romanticization of prior labour processes (despite the fact that romanticization frequently proved to be an important mediational resource in many workers' learning we saw here) we can note the fact that the possibilities for worker resistance, and the potential for workers to learn to expand upon their own humanizing impulses, have been narrowed considerably. That is, the opportunities for workers to respond effectively to the many expressions of contradiction between use-value and exchange-value generation in their occupational learning lives have become significantly more constrained. The difference between former and current learning/labour processes thus pivots on the recognition that greater power to realize austerity goals – and to mediate the lives of workers and through this more harshly discipline the poor – now rests in the hands of the capitalist state. With the power of the state, itself under siege at the hands of a system of monopoly-finance capital, both workers and clients are markedly more vulnerable.

The governance of learning life by exchange-value is intensifying for these workers. This is the political economy of distrust and vulnerability as well as potentiality within the learning lives of state welfare workers. Forms of occupational knowledge themselves are being altered. Deepening the point, it should not go without mentioning that across these battle-lines there are growing patterns of breakdown, floundering, instrumentalism, careerism and human alienation. In Chapter 4 of the book I referenced Ferguson and Lavalette (2004) and others in connection to this very issue. The systemic changes to the labour process are persistently undermining the otherwise de-alienating potentialities of the use-value of the lives of state welfare workers and the lives of the poor. This is an intensifying, contradictory, structural condition of occupational learning lives in which workers themselves – as living, breathing, and indeterminate *labour power* – play a crucial role. As an expression of core dimensions of contradiction between, for example, the socialization of the forces of production and capitalist relations of production, we see many state welfare workers engaged in the struggle to re-inherit the progressive possibilities of their occupation in which the *failure* to serve the direct needs of the fully biographical client-person is a form of *success* for state actors seeking both cost avoidance and reduced welfare rolls.[4] What is made equally clear is that no such failures/successes occur in the absence of the participation of concrete individuals thinking, feeling, knowing, and acting within labour process activity. Choices, and inherent to them responsibilities, are implicated in a Use-Value Thesis of occupational learning in this sense.

In efforts to seek a more fully humanized appreciation for the everyday triumphs and tragedies of occupational learning amongst the contemporary state welfare workers we met in this book, we cannot afford to lose the point raised by Baines (2008) at the beginning of this sub-section. It revolves around the accumulating, structural potential for political resistance, the notion of a *trench warfare* (the grinding "war of position" as opposed to mobilization or movement), and the transformational inter-dependencies that emerge from an increasingly shared experience of deepening contradiction at work. While the dynamics of austerity impact workers, workers vis-à-vis their learning lives may also impact the shape and future of austerity in potentially progressive ways. This too is a thematic that links the machineries of occupational knowledge construction directly to the broader dynamics of political economy of the state and beyond.

In the end, inherent to the theme synthesized in this sub-section is the question of political economic transformation. I am not alone in arguing this is an unavoidable question if we are to appreciate the fullness of occupational learning in activity (Chapter 2), and I claim a Use-Value Thesis on mind in political economy may be helpful in answering it. Fundamental transformation is obviously not the sole preserve or responsibility of any particular sector of workers. In advanced capitalism, both post-industrialism and non-Marxist streams of LPT helped to emphasize the failures (e.g., the over-emphasis on the role of factory workers) associated with this type of thinking. Yet still we can say, state welfare work does lie at a unique intersection of citizens, the capitalist state, and the violent workings of capitalist political economy. At the very least, on the basis of minimal income support, the services state welfare workers provide either support or undermine the capacity for the poor (those who have the very least to lose from broader transformation) to stabilize their lives and, possibly, respond. Of course alternatively these same forms of support may be used to purchase consent (cf. Piven and Cloward 1971). Either way, the core dimensions of the contradiction of capitalism converge here in especially sharp relief, and there is an enormous amount to be learned from the response of these workers among many others.

Thus even as social change comes about by the accumulation of many sources of organization, mobilization, and action within and beyond the workplace – at the crux of the matter rest several questions as it regards the research in this book. What exactly is the contribution of learning at the point of production in social change? May there still be something left to be said about the relationship among occupationally specific knowledge, the persistence of use-value, and (what scholars used to refer to as) *worker militancy*? For both better and worse, is it the case that working knowledge is a crucial political and economic knowledge as well? There are clues as to the latent potential of the types of genuine up-skilling processes described in this research that suggest a variety of answers to just these types of questions. A defining feature of up-skilling and what Leontiev referred to as consolidating knowledge forms, as we have seen in Chapter 8, is an expansive knowledge production process that entails a type of broader perspective on the role, for example, of the state and financialization in people's lives. Indeed, a Use-Value Thesis suggests this expansion emerges out of the micro-anatomies of activity, what Vygotsky earlier spoke of as the "murky tangle of tiny details" that make up the contradictory occupational life of the thinking, feeling, knowing, and acting subject. At the same time, these details account for a very different mode of participation in activity as well: i.e., one that produces the fractionalization of learning (Chapter 7). Learning the arts of making out and engrossment, games, relative/repressive satisfactions, as well as Luedtke's (1986) notion of *eigensinn* (cf. notes, Chapter 7), all suggest individuation processes and the establishment of an increasingly "privatized politics" rooted in the labour/learning process. In the term *eigensinn*, as with several other concepts I apply more widely, we can distill, for example, that the true meanings of worker re-appropriation of time and space in the labour process actually revolve around the seemingly basic question of purpose, learning, and the broader object-relatedness of activity. Again, this is a matter inseparable from political economy and the relations of contradiction of use- and exchange-value as well.

Understanding the "how" of learning in these ways, I argue, is likely one of the most under-utilized stepping stones to appreciating the processes of making and re-making an occupation vis-à-vis the dynamics of consent, accommodation and resistance. And where occupational learning is not simply written off as a site in which workers are presumed to either simply learn to be dominated, or simply learn to exercise their apparently natural proclivities as acquisitive and un-restrained free agents, I argue the deeply humanized impulses associated with use-value production emerge time and time again. Indeed, from the belly of protests that are marking the battle with austerity today – whether it has been in Wisconsin, Québec or elsewhere in North America, or in Belgium, France, Greece, Portugal, the United Kingdom – the knowledge and experiences of public sector workers, normally well sequestered within in administrative lives, are changing. More than likely this learning is taking on new, more consolidated, and possibly more radical forms, as the sounds of price and worth – of use-value and exchange-value – clash.

Conclusions

It would be nice if meeting the basic needs of human beings – those of workers and the poor – were not subject to the types of deeply contradictory dynamics that I have tried to explore in this book. This is a general point made by Eagleton:

> The hope for a better future cannot just be a wistful "wouldn't it be nice if…" If it is to be more than an ideal fantasy, a radically different future must be not only desirable but feasible; and to be feasible it has to be anchored in the *realities of the present*. It cannot just be dropped into the present from some political outer space. *There must be a way of scanning or X-raying the present which shows up a certain future as a potential within it.*… Starting from where we are may not sound the best recipe for political transformation. The present seems more an obstacle to such change than an occasion for it. As the stereotypically thick-headed Irishman remarked when asked the way to the railway station: "Well, I wouldn't start from here." The comment is not as illogical as some might think, which is also true of the Irish. It means "You'd get there quicker and more directly if you weren't starting from the awkward, out-of-the-way spot." … Only by accepting that *contradictions are the nature of class-society*, not by denying them in a spirit of serene disinterestedness, can you unlock the human wealth they hold back. It is at the points where the logic of the

> present comes unstuck, runs into impasse and incoherence, that Marx, surprisingly enough, finds the outline of a transfigured future. (Eagleton 2009, pp. 69–71, 79; emphasis added)

We can always only start from precisely where we are. Luckily there are a range of resources available to us to do precisely what Eagleton has in mind when he speaks about the need for "X-raying the present" in order to find the "future potential within it".

As regards research on work and learning, Adler (2004) points out, "[a] good theory of skill is needed" (p. 258), and he says this in the context of a number of broader concerns. However, setting aside the obvious value of much sociology of work and LPT research specifically, I argue we should wonder what kind of visions of skill and knowledge are allowed to stand-in for the dynamic processes concerning how these skills and knowledge actually emerge (or are made to disappear) in the *concrete doings* of people's occupational lives. Researchers are faced with something of a choice. We can continue to construct and name an ever proliferating set of work/skill types and correlate their appearance with different elements of labour process; *or*, we can more diligently seek to inform these otherwise useful observations with a turn toward critical analyses of practice. Such a turn might demonstrate how capitalist political economy, the labour process, and the learning process can be understood within the same unit of analysis. And it it might do something more than just undermine the dominance of proxy references to challenge the type of skills impasse I described early on.

It is in this sense that beneath the basic attention to the principles that define capitalism, this book has tried to offer a presentation of occupational learning that doggedly attempts to keep real, living human beings at the centre. The book can be said to presume the standpoint of Marxist Humanism in this way. It presumes that people must – in all their bravery, commitment, frustration, mania, shirking, joy, fascination, failure, and exhaustion – learn to accomplish the task of historical change, and they do so *because of and despite* the contradictions they face.

Even limited to the sphere of a particular occupation, a particular labour process, and a particular national context, such concerns point to the significant challenge of inter-disciplinary dialogue. It is not unlike the impulse that Leontiev (1978) was responding to in the final words of *Activity, Personality and Consciousness*: "thinking about the perspectives of psychological science as centering in itself multifaceted approaches to man [*sic*], one must not be distracted from that fact that this *centering* takes place on the *social* level – just as it is at this level that human fate is decided" (p. 143; emphasis in original). In terms of a particular type of inter-disciplinary dialogue, I have argued that an unflagging orientation to *use-value* – that is, *people* and the trans-historical life energies that persistently motivate their action and realize what Marx called their "species being" – allows the linkage of critical labour process analysis to robust theories of activity and mind in political economy.

Appendix: List of Interviewees and Demographic Information

Interview Code	Education Level	Union Activism Level	Age	Gender	Seniority	Dis-ability	Self-Described Social Class	Job Title	Self-Described Race/Ethnicity
B1PS0303	High school diploma and several certificates	Medium	59	F	18	Yes	Middle-class	Consolidated Verification Process worker	Caucasian Canadian
B2PS0303	High school diploma, 2 yrs. University	High	36	M	12	No	refused	Consolidated Verification Process worker	Canadian
B3PS0303	Bachelor of Arts, Psychology	High	42	F	12	No	Middle-class	Case Manager	Caucasian Anglo Saxon
BBATH0303	College diploma in human resources management	Low	25	F	4	No	Middle-class	Case Manager	Refused
BCBBP0704a	High school diploma	n/a	n/a	F	25	n/a	refused	Case Manager	Caucasian
BCBBP0704b	College diploma in General Arts	High	n/a	F	11	n/a	refused	Employment Services Worker	Caucasian
BDBTH0303	Bachelor of Arts Social Work	Low	40	F	14	No	Middle-class	Intake Screening Worker, former Case Manager	Caucasian
BEMAT0303	High school diploma, Course certificates from college	High	44	F	11	No	Middle-class	Case Manager	Caucasian

BGPS203	High school completion	Low	23	F	1	No	Middle-class	Case Manager	White
BHSPS0903	BA in social work	Medium	25	F	3	No	Professional	Case Manager	Caucasian
BJG303PS	BA social work	Low	39	M	8	No	Middle-class	Intake Screening Worker	White
BJGTH0303	High school diploma	Medium	55	F	4	No	Middle-class	Clerical support worker	Caucasian
BKRTH0303	Social Service diploma	Low	25	F	3	No	Middle-class	Case Manager	Caucasian
BKSAT0303	Early childhood education college diploma	Medium	39	F	14	No	Middle-class	Employment Services Worker	Anglo- Saxon
BPPPS0903	BA in sociology and MA in social work	Medium	37	F	14	No	Middle-class	Consolidated Verification Process worker	White Anglo-Saxon English Canadian
BSLAT0303	College diploma and university degree	Low	49	F	13	No	Middle-class	Case Manager	refused
BPSBP1009	College diploma in social services	High	47	F	16	No	Middle-class	Employment Services Worker	Canadian
HABAT0503	College diploma in social work	Medium	27	F	3	No	Middle-class	Case Manager	Caucasian
HAT22404	BA psychology	Medium	33	M	5	No	Middle-class	Consolidated Verification Process worker	refused
HBBAT0403	BA economics	Medium	46	M	11	No	Middle and working-class	Intake Screening Worker	Caucasian

(continued)

Interview Code	Education Level	Union Activism Level	Age	Gender	Seniority	Dis-ability	Self-Described Social Class	Job Title	Self-Described Race/Ethnicity
HBNAT503	College diploma incomplete	Low	26	F	2	No	Professional	Consolidated Verification Process worker	Canadian
HCAAT0303	College diploma in social services; currently completing a BA	Low	26	M	2.5	No	Middle-class	Case Manager	Caucasian
HCWAT0303	BA in social work	Medium	44	F	17	Yes arthritis	Working-class	Case Manager	Caucasian
HDKAT0404[1]	College diploma in social services	Low	39	F	5	No	Middle-class	Consolidated Verification Process Worker	White
HDSAT0404[1]	BA in social work and college diploma in social welfare	Medium	55	M	15	No	Middle-class	Employment Services Worker	White
HGAAT0404[1]	College diploma in social work	Low	46	F	13	No	Middle-class/ working-class	Case Manager	Caucasian
HGWAT0404	BA in political science	Low	36	M	2	No	Middle-class	Case Manager	refused
HIMAT0404	High school diploma	Low	38	F	13	No	Just normal	Consolidated Verification Process worker	German-Canadian

HJBAT0104	BA in English and college diploma in social services	Low	43	F	21	No	Lower middle-class	Consolidated Verification Process worker	Caucasian
HJIDAT0404	BA in anthropology and college diploma in computer science	Medium	44	F	13	No	Middle-class / working-class	Case Manager	Ethnically diverse
HJKAT0404	Completing BA and holds college certificate in accounting	Low	38	M	13	No	Middle-class	Consolidated Verification Process worker	Slavic/Eastern European
HJMAT0903	BA in history	Medium	58	M	18	No	Middle-class	Eligibility Review Officer	White
HJSAT0104	College diploma (unspecified)	Low	30	F	6	No	Middle-class	Employment Services Worker	refused
HKMAT0404	BA in social work	Medium	47	F	13	Yes (repetitive strain injury in wrist)	Middle-class	Employment Services Worker	British
HLPAT0903	BA in history; BA in psychology; college diploma in counselling; MA in history incomplete	Medium	40	M	2.5	No	Middle-class	Case Manager	Welsh
HMBAT0404	MA in economics and college diploma in social work	Low	54	M	16	No	Middle-class	Case Manager	East Indian

(continued)

Interview Code	Education Level	Union Activism Level	Age	Gender	Seniority	Dis-ability	Self-Described Social Class	Job Title	Self-Described Race/Ethnicity
HMLAT0303	BA in social work and BA in sign language	High	36	F	11	Yes (hard of hearing)	Middle-class	Eligibility Review Officer/ Consolidated Verification Process Worker	White French
HMMAT0903	BA in sociology	Medium	59	M	13 (+10)	No	Working-class	Intake Screening Worker	Light-skinned
HMRAT1003	BA in economics	Low	32	M	3	No	Professional	Case Manager	White
HNMAT0603	BA in PHE and B.Ed. and College diploma in fitness	Low	27	F	1.5	No	Lower middle-class	Consolidated Verification Process worker	White
HSAAT0903	High School	Medium	57	F	7	No	Working-class	Case Manager	Canadian
HTHAT0503	BA sociology and diploma in early childhood education	Medium	38	F	12	No	Middle-class	Case Manager	Eastern European
HTTAT1003	BA in sociology	Medium	44	F	19	No	Middle-class	Consolidated Verification Process worker	Canadian
HTTPS404[2]	BA social work	Low	56	F	19	No	Middle-class	Case Manager	White
NBW403DB[2]	Highschool + certificate in human services	Low	25	F	2	No	Middle-class	Clerical support worker	Black
NF15DB0303	BA in social work	Medium	38	F	10	No	Working-class	Employment Services Worker	Canadian

NF16DB0403	College diploma in social services and incomplete BA	Medium	41	F	11	No	Middle-class	Consolidated Verification Process Worker	White
NF17DB0304	College diploma in social work; part way through a degree in human resources	Medium	46	F	11	No	Middle-class	Case Manager	First Nations Aboriginal
NF18DB0304	College diploma in social work; some university education	Medium	56	F	18	No	Middle-class	Case Manager	Canadian
NHYAT404[1]	College diploma	Medium	32	M	7	No	Working-class	Employment Services Worker	Afro-Canadian
NTG203DB	BA sociology	Medium	47	F	19	Repetitive strain in wrist	Professional	Case Manager	Caucasian
O1PS0210	College diploma in social work	High	52	F	19	No	Working-class	Case Manager	White
O2PS0310	BA in social work	High	44	F	14	No	Working-class	Case Manager	Canadian
O3PS0403	College certificate in HR and MA (unspecified)	Low	30	F	7	No	White-collar professional	Former Intake Screening Worker; Case Manager; system tester for provincial government	Irish Canadian

(continued)

Interview Code	Education Level	Union Activism Level	Age	Gender	Seniority	Dis-ability	Self-Described Social Class	Job Title	Self-Described Race/Ethnicity
SC01DB0303	BA in sociology	Medium	40	F	12 (additional 7 years as a job councillor in welfare services)	No	Middle-class	Employment Services Worker	White
SC02DB0303	BA sociology; MA social work; employment counselling certificate	Low	29	F	3	No	Middle-class	Case Manager	White Anglo- Saxon
SC03DB0303	BA in psychology	Low	33	F	3.5	No	Middle-class	Case Manager	Beige
SC04DB0303	BA in humanities	refused	refused	M	4	refused	refused	Case Manager	refused
SC06DB0303	BA in psychology	refused	refused	F	4	refused	refused	Case Manager	refused
SC07DB0303	BA in theology	High	59	M	4	No	refused	Case Manager	refused
SC08DB0303	College diploma social work and some university (unspecified)	Low	32	M	3	No	Middle-class	Case Manager	French
SC09DB0603	high school	refused	33	refused	refused	refused	refused	Case Manager	refused
SC10DB0603	BA in psychology	refused	refused	refused	13	refused	refused	Case Manager	refused
SC11DB0603	BA in child studies	Medium	41	F	14	No	Middle-class	Case Manager	Caucasian
SC12DB0603	BA in psychology and college diploma in early childhood education	Medium	39	F	15	Yes dyslexia	Middle-class	Case Manager	Caucasian Canadian

SC13DB0603	BA in sociology	Medium	43	M	17	No	Middle-class	Intake Screening Worker	Canadian
SC21DB0503	High school and incomplete university	Low	29	F	7	No	Professional	Intake Screening Worker	Canadian
SC25DB0503	BA social work	Medium	30	F	8	No	Middle-class	Case Manager	Asian-Canadian
SC26DB0303	College diploma in human resources	Low	23	M	3	No	Middle-class	Employment Services Worker	Canadian
SC27DB0603	High school and certificate in social services	Low	24	F	1	Yes	Middle-class	Case Manager	Canadian
SC27PS0103	College diploma in social services and some university	Medium	29	F	4	No	Lower middle-class	Case Manager	White
SC5DB0303	BA in psychology	Low	36	M	14	No	Middle-class	Case Manager	White
SYTH203[1]	College diploma in counselling	Low	28	M	4	No	White-collar	Case Manager	Chinese-Canadian
WHH303DB	College diploma in fine arts	Low	28	F	4	No	Middle-class	Case Manager	White

Notes

1. Introduction

1. From *Elmer Rice: Three Plays: The Adding Machine, Street Scene and Dream Girl.* New York: Hill & Wang, 1965 (all quoted material from p. 220).
2. Frigga Haug (1987, 1992, 2008) explains this memory work method and its origin.
3. As this concern relates to everyday learning: see Sawchuk (2003b).
4. The funding for the study "Working IT in Welfare Work" (Sawchuk, Principal Investigator) was linked to a large national research network, headed by D. W. Livingstone, called the Work and Lifelong Learning Network (WALL) (www.wallnetwork.ca). Both were funded by the Social Science and Humanities Research Council of Canada and housed at the University of Toronto's Centre for the Study of Education and Work.

2. The Skills Impasse and an Activity Approach

1. This was research primarily associated with the, at the time, emerging Chicago School of Sociology, which dealt with detailed studies of particular occupational groups and individuals in those occupations.
2. Despite his attention to social movements and culture, Touraine was versed originally in the sociology of work and occupations influenced by Georges Friedman's critique of the fragmentation of work processes and, initially, the centrality of craft knowledge (cf. Clark and Diani 1996). Touraine's earlier perspectives recognized the overlaps between independent worker culture and the social movement potential of organized labour no doubt in part because of events of the period in France. However, he ultimately oriented toward the notion of a post-industrial or programmed society in which general forms of social alienation (led by a broader technocracy) largely trumped exploitation in economic life and contradictions (and technocracies) of work as the key driver for change (Touraine 1971). The problems of work, in other words, were to be solved outside it.

3.   Many of Alain Touraine's works (indeed, a great deal of French sociology of work research generally) had not been translated at this time (1970s). Had they been, as several contributors to Clark and Diani (1996) have duly noted, the major *turn* represented by Braverman would not have appeared quite so abrupt.

4.   E.g., see Braverman (1974/1998), chapter 20, 'A Final Note on Skill'.

5.   See volume 28, issue 9 of *Organization Studies*, where an article by Adler, followed by critiques and a rejoinder, generated what could be thought of as a contemporary roll-call of the basic positions across the different streams of LPT. Arguments regarding whether aggregate skill processes were flattening, producing pyramids, or producing hourglass shapes are offered and continue to bump up against what I am referring to as the skills impasse; likewise, there is a series of repeated calls for better understanding of the dynamics of skill/ knowledge formation, socialization, and identity within the labour process which remain, as the contributors admit, underdeveloped, a point which to my mind likewise confirms a type of impasse.

6.   I am well aware of the history of debates regarding the naming of this tradition (e.g., cultural historical activity theory, socio-cultural activity theory, the activity approach, activity theory). The resolution of these matters is not an issue I pursue here. The term "Cultural Historical Activity Theory" here is meant to reflect simply a basic level of continuity from the work of Vygotsky and collaborators through to contemporary research. Additional claims as to the history and contemporary framing of studies of activity as either a matter of generational development or the product of an ongoing paradigmatic tension are addressed in Fenwick, Edwards, and Sawchuk (2011; see also Sawchuk and Stetsenko 2008, Lompscher 2006).

7.   See Newman and Holzman (1993), Au (2007), Elhammoumi (2006), and Vygotsky's own "The Socialist Alteration of Man" (1930; e.g., re-printed in van der Veer and Valsiner 1994).

8.   CNC refers to Computer Numerical Control (a particular prominent form of automation dealt with in early labour process research).

9.   The analysis of play by Vygotsky was one of a number of key areas through which the role of activity as a whole (what Leontiev later referred to in terms of the minimal, meaningful unit of analysis) was strongly suggested. However, there are a variety of other linkages between play and games that could be explored. A CHAT perspective on play, from Vygotsky and Leontiev, for example, emphasizes the point that it expresses an attempt to bring an otherwise unmanageable reality (e.g., in the case of a child, realities of an adult world) into a form that allows meaningful, albeit very limited, participation (the creation of a zone of proximal development). Similar dynamics regarding making an unmanageable reality open to meaningful participation are involved in workplace games that are discussed later in this book. At the same time, however, not all development and zones of proximal development are the same. As we will see, from a mind in political economy perspective on the labour process, trajectories of development can foment and solidify some dimensions of contradictions while resolving others and may or may not be governed by use-value generation. Here I use the terms *engrossment* and *games* to depict a particular type of a zone of proximal development in which

peripheral dimensions of contradiction, notably those limited to relations of operations and actions, become a fixture of learning and development. In this research, as we will see in Chapter 7, this specific type of process regularly depended on a type of engrossment through which collective resources (e.g., zones of proximal development, group formation) ultimately confirm forms of individuated control, a particular means/end relation that is fundamental to the social practices of alienated learning. Engrossment and games, in other words, may have many of the trappings of play in general as well as the trappings of engagement in practice *for its own sake* (the appearance of a personal use-value), but it is arguably its most depleted expression.

10. Across the empirical analysis in the book and again in the review/synthesis in the closing chapter in fact we will be able to recognize the full range of what Ollman (1993) refers to as the (five) different "movements" of contradiction, and most notably perhaps the notion of "immanent unfolding" being expressed by the notion of "trajectories" as well as what I term in Chapters 7 and 8 the "realization" of these trajectories as new "knowledge forms", partial resolutions of contradiction, and so on; i.e.:

    > Of the five movements found in contradiction, the two most important ones are the movements of *mutual support* and *mutual undermining*. Pulling in opposite directions, each of these movements exercises a constant, if not even or always evident, pressure on events. The uneasy equilibrium that results lasts until one or the other of these movements predominates.... A third movement present in contradictions is the *immanent unfolding* of the processes that make up the "legs" of any contradiction. In this way, a contradiction becomes bigger, sharper, more explosive; both supporting and undermining movements become more intense, though not necessarily to the same degree. According to Marx, the capitalist contradictions "of use-exchange-value, commodity and money, capital and wage-labor, etc., assume ever greater dimensions as productive power develops" (1971, 55). The very growth of the system that contains these contradictions leads to their own growth.... A fourth movement found in contradictions is the *change in overall form* that many undergo through their interaction with other process in the larger system of which they are part.... The fifth and final movement contained in contradiction occurs in its *resolution* when one side overwhelms what has hitherto been holding it in check, transforming both itself and all its relationships in the process. The resolution of a contradiction can be of two sorts, either temporary and partial or permanent and total. (Ollman 1993, pp. 51–2; emphasis added)

11. Adler (2006, p. 188) actually specifies the need for a "paleo-Marxist version of activity theory" in fact while offering a well-developed, if brief, example of such an analysis.

12. It may be helpful for some readers that I note here that there is no reason to believe, in my view, that these three work/skill types do not have some natural affiliation to Gregory Bateson's three levels of learning (e.g., 1973) and, in some ways also with the work of Argyris and Schön (e.g., 1974). A recent article by Tosey, Visser, and Saunders (2012), however, outlines in significant detail how notions of, for example, either "Level III" learning or "triple-loop

learning" have been subject to a good deal of confusion and uneven conceptual development over the years. I use the alternative terms of repair-work/skill, sense-repair-work/skill, and object-work/skill in order to achieve stronger coherence between analyses of skill and activity specifically, while avoiding the confusion related to these other approaches.

3. Taylorism – An Enduring Influence

1.	Statement from Taylor in the transcript from *Hearings before Special Committee of the House of Representatives to Investigate the Taylor and Other System of Shop Management under the Authority of House Resolution 90*, 1912/1947, p. 57. Hereafter this transcript is simply cited in the text as *Testimony*.

2.	While not a statement amenable to all forms of Marxist analysis and quite separate from the more obvious cases of privatization of public sector services, here the concern for "surplus value" (exploitation) is an important element of the argument that *profitability* (associated with private sector production) and *austerity* (associated with public sector production) are parallel terms. In the era of monopoly-finance capitalism the separations are challenged further (Bellamy Foster and McChesney 2009; Bellamy Foster and Magdoff 2009).

3.	The 1910 Eastern Railroad case (a.k.a. the Eastern Rate case) was essentially one of the first formal public hearings on the purposes and effects of Taylorism; it offered an early opportunity to clarify the nature of Taylorism, in this instance, in front of the U.S. Interstate Commerce Commission. It is typically dubbed the dawn of public awareness of Taylorism. It was initiated by a request to the railroad owners to increase freight rates by 10%. Presented by the Taylor Society member and a man later to become a supporter of the U.S. president Theodore Roosevelt's anti-trust initiatives (and eventually a United States Supreme Court judge) Louis Brandeis, the case became a key element of our historical understanding of Taylorism while also granting Taylor's system the moniker "Scientific Management". Retained by firms using the railways to ship their goods, Brandeis argued by utilizing Taylor's method to persuade the commission that, in light of the potential for making efficiency gains (producing, according to Brandeis, "at least a million dollars a day" if Taylorist techniques were applied), freight rate hikes did not have to accompany wage increases. According to Kraines (1960), "up to this time not even one article had been published in any of the generally accessible periodicals containing in its title the term 'scientific management'" (p. 191). The public discussion over the Watertown Arsenal application of Taylorism which led to both wildcat strikes and, in turn, the U.S. House of Representative Committee Hearings referenced in this chapter offered an additional instance of public engagement and politicization. Never before or since has work re-organization been the subject of contention in popular political discourse in North America.

4.	Here we might compare, for example, the set of principles offered in *Principles* (1912/1947) with those offered in *Shop Management* (1903/1947). The former are listed by Taylor as follows: shift decision-making from worker to management; use scientific methods to analyze work and re-design; provide detailed description of best practice and establish production outputs/wage system;

select the best worker for the job; train workers; monitor their activities. In *Shop Management* they appear as follows: assignment of large daily task to individual workers; standardization of conditions through initial task analysis; high pay for success of individual worker; and, loss of pay by individual worker in case of failure (e.g., pp. 63–4). The second list stands out somewhat with its framing of standards work as an initial redesign.

5. Both Kakar (1970) and Bahnisch (2000) give considerable evidence of the obsessive-compulsive dimensions of Taylor's system and personal life style.

6. Indicative examples of Taylor's reference to the matter of occupational learning as such can be found, for example, in *Testimony* (pp. 35–44), *Principles* (pp. 122–31), and *Shop Management* (e.g., pp. 70–3, pp. 108–10), although in general references to his view on learning are scattered regularly throughout his writings.

7. Meiksins Wood (1999) offers a contemporary summary and clarification of the literature regarding the point that changes in production (as opposed to the functioning of capitalist markets as such) was the central defining feature of capitalism historically beginning with changes in English agriculture and competitive land-leasing. Here she makes an important distinction between the birth of capitalism and modernism.

8. The Taylor Society, which merged with the Society of Industrial Engineers in 1936, lives on today as the Society for Advancement of Management.

9. However, it is important to note that questioning of Taylor by the committee chair William Wilson (Democrat, former secretary treasurer of the United Mine Workers Union; later to become secretary of labor under Woodrow Wilson) revealed that wage gains were never to be equal to the actual increases in productivity achieved (*Testimony*, pp. 126–8) despite Taylor's claims.

10. While his focus on appropriating working knowledge vis-à-vis the separation of design and execution is well known, Taylor admits regularly that "our difficulties are almost entirely with the [learning of] management" (*Testimony*, p. 153), a point he elaborates on considerably in *Shop Management* (e.g., pp. 93–4).

11. We can note in this regard that the so-named "brain workers" were also to be subject to the rigors of Taylorist task design and strict divisions of labour (see *Shop Management*).

12. It is likely no coincidence that, as Taylor indicated in his testimony to the U.S. House of Representatives, his early educational experience played a crucial role in the development of his thinking around notions of learning in doing (rather than "book learning"), thinking that (also according to his testimony and in keeping with his personality) had taken him exactly "29 years and three to four months" to develop (*Testimony*, p. 132).

13. Taylor specifically addresses the need for a standardizing psycho-social science of work as well (in terms of mental activities such as the reading of drawings, but also attention and motivation more generally). In conjunction with his practical knowledge of worker learning culture, it pre-figured and was likely more advanced than the work of Elton Mayo and others of the Human Relations Movement (e.g., see *Testimony*, pp. 257–63, for a concise statement by Taylor on time-study of mental work).

14. References of this type appear across most of Taylor's writing. In them, he often identified the power of workers' collective learning explicitly, and it

is clear that the assignment of group task assignments was to be avoided because of the power of collective dynamics. That is, gang work would, he concluded, virtually always seed alternative learning, and thus there is a clear awareness of the link between autonomous knowledge-making and groups. It is interesting in this context to contrast Taylor's warnings against group work among laborers, on the one hand, and his strong advocacy for close interaction and physical proximity across the (albeit well-defined) tasks and division of labour of those in the planning office (see, for example, *Shop Management*, pp. 109–10).

15. Taylor's terminology for the second phase/class of time study was typically *unit time study* (see, for example, *Shop Management*, p. 65; but in many other places as well). In contrast, there was also the initial phase of analysis upon which these unit time studies were based: i.e., initial standardization as well as broader task sequencing could be established, producing, for example, the initial individual worker (and supervisor) instruction cards. The discussions of preliminary analysis, even in the lengthy sections where he outlines in detail the functions of the planning department in *Shop Management* (e.g. pp. 110–23), were elusive however. Still, we can observe references to *standards work* by the planning office that is "an absolutely necessary preliminary to success in assigning daily tasks" (as well as most of the other functions associated with Taylorism) (*Shop Management*, pp. 116, 123). Indeed, this *standards work* is distinguished clearly by Taylor from *improvement of system or plant work* in which more detailed unit time study took place (e.g., p. 120). I argue that *standards work* remains a key, under-appreciated element of the Taylorist system as well as the one that was virtually always completed (unlike the detailed unit time studies). In this context we can also note that it is *standards work* that Taylor explicitly credits for the invention of high-speed steel (p. 124), arguably the invention that was most central to bringing his work to prominence generally.

16. The basic identification of these types of workaround practices is far from novel and will be discussed further on in the book. Particularly relevant to the current study, however, is the summary of the basic argument provided in, for example, Button, Mason, and Sharrock (2003). They challenge simplistic applications of both the disempowerment and the resistance theories of technological change. Button et al. (2003) focus on the tendency for workers and management to respond pragmatically and cooperatively to work around a technological system in order to achieve basic functional goals of the organization, despite the often deep-seated political economic contradictions.

17. I.e., Burawoy (1979), Edwards (1979), and Littler (1982).

18. Recall that prior to the Eastern Railroad Case hearings and Brandeis's popularization of the term "Scientific Management", Taylor himself typically referred to his system as "Task Management", which, likewise, inherently undermines the notion that systematization, rather than task design, was central to the approach even if, admittedly, Taylor himself spent a disproportionate time discussing its systemization in his most widely available writings.

19. Herbert Hoover (American president, 1929–33) was himself a professional engineer and a staunch advocate of the Efficiency Movement of the period

in which the work of Taylor, associates, and disciples figured prominently. Following World War II he was appointed to lead what became called the First and Second Hoover Commissions, which had as their aim to improve efficiency of the executive branch of government service. Appointing Hoover in the First Commission was President Truman, likewise virtually a life-time advocate of scientific management (Pemberton 1989).

20. These are largely attempts at socio-technical system (STS) design (cf. Niepce and Molleman, 1998).

21. Adler's notion of 'democratic Taylorism' is said to provide greater job satisfaction and learning opportunities than traditional Taylorism. In part this raises though it does not resolve the types of concerns dealt with in the rest of this book concerning autonomy under contemporary Taylorized labour processes. Further insights on this point can be gleaned from the Berggren versus Alder and Cole debate of 1993–4 in the pages of the *Sloan Management Review*.

22. In point of fact, Taylor's own comments on this matter are rather confusing in themselves. Looking across his testimony to the U.S. House of Representatives Committee, for example, he clearly balked at the question of whether his system had actually ever been fully realized. The status of Taylorism is made even more ambiguous if we take seriously his regular statements that "it cannot be said to exist … in any establishment until after [a complete mental revolution] has taken place" (*Testimony*, p. 31) along with his admission that to his knowledge such a transformation had never occurred.

23. In this book, the "Consolidated Verification Process" (CVP) is a specific series of tasks and a job within which client files are flagged and reviewed for possible inaccuracies, inconsistencies, or changes in circumstance through which cost savings are identified. As of 2012, this process was re-designed (and named the "Eligibility Verification Process") to link with a consumer information credit risk management database company called Equifax. As detailed later on in the book, the verification process was also a key means through which the work re-organization initiative was financed by the government vis-à-vis a private-public sector partnership agreement.

24. This was a type of steel developed by Taylor and a metallurgist named Maunsel White at Bethlehem Iron Company in 1898. It represented a major change in work associated with metal cutting tools.

25. Taylor noted that under the wrong organizational conditions (e.g., a failure to move related materials and outputs effectively to keep up) the gains made possible through the use of high-speed steel were mostly lost. In this context, although both Taylor and White are credited with inventing high-speed steel, Taylor's contribution, over White's technical expertise, is critical, for it was Taylor who identified that, according to overall cost reduction, high-speed steel could make an enormous contribution, *but only if task re-organization in the labour process were carried out*. White, on the other hand, only observed that all that high-speed steel could contribute was a reduction in tool re-grinding time, which, to the aggravation of Taylor, often led (in companies that used it without attention to Taylorism) only to more free time for workers and no gain in profitability in an organization overall (see Aitken 1960, pp. 29–31).

4. Historical Mediations in the Making of Taylorism in Contemporary State Social Services Work

1. "Dig where you stand" is a phrase called to my attention in the writings of Yrjö Engeström, but it is based on a Swedish social democratic movement. According to an excellent Lund University doctoral dissertation by Pär-Ola Zander (2007, pp. 161–2), this notion of digging where you stand (Swedish: Grävdär du står) was at one time the focus of more than 10,000 study circles in Sweden through which workers were explicitly encouraged to explore political economic systems more broadly beginning with the history of their particular work context.

2. Historically, notions of welfare benefits services as we know them today in Canada have their roots in social issues such as unemployment and, to some degree, child-care and support for single mothers. In this context, arguably the early makings of the state welfare work occupation have their roots in either the work of the National Employment Commission immediately prior to World War II or the Canadian government's short-lived and largely rhetorical 1945 Green Book proposals to expand welfare provision (the latter turning out to be an initiative that ended up dissuading involvement in welfare provision at the provincial and municipal levels while increasing the burden on religious and other private charities) (e.g., Struthers 1987). More cleanly, we could instead look toward the events leading up to the federal government's 1956 Unemployment Assistance Act, itself phased out in 1966 but enmeshed within discussions of general welfare provision which included significant pressure from the field of social work itself. In this context, Jennissen and Lundy outline the specific relationship between the occupations of social work and state welfare work in Canada in their excellent 2011 book somewhat more thoroughly. In it we see how the issue was addressed by the Canadian Association of Social Workers (CASW) beginning in the 1950s under discussions of the skilled labour shortage for public sector work related to welfare services during the 1961 membership criteria discussion and that leading up to the 1963 CASW Delegate Conference a range of reports had been circulated on the matter. At about this time, several provinces had also produced reports on labour force shortages in social work and welfare benefits work as well. The CASW would eventually adopt a policy regarding minimum training. Interestingly for us here, their policy also established a division between social work and state welfare work as revolving around the use (or lack of use) of professional judgment.

3. Evetts (2003, 2006) offers a summary of the features of the professional according to the sociology of professions. It typically includes the possession and application of a specialized body of knowledge, almost universally gleaned from extensive formal education and a specific vocational training period. It also involves self-regulating association, which either dictates or provides input into educational preparation, produces a code of conduct offering protection to the public and mechanisms for disciplinary action, and generally promotes the profession as well. Together, these features effect what is typically referred to as occupational closure, supported by state legislation, certification, and so on.

4. In terms of the writings of Antonio Gramsci through to Raymond Williams's commentary on the state and culture, but most directly perhaps in the work of Ralph Miliband (e.g., 1973) and Nicos Poulantzas (e.g., 1973) (who both drew on the works of both Gramsci and Williams), it is important to specify Carey's observations further in the sense that the contradictory role of the capitalist state in Western democracies has always pivoted on meeting the needs of capital, maintaining an adequate environment for capital accumulation as set against the needs of maintaining public legitimacy (one of the most important means of the latter being the provision, or appearance of provision, of public services). In this sense, it is the changing conditions through which workers consent, accommodate, or resist aspects of their work, and thus the labour process, that likely defines the differences we see across the periods Carey addresses. Cousins (1987) is more explicit in this regard, devoting more sustained discussion to theories of the state and social services change, although for her, reflecting on the field of industrial sociology and Labour Process Theory, a combination of the work of the Marxist political sociologist Claus Offe and the sociological theory of bureaucracy of Max Weber figures more prominently.

5. Making a relevant distinction for us here, however, White (2005) links the CAP era with "pre-welfare state institutional relations" (p. 6). In discussion of Ontario specifically, she compares the CAP era to the much earlier era associated with the Ontario Charities Act of 1874. She goes on to note that, despite the attempts of the Canadian federal government at constructing a more elaborate welfare state apparatus, most of the provinces in Canada (outside the unique case of Québec) in fact were not seeking to "fashion themselves as welfare states" at all (p. 7). The role of municipalities in this, however, was a complicated one in provinces such as Ontario, a point that will emerge again in Chapter 9 regarding occupational enculturation, professionalization, and occupational entry.

6. That is, it began to disintegrate roughly by 1973 in connection with broader economic crises of Western capitalism.

7. This was done through legislation such as the Family Benefits Act of 1966, for example.

8. The focus here concerns the relationship between cost avoidance and change in the labour process primarily. As such, while they are hardly inconsequential, I leave aside a number of sources of projected reduction of state expenditures including changes to the disability adjudication regulations embedded in the Ontario Disability Support Program Act established at the launch of the new work/computer system. As the HLB (2002) report indicates, this amount was projected to be $42.3M year by year (this was essentially based on legislatively removing disability claimants from the benefit rolls). Likewise, we can leave to one side the fact that the SDMT system incorporated new rules for calculating net chargeable income deductions (reducing the types and amounts of eligible income deductions) which were projected to amount to cost reductions of $10.6M year by year and which reduced payments to clients but otherwise were not directly implicated in the labour process change. Thus, by excluding these two sources of cost reduction, we can see in the HLB (2002) report that

the labour process re-design in general welfare services itself was intended to reduce costs by $324.6M annually.

9. The "Consolidated Verification Process" (CVP) is an eligibility verification task process that standardized and monitored closely the case review process. It was one of the key areas in which municipal governments could realize the benefits of cost avoidance particularly in light of the eligibility review incentive program that was later established. As of 2012, this verification task process was in the course of re-organization into something the Ontario Ministry of Community and Social Services named the "Eligibility Verification Process" (EVP). Notably, it expands the use of third party information considerably on the basis of the government's Integrated Social Assistance Monitoring Framework (ISAMF), which is a risk analysis based oversight framework and involves contracting with the private sector company Equifax (specializing in consumer credit rating).

10. The 2001 Ontario Budget provides a brief history and confirms that significant reduction in corporate and individual tax rates (the latter reduced by 30%) as well as the increased pace of public debt repayment (rationalized by the fact that the provincial debt roughly doubled during the 1995–9 term). These occurred in Ontario during the lead up to and following the implementation of the new welfare services labour process change and were central to the Conservative government's policy over the length of its two terms in power (1995–2002). Additional cost avoidance as it related to general welfare services also included the cutting of the welfare roll significantly even prior to the implementation of the new work system (i.e., between 1995 and 2001). Over the period of this study itself, between 2002 and 2009 personal tax rates were raised slightly while the corporate tax rates were further lowered (via capital gains tax adjustment) by the Liberal provincial government that preceded the Conservatives (Ontario Provincial Budget, e.g., 2003, 2009).

Importantly, government costs for the initial re-design and implementation of the Ontario welfare service labour process amounted to more than $400M up to 2003, a sum that included more than $250M in payments to the main private sector consultant company which over-ran the original contract costing agreement significantly (projected at $70M; see Office of the Ontario Auditor General 2003). As regards this consultant company, this was not a unique situation. As reported by the National Union of Public and General Employees (NUPGE-Canada) in their 2000 report on the same company used in the welfare re-design investigated here, a track record of cost overruns, uneven job and technological re-design, as well as job-cutting was found in similar re-organization initiatives in the United States, Britain, Ireland, and Canada: for example: a) as reported in the *Omaha World Herald* (21 November 1997) where the Nebraska state auditor was quoted, "I've been auditor for six years now and this is the most wasteful project I have ever heard of. It's like pouring money down a deep, dark hole" in his examination of a government contract; b) as reported in the *San Antonio Express-News* (23 January 1997), where the state auditor's report found ballooning cost overruns and an under-estimation of the complexity of the tasks involved in fulfilling a Texas government service re-organization project; c) as reported in the *Washington Post* (29 October

1996), the consultant contract produced 150% cost overruns in a Virginia social service re-organization project; d) the 1996 British government's levying of financial penalties on the same private contractor for failing to deliver on the UK National Insurance System re-design; e) between 1994 and 1996, the Irish government auditor conclusions of the company's involvement in cost overruns and failures to re-design social services effectively; f) in 1995 the Canadian Department of Public Works and Government Services was forced to cancel a $44M (Cdn) contract after the consultant company failed to deliver a re-design plan on budget (see *Computing Canada*, 10 May 1996); and g) the provincial auditor in New Brunswick (Canada) concluded that there were inappropriate cost overruns in re-organizing the province's justice work/computer system.

11. Municipal reporting over the period of this study (2002–9) provides additional detail on how pressures were managed locally. For example, beginning with an early report from the York Region municipality we find the following:

> In 2003, a provincial baseline target of 118 cases per month was established for CVPreviews for York Region. The Social Assistance Division exceeded this target, achieving on average 200 reviews per month and received $205,175, the maximum available incentive payment for York Region. This incentive funding will continue in 2004 and York Region's Ontario Works Program is on track to, once again, exceed the baseline target ... in 2005 and beyond.... The effective review of social assistance case files through CVP, supported by provincial technology and third party validation of information, resulted in 349 participants exiting the Ontario Works Program in 2003. An analysis of gross and net (Regional) social assistance savings resulting from exits as a result of CVP (based on a calculation of six months of savings), demonstrates the cost avoidance associated with this approach. (York Region Community Services and Housing Committee 2004, pp. 2, 4)

In this report we see the key mediations and dynamics of austerity and cost avoidance the new system supports. These dynamics have only intensified in the succeeding years. A key example of how the infrastructure of the SDMT labour process has been effective in achieving austerity/cost avoidance goals in the critical period of economic downturn beginning in 2008 is provided by similar municipal level documentation from the Peel Region (one of the most aggressive municipalities in this regard). Peel Region reported as the economic downturn was taking hold that "OW will incur lower net social assistance and employment benefit costs due to social assistance caseload being lower than projected" (Peel Region 2008, p. 3). As in the earlier excerpt from the York Region and throughout the province, in fact, a key lever of cost avoidance has remained the Consolidated Verification Process (CVP) tracking system. Developing its own, more stringent algorithm tool for the purposes of cost avoidance, between 2005 and 2007 the Peel Region had already begun outperforming the provincial average with a "termination rate averag[ing] 29 per cent of all cases reviewed versus the provincial average of 14 per cent" (Peel Region 2008, p. 6). This led to $8.5M in cost avoidance in 2007 as well as maximization of its available share of provincial incentive funding to cut, producing an additional half million dollars. Moving through 2008 this municipality projected a stabilization of caseloads that, in the context of rapidly spiking unemployment (increasing by as much as 50% over the course of 2008), was remarkable. Setting aside inflation affecting salary increases, the Peel Region projected further increases in unemployment and poverty in the region, including an increase in caseload, *but* an overall decrease in cost per case, which, in combination with changes to the Ontario Child Benefit funding program, resulted in a projected $0.1M savings despite radically changing economic fortunes in 2009. Each of these achievements lies in direct contrast to the municipality's experiences in 1994–9 under the previous work system, when unemployment rates outstripped caseload levels to increase the overall cost of welfare service administration (p. 10). In dealing with cost avoidance and austerity at the municipal level, York and Peel Regions were far from unusual. Data from the City of Hamilton and the Niagara Region, for example, demonstrate the same dynamics. In the case of Hamilton (City of Hamilton Community Services Department 2009), as with Peel and again in the midst of severe economic downturn, increases in unemployment, poverty, and economic downturn generally likewise produced an increase in caseload generally, *but also* a decrease in client time spent on OW assistance, resulting in an overall cost-per-case decrease (e.g., $757 per case cost in 2007 versus $684 per case cost in 2009). As it was throughout the province, the many changes in the welfare work labour process discussed in this book were central, and played a significant role in producing higher rates of ineligibility.

12. We can note here that the specific job names often varied somewhat from municipality to municipality and likewise vary in the talk of workers themselves (also from different municipalities) excerpted in this research.

13. SDMT was a custom-developed system that was intended to create a real-time, Web-enabled application that was designed to support case processing and initially embedded some 800 rules (this has expanded since implementation with a series of new editions) governing eligibility for social services payments. It was a software system based on a mainframe running a platform known as OS/390. At the time of development it was designed to replace eight incompatible applications in use in the prior labour process (see Figure 4.1). Through it was essentially an intra-net design, workers accessed data via Internet Explorer using Microsoft's Active Server Pages technology. The system also initially included Business Objects SA's reporting tools to enhance managerial practice. It was supported by network hardware from Cisco Systems (see Songini 2004).

14. This is an excerpt from the interviews completed for the research project reported in this book, and going forward I use these interviewee codes, for which additional biographical information can be found in the Appendix. In this particular instance and in keeping with the point that the work of Carey raises concerning the use of the term "Case Manager" (cf. Postle [2001]) – for the sake of consistency, my own reference to this particular job category in the new SDMT labour process is as "Case Manager". Where interviewees use the terms "Case Manager" and "Case Worker" themselves, the text has been left unchanged.

15. Lewchuk (2002) dealt with workers in specialized (i.e., disability benefits delivery; Ontario Disability Support Program), as opposed to those working

in general welfare services (Ontario Works). They are distinctive jobs but were built on virtually the same labour process and utilized the same SDMT technology.

5. Experiencing the De-Skilling Premises of Welfare Work

1. Some readers may have questions regarding the uses of the terms "un-self-consciousness" as distinct from "self-conscious". This is a phrasing meant to recognize the relevance of the claim that Vygotsky addressed some time ago:

    > there is a great difference between the concepts of "unconscious" and "lack of conscious awareness." Lack of conscious awareness is not simply part of the conscious or unconscious. It does not designate a level of consciousness. It designates a different process in the activity of consciousness. I tie a knot. I do it consciously. I cannot, however, say precisely how I have done it. My action, which is conscious, turns out to be lacking in conscious awareness because my attention is directed toward the act of tying, not on *how* I carry out that act. Consciousness always represents some piece of reality. The object of my consciousness in this example is the tying of the knot, that is, the knot and what I do with it. However, the actions that I carry out in tying the knot – what I am doing – is not the object of my consciousness.… Conscious awareness is an act of consciousness whose object is the activity of consciousness itself. (Vygotsky 1987, p. 190; emphasis in original)

    This is a point that some forms of sociology (as well as social phenomenology) have likewise taken seriously (e.g., Garfinkel and Goffman on the one hand; Husserl and Schutz on the other). Central to the distinctions in Vygotsky's comments above is the configuration of relations involving the self (i.e., "what *I* am doing"). We have here, of course, some key schematics of object-relatedness and the theory of activity more broadly. While this use of terminology may seem like a small point, I hope it is clear that it speaks to matters deeply embedded in a theory of activity. Shifts in consciousness in relation to the self specifically are, in other words, key entry points for empirical exploration of changes in learning and the object-relatedness of the activity.

2. Going forward, the reader is invited to reference the list of abbreviations as necessary (provided in the front matter) for terms used by interviewees where the terms are otherwise not defined in the text.

3. Throughout the remainder of the book, interview excerpts involving exchanges between interviewer and subject are marked as "I" (interviewer) and "S" (subject). It is also important to note that italicized words or phrases within interview excerpts do not represent points of emphasis provided by interviewees, but rather have been added to assist particular points of analysis in the body of the text.

4. This need for an elaborate infrastructure of control was, of course, one of the very first *object lessons* that Frederick Taylor learned in attempting to control a team of ore shovellers at Bethlehem Steel. (I see it as worthwhile to note this because in doing so we support the attempt to de-reify and de-naturalize

the modes of control in the labour process). Taylor's report on experiments in re-organizing this ore-shovelling work over a *three year period* showed how efforts at the control of seemingly simple task in fact required mammoth efforts and organizational resources. Specifically the shovelling work experiment required a new division of *supervisory labour* as well as bureaucratic re-organization responding to, for example, issues of worker literacy (resolved with colour-coded slips), the means of keeping track of who physically went where (this included supervisors, time-study personnel, and the shovellers themselves), as well as the creation of planning centralized to an office containing all the necessary maps of Bethlehem Works, charts, and other data needed to generate an account of the broader flow of shovelling work. Indeed, special phones and messenger services were also created for this purpose. Taylor remarked on this in his testimony to the Special House Committee in 1912 (see the opening quotation of Chapter 3 which specifically refers to this three year experiment). And, the point here is that many of the seemingly common-sense qualities of the labour process, and specifically the capacities of computer systems such as SDMT, belie an enormous accumulation of efforts and inventions that have been capitalized upon and embedded in socio-organizational technologies such as those in this example of state welfare work.

5. That is, according to the Ontario Government's "Transforming Ontario's Social Assistance Delivery System" statement in 2002: "… goal of creating efficient programs that would save taxpayers money and provide excellent customer service, information on demand, and modern technology".

6. De-Skilling – Learning Welfare Work and the Mediations of Space, Time, and Distance

1. This phrase *"seen but unnoticed"* is drawn from studies of ethnomethodology and conversational analysis (EM/CA). In brief, EM/CA, founded by Harold Garfinkel, on the one hand, and the work of Harvey Sacks, Emmanuel Schegloff and Gail Jefferson, on the other, have as one of their key domains of interest the tacit, seen but unnoticed social accomplishment of everyday life. Dealing with many of the most minute levels of interaction, EM/CA has made valuable insights on the nature of social order in the seriousness it grants to its material nature (whether this is revealed through people's interactive arrangement of their bodies, gestures, voice tone, gaze, or sight-lines or how a work space is configured, etc.). It is a phenomenon conceptualized in the CHAT tradition as well:

    > Thus when we are dealing with any activity – for example, learning – very little of what is perceived by the subject, and without which the carrying out of activity is impossible, is also actually recognized by him [*sic*]. In spite of what is apparent, what is actually recognized is only that which enters into the activity as a subject of one or another action that is carried out as its direct goal. (Leontiev 1978, p. 155)

2. See also the special issue of the journal *Computer Supported Cooperative Work* (1999, vol. 8) and likewise the special issue of *Mind, Culture and Activity* (vol.

14[1/2] 2007) for further examples, while Elhammoumi (2006) offers an extended discussion of spatio-temporal dimensions of CHAT in terms of a Marxist approach specifically.

3. In terms of this notion of the virtual/material: among others, Huws (1999, 2003) makes the point quite clearly that despite the appearances of *virtual* worlds of work, the labour processes involving virtual work remain deeply entwined by basic material mediations of time, space, and distance, as well as scales.

4. Here it makes sense to note specifically how the prior welfare work computer system called Case Worker Technology *did not* function as a work routing system. The ability of workers to switch and re-sequence tasks as this worker describes is a clear illustration in this regard.

7. Re-skilling, Consenting, and the Engrossments of Administrative Knowledge

1. As I have already noted in this book generally, it is important to avoid the romanticization of past forms of welfare work. Here it seems obvious that this is the case. Elsewhere, for example, in discussions of those oriented toward a type of social work ideal, welfare work craft, and so on, it is equally necessary. Piven and Cloward (1971), and more recently in the Canadian context Herd and Mitchell (2005), have noted the dynamics of surveillance involved but also see Hier (2003) Eaton Mosher, Evans, and Little (2004); as well as Chunn and Gavigan (2004, 2010) for further insights on welfare work and its highly contradictory political position in the contemporary and historical Canadian context.

2. Burawoy's theory of games has nothing to do with the version of game theory associated with the Rational Choice theorists, and my use of the term "humanist" (and elsewhere in the book "humanizing") has nothing to do with of liberal humanist thought (see Chapter 11).

3. For Burawoy (1979, pp. 77–81), the definition of games is linked to the notion of "relative satisfactions" in the work of the industrial sociologist William Baldamus; however it owes more, as he notes, to Herbert Marcuse's analysis of "repressive satisfactions", i.e.,

    > The stimulus to engage in such work games derives as much from the inexorable coercion of coming to work, and subordination to the dictates of the labor process once there, as from the emergence of 'radical needs,' 'a new vision of work,' or 'nonlogical code.' The game is entered into for its *relative* satisfactions, or what Herbert Marcuse calls *repressive* satisfactions. The game represents a need that is strictly the product of a society 'whose dominant interests demand repression.' The satisfaction of that need reproduces not only 'voluntary servitude' (consent) but also greater material wealth. (Burawoy 1979, p. 81)

4. See Ben Hamper's classic *Rivethead* (1986) for an extreme set of examples in manufacturing.

5. Roy (1952) and Burawoy (1979) were based on research conducted at the same facility, albeit decades apart.

6.   The identification of these processes as involving a "marginalization of con-
     tradictions" is owed to discussions with Arlo Kempf. They link closely to the
     notion of relative/repressive satisfactions discussed elsewhere.

7.   Brought to the fore by Knorr Cetina's comparative approach (1999), there
     are more parallels perhaps than meet the eye at first glance. In High-Energy
     Physics (HEP) labs, for example, we discover workers are constantly engrossed
     in the elimination of all factors potentially affecting their instruments and
     results/phenomena of interest. Every source of outside variation is constantly
     "beaten down", and they spend their time interpreting what is not present or
     associated with the results of an experiment in order to arrive at what is. This is
     something referred to by Knorr Cetina as negative knowledge producing posi-
     tive knowledge. By contrast, Microbiology (MB) lab work involves an explora-
     tion of these sources of variation. Scientists within this form of labour process
     activity maximize engagement with their phenomenon of interest much more
     so as it exists in relations with the natural environment. In response to chal-
     lenges, MB scientists begin manipulating and testing a vast array of relation-
     ships in order to generate relevant experimental outcomes. In the case of
     state welfare workers, it does seem plausible that what I term "administrative
     object-relatedness in activity" parallels a culture of *negative epistemics* as seen
     in the HEP labs while what I discuss in Chapter 8 as "craft object-relatedness
     in activity" seems more akin to MB lab culture (presumably we would call it
     a culture of *positive epistemics* though I do not recall that Knorr Cetina does
     this). Here, however, the parallel likely ends. The means for addressing issues
     of regulation and control through to, for example, the typologies of 'commu-
     nitarian' versus 'competitive' styles of work that Knorr Cetina (1999) discusses
     are not adequate to my purposes here.

8.   The *structure of wanting/lacking* (1997; Knorr Cetina and Bruegger 2002) within
     processes of engrossment is largely premised on the work of Lacan and Freud.
     While, vis-à-vis the entertainment of Marcuse's notion of repressive satisfac-
     tions, Freudian thought is not altogether eschewed here, in general, the use of
     Freud can be seen to be at odds with key aspects of Vygotskian analysis. That
     is, naturalistic forms of psychology including Freud's [e.g., "represent[ing] man
     as a being whose initial development is not social, as a being for whom social
     activity is something brought in from without, this perspective seems to have
     been dominated by ultra biological views" (Vygotsky 1987, p. 344)] are not
     consistent with the CHAT approach. To the degree a version of the structure
     of wanting/lacking is detectable amongst the findings in this book however,
     a CHAT perspective would interpret it (as I do here) as a thoroughly his-
     torical, cultural, political economic as well as an agentive phenomenon rather
     than a trans-historical and biological one [see chapters 1 and 2 of Vygotsky
     (1987) for further detailing of his concerns about Freud]. In addition to these
     dis-continuities, there are also some minor challenges that are rooted in differ-
     ences in conceptual vocabulary. In Knorr Cetina's framework an *object* refers to
     a concept that in CHAT terms would likely be described as a *goal*. She says, for
     example, "[objects] are the *goal* of expert work; and they are also what experts,
     scientists, etc. *regularly profess themselves to be interested in*, attracted by, seduced
     into and attached to" (1997, p. 12; emphasis added). Self-conscious expressions

of this kind are, for CHAT, reflective of goal-directed actions, though in some instances if understood as a projected outcome (Russian word *objekt* as opposed to *predmet*: see Chapter 2) the different usages here might be reconciled.

9. On the one hand, Vygotsky's approach owes something to the work of Kurt Lewin in relation to the significance of the internalization and the mimicking of the social (e.g., Vygotsky 1987, pp. 74–5) and we also see a key parallel with Mead's work (cf. Edwards 2007b). Writings in the distributed cognition tradition were, on the other hand, directly influenced by Vygtosky, among others.

10. There are many differences to be seen, but here I am describing a notion of engrossment that comes closer in some respects to what, for example, Stromberg (2000) described as the "*I* of enthrallment" in a "limited section of the world" involving "immersion in culturally available fictions" (p. 491). There are many parallels to be drawn here as well to Vygotsky's theory of play (see the notes for Chapter 2). Moreover, as Burawoy (1979) says directly: "the feature responsible for drawing workers into the game is their lack of complete control over outcomes" (p. 149), and this too evokes the kind of discussion of play that Vygotsky presented.

11. As I do where relevant going forward in the remainder of the book, I use line-numbering to support a more detailed explanation of certain key (and lengthy) excerpts such as this.

12. I do not intend any spiritual connotations in the use of this term "mantra", though I do intend to imply the basic notion of a particular phrase that may support a form of transformation.

13. These same dynamics of engrossment dealing with computer technology were seen among male factory workers in Sawchuk (2003a).

14. Although this worker holds only four years seniority in his current bargaining unit (see Appendix), he has actually worked in welfare services as a Case Manager for more than 20 years.

15. While obviously not proving the point on its own, it is still worthwhile noting that in the research interview with this Case Manager he went on to reminisce about his engagements with clients and concerns about the new labour process in the following way which supports the notion that he has not likely "always felt that way" at all:

> You know, occasionally I do think about how important really counselling clients is, but the word counselling is not really used a whole lot around here now because it's seen more as a separate profession. And you, well, for me it's something that I think of as part of another life. I actually used to do a lot of family counselling but I'm not allowed to do that here now.… I used to work in co-operation with and in touch with physicians, surgeons, disability office. I advocated very strongly on behalf of my clients but now things have changed. (SC07DB0303, Case Manager)

16. In an ancillary sense in this analysis, the necessary linkage between social order and morality (or what is here considered as an feature of different types of occupational ethics) is a fundamental feature of socially contingent, interactive accomplishment of human sense-making as described in variety of places, but most directly and unequivocally to my mind in the work of Harold Garfinkel (e.g., 1967), where he took up the matter in, for example, his famous breeching

experiments. In relation to Garfinkel's formulation it is suggested here that part of this dynamic depends on the matter of the actor's interpretive trust, a feature indelibly linked to anxieties from which it emerges and to which it contributes. That is, the suggestion is that heightened anxieties linked to biography/history/activity parallel heightened concerns for trust and the invocation of more strongly felt practical moral/ethical claims. This set of relationships, too, can be meshed with either Knorr Cetina's concern for the structure of wanting/lacking under a certain formulation of them or, better still in my view, CHAT's concern for the dynamics of contradictions.

17. By the close of the research these types of local financial backup systems had been established in most municipalities (key informant interview).

18. There is yet another term and series of observations which can be provided here which will be of some value to the broader synthesis later in Chapter 11. Luedtke's (1986) detailed study of late nineteenth century machinists in Germany produced the notion of *Eigensinn*: "interactions and expressions not meant primarily as direct resistance to demands 'from above'; instead, they expressed a space of their own – *Eigensinn* (self-will or self-reliance)"; "individualist withdrawal"; "being-with-others" on the basis of "being-with-oneself"; and rooted in "longings and desires as well as anxieties" (pp. 79, 80, 81). Of course, many researchers have, for some time, enjoyed the discovery and re-discovery of resistance generally. They have also seemed to relish the discovery of even the most minute expressions of autonomy, which are, in turn, very different from a type of politicized resistance and, for example, *fully developed* (rather than *false* or *contradictory*) class consciousness. Researchers and particularly historians do not, of course, offer much if any explanation of the processes through which one or the other (that is, true, false, or contradictory consciousness) emerges, though to be sure it is not uncommon for them to take off on flights of lay psychological and cultural analysis. But, while many historians (in the German micro-history tradition), like Luedtke, reject the general notion of the irrational and deviant implication of *Eigensinn*, in general what we find is a term that is juxtaposed to *resistance* and in this context can be brought very close to the concept of games, relative/repressive satisfactions. Luedtke himself demonstrates amongst his machinists a very narrow political consciousness and, important to us here, a "privatization of politics" (that which is typically associated with craft unionism) rooted in *Eigensinn* (pp. 82–5). In the term *Eigensinn*, as in these other concepts, we can distill, in fact, that notions of worker re-appropriation of time and space in the labour process really do revolves around the seemingly basic question of purpose, an issue that CHAT has theorized extensively in term of object/motive and object-relatedness of activity for example.

19. An earlier version of this article was published as follows: McDermott, R. and Lave, J. (2002). "Estranged ~~Labor~~ Learning", *Outlines: Critical Social Studies*, 4(1), pp. 19–48.

8. Up-Skilling, Resisting, and Re-Keying for Craft Knowledge

1. In most streams of sociology of work including in Labour Process Theory (LPT) research specifically (in the case of LPT, in part because of the centrality

in Braverman's work and his oft-cited preoccupation with craft workers) the term "craft" is heavily loaded. It is more than reasonable, in my view, that one would hesitate to use it. It has been the subject of debate in terms of whether or not a certain type of labour process, knowledge form, and dynamic of worker control existed, and, if so, when and how it emerged, changed or disappeared. It has been associated with conflations across analysis of worker capacities, job and task, complexity, autonomy, labour market value and labour market structure, and more. As recently as 2007 (but following in a longer tradition of diversely focused critique that has not exclusively been animated by Braverman alone, e.g., Turner 1962; Lee 1981; Littler 1982), Adler confirms an important point in framing of craft work/knowledge as *craft idiocy* (re-working Marx's notion of rural idiocy): e.g., "the autonomous craftsman (or alternatively, reflecting the ideal of alienated, self-sufficient individualism that is the spontaneous ideology of market society)" (Adler 2007a, p. 1319). It speaks to an important point regarding individuation and isolation (including the isolation of some groups from others within processes of occupational closure). This critique thus has included the notion of traditional craft unionism: the concentration of control of work knowledge amongst a specific (relatively privileged white male) group of workers historically. Thus, it has regularly served as platform for charges of idealization related to gendered and racialized dimensions as well. However, in my use of the term as name for a specific mode of participation in activity (and potentially a form of activity itself) I wish to designate first and foremost the dynamics of learning and knowledge construction. And, in my usage the notion of craft knowledge and learning are treated as the opposite of alienated, self-sufficient individualism or even group-based isolations. Moreover, my use of the term does not differentiate notions of craft from science (as Knorr Cetina and others in the sociology of science or lab studies tradition show; science is every bit as much a craft in this sense), and it has the added feature (important in this specific analysis) of side-stepping the potential confusion with notions of professionalization (a likewise heavily loaded term).

2. Beyond referencing Vygotsky, in *Frame Analysis* Goffman also references the works of Vološinov and Labov, whose works have also been considered in close connection to Cultural Historical Psychology in a variety of ways. Even still, claims that Goffman's thinking has been influenced by Cultural Historical perspectives should be tempered (after all, Lenny Bruce, Raymond Massey, and Allen Funt are referenced in *Frame Analysis* just as often).

3. That is, it is recognisable despite the fact that Goffman regularly turns to phenomenology in a way that Vygotsky and colleagues never did. That is, at a variety of key junctures, Goffman's argument relies upon, for example, Schutz, Merleau-Ponty, Husserl, and Wittgenstein as well as phenomenologically informed sociology (e.g., Cicourel, Gurwitsch, and Luckmann). Because of this, additional conceptual translation is required alongside the management of some conceptual tensions. I find that neither is unusually difficult. For example, "To experience an object amounts to being confronted with a certain order of existence" (a quote Goffman takes from Aaron Gurwitsch's study of consciousness and unconsciousness [1974, p. 308]) likely parallels the sentiments of Vygotsky and Leontiev quite closely. For a discussion of the poten-

tial links between the work of Schutz and CHAT see Sawchuk and Stetsenko (2008), or, more definitively, Russell (2010).

4. This is also a conceptualization he links with different forms of engrossment.

5. See the section entitled "Data Sources and Interpretation".

6. This distinction is an important one dealt with by Vygotsky, as we have seen earlier, e.g., Chapter 2. It also emerges independently, at approximately the same time, in the work of Mead: "significant symbols [and] communication which is directed not only to others but also to the individual himself [*sic*] ... where he talks and replies to himself as truly as the other person replies to him" as a means by which the self is made "as an object to itself". Mead likewise talks about the moments of reflexivity that demonstrate how the self "can be both subject and object", and these are processes, he goes on to confirm dependent on the nature of "social conduct or activity in which the given person or individual is implicated" (*Mind, Self and Society*, 1934/1967, pp. 135–9).

7. While the notion of mantra is an additional element, in broad terms, the significance of this concept of the "we-talk" artefact in this analysis emerges from an interpretation of two sets of work. First, there are a number of socio-cultural analyses of learning that have dealt with the general idea. Holland et al. (1998), for example, address how important the production of similar types of artefacts are for significant changes in people's lives (e.g., in analysis of non-drinking alcoholics); in a related way Orr (1996) discusses the production of "war stories" and other narrative/artefacts that mediate occupational development (and the development of an occupation as a whole) in the case of photocopy repair personnel; and Lave and Wenger (1991) refer to the importance of re-telling stories about work in their series of studies which include occupations. Second and somewhat more directly important to my use of the term "we-talk" is the work of Basil Bernstein. His early work on schoolchildren specifically highlighted class-based differences in elaborated and restricted linguistic codes which linked to differential levels of routinization and predictability of speech and the formation of social groups, i.e., "the extent to which each facilitates (elaborated code) or inhibits (restricted code) an orientation to symbolize intent in a verbally explicit form" (1971, pp. 98–9). For Bernstein, these were important windows into social capacities for expression and self-control, which are rewarded and punished in school-based pedagogical forms. However, as we broaden the application of these concepts to the labour process we reveal the cultural/institutional presumptions of schooling and pedagogy to ask additional questions. That is, elaborated codes align with the assumption of individualist, even competitive contexts; restricted codes align with social cohesion and consensual/negotiated contexts. Here implications of "elaborated" and "restricted" are cast in a somewhat different light. While fuller critique of Bernstein's work can be found in, for example, Sadovnik (1995), the underlying dynamic of interest here is captured by White and Siegel (1984, p. 275) in their comment that the former emphasizes the "I" while the latter emphasizes the "we" orientation toward social action. I contend that with help of a CHAT perspective we can extend this further by saying these contribute to distinctive outcomes based on the broader structure of activity. In either case, the link to forms of teaching and learning (broadly

conceived) is not coincidental. In *Pedagogy, Symbolic Control and Identity* (2000) Bernstein begins and ends with a focus on the principles of communication as the nexus of the reproduction of modes of control in learning, which, unavoidably, applies here.

8. Referenced elsewhere in this book, on this (and a variety of other points in fact) the edited collection by Seddon, Henriksson, and Niemeyer (2010) offers a variety of superb observations that are in my view worthwhile reading in parallel to this analysis.

9. It is unlikely that interviewing workers in pairs (as was done from time to time in this research) did not have a positive effect on the capacity, in the course of generating the interview account, to construct clear evidence of the types of alternative perspective within the labour process that re-keying represents. I do not, however, suggest that this is only a product of paired interview methods.

10. Indeed, there is ample evidence beyond what has been noted here that these specific types of workarounds used by workers regularly involved collaboration with clients. An excerpt from a client interview in Herd and Mitchell's excellent research on experiences in the general welfare program in Ontario (OW) covering the same period, for example, indicates the following:

> I asked them exactly how I was supposed to go about getting my landlord's address and phone number and what not. And she told me, 'Lie to him.' She said to say you're filling out your income tax…. 'Tell him what you have to tell him. But we have to have his address and phone number'…. I was kind of shocked when they said that I was supposed to lie to my landlord. (Welfare Client Interviewed in Herd and Mitchell 2005, p. 23)

11. This is a pseudonym.

9. Divisions of Knowledge Production, Group Formation, and Occupational Enculturation

1. Edwards's work here is connected to the "Learning in and for Interagency Working" (LIW) project (e.g., Edwards 2004, 2007a; Daniels 2004; Daniels, Leadbetter, Warmington, Edwards, Martin, Popova, Apostolov, Middleton and Brown 2007), which had as its focus not a specific occupation as much as the inter-action between several (multi-professional) teams as well as the notion of co-configuration work specifically. The LIW research has, however, shed light on the dynamics of the reproduction, transformation, and alignments of objects of professional activity in public sector human services work (in Britain). Likewise, the LIW project addressed the degree to which social service work learning depends on non-routine, improvised decision-making, navigation of bureaucratic hurdles, and, in a range of practices, mundane rule-bending/ breaking. As shown in the LIW research as well as here, these practices are made more understandable when they are conceived as object-related activity. Moreover, Daniels et al. (2007) have also found significance in the role of "client needs and/or rapidly changing situations" and notions of the "whole child" (p. 534) which parallels my interest in the status and role of the "fully

biographical client-person". It offers a crucial interventionist perspective (stemming from Engestrom's Change Laboratory methods) that is absent in the research of the present book. There are in fact several different points of emphasis found between the LIW research writings currently available and the observations offered in this book that taken together would likely form some useful points of departure for future work.

2. The description of the survey data method provided in Chapter 1 is not repeated here beyond noting that where cross-tabulation was carried out chi square tests of significance were used to confirm the strength of the association between variables in the bivariate results offered.

3. When analysing the survey data here and in the next chapter, in some instances levels of experience are profiled in terms of generalized veteran/newcomer distinctions. When this is the case, veterans are those who have state welfare work experience that stretches (sometimes a good deal) beyond the current SDMT labour process era; newcomers are defined as having experienced *only* the SDMT labour process era. In other instances, as we will see, it makes more sense to profile levels of welfare work experience in a slightly more detail way. When this is the case, "low levels of experience" refer to those hired from 2002 forward (the SDMT era), "medium levels of experience" to those hired between 1990–2002, and "high levels of experience" to those hired prior to 1990 (cf. Figure 4.1, Chapter 4).

4. There was only one case in the survey data (n = 339) of a newcomer who was an Employment Services Worker and there were no instances of a newcomer who worked as an Eligibility Review Officer.

5. A small number of respondents in the survey also had a master's degree in social work, but the number is too small to be helpful to statistical comparisons.

6. The estimate of just below 10% is approximate in part because on this particular question in the survey the missing values count was uncharacteristically high (40% of the sample).

7. Likert-style question choices were as follows: very easy to learn, easy to learn, not particularly easy or hard to learn, hard to learn, very hard to learn.

8. The question measuring computer literacy level on the survey was based on indicating an ability to carry out computer-based tasks that were progressively more complicated (e.g., from using basic software, checking e-mail, and searching the Internet effectively to trouble-shooting technical problems, fixing viruses, and so on) (see discussions of functional computer literacy definition/testing, e.g., Morgan 1998; Charp 1999).

9. Though an ancillary point, I can add here that as far as the effects of prior educational attainment are concerned: *irrespective of work experience*, those with higher educational attainment exhibited greater levels of additional course work (e.g., 95% of all additional training courses taken were taken by those with post-secondary education).

10. Based on paired Likert-style questions: "In your own experience, how important have these organized training courses been for the overall learning required to do your job?" and "In your own experience, how important has the informal on-the-job learning you have done over the last year been for the overall learning required to do your job?".

10. Understanding Prevalence, Roots, and Factors of Trajectories of Knowledge Production

1. As in the previous chapter, I refer the reader to the general description of the survey data provided in Chapter 1 while also noting that where cross-tabulation was carried out chi square tests of significance were used to confirm the strength of the association between variables in the bivariate treatments.

2. Here I am referring primarily to Chapter 9 of *Manufacturing Consent: Changes in the Labor Process under Monopoly Capitalism* (1979) where Burawoy examines the claim that "whatever consent is necessary for the obscuring and securing of surplus value is generated at the point of production rather than imported into the workplace from outside" (p. 135). He does so through a series of regression analyses involving work output in relation to variables said to be internal to the social relations of production and those such as race, education, age, and marital status said to be external to production. My analysis does not include production output, and I do not find the types of hypotheses that regression analysis affords to be very helpful analytically. Thus, in taking up a factor analysis I seek to explore and compare (and examine possible inter-relations between) sets of internal and external variables *in terms of* the types of occupational learning dynamics demonstrated in the qualitative analysis. Even still, Burawoy's conclusions parallel many of those I will offer here:

    > From these results it is clear that the labor process is not autonomous with respect to the translation of relations into activities. Consciousness molded in practices outside the factory do affect, although within narrow limits, the way operators respond to production relations. However, if the labor process is not autonomous, it may be *relatively autonomous*. That is, the labor process may itself determine the effect of imported consciousness. (Burawoy 1979, p. 152; emphasis in original)

    He goes on to warn us that "the more we dissociate the experiences of workers outside work from the responses in work, the more we are forced toward postulating invariant human characteristics – that is, the more we are driven toward outlining a theory of human nature" (p. 156). A suitable warning to which, in my view at least, detailed attention to the processes of learning and human development responds. Overall, both sets of results suggest a complex series of mediated processes. Therefore, while the exact level of relativity involved in a *relatively autonomous* labour process will likely always prove difficult to establish, here the basic claim relates to the more general need for detailed attention to concrete dynamics of occupational knowledge production, beginning from the practices of working themselves.

3. From the perspective of the provincial government and state austerity, the ISU call centre system was seen as ineffective because of its limited ability to generate reduction in expenditures, i.e.:

    > provincial review identified two major problems with the intake screening units: too many applicants (40%) were bypassing the ISU and applying directly; and "only" 12% of applicants were being screened out at the telephone pre-screening stage. Suggested strategies for increasing the

screen out rate included instructing "screeners to complete Stage 1 (telephone interview), including making conclusions of ineligibility where appropriate, *for as many applicants as possible*" (emphasis added), and to have screeners exercise greater discretion to make conclusions of ineligibility for people whose income and assets fall within 15% of the allowable limit and forward only those whose income and/or assets are likely to decrease. (Herd and Mitchell 2005, p. 11; emphasis in original)

4. Much later it was determined that a more localized version of call screening would be implemented, but this decision had not yet been made at the time of the survey administration.

5. Questions: Fixed-choice – "If the Intake Screening Unit centres were to be closed, what kind of effect do you think it would have on your daily work?" (very positive; positive; no effect; negative; very negative); Open-ended – "Please indicate the top three ways that the closure of the Intake Screening Unit centres would affect your work."

6. Responses to the series of questions dealing with views on the labour process (referenced both in Chapter 9 and 10) were slightly less consistent in fact, owing in some ways to the types of idioms (relating to the meaning of effectiveness) that different workers used. Of course, individual variables within the set of variables dealing with views and outcomes of the labour process were still useful but within limits (in part this is why I develop this broader term called "amalgamated critique"). But, as a case in point here, responses to the direct question on the effectiveness of the division of labour co-varied much more loosely (with less instances of statistical significance) across other variables than did the ISU closure variable. I argue this is because the ISU closure was not only an immediately pending issue that focused attention of respondents uniquely, but it was also more easily interpreted by workers and it connected in a far more tangible and concrete way to their practices (bypassing many of the idiomatic effects).

7. The one exception here is the small number of those respondents describing themselves as "blue collar". These respondents disproportionately felt their daily work would be positively affected by the closure (66.7%; $p < 0.05$). (Though not statistically significant, by comparison, less than a third [30%] of those workers referring to themselves as "professional class" said the same thing.)

8. Survey question: "Please indicate by your response below your level of participation in your union." On the basis of the fixed choices provided, *low level of participation* was defined by respondent selections one of the following statements: "I pay no attention to union materials", "I pay attention to union materials", or "I attend union meetings occasionally or often". *High level of union participation* was defined by selection of one of these statements: "I volunteer for some form of union activity" or "I hold or have held an elected or appointed position within my union".

9. We can note here, however, that respondents' selected social class identity (fixed-choice list including working-class, blue-collar, white-collar, middle-class, upper-class, professional class) does not relate statistically to union participation in this survey.

10. Further to the definition of factor analysis, as Tabachnick and Fidell (2007) explain, it is a statistical technique "applied to a single set of variables when the

researcher is interested in disovering which variables in the set form coherent subsets that are relatively independent of one another. Variables that are correlated with one another but largely independent of other subsets of variables are combined into factors." In the case of this research, SPSS Version 19 was used to carry out the analyses. The Kaiser-Meyer-Olkin (KMO), a measure of sampling adequacy, and Bartlett's test of sphericity, a measure of the strength of intercorrelations among variables included in factorization, demonstrate that the selected sets of variables are suitable for factorization. Though the conventions surrounding statistical significance vary somewhat in the literature using factor analysis, in principle KMO values greater than 0.5 represent the minimal basis for beginning to claim the existence of valid relationship sets; values between 0.5 and 0.7 are seen as moderately strong relationships; values between 0.7 and 0.8 are considered strong relationships; and values above 0.8 are considered very strong relationships statistically (Field 2005). In both analyses carried out in this chapter, the scores on these tests establish that factor analysis is appropriate (though these measures are stronger for the first factor analysis), while we also see that the ratio of sample size to the number of variables is acceptable in terms of standard premises (e.g., Tabachnick and Fidell 2007). Finally, an inspection of the correlation matrix for the variables in the two analyses (with the exception noted in the second analysis) shows appropriate levels of inter-correlation and no instances of inappropriately strong inter-correlation (i.e., no singularity).

11. Over the last three decades or more, research on this issue generally has demonstrated association between demographic/broader identity issues and union participation (measured in various ways), e.g., Gordon, Philpot, Burt, Thompson and Spiller (1980); Fullagar (1986); Fullagar, Gallagher, Clark and Carroll (2004); Gallagher and Clark (1989); Sverke and Kuruvilla (1995). Fullagar (1986) stands out in relation to this study since he specifically used factor analysis to explore the relationship between demographics (i.e. race) and union attitudes (amongst blue-collar workers), and, as here, discovered a series of complex relationships.

12. The initial set of variables included in the "labour process set" were as follows: current position; rating of general effectiveness of present tech/work system; rating of effectiveness of work organization in present tech/work system; rating of effectiveness of division of labour in present tech/work system; rating of level of worker control/decision-making in the present tech/work system; rating of how well present tech/work system allows worker skill development; rating of workload in present tech/work system; rating of level of support from management in present tech/work system; rating of level of support from co-workers in present tech/work system; rating of quality of worker/client communication in present tech/work system; rating of contribution to quality of work by present tech/work system; rating of contribution to client's lives of present tech/work system; rating of contribution to ease/difficulty learning of present tech/work system; rating of contribution to flexibility of present tech/work system; rating of contribution to management surveillance of present tech/work system; rating of contribution to worker accountability of present tech/work system; rating of contribution to management understanding of work of present tech/work system; frequency of use of workarounds; anticipated effect of closure of the intake screening unit system.

13. KMO score of 0.845; Bartlett's Chi-Square 608.232, p < 0.001.
14. Because social withdrawal is a key practice in all of this, obviously it also makes some sense that workers experiencing the most difficulties were essentially un-represented in the interview research.
15. The initial set of variables included in the "broader experiences, attitudes and demographics set" were as follows: age, gender, race/ethnicity, disability, self-designated social class description, union seniority, union participation level, welfare work background experience, educational attainment level, educational attainment field of study, general computer literacy, prior training participation, prior involvement in work change planning process.
16. KMO score of 0.507; Bartlett's Chi-Square 65.008, p < 0.001. I note, however, the second factor analysis is less conventional (i.e. the inclusion of a factor with one variable), more complicated, and because of this some additional comments are relevant. Specifically, eigenvalues dropped below 1.0 after the first four variables in the analysis. The next four that were retained had values between 1.0 and 0.623 (while the last five variables clearly had to be excluded). Normally, we might only extract/retain the first four variables. In fact, the total variance reported in the body of the text (more than 61%) is based on these first four variables only in order to offer a more conservative portrait of the analysis (i.e., the total variance accounted for by all eight of the extracted variables was quite high at greater than 80%). Particularly in the case of the second factor analysis, since this is an exploratory effort I turned with special attention to the scree plot for additional support for interpretation, and a clear flattening out following the eight retained variables (less so following only the first four variables) was seen. In order to assist analysis in this context the minimal loading level for this analysis was set at 0.45.
17. Here we should recall, as mentioned earlier, that I have folded both those selecting "professional class" as well as "middle-class" responses into this variable. For the purposes of factor analysis, however, we can note also that the variable is understood as a scaled (not a nominal) variable, i.e., it is interpreted as differing levels of class consciousness. For this particular statistical procedure race and gender are treated the same way (i.e., in terms of a scaled variable of racial and gendered privilege).
18. Indeed, those survey respondents choosing a middle-class designation did not even differ from those identifying as working-class in terms of reports of the occupation of their parent growing up (head of household).

11. Mind in Political Economy and the Labour Process – A Use-Value Thesis

1. See Bellamy Foster and McChesney (2009). See also the earlier reflections on the changes from monopoly capitalism to monopoly-finance capitalism in Sweezy (1994).
2. Aronowitz and Bratsis (2002) draw together a host of reconsiderations of theories of state in their edited collection including re-interpretations of the Miliband/Poulantzas debate (a re-enactment, according to the editors, of the

Lenin-Luxemburg debate) which are particularly helpful on this point regarding the nature of hegemony and the relative autonomy of governments in advanced capitalism.

3. Inclusive of analysis of the changes in Ontario welfare system specifically, see Chunn and Gavigan (2004, 2010).

4. Indeed, as mentioned earlier, evidence shows that as the system was finishing its first year of operation in 2003 some of the most startling directives on welfare worker practices were issued by the government to ISU workers, who were encouraged to use their own discretion as much as possible to reduce the number of clients who could or would make a claim (Government of Ontario, Ministry of Community and Social Services 2001; see further discussion in Herd and Mitchell 2005, pp. 19–20).

References

Abbott, A. (1986). "Jurisdictional Conflicts: A New Approach to the Development of the Legal Profession", *Law and Social Inquiry*, 11, 187–224.

(1988). *The System of Professions: Essay on the Division of Expert Labour*. Chicago: University of Chicago Press.

(2009). "Organizations and the Chicago School". In P. Adler (ed.) *The Oxford Handbook of Sociology and Organizational Studies*. New York: Oxford University Press.

Ackroyd, S. (2009). 'Labor Process Theory as "Normal Science"', *Employee Responsibilities and Rights Journal*, 21(3): 263–272.

Ackroyd, S. and Bolton, S. (1999). "It Is Not Taylorism: Mechanisms of Work Intensification in the Provision of Gynaecological Services in a NHS Hospital", *Work, Employment and Society*, 13(2), 369–387.

Ackroyd, S. and Thompson, P. (1999). *Organisational (Mis)Behaviour*. London: Sage.

Adler, P. (1993). "Time-and-Motion Regained", *Harvard Business Review*, January–February, pp. 97–108.

(1995). "'Democratic Taylorism': The Toyota Production System at NUMMI". In S. Babson (ed.) *Lean Work: Empowerment and Exploitation in the Global Auto Industry* (pp. 207–219). Detroit: Wayne State University Press.

(2004). "Skill Trends under Capitalism and the Socialisation of Production". In C. Warhurst, I. Grugulis and E. Keep (eds.) *The Skills That Matter* (pp. 242–260). London: Palgrave Macmillan.

(2005). "The Evolving Object of Software Development", *Organization*, 12(3), 401–435.

(2006). "From labour process to activity theory". In P. H. Sawchuk, N. Duarte and M. Elhammoumi (eds.) *Critical Perspectives on Activity: Explorations Across Education, Work and Everyday Life* (pp. 160–192). New York: Cambridge University Press.

(2007a). "The Future of Critical Management Studies: A Paleo-Marxist Critique of Labour Process Theory", *Organization Studies*, 28(09), 1313–1345.

(2007b) "Marx, Socialization and Labour Process Theory: A Rejoinder", *Organization Studies*, 28(09), 1387–1394.

Adler, P. and Borys, B. (1996). "Two Types of Bureaucracy: Enabling and Coercive", *Administrative Science Quarterly*, 41, 61–89.

Aitkin, H. (1960). *Scientific Management in Action: Taylorism at Watertown Arsenal, 1908–1915*. Princeton, NJ: Princeton University Press.

Argyris, C. and Schön, D. (1974). *Theory in Practice: Increasing Professional Effectiveness*. San Francisco: Jossey-Bass.

Arievitch, I. (2003). "A Potential for an Integrated View of Development and Learning: Galperin's Contribution to Sociocultural Psychology", *Mind, Culture, and Activity*, 10, 278–288.

Armstrong, P. and Armstrong, H. (2001). *Thinking It Through: Women, Work and Caring in the New Millennium*. Halifax: Atlantic Centre of Excellence in Women's Health.

Aronowitz, S. and Bratsis, P. (eds.) (2002). *Paradigm Lost: State Theory Reconsidered*. Minneapolis: University of Minnesota Press.

Arthur, M. and Rousseau, D. (eds.) (1996). *The Boundaryless Career*. New York: Oxford University Press.

Arthur, M., Hall, D., and Lawrence, B. (eds.) (1989). *Handbook of Career Theory*. Cambridge: Cambridge University Press.

Attewell, P. (1987). "The De-skilling Controversy", *Work and Occupations* 14(3), 323–346.

Au, W. (2007). "Vygotsky and Lenin on Learning: The Parallel Structures of Individual and Social Development", *Science and Society*, 71(3): 273–298.

Avis, J. (2007). "Engeström's Version of Activity Theory: A Conservative Praxis?" *Journal of Education and Work*, 20(3), 161–177.

  (2009). "Transformation or Transformism: Engestrom's Version of Activity Theory", *Educational Review*, 61(2), 151–165.

Bahnisch, M. (2000). "Embodied Work, Divided Labour: Subjectivity and the Scientific Management of the Body in Frederick W. Taylor's 1907 'Lecture on Management'", *Body & Society*, 6(1), 51–68.

Bailey, R. and Brake, M. (eds.) (1975). *Radical Social Work*. London: Edward Elgar.

Baines, C., Evans, P.M. and Neysmith, S. M. (1998). "Caring: Its Impact on the Lives of Women". in C. Baines, P. M. Evans and S. M. Neysmith (eds.) *Women's Caring. Feminist Perspectives on Social Welfare* (pp. 3–22). Toronto: Oxford University Press.

Baines, D. (2004a). "Pro-Market, Non-Market: The Dual Nature of Organizational Change in Social Services Delivery", *Critical Social Policy*, 24(1), 5–29.

  (2004b). "Caring for Nothing: Work Organization and Unwaged Labour in Social Services", *Work, Employment and Society*, 18(2), 267–295.

  (2004c). "Seven Kinds of Work, Only One Paid: Raced, Gendered and Restructures Care in the Social Services Sector", *Atlantis: A Women's Studies Journal*, 28(2), 19–28.

  (2008). "Race, Resistance, and Restructuring: Emerging Skills in the New Social Services", *Social Work*, 53(2), 123–131.

Baldry, C., Bain, P. and Taylor, P. (1998). "Bright Satanic Offices: Intensification, Control and Team Taylorism". In P. Thompson and C. Warhurst (eds.) *Workplaces of the Future* (pp. 163–183). London: Macmillan.

Barley, S. (2005). "What We Know and Mostly Don't Know about Technical Workers". In S. Ackroyd, R. Batt, P. Thompson and P. Tolbert (eds.) *The Handbook of Work and Organizations* (376–403). Oxford: Oxford University Press.

Baruch, Y. (2006). "Career Development in Organizations and beyond: Balancing Traditional and Contemporary Viewpoints", *Human Resource Management Review*, 16, 125–138.

Bashevkin, S. (2002). *Welfare Hot Buttons: Women, Work, and Social Policy Reform*. Toronto: University of Toronto Press.

Bateson, G. (1973). *Steps to an Ecology of Mind: Collected Essays in Anthropology, Psychiatry, Evolution and Epistemology*. London: Paladin.

Battle, K. and Torjman, S. (1995). *How Finance Re-Formed Social Policy*. Caledon Institute of Social Policy, Ottawa.

Becker, G. (1964). *Human Capital: A Theoretical Analysis with Special Reference to Education*. New York: Columbia University Press.

Beirne, M., Ramsay, H. and Pantelli, A. (1998). "Developments in Computing Work: Control and Contradiction in the Software Labour Process". In P. Thompson and C. Warhurst (eds.) *Workplaces of the Future* (pp. 142–162). London: Macmillan.

Bell, D. (1973). *The Coming of the Post-Industrial Society*. New York: Basic Books.
  (1976). *The Cultural Contradictions of Capitalism*. New York: Basic Books.

Bellamy Foster, J. and Magdoff, F. (2009). *The Great Financial Crisis: Causes and Consequences*. New York: Monthly Review Press.

Bellamy Foster, J. and McChesney, R. (2009). "Monopoly-Finance Capital and the Paradox of Accumulation", *Monthly Review*, 61(5), 1–20.

Bernstein, B. (1971). *Class, Codes and Control.* Vol. 1. *Theoretical Studies towards a Sociology of Language*. London: Routledge and Kegan Paul.

Bernstein, Basil (2000). *Pedagogy, Symbolic Control and Identity: Theory, Research, Critique*. New York: Rowman & Littlefield.

Blanck, G. (1993). "Vygotsky: The Man and His Cause". In Luis C. Mol (ed.) *Vygotsky and Education: Instructional Implications and Applications of Sociohistorical Psychology*. Cambridge: Cambridge University Press.

Blau, P. (1955/1963). *The Dynamics of Bureaucracy: A Study of Interpersonal Relationships in Two Government Agencies*. London: University of Chicago Press.

Blauner, R. (1964). *Alienation and Freedom*. Chicago: Chicago University Press.

Blunden, A. (2010). *An Interdisciplinary Theory of Activity*. Boston: Brill.

Boland, R. and Pondy, L. (1983). "Accounting in Organizations: A Union of Natural and Rational Perspectives", *Accounting, Organizations and Society*, 8, 223–234.

Bolton, S. (2004). "Conceptual Confusions: Emotion Work as Skilled Work". In C. Warhurst, I. Grugulis and E. Keep (eds.) *The Skills That Matter* (pp. 19–37). London: Palgrave Macmillan.

Boutilier, D. (2009). *A Symbolic Interactionist Perspective on Work and Learning in Social Benefits Delivery in Ontario*. Unpublished Doctoral Thesis, University of Toronto, Canada.

Bowker, G. C. and Star, S. L. (1999). *Sorting things out: Classification and Its Consequences*. Cambridge, MA: MIT Press.

Braverman, H. (1974/1998). *Labor and Monopoly Capitalism: The Degradation of Work in the 20th Century*. New York: Monthly Review Press.

Bruni, A., Gherardi, S. and Parolin, L. (2007). "Knowing in a System of Fragmented Knowledge", *Mind, Culture, and Activity*, 14(1), 83–102.

Bryman, A. (1992). "Quantitative and Qualitative Research: Further Reflections on Their Integration". In J. Brannen (ed.) *Mixing Methods: Qualitative and Quantitative Research* (pp. 57–78). Aldershot, UK: Ashgate.

Burawoy, M. (1979). *Manufacturing Consent: Changes in the Labour Process under Monopoly Capitalism*. Chicago: University of Chicago Press.

(1985). *The Politics of Production*. London: Verso.

Burns, L. (1980). "The Chicago School and the Study of Organizational-Environment Relations", *Journal of the History of Behavioral Sciences*, 16, 342–358.

Burrell, G. and Dale, K. (2003). "Building Better World: Architecture and Critical Management Studies". in M. Alvesson and H. Willmott (eds.) *Studying Management Critically*. London: Sage.

Button, G., Mason, D. and Sharrock, W. (2003). "Disempowerment and resistance in the print industry? Reactions to surveillance-capable technology", *New Technology, Work and Employment*, 18(1), 50–61.

Carey, M. (2003). "Anatomy of a Care Manager", *Work, Employment and Society*, 17(1), 121–35.

(2004). *The Care Managers: Life on the Front-Line After Social Work*. Unpublished Ph.D. Thesis, University of Liverpool, UK.

(2008). "The Quasi-Market Revolution in the Head: Ideology, Discourse, Care Management", *Journal of Social Work*, 8(4), 341–362.

(2009). "'It's a Bit Like Being a Robot or Working in a Factory': Does Braverman Help Explain the Experiences of State Social Workers in Britain since 1971?", *Organization*, 16(4), 505–527.

Carr, A. and Hancock, P. (2006). "Another Time, Another Place: Space and Time in Organizational Studies", *TAMARA: Journal of Critical Postmodern Organizational Science*, 5(1/2), 91–95.

Charp, S. (1999). "Technical Literacy-Where Are We?" *T.H.E. Journal*, 27(3), 6–8.

Chunn, D. and Gavigan, S. (2004). "Welfare Law, Welfare Fraud, and the Moral Regulation of the 'Never Deserving' Poor", *Social Legal Studies*, 13(4), 219–243.

Chunn, D. and Gavigan, S. (eds.) (2010). *The Legal Tender of Gender: Law, Welfare and the Regulation of Women's Poverty*. Oxford: Hart.

City of Hamilton Community Services Department (2009). *Ontario Works Caseload Contingency Plan (CS09021) (City Wide)*. Hamilton, Canada: City of Hamilton.

Clark, J. and Diani, M. (eds.) (1996). *Alain Touraine*. London: Falmer.

Clarke, J. and Newman, J. (1993). "Managing to Survive: Dilemmas of Changing Organisational Forms in the Public Sector". In N. Deakin and R. Page (eds.) *The Costs of Welfare* (46–64). Aldershot: Avebury.

(1997). *The Managerial State: Power, Politics and Ideology in the Remaking of Social Welfare*. London: Sage.

Cockburn, C. (1985). *Machinery of Dominance: Women, Men and Technical Know-How*. London: Pluto Press.

Cockburn, C. and Ormrod, S. (1993). *Gender and Technology in the Making*. Newbury Park, CA: Sage.

Cole, M. (1996). *Cultural Psychology: A Once and Future Discipline*. Cambridge, MA: Harvard University Press.

Coleman, N. and Harris, J. (2008). "Calling Social Work", *British Journal of Social Work*, 38, 580–599.

Corrigan, P. and Leonard, P. (1978). *Social Work Practice under Capitalism: A Marxist Approach*. Basingstoke: Macmillan.

Cousins, C. (1987). *Controlling Social Welfare: A Sociology of State Welfare Work and Organisation*. Sussex: Wheatsheaf.

Cressey, P. and MacInnes, J. (1980). "Voting for Ford: Industrial Democracy and the Control of Labour", *Capital & Class* 11, 5–53.

Dahrendorf, R. (1959). *Class and Class Conflict in An Industrial Society*. London: Routledge & Kegan Paul.

Daniels, H. (2004). "Cultural Historical Activity Theory and Professional Learning", *International Journal of Disability, Development & Education*, 51(2), 185–200.

Daniels, H. and Warmington, P. (2007). "Analysing Third Generation Activity Systems: Labour-Power, Subject Position and Personal Transformation", *Journal of Workplace Learning*, 19(6), 377–391.

Daniels, H., Leadbetter, J., Warmington, P., Edwards, A., Martin, D., Popova, A., Apostolov, A., Middleton, D. and Brown, S. (2007). "Learning in and for Multi-Agency Working", *Oxford Review of Education*, 33(4), 521–538.

Delbridge, R. (2000). *Life on the Line in Contemporary Manufacturing*. Oxford: Oxford University Press.

(2006). "Extended Review: The Vitality of Labor Process Analysis", *Organization Studies*, 27(8), 1209–1219.

Demazière, D., Horn, F. and Zune, M. (2007). "The Functioning of a Free Software Community: Entanglement of Three Regulation Modes – Control, Autonomous and Distributed", *Science Studies*, 20(2), 34–54.

Derber, C. (1982). *Professionals as Workers: Mental Labor in Advanced Capitalism*. Boston: G. K. Hall.

Dominelli, L. (2002). *Feminist Social Work Theory and Practice*. New York: Palgrave Press.

Dominelli, L. and Hoogvelt, A. (1996). "Globalization and the Technocratization of Social Work", *Critical Social Policy* 16, 45–62.

Durand, J-P. (1990). "Information Technology and the Legacy of Taylorism in France", *Work, Employment and Society*, 4(3), 407–427.

Eagleton, T. (2011). *Why Marx Was Right*. New Haven, CT: Yale University Press.

Eaton Mosher, J., Evans, P. and Little, M. (2004). *Walking on Eggshells: Abused Women's Experiences of Ontario's Welfare System*. Toronto: Ontario Association of Interval and Transition Houses & Ontario Social Safety Network.

The Economist (2011). "Schumpeter – Ahead of the Curve: Daniel Bell, Who Died on January 25th, Was One of the Great Sociologists of Capitalism", The Economist (February 3).

Edwards, A. (2004). "The New Multi-Agency Working: Collaborating to Prevent the Social Exclusion of Children and Families". *Journal of Integrated Care*, 12(5), 3–9.

(2005). "Relational Agency: Learning to Be a Resourceful Practitioner", *International Journal of Educational Research*, 43, 168–182.

(2007a). "Working Collaboratively to Build Resilience: A CHAT Approach", *Social Policy & Society*, 6(2), 255–264.

(2007b). "An Interesting Resemblance: Vygotsky, Mead and American Pragmatism". In H. Daniels, M. Cole, and J. Wertsch (eds.) *The Cambridge Companion to Vygotsky* (pp. 77–100). New York: Cambridge University Press.

Edwards, A. and Mackenzie, L. (2005). "Steps Towards Participation: The Social Support of Learning Trajectories", *International Journal of Lifelong Education*, 24(4), 287–302.

(2008). "Identity Shifts in Informal Learning Trajectories". In B. van Oers, E. Elbers, R. van der Veer and W. Wardekker (eds.) *The Transformation of Learning*. Cambridge: Cambridge University Press.

Edwards, P. and Collinson, M. (2002). "Empowerment and Managerial Labor Strategies: Pragmatism Regained", *Work and Occupations*, 29(3), 272–99.

Edwards, R. (1975). "The Social Relations of Production in the Firm and Labor Market Structure". *Politics and Society*, 5, 83–108.

(1979). *Contested Terrain: The Transformation of the Workplace in the Twentieth Century*. London: Heinemann.

Elhammoumi, M. (2006). "Is There a Marxist Psychology?" In P. H. Sawchuk, N. Duarte and M. Elhammoumi (eds.) *Critical Perspectives on Activity: Explorations across Education, Work and Everyday Life* (pp. 23–34). New York: Cambridge University Press.

Engeström, Y. (1987). *Learning by Expanding: An Activity-theoretical Approach to Development Research*. Helsinki: Orienta-Konsultit.

(1990). *Learning, Working and Imagining: Twelve Studies in Activity Theory*. Helsinki: Orienta-Konsultit.

(1999). "Expansive Visibilisation of Work: An Activity-Theoretical Perspective", *Computer Supported Cooperative Work*, 8, 63–93.

(2001). "Expansive Learning at Work: Toward an Activity Theoretical Reconceptualization", *Journal of Education and Work* 14(1), 133–56.

(2006). "Values, Rubbish and Workplace Learning". In P. H. Sawchuk, N. Duarte and M. Elhammoumi (eds.) *Critical Perspectives on Activity: Explorations across Learning, Work and Everyday Life* (pp. 193–207). New York: Cambridge University Press.

(2007). "Enriching the Theory of Expansive Learning: Lessons from Journeys toward Co-configuration", *Mind, Culture, and Activity*, 14(1), 23–39.

Engeström, Y., Engeström, R. and Vähäaho, T. (1999). "When the Center Does Not Hold: The Importance of Knotworking". In S. Chaiklin, M. Hedegaard, U. J. Jensen (eds.) *Activity Theory and Social Practice: Cultural–Historical Approaches*. Aarhus: Aarhus University Press.

Engeström, Y., Lompscher, J., and Rückriem, G. (eds.) (2005). *Putting Activity Theory to Work: Contributions from Developmental Work Research*. Berlin: Lehmanns Media.

Engeström Y. and Middleton D. (1996). *Communication and Cognition at Work*. New York: Cambridge University Press.

Engeström, Y. and Sannino, A. (2010). "Studies of Expansive Learning: Foundations, Findings and Future Challenges", *Educational Research Review*, 5, 1–24.

Evetts, J. (2003). "The Sociological Analysis of Professionalism". *International Sociology*, 18(2), 395–415.

(2006). "Short Note: The Sociology of Professional Groups: New Directions", *Current Sociology*, 54(1), 133.

Feenberg, A. (1991). *Critical Theory of Technology*. New York: Oxford University Press.

Feldman, D. (ed.) (2002). *Work Careers: A Developmental Perspective*. San Francisco: Jossey-Bass.

Felstead, A., Gallie, D. and Green, F. (2002). *Work Skills in Britain 1986–2001*. London: Department for Education and Skills.

(2004). "Job Complexity and Task Discretion: Tracking the Direction of Skills at Work in Britain". In C. Warhurst, I. Grugulis and E. Keep (eds.) *The Skills That Matter* (pp. 148–169). London: Palgrave Macmillan.

Fenwick, T., Edwards, R. and Sawchuk, P. H. (2011). *Emergence, Expansion, Translation: New Approaches to Educational Research*. New York: Routledge.

Ferguson, I. and Lavalette, M. (2004). "Beyond Power Discourse: Alienation and Social Work", *British Journal of Social Work*, 34, 297–312.

Field, A. (2005). *Discovering Statistics Using SPSS* (2nd ed.) London: Sage.

Fitzgibbon, D. (2008). "Deconstructing Probation: Risk and Developments in Practice", *Journal of Social Work Practice*, 22(1), 85–101.

Florida, R. (2002). *The Rise of the Creative Class: And How It's Transforming Work, Leisure, Community and Everyday Life*. New York: Basic Books.

Foster, D. and Hoggett, P. (1999). "Change in the Benefits Agency: Empowering the Exhausted Work?", *Work, Employment and Society*, 13(1): 19–31.

Form, W. (2002). *Work and Academic Politics: A Journeyman's Story*. New Brunswick, NJ: Transaction Books.

Frenkel S., Korczynski M., Shire, K. and Tam, M. (1999). *On the Front Line: Organization of Work in the Information Economy*. Ithaca, NY: Cornell University Press.

Friedman, A. (1977). *Industry and Labour: Class Struggle at Work and Monopoly Capitalism*. London: Macmillan.

Friedmann, G. (1961). *The Anatomy of Work*. London: Heinemann.

Fullagar, C. (1986). "A Factor Analytic Study on the Validity of a Union Commitment Scale", *Journal of Applied Psychology*, 71(1), 129–136.

Fullagar, C., Gallagher, D., Clark, P. and Carroll, A. (2004). "Union Commitment and Participation: A Ten-Year Longitudinal Study", *Journal of Applied Psychology*, 89, 730–737.

Galabuzi, G.E. (2006). *Canada's Economic Apartheid*. Toronto: Canadian Scholar's Press.

Gallagher, D. and Clark, P. (1989). "Research on Union Commitment: Implications for Labor". *Labor Studies Journal*, 14(1), 52–71.

Gallie, D., Felstead, A. and Green, F. (2003). "Skill, Task Discretion and New Technology: Trends in Britain 1986–2001", *L'Année sociologique*, 53(2), 401–430.

Garfinkel, H. (1967). *Studies in Ethnomethodology*. Englewood Cliffs, NJ: Prentice-Hall.

Gavigan, S. and Chunn, D. (2007). "From Mothers' Allowance to Mothers Need not Apply: Canadian Welfare as Liberal and Neo-Liberal Reforms", *Osgoode Hall Law Journal*, 45(4), 733–771.

Gilroy, J. (2000). "Critical Issues in Child Welfare: Perspective from the Field". In M. Callahan and S. Hessle (eds.) *International Child Welfare: Valuing the Field* (pp. 23–45). London: Ashgate.

Giordano, L. (1992). *Beyond Taylorism*. London: Macmillan.

Glisson, C. and Hemmelgarn, A. (1998). "The Effects of Organizational Climate and Interorganisational Coordination on the Quality and Outcomes of Children's Service System", *Child Abuse and Neglect*, 22(5), 401–421.

Goffman, E. (1974). *Frame Analysis*. New York: Harper & Row.

(1981). *Forms of Talk*. Philadeplhia: University of Pennsylvania Press.

Gordon, M., Philpot, J., Burt, R., Thompson, C. and Spiller, W. (1980). "Commitment to the Union: Development of a Measure and an Examination of Its Correlates", *Journal of Applied Psychology*, 65, 479–499.

Government of Ontario, Ministry of Community and Social Services (2001). *Intake Study – Final Report: Study of the Ontario Works New Application Process* (December). Toronto: Government of Ontario.

Graham, K. and Phillips, S. (1998). "Who Does What in Ontario: Disentangling Provincial-Municipal Relations," *Canadian Public Administration*, 41(2), 175–209.

Gramsci, A. (1971). *Selections from the Prison Notebooks*. New York: International.

Hales, M. (1980). *Living Thinkwork: Where Do Labour Processes Come From?* London: CSE Books.

Hamper, B. (1986). *Rivethead: Tales from the Assembly Line*. New York: Warner.

Hampson, I. and Junor, A. (2005). "Invisible Work, Invisible Skills: Interactive Customer Service as Articulation Work", *New Technology, Work and Employment* 20(2), 166–81.

(2010). "Putting the Process Back In: Rethinking Service Sector Skill", *Work, Employment and Society*, 24(3), 526–545.

Harris, J. (1998). "Scientific Management, Bureau-Professionalism and New Managerialism. The Labour Process of State Social Work", *British Journal of Social Work* 29: 915–37.

(2003). *The Social Work Business*. London: Routledge.

Haug, F. (1992). *Beyond Female Masochism: Memory-Work and Politics*. (R. Livingstone, Trans.). London: Verso.

(2008). "Memory Work", *Australian Feminist Studies*, 23(58), 537–541.

(2010). "A Politics of Working Life". In T. Seddon, L. Henriksson and B. Niemeyer (eds.) *Learning and Work and the Politics of Working Life: Global Transformations and Collective Identities in Teaching, Nursing and Social Work* (pp. 217–225). New York: Routledge.

Haug, F. et al. (1987). *Female Sexualization: A Collective Work of Memory*. (E. Carter, Trans.). London: Verso.

Haug, M. (1973). "Deprofessionalization: An Alternative Hypothesis for the Future", *Sociological Review Monograph*, 20, 195–211.

Hennessy, T. and Sawchuk, P. H. (2003). "Worker Responses to Technological Change in the Canadian Public Sector: Issues of Learning and Labour Process", *Journal of Workplace Learning*, 15(7), 319–25.

Herd, D. and Mitchell, A. (2005). *Discouraged, Diverted and Disentitled: Ontario Works' New Service Delivery Model*. Toronto: Community Social Planning Council of Toronto.

Herd, D., Mitchell, A. and Lightman, E. (2003). "Rituals of Degradation: How Ontario Works' Administrative Process Discourages, Diverts and Disentitles", *Welfare-to-Work: The Next Generation: A National Forum*, (November 16–18). St John's, Newfoundland and Labrador, Canada.

Heritage, J. (1984). *Garfinkel and Ethnomethodology*. London: Polity Press.

Hier, S. (2003). "Probing the Surveillant Assemblage: On the Dialectics of Surveillance Practices as Processes of Social Control", *Surveillance & Society*, 1(3), 399–411.

Hirschhorn, L. (1984). *Beyond Mechanization: Work and Technology in a Postindustrial Age*. Cambridge, MA: MIT Press.

Hitchens, C. (2010). *Hitch 22: A Memoir*. Toronto: McClelland & Stewart.

HLB Decision Economics Incorporated (2002). *Review and Update of the Business Transformation Project Business Case and Risk Analysis*. A Publication of HLB Decision Economics Incorporated.

Hochschild, A. (1979). "Emotion Work, Feeling Rules, and Social Structure", *American Journal of Sociology*, 85(3), 551–575.

(1983). *The Managed Heart: Commercialisation of Human Feeling*. Berkeley: University of California Press.

Holland, D., Lachicotte, W., Skinner, D. and Cain, C. (1998). *Identity and Agency in Cultural Worlds*. Cambridge, Ma: Harvard University Press.

Holosko, M. and Leslie, D. (2001). "Is Social Work a Profession? The Canadian Response", *Research on Social Work Practice*, 11(2), 201–209.

Hutchins, E. (1995). *Cognition in the Wild*. Cambridge, MA: MIT Press.

Huws, U. (1999). "Material World: The Myth of the Weightless Economy". In L. Panitch and C. Leys (eds.) *Socialist Register 1999* (pp. 29–55). Suffolk: Merlin Press.

(2003). *The Making of a Cybertariat: Virtual Work in a Real World*. New York: Monthly Review Press.

Illeris, K. (2002). *The Three Dimensions of Learning: Contemporary Learning Theory in the Tension Field between the Cognitive, the Emotional, and the Social*. Frederiksberg, Denmark: Roskilde University Press.

Ilyenkov, E. (1982). *The Dialectics of the Abstract and the Concrete in Marx's Capital*. Moscow: Progress.

Jackson, N. (1994). "Rethinking Vocational Learning: The Case of Clerical Skills". In L. Erwin and D. MacLennan (eds.) *Sociology of Education in Canada: Critical Perspectives on Theory, Research and Practice* (pp. 341–51). Toronto: Copp Clark Longman.

Jennissen, T. and Lundy, C. (2008). *Keeping Sight of Social Justice: 80 Years of Building CASW*. Ottawa: Canadian Association of Social Workers. [downloaded January 2, 2008 from http://www.casw-acts.ca/aboutcasw/building_e.pdf].

(2011). *One Hundred Years of Social Work: A History of the Profession in English Canada 1900–2000*. Waterloo, Canada: Wilfred Laurier University Press.

Jensen, K. (2007). "The Desire to Learn: An Analysis of Knowledge-Seeking Practices among Professionals", *Oxford Review of Education*, 33(4), 489–502.

Jones, C. (1983). *State Social Work and the Working Class*. London: Macmillan.

(1999). "Social Work: Regulation and Managerialism". In M. Exworthy and S. Halford (eds.) *Professionals and the New Managerialism in the Public Sector*. Buckingham: Open University Press.

(2001). "Voices from the Front-Line: State Social Workers and New Labour", *British Journal of Social Work*, 31, 547–62.

Jones, O. (1997). "Changing the Balance? Taylorism, TQM and Work Organisation", *New Technology Work and Employment*, 12(1), 13–24.

(2000). "Scientific Management, Culture and Control: A First-Hand Account of Taylorism in Practice", *Human Relations*, 53(5), 631–653.

Kakar, S. (1970). *Frederick Taylor: A Study in Personality and Innovation*. Boston: Heffernan Press.

Kaptelinin, V. (2005). "The Object of Activity: Making Sense of the Sense-Maker", *Mind, Culture and Activity*, 12(1), 4–18.

Keep, E. (2000a). "Creating a Knowledge-Driven Economy: Definitions, Challenges and Opportunities", *SKOPE Policy Paper* No. 2, University of Warwick, UK.

(2000b). *Upskilling Scotland*. Edinburgh: Centre for Scottish Public Policy.

Kerr, C., Dunlop, J., Harbison, F. and Myers, C. (1962). *Industrialism and Industrial Man*. London: Heinemann.

Kincheloe, J. (1999). *How Do We Tell the Workers? The Socioeconomic Foundations of Work and Vocational Education*. Boulder, CO: Westview Press.

Kirst-Ashman, K. (1992). "Feminist Values and Social Work: A Model for Educating Non-Feminists", *Arete*, 17, 13–25.

Knights, D. and Willmott, H. (eds.) (1990). *Labor Process Theory*. London: Macmillan.

Knights, D. and Willmott, H. (2007). "Socialization, Yes. Skill Upgrading, Probably. Robust Theory of the Capitalist Labour Process, No.", *Organization Studies*, 28(9), 1369–1378.

Knorr Cetina, K. (1981). *The Manufacture of Knowledge – an Essay on the Constructivist and contextual Nature of Science*. Oxford: Pergamon Press.

(1999). *Epistemic Cultures: How the Sciences Make Knowledge*. Cambridge, MA: Harvard University Press.

(1997). "Sociality with Objects: Social Relations in Postsocial Knowledge Societies". *Theory, Culture & Society*, 14(4), 1–30.

(1999). *Epistemic Cultures: How Sciences Make Knowledge*. Cambridge MA: Harvard University Press.

Knorr Cetina, K. and Brueggar, U. (2002). Traders' Engagement with Markets: A Postsocial Relationship. *Theory Culture and Society*, 19(5–6), 161–185.

Kostogriz, A. (2006). "Putting 'Space' on the Agenda of Sociocultural Research", *Mind, Culture and Activity*, 13(3), 176–190.

Kraines, O. (1960). "Brandeis' Philosophy of Scientific Management", *Political Research Quarterly*, 13(1), 191–201.

Kreis, S. (1990). "The Diffusion of Scientific Management: The Bedaux Company in America and Britain, 1926–1945", in D. Nelson (ed.) *A Mental Revolution:*

Scientific Management since Taylor (pp. 156–174). Columbus: The Ohio State University Press.

Kummerow, J. (ed.). (2000). *New Directions in Career Planning and the Workplace* (2nd ed.). Palo Alto, CA: Davies-Black.

Lafer, G. (2004). "'What Is Skill?' Training for Discipline in the Low-wage Labour Market". In C. Warhurst, I. Grugulis and E. Keep (eds.) *The Skills That Matter* (pp. 109–127). London: Palgrave Macmillan.

Langemeyer, I. and Roth, W.M. (2006). "Is Cultural-Historical Activity Theory Threatened to Fall Short of Its Own Principles and Possibilities in Empirical Research?" *Outlines. Critical Social Studies*, 8(2), 20–42.

Lavalette, M. (ed.) (2011). *Radical Social Work Today: Social Work at the Crossroads*. Bristol: Policy Press.

Lave, J. and Wenger, E. (1991). *Situated Learning: Legitimate Peripheral Participation*. New York: Cambridge University Press.

Lazzari, M. M., Colarossi, L., and Collins, K. S. (2009). "Feminists in Social Work: Where Have All the Leaders Gone?" *Affilia*, 24, 348–359.

Lefebvre, H. (1991). *The Production of Space* (D. Nicholson-Smith, Trans.). Malden, MA: Blackwell.

Lehmann, W. (2000). "Is Germany's Dual System Still a Model for Canadian Youth Apprenticeship Initiatives?" *Canadian Public Policy-Analyse de Politiques*, 26(2), 225–240.

Lehmann, W. and Taylor, A. (2003). "Giving Employers What They Want? New Vocationalism in Alberta", *Journal of Education and Work*, 16(1), 45–67.

Leontiev, A.N. (1978). *Activity, Consciousness, and Personality*. Englewood Cliffs, NJ: Prentice Hall.

(1981). *Problems of the Development of the Mind*. Moscow: Progress.

Lewchuk, W. (2002). Workload, Work Organization and Health Outcomes: The Ontario Disability Support Program. Report Submitted to the Ontario Public Service Employees Union.

Lightman, E., Herd, D. and Mitchell, A. (2006). "Exploring the Local Implementation of Ontario Works", *Studies in Political Economy*, 78, 119–143.

Lipsky, M. (1980). *Street-Level Bureaucracy: Dilemmas of the Individual in Public Services*. New York: Russell Sage.

Littler, C. (1982). *The Development of the Labour Process in Capitalist Societies: A Comparative Analysis of Work Organization in Britain, the USA and Japan*. London: Heinemann.

Livingstone, D. (2004). *The Education–Jobs Gap*. Toronto: University of Toronto Press.

Livingstone, D. and Sawchuk, P. H. (2004). *Hidden Knowledge: Organized Labour in the Information Age*. Toronto: University of Toronto Press.

Lomba, C. (2005). "Beyond the Debate over 'Post'- vs 'Neo'-Taylorism: The Contrasting Evolution of Industrial Work Practices", *International Sociology*, 20(1), 71–91.

Lompscher, J. (2006). "The Cultural Historical Activity Theory: Some Aspects of Development". In P. H. Sawchuk, N. Duarte and M. Elhammoumi (eds.) *Critical Perspectives on Activity: Explorations Across Education, Work and the Everyday* (pp. 35–51). New York: Cambridge University Press.

Luedtke, A. (1986). "Cash, Coffee-Breaks, Horseplay: Eigensinn and Politics among Factory Workers in Germany circa 1900". In M. Hanagan and C. Stephenson (eds.) *Confrontation, Class Consciousness and the Labor Process: Studies in Proletarian Class Formation* (pp. 65–95). New York: Greenwood Press.

Luff, P., Hindmarsh, J. and Heath, C. (eds.) (2000). *Workplace Studies: Recovering Work Practice and Informing System Design*. New York: Cambridge University Press.

Lundy, C. and van Wormer, K. (2007). "Social and Economic Justice, Human Rights and Peace the Challenge for Social Work in Canada and the USA", *International Social Work*, 50(6), 727–739.

Luria, A. R. (1976). *Cognitive Development: Its Cultural and Social Foundations*. Cambridge, MA: Harvard University Press.

Macdonald, K. (1995). *The Sociology of the Professions*. London: Sage.

Martin, D. and Peim, N. (2009). "Critical Perspectives on Activity Theory", *Educational Review*, 61(2), 131–138.

Marx, K. (1845/1996). *Theses on Feuerbach* (Robert C. Tucker). New York: Norton.

   (1845–46/1996). *The German Ideology* (Robert C. Tucker). New York: Norton.

   (1867–68/1990). *Capital* (Vols. 1–3). New York: International.

Marx, Karl (1844/1978). *Economic and Philosophical Manuscripts of 1844* (Robert C. Tucker). New York: Norton.

McDermott, R. and Lave, J. (2006). "Estranged ~~Labor~~ Learning". In Peter H. Sawchuk, Newton Duarte and Mohamed Elhammoumi (eds.) *Critical Perspectives on Activity: Explorations across Education, Work and the Everyday* (pp. 89–122). New York: Cambridge University Press.

Mead, G. H. (1934/1967). *Mind, Self and Society: From the Standpoint of a Social Behaviorist*. Chicago: University of Chicago Press.

Meiksins Wood, E. (1999). *The Origins of Capitalism*. New York: Monthly Review Press.

Miettinen, R. (2005). "Object of Activity and Individual Motivation", *Mind, Culture and Activity*, 12(1), 220–229.

Miettinen, R. and Virkkunen, J. (2005). "Epistemic Objects, Artefacts and Organizational Change", *Organization*, 12(3), 437–456.

Miliband, R. (1973). *The State in Capitalist Society: The Analysis of the Western System of Power*. London: Quartet Books.

Milkman, R. (1998). "The New American Workplace: High Road or Low Road?" In P. Thompson and C. Warhurst (eds.) *Workplaces of the Future* (pp. 25–39). London: Macmillan.

Mirchandani, K. (2012). *Phone Clones*. Ithaca, NY: Cornell University Press.

Moffat, K. (2001). *A Poetics of Social Work: Personal Agency and Social Transformation in Canada, 1920–1939*. Toronto: University of Toronto Press.

Morgan, E. (1998). "Computer Literacy for Librarians", *Computers in Libraries*, 18(1), 39–41.

Myles, J. (1988). *The Expanding Middle: Some Canadian Evidence on the Deskilling Debate* (No. 9). Ottawa: Statistics Canada.

Nardi, B. (ed.) (1996). *Context and Consciousness: Activity Theory and Human-Computer Interaction*. Cambridge, Ma: MIT Press.

Nardi, B. and Engeström, Y. (1999). "A Web on the Wind: The Structure of Invisible Work", *Computer Supported Cooperative Work*, 8, 1–8.

Nelson, D. (1980). *Frederick W. Taylor and the Rise of Scientific Management*. Madison: University of Wisconsin Press.

Newman, F. and Holzman, L. (1993). *Lev Vygotsky: Revolutionary Scientist*. London: Routledge.

Niepce, W. and Molleman, E. (1998). "Work Design Issues in Lean Production from a Sociotechnical Systems Perspective: Neo-Taylorism or the Next Step in Sociotechnical Design?" *Human Relations*, 51(3), 259–287.

Niewolny, K. and Wilson, A. (2009). "What Happened to the Promise? A Critical (Re)Orientation of Two Sociocultural Learning Traditions", *Adult Education Quarterly*, 60(1), 26–45.

Noble, D. (1984). *The Forces of Production: A Social History of Industrial Automation*. New York: Alfred A. Knopf.

Nolan, P. (2003). Reconnecting with History: The ESRC Future of Work Programme, *Work, Employment and Society*, 17(3), 473–480.

Nolan, P. and Slater, G. (2003). "The Labour Market: History, Structure and Prospects". In P. Edwards (ed.) *Industrial Relations: Theory and Practice*. Oxford, UK: Blackwell.

Nonaka, I. and Takeuchi, H. (1995). *The Knowledge Creating Company: How Japanese Companies Create the Dynamics of Innovation*. New York: Oxford University Press.

NUPGE (2000). *Andersen Consulting: Living High on the Hog on the Backs of Ontario's Poor*. Ottawa: NUPGE.

Nyland, C. (1996). "Taylorism, John R. Commons, and the Hoxie Report", *Journal of Economic Issues*, 30(4), 985–1016.

(1998). "Taylorism and the Mutual-gains Strategy", *Industrial Relations*, 37(4), 519–542.

O'Doherty, D. and Willmott, H. (2001). "Debating Labour Process Theory: The Issue of Subjectivity and the Relevance of Poststructuralism", *Sociology*, 35(2), 457–476.

Offe, C. (1984). *Contradictions of the Welfare State*. London: Hutchinson.

Office of the Ontario Auditor General (2003). *2003 Annual Report*. Toronto: Queen's Printer for Ontario.

Ollman, B. (1976). *Alienation: Marx's Conception of Man in Capitalist Society*. London: Cambridge University Press.

(1993). *Dialectical Investigations*. New York: Routledge.

Orr, J. (1996). *Talking about Machines*. Ithaca, NY: IRL Press.

Osterman, P. (1996). *Broken Ladders: Managerial Careers in the New Economy*. New York: Oxford University Press.

Pabon, C.E. (1992). *Regulating Capitalism: The Taylor Society and Political Economy in the Interwar Period*. Unpublished doctoral dissertation, University of Massachusetts-Amherst.

Paradeise, C. (2003). "French Sociology of Work and Labor: From Shop Floor to Labor Markets to Networked Careers", *Organization Studies*, 24(4), 633–653.

Parsloe, P. (1981). *Social Service Area Teams*. London: Allen and Unwin.

Parsloe, P. and Stevenson, O. (eds.) (1978). *Social Services Teams: The Practitioners View*. London: OHMS.

Parsons, T. (1954). *Essays in Sociological Theory*. New York: Free Press.

Peel Region (2008). *Ontario Works Budget Document*. Toronto: Peel Region Municipal Government.

Peim, N. (2009). "Activity Theory and Ontology", *Educational Review*, 61(2), 167–180.

Pemberton, W. (1989). *Harry S. Truman: Fair Dealer and Cold Warrior*. Boston: Twayne.

Piore, M. and Sabel, C. (1984). *The Second Industrial Divide: Possibilities for Prosperity*. New York: Basic Books.

Pithouse, A. (1987). *Social Work: The Social Organisation of an Invisible Trade*. Aldershot: Avebury.

Piven, F. and Cloward, R. (1971). *Regulating the Poor: The Function of Public Welfare*. London: Tavistock.

Pollert, A. (1981). *Girls, Wives, Factory Lives*. London: Macmillan.

Postle, K. (2001). "The Social Work Side Is Disappearing: I Guess It Started with Us Being Called Care Managers", *Practice*, 13(1), 3–18.

Poulantzas, N. (1973). *Political Power and Social Classes*. London: NLB.

Pruijt, H. (1997). *Job Design and Technology: Taylorism versus Anti-Taylorism*, New York: Routledge.

    (2000). "Repainting, Modifying, Smashing Taylorism", *Journal of Organizational Change*, 13(5), 439–451.

Psathas, G. (1996). "Theoretical Perspectives on Goffman: Critique and Commentary", *Sociological Perspectives*, 39(3), 383–391.

Reisch, M. and Andrews, J. (2001). *The Road Not Taken: A History of Radical Social Work in the United States*. Philadelphia: Brunner-Routledge.

Reich, R. (1991). *The Work of Nations: Preparing Ourselves for 21st Century Capitalism*. New York: Knopf.

Rice, J. and Prince, M. (2000). *Changing Politics of Canadian Social Policy*. Toronto: University of Toronto Press.

Rikowski, G. (2002a). "Methods for Researching the Social Production of Labour Power in Capitalism", *University College Northampton School of Education Research Seminar* (March 7).

    (2002b) "Fuel for the Living Fire: Labour-power!" In A. Dinerstein and M. Neary (eds.) *The Labour Debate: An Investigation into the Theory and Reality of Capitalist Work*. Aldershot: Ashgate.

Ritzer, G. (1989). "Sociology of Work: A Metatheoretical Analysis", *Social Forces*, 67(3), 593–604.

Ritzer, G (1998). *The McDonaldisation Thesis*. London: Sage.

Roach Anleu, s. (1992). "The Professionalization of Social Work? A Case Study of Three Organizational Settings", *Sociology*, 26(1): 23–44.

Rogoff, B. and Lave, J. (eds.) (1984). *Everyday Cognition: Its Development in Social Context*. Cambridge, MA: Harvard University Press.

Rojewski, J. (2002). "Preparing the Workforce of Tomorrow: A Conceptual Framework for Career and Technical Education", *Journal of Vocational Education Research*, 27(1), 7–35.

Roy, D. (1952). *Restriction of Output in a Piecework Machine Shop*. Unpublished Ph.D. Dissertation, University of Chicago.

Russell, D. (2010). "Writing in Multiple Contexts: Vygotskian CHAT Meets the Phenomenology of Genre". In C. Bazerman et al. (eds.) *Traditions of Writing Research* (353–364). New York: Routledge.

Sadovnik, A. (ed.) (1995). *Knowledge and Pedagogy: The Sociology of Basil Bernstein.* Norwood, NJ: Ablex.

Sannino, A., Daniels, H. and Gutiérrez, K. (eds.) (2009). *Learning and Expanding with Activity Theory.* New York: Cambridge University Press.

Sawchuk, P. H. (2002). "Review of Basil Bernstein's 'Pedagogy, Symbolic Control and Identity'" *Discourse and Society*, 13(4), 572–573.

(2003a). *Adult Learning and Technology in Working-Class Life.* New York: Cambridge University Press.

(2003b). "Informal Learning as a Speech-Exchange System: Implications for Knowledge Production, Power and Social Transformation", *Discourse and Society*, 14(3), 291–307.

(2006a). "Activity and Power: Everyday Life and Development of Working-class Groups". In P. H. Sawchuk, N. Duarte and M. Elhammoumi (eds.) *Critical Perspectives on Activity: Explorations across Education, Work and the Everyday*, (pp. 238–67). New York: Cambridge University Press.

(2006b) "Frameworks for Synthesis of the Field of Adult Learning Theory". In T. Fenwick, T. Nesbit and B. Spencer (eds.) *Contexts of Adult Education: Canadian Perspective* (pp. 140–52). Toronto: Thompson.

(2006c). "'Use-Value' and the Re-thinking of Skills, Learning and the Labour Process", *Journal of Industrial Relations*, 48(5), 593–617.

(2007a). "Understanding Diverse Outcomes for Working-Class Learning: Conceptualizing Class Consciousness as Knowledge Activity", *Economic and Labour Relations Review*, 17(2), 199–216.

(2007b). "Theories and Methods for Research on Informal Learning and Work: Towards Cross-fertilization", *Studies in Continuing Education*, 29(3), 34–48.

(2008). "Lifelong Learning and Work as 'Value Production': Combining Work and Learning Analysis from a Cultural-historical Perspective". In D. W. Livingstone, K. Mirchandani and P. H. Sawchuk (eds.) *The Future of Lifelong Learning and Work: Critical Perspectives*, Rotterdam, Netherlands: Sense.

(2009). "Occupational Transitions within Workplaces Undergoing Change: A Case from the Public Sector". In P. H. Sawchuk and A. Taylor (eds.) *Challenging Transitions in Learning and Work: Perspectives on Policy and Practice*. Rotterdam: Sense.

(2010a). "Researching Workplace Learning – an Overview and Critique". In M. Malloch, L. Cairns, K. Evans and B. O'Connor (eds.) *The International Handbook of Workplace Learning*. London: Sage.

(2010b). "Reading across Workplace Learning Research to Build Dialogue", *Frontiers of Education in China*, 5(3), 365–381.

Sawchuk, P. H., Duarte, N. and Elhammoumi, M. (2006). *Critical Perspectives on Activity: Explorations across Education, Work and Everyday Life*. New York: Cambridge University Press.

Sawchuk, P. H. and Stetsenko, A. (2008). "Sociological Understandings of Conduct for a Non-Canonical Activity Theory: Exploring Intersections and Complementarities" *Mind Culture and Activity*, 15(4), 339–360.

Seddon, T., Henriksson, L. and Niemeyer, B. (eds.) (2010). *Learning and Work and the Politics of Working Life: Global Transformations and Collective Identities in Teaching, Nursing and Social Work*. New York: Routledge.

Scott, W. (1966). "Professionals in Bureaucracies: Areas of Conflict". In H. Vollmer and D. Mills (eds.) *Professionalization* (pp. 265–275) Englewood Cliffs, NY: Prentice-Hall.

Simpkin, M. (1983). *Trapped within Welfare: Surviving Social Work* (2nd ed.). London: Macmillan.

Simpson, I. (1989). "Sociology of Work: Where Have the Workers Gone?" *Social Forces*, 67(1), 563–581.

Slavin, P. (2002). "Profession Strained in Canada", *NASW News* (March), p. 15.

Smith, C. and Thompson P. (1999). "Re-Evaluating the Labor Process Debate". In M. Wardell, T. Steiger and P. Meiksins (eds.) *Rethinking the Labor Process* (pp. 205–232). Albany: State University of New York Press.

Smith, D. (1987). *The Everyday World as Problematic: A Feminist Sociology*. Toronto: University of Toronto Press.

Songini, M. (2004). "Accenture IT System under Fire in Ontario: Upgrade Needed to Calculate Welfare Benefit Changes; Inquiry Sought into Deal with Vendor", *Computer World*, (August 2nd). [downloaded March 2008 from http://www.computerworld.com/careertopics/careers/consulting/story/0,10801,94951,00.html]

Spenner, K. (1983). "Deciphering Prometheus: Temporal Change in the Skill Level of Work", *American Sociological Review*, 48(6), 824–37.

(1988). "Technological Change, Skill Requirements, and Education: The Case for Uncertainty". In R. Cyert and D. Mowery (eds.) *The Impact of Technological Change on Employment and Economic Growth* (pp. 131–184). Cambridge, MA: Ballinger.

Spinuzzi, C. (2009). *Tracing Genres through Organizations: A Sociocultural Approach to Information Design*. Cambridge, MA: The MIT Press.

Stalker, C., Mandell, D., Frensch, K., Harvery, C. and Wright, M. (2007). "Child Welfare Workers Who Are Exhausted Yet Satisfied with Their Jobs: How Do They Do It?" *Child & Family Social Work*, 12 (2), 182–191.

Star, S. L. (1995). *Ecologies of Knowledge: Work and Politics in Science and Technology*. Albany: State University of New York Press.

Star, S. L. and Griesemer, J. (1989). "Institutional Ecology, 'Translations,' and Boundary Objects: Amateurs and Professionals in Berkeley's Museum of Vertebrate Zoology, 1907–1939", *Social Studies of Science*, 19, 387–420.

Stetsenko, A. (2005). "Activity as Object-Related: Resolving the Dichotomy of Individual and Collective Planes of Activity", *Mind, Culture and Activity*, 12(1), 70–88.

(2008). "Collaboration and Cogenerativity: On Bridging the Gaps Separating Theory-Practice and Cognition-Emotion", *Cultural Studies of Science Education*, 3, 521–533.

(2009). "Vygotsky and the Conceptual Revolution in Developmental Sciences: Towards a Unified (Non-Additive) Account of Human Development". In M. Fleer, M. Hedegaard, and J. Tudge (eds.) *Childhood Studies and the Impact of Globalization: Policies and Practices at Global and Local Levels* (pp. 125–141) New York: Routledge.

(2010). "Teaching–learning and development as activist projects of historical Becoming: expanding Vygotsky's approach to pedagogy", *Pedagogies: An International Journal*, 5(1), 6–16.

Stetsenko, A. and Arievitch, I. (2004). "The Self in Cultural-historical Activity Theory: Reclaiming the Unity of Social and Individual Dimensions of Human Development", *Theory & Psychology*, 14(4), 475–503.

Stoney, C. (2001). "Strategic Management or Strategic Taylorism? A Case Study into Changes in a UK Local Authority", *The International Journal of Public Sector Management*, 14(1), 27–42.

Storey, J. (1985). "The means of management control", *Sociology* 19(2), 193–211.

Streeck, W. (1989). "Skills and the Limits of Neo-liberalism: The Enterprise of the Future Place of Learning", *Work, Employment and Society* 3(1), 89–104.

Stromberg, P. (2000). "The I of Enthrallment", *Ethos*, 27(4), 490–504.

Struthers, J. (1987). "Shadows from the Thirties: The Federal Government and Unemployment Assistance, 1941–1956". In J. Ismael (ed.) *The Canadian Welfare State: Evolution and Transition* (pp. 3–32) Edmonton: The University of Alberta Press.

(1994). *The Limits of Affluence: Welfare in Ontario, 1920–1970.* Toronto: University of Toronto Press.

Suchman, L. and Jordan, B. (1990). "Interactional Troubles in Face-to-Face Survey Interviews", *Journal of the American Statistical Association*, 85(409), 232–241.

Sverke, M. and Kuruvilla, S. (1995). "A New Conceptualization of Union Commitment", *Journal of Organizational Behavior*, 16, 505–532.

Sweezy, P. (1994). "The Triumph of Financial Capital," *Monthly Review*, 46(2), 1–11.

Symes, C. and McIntyre, J. (eds.) (2000). *Working Knowledge: The New Vocationalism and Higher Education.* New York: Routledge.

Szymanski, M. and Whalen, J. (eds.) (2011). *Making Work Visible: Ethnographically Grounded Case Studies of Work Practice.* New York: Cambridge University Press.

Tabachnick, B. and Fidell, L. (2007). *Using Multivariate Statistics* (5th ed.) Boston: Pearson/Allyn & Bacon.

Taylor, F.W. (1895/1919) *Two Papers on Scientific Management: A Piece Rate System and Notes on Belting.* New York: G. Routledge and Sons.

(1903/1947) *Shop Management.* New York: Harper and Brothers.

(1911/1947) *Principles of Scientific Management.* New York: Harper and Brothers.

(1912/1947) *Hearings before Special Committee of the House of Representatives to Investigate the Taylor and Other System of Shop Management under the Authority of House Resolution 90,* New York: Harper and Brothers.

Taylor, R. (2004). "Extending Conceptual Boundaries: Work, Voluntary Work and Employment", *Work, Employment and Society*, 18(1), 29–49.

Thompson, P. (1989). *The Nature of Work: An Introduction to Debates on the Labour Process.* London: Macmillan.

(2003). "Disconnected Capitalism: Or Why Employers Can't Keep Their Side of the Bargain", *Work, Employment and Society*, 17(2), 359–378.

Tinker, T. (2002). "Spectres of Marx and Braverman in the Twilight of Postmodernist Labour Process Research", *Work, Employment and Society* 16(2), 251–81.

Tosey, P., Visser, M. and Saunders, M. (2012). "The Origins and Conceptualizations of 'Triple-Loop' Learning: A Critical Review", *Management Learning*, 43(3), 291–307.

Touraine, A. (1971). *The Post-Industrial Society: Tomorrow's Social History: Classes, Conflicts and Culture in the Programmed Society*. New York: Random House.

Tsui, M-S. (1997). "The Roots of Social Work Supervision: A Historical Review", *The Clinical Supervisor*, 15(2), 191–198.

Tudiver, N. (1982). "Business Ideology and Management in Social Work: The Limits of Cost Control", *Catalyst*, 4(1), 25–48.

Turner, H. (1962). *Trade Union Growth, Structure and Policy*. London: Allen and Unwin.

Van der Veer, R. and Valsiner, J. (eds.) (1994). *The Vygotsky Reader*. New York: Blackwell.

Vasilyuk, F. (1991). *The Psychology of Experiencing: the Resolution of Life's Critical Situations*. London: Hemel Hempstead, Harvester.

Vygotsky, L.S. (1978). *Mind in Society: The Development of Higher Psychological Processes*. Cambridge, MA: Harvard University Press.

　(1987). *The Collected Works of L. S. Vygotsky*. Vol. 1. *Problems of General Psychology*. New York: Plenum Press.

　(1997). *The Collected Works of L.S. Vygotsky*. Vol. 4. *The History of the Development of the Higher Mental Functions*. New York: Plenum Press.

　(1998). *The Collected Works of L. S. Vygotsky*. Vol. 5. *Child Psychology*. New York: Plenum Press.

Vygotsky, L. S. (1994). "The Problem of the Environment". In R. Vander Veer and J. Vlasiner (eds.) *The Vygotsky Reader* (pp. 338–354). Cambridge: Blackwell.

Wagner-Tsukamoto, S. (2007). "An Institutional Economic Reconstruction of ScientificManagement: On the Lost Theoretical Logic of Taylorism", *Academy of Management Review*, 32(1), 105–117.

Wardell, M., Steiger, T. and Meiksins, P. (1999). *Rethinking the Labor Process*. Albany, NY: SUNY Press.

Warhurst, C., Grugulis, I. and Keep, E. (eds.) (2004). *The Skills That Matter*. London: Palgrave Macmillan.

Warhurst, C. and Thompson, P. (2006). "Mapping Knowledge in Work: Proxies or Practices?" *Work, Employment and Society*, 20(4), 787–800.

Warhurst, C., Thompson, P. and Nickson, D. (2008). "Labour Process Theory: Putting the Materialism Back into the Meaning of Service Work". In M. Korczynski and C. Macdonald, C. (eds.) *Service Work: Critical Perspectives* (pp. 91–112). London: Routledge.

Waring, S. (1990). "Peter Drucker, MBO, and the Corporatist Critique of Scientific Management". In D. Nelson (ed.) *A Mental Revolution: Scientific Management since Taylor* (pp. 205–236), Columbus: The Ohio State University Press.

　(1991). *Taylorism Transformed: Scientific Management Theory since 1945*, Chapel Hill: University of North Carolina Press.

Warmington, P. (2008). "From 'Activity' to 'Labour' : Commodification, Labour-power and Contradiction in Engeström's Activity Theory", *Critical Social Studies* No. 2, 13.

Webb, J. (2001). "Gender, Work and Transitions in the Local State", *Work, Employment and Society* 15(4), 825–44.

Wertsch, J. (1991). *Voices of the Mind: a Sociocultural Approach to Mediated Action.* Cambridge, MA: Harvard University Press.

Westwood, S. (1984). *All Day Every Day: Factory and Family in the Making of Women's Lives.* London: Pluto Press.

White, D. (2005). *New Relations of Welfare Governance in Canada: Shifting Boundaries between State and Civil Society.* Montréal: Centre de recherche sur les politiques et le développement social, Université de Montréal.

White, S. and Siegel, A. (1984). "Cognitive Development Is Space and Time". In B. Rogoff and J. Lave (eds.) *Everyday Cognition: Its Development in Social Context.* Cambridge, MA: Harvard University Press.

White, V. (2006). *The State of Feminist Social Work.* New York: Routledge.

Wilensky, H. (1961). "Careers, Lifestyles, and Social Integration", *International Social Science Journal*, 12, 553–558.

(1964). "The professionalization of everyone?" *The American Journal of Sociology*, 70(2), 137–158.

Williams, R. (1977). *Marxism and Literature.* New York: Oxford University Press.

Willmott, H. (2005). "Theorizing Contemporary Control: Some Poststructuralist Responses to Some Critical Realist Questions", *Organization*, 2(5), 747–780.

Womack, J. P., Roos, D. and Jones, D. (1990). *The Machine That Changed the World.* New York: Rawson Associates.

Wood, S. (ed.) (1982). *The Degradation of Work? Skill, Deskilling and the Labour Process.* London: Hutchinson.

Worthen, H. (2001). The Working Knowledge of Union Representatives in Piece Rate Apparel Shops: An Activity-Theoretical Analysis. Unpublished Manuscript, University of Illinois, Chicago.

(2008). "Using Activity Theory to Understand How People Learn to Negotiate the Conditions of Work", *Mind, Culture and Activity*, 15(4), 322–338.

Worthen, H. and Berry, J. (2006). "'Our Working Conditions Are Our Students' Learning Conditions': A CHAT Analysis of College Teaching". In P. H. Sawchuk, N. Duarte, M. Elhammoumi (eds.) *Critical Perspectives on Activity: Explorations Across Education, Work and Everyday Life* (pp. 123–142). New York: Cambridge University Press.

Wrege, C. and Greenwood, R. (1991). *Frederick W. Taylor, the Father of Scientific Management: Myth and Reality.* Homewood. IL: Richard D. Irwin.

York Region Community Services and Housing Committee (2004). *Report No. 10 of the Community Services and Housing Committee* (Section 3: Ontario Works Program Consolidated Verification Process Program Report). Toronto: York Region Municipal Government.

Zander, P-O. (2007). *Collaborative Process Change by Inscription – a Contested Terrain for Interaction Designers.* Unpublished Doctoral Dissertation, Department of Informatics, Lund University, Sweden.

Zinchenko, V. (2002). "From Classical to Organic Psychology: In Commemoration of the Centennial of Lev Vygotsky's Birth". In S. Shohov (ed.) *Advances in Psychology Research: Volume 18* (pp. 3–26). New York: Nova Science.

Zimbalist, A. (ed.) (1979). *Case Studies on the Labor Process*. London: Monthly Review Press.
Zuboff, S. (1988). *In the Age of the Smart Machine: The Future of Work and Power*. New York: Basic Books.

Index

The Learning in Doing series was founded in 1987 by Roy Pea and John Seely Brown.